Globalisation, Environment and Social Justice

T0298447

This volume provides a comprehensive account of the connections between globalisation, environment and social justice. It examines varied dimensions of environmental sustainability; the adverse impact of globalisation on environment and its consequences for poverty, unemployment and displacement; the impacts on marginalised sections such as scheduled castes and tribes and women; and policy frameworks for ensuring environmental sustainability and social justice.

The chapters build on detailed case studies from different parts of the world and deal with critical environmental issues such as global emissions, climate change, sustainable development, green politics, species protection, water governance, waste management, food production and governance besides education, inclusivity and human rights.

Presenting a range of topics alongside new perspectives and discourses, this interdisciplinary book will be useful to students and researchers of political studies, sociology and environmental studies as well as policymakers and those working in the government and civil society organisations.

Manish K. Verma is Professor, Head and Deputy Coordinator of the UGC–Special Assistance Programme in the Department of Sociology at Babasaheb Bhimrao Ambedkar (Central) University, Lucknow, India. Previously he served in the Department of College Education, Rajasthan, as Lecturer, Senior Lecturer and Lecturer in Selection Grade for 10 years and briefly at NTPC, Corporate Office, New Delhi, as Sociologist. With a doctorate from Jawaharlal Nehru University, New Delhi, he has more than 22 years of teaching and research experience. He has published many books, including *Globalisation, Social Justice and Sustainable Development in India* (2017), *Peri-urban Environment* (2017), *Globalization and Environment: Discourse, Policies and Practices* (2015) and *Development, Displacement and Resettlement* (2004). Several of his research papers and chapters have been published in journals and edited volumes. He is a member of various professional bodies such as the International Sociological Association, Indian Sociological Society and Rajasthan Sociological Association. At present, he is a member of the Managing Committee of the Indian Sociological Society. His main research interests include environment and development, involuntary displacement, urban ecology, social justice and globalisation.

Globalisation, Environment and Social Justice
Perspectives, Issues and Concerns

Edited by Manish K. Verma

Routledge
Taylor & Francis Group

LONDON AND NEW YORK

First published 2019
by Routledge

2 Park Square, Milton Park, Abingdon, Oxfordshire OX14 4RN
52 Vanderbilt Avenue, New York, NY 10017

Routledge is an imprint of the Taylor & Francis Group, an informa business

First issued in paperback 2019

British Library Cataloguing-in-Publication Data
A catalogue record for this book is available from the British Library

Library of Congress Cataloging-in-Publication Data
A catalog record for this book has been requested

ISBN: 978-0-8153-6887-8 (hbk)
ISBN: 978-0-367-47924-4 (pbk)

Typeset in Sabon
by Apex CoVantage, LLC

Contents

Figures

Tables

Contributors

Benson M. O. Agaya is Lecturer at the Department of Sociology, University of Nairobi, Kenya.

Purba Chattopadhyay is Assistant Professor of Economics at the Department of Home Science, Viharilal Campus, Calcutta University, Kolkata, India.

S. N. Chaudhary is Professor of Sociology and Rajiv Gandhi Chair in Contemporary Studies at Barkatulla University, Bhopal, India.

Venkatesh Dutta is British Chevening Scholar, University of Wales, UK; Fulbright Scholar, University of Maryland, USA; Member, Core Group, State Science and Technology Programme, Ministry of Science and Technology, Government of India is Faculty (Environment Management Planning) and Coordinator, DST Centre for Policy Research, Babasaheb Bhimrao Ambedkar (Central) University, Lucknow, India.

Jan Marie Fritz is Vice President of Finance, International Sociological Association (ISA); Professor, Department of Architecture, Art and Planning, University of Cincinnati, USA; and Visiting Professor, Department of Sociology, University of Johannesburg, South Africa.

Siri Gamage is Senior Lecturer, Education Context Team, School of Education, University of New England, Armidale, NSW, Australia.

Ramanuj Ganguly is Professor of Sociology at the Department of Sociology, West Bengal State University, Barasat, Kolkata, India.

Marco Grasso is Associate Professor of Political Geography at the Universitadegli Studi di Milano-Bicocca, Italy. He is also UNEP (UNEP) GEO (Global Environmental Outlook) expert and Lead Author in the Climate Section of the Regional Assessment for Europe.

Gomati Bodra Hembrom is Assistant Professor at the Department of Sociology, Jamia Millia Islamia, New Delhi, India.

Amlendu Jyotishi is Professor at Amrita School of Business, Amrita Viswa Vidyapeetham (University), Bangalore Campus, India.

Sajiv Madhavan is a part-time PhD Research Scholar at Amrita School of Business, Amrita University, Coimbatore Campus and Heads Business Excellence in Tata Elxsi, Bangalore, India.

Siddhartha Mukerji is Assistant Professor at the Department of Political Science, Babasaheb Bhimrao Ambedkar (Central) University, Lucknow, India. He was extensively engaged in the EECURI (India-Europe Network) Project involving UK, India and France for which he visited King's College London and London School of Economics and Political Science.

Sudeshna Mukherjee is an alumnus of Jawaharlal Nehru University, New Delhi, and a member of the faculty at the Centre for Women's Studies, Bangalore University, Bangalore, India. Her primary area of research includes gender, health, development and environment.

B.K. Nagla is former Professor of Maharshi Dayanand Rohtak University, Haryana, India.

Edgard Leite Ferreira Neto is Executive Director of Realitas Institute, Rio de Janeiro, Director of the Indian Studies Program at Rio de Janeiro State University and Executive Director of the Center for Jewish History and Culture, Rio de Janeiro. Currently he also holds the position of Director of Rio de Janeiro's History of Religions Group at the National Association of History. Further, he is Associate Professor at the Rio de Janeiro State University and at the Rio de Janeiro State Federal University. In 2013 he was elected a full member of the Brazilian Academy of Philosophy.

Manisha Tripathy Pandey is Associate Professor at the Department of Sociology, Jamia Millia Islamia, New Delhi, India.

R. Parthasarthy is Professor and Director, Gujarat Institute of Development Research, Gota, Ahmedabad, India.

B.N. Prasad is Professor and Head at the Department of Sociology and Social Anthropology, A.N. Sinha Institute of Social Studies, Patna, India.

Aditya Raj is Assistant Professor at the Department of Humanities and Social Sciences (HSS), Indian Institute of Technology Patna, India.

He completed his PhD as Commonwealth Fellow from the McGill University. He was also at the University of British Columbia, Vancouver, before joining IIT Patna.

Papia Raj is Assistant Professor at the Humanities and Social Sciences Department at IIT Patna, India. She was the recipient of Canadian Commonwealth Scholarship and completed her PhD degree from McGill University, Montreal. She was a post-doctoral fellow in the School of Population and Public Health at University of British Columbia, Vancouver.

Antara Ray is Assistant Professor of Sociology at the Department of Sociology, Presidency University, Kolkata, India.

Dipankar Roy is UGC Research Fellow at the Department of Geography, Faculty of Science, Banaras Hindu University, Varanasi, India.

Sheetal Sharma is Assistant Professor at the Centre for European Studies, School of International Studies, Jawaharlal Nehru University, New Delhi, India.

Ravi S. Singh is Professor at the Department of Geography, Faculty of Science, Banaras Hindu University, Varanasi, India.

Manish K. Verma is Professor, Head and Deputy Coordinator of UGC-Special Assistance Programme in the Department of Sociology at Babasaheb Bhimrao Ambedkar (Central) University, Lucknow, India.

Foreword

Globalisation is an all-encompassing process of change in economic and market interactions and their implication on policy and political choice, which together constitute dimensions of change affecting the physical, cultural and social aspects of society. These directly and indirectly trigger the process of resource utilisation that has a direct bearing upon the theory and issues of social justice and changes in environment. Environmental factors accompany processes related to factors determining demand and supply of environmental resources, their distribution across sections of society and issues of social justice. In fact, globalisation in India can be distinguished between traditional and contemporary forms. The traditional form, for instance, is manifested in the message of non-violence and cultural tolerance propounded by the Buddhist philosophy, the transformation of economy and orientation to other societies to adjust with the forces in India, particularly in the domains of the market economy and commensurate forms of production. Contemporary processes of globalisation both in the economic domain and culture have a high rate of acceleration and intensification of symbolic and ideological forms because of new forms of technological advancement. Contemporary technology, such as telephony, internet, and related technologies, has given new wings to the cultural, social and economic process of growth and transformation. These processes in totality affect environment deeply. They are also germane to issues of social justice because the new forces of change necessitate certain ancillary changes in society, such as the expansion of education and its rate of distribution among various classes and communities and making economic resources available to the weaker sections of society to be able to absorb skills and new perspectives of change. It is in this sense that globalisation and adaptive changes in resource utilisation connect with environmental factors and generate the ability to make these changes available to people in a meaningful manner. This reinforces social justice. Thus a meaningful connection between globalisation, environmental factors and social change can be established in the perspective of social growth and justice.

Manish K. Verma's volume, *Globalisation, Environment and Social Justice: Perspectives, Issues and Concerns*, is a meaningful effort to analyse these factors through his own writing in the volume and through a collection of other chapters configuring the relevant ideas of a large number of social scientists who are engaged in studies in this field. As we read through the collection of these chapters, we cannot but be impressed by their purposiveness and meaningful orientation in regard to issues. The book is of a wider interest to researchers, policymakers, development practitioners, social workers and post-graduate students and research scholars. I highly commend the effort that Dr. Verma has made in collecting these chapters and for his own observations relevant to the field. I am sure the book will be received with keen interest and will have meaningful contribution to make in the field.

Yogendra Singh
Professor Emeritus, Centre for the Study of Social Systems,
School of Social Sciences, Jawaharlal Nehru
University, New Delhi, India

Preface

As the most powerful agent of change the world has ever experienced, globalisation has not only swept the entire planet in its strong currents but has also attempted to integrate it socially, economically, culturally, politically, commercially and technologically up to a large extent. India, being the fastest growing economy and largest democratic country having the second largest population in the world, is also equally affected by the globalisation process. The transformation of society and its various domains due to the neo-liberal globalisation process during the last couple of decades have been so swift and forceful that they astonished everyone including academicians, social scientists, policymakers, planners and people at large. Therefore the nature, scope and form of globalisation are under intense deliberation as scholars hold divergent views over their impact on environment and society. Similarly, the direction of change that globalisation has brought is also a matter of discussion. The intelligentsia is pondering to ascertain whether globalisation is just an extension of the modernisation process, or whether it is a new model of development. A group of scholars considers globalisation as historically rooted and entrenched, in some implicit form, during the early modern age. Another school, on the contrary, holds that globalisation is a completely recent phenomenon the world has come across. For them, the process of liberalisation, privatisation and globalisation (LPG), initiated at the global level since the 1980s (or the early 1990s in India) has played a pivotal role in terms of unification of the world in general and the market in particular. Down the line, it is a perennial issue of concern whether to consider the globalisation processes benevolent and beneficial to human beings, or contrarily detrimental due to being instrumental for environmental degradation and creating exclusion and injustice, especially for those who are at the margins of the society. Further, another school of thought views globalisation as a Western hegemonic project causing imbalance to the global equilibrium and as a tool to amplify the colonial pursuit of hunger and greed for profit maximisation. For them, the powerful, hegemonic, influential, advanced and technological savvy Western countries are using globalisation as a tool to augment their control over not only the allocation of scant resources and goods globally but also driving the ecology, environment, economy, governance, society and culture of the developing and under-developed third world countries. Therefore, from this perspective, the Western countries are cleverly using their long-standing colonial policy of drain of wealth and plunder but masking that in the talk of a new humane face of globalisation. Most alarmingly, by extending its ambit further and evolving the globalisation project much sharper than ever before, the hegemonic Western countries are now, by and large, intending to control knowledge, information, technology, economy, society, culture and eventually environment and the possibility of a just social order. Now neo-liberal globalisation has emerged as a prime source of distress, disparity, discrimination, deprivation, marginalisation, exclusion, ecological imbalance and environmental catastrophe.

Thus it is clearly evident that there are as many interpretations of globalisation as its interpreters, and there should not be any surprise given its multifaceted and dynamic nature. However, most recently, the debate of globalisation per se has been shifted on to examine the convergence and divergence between globalisation, environment and social justice. In what way and up to what extent globalisation is using nature and environment, the most important building block of any development endeavour, and how environmental catastrophe and ecological imbalance is creating a question mark on the possibility of environmental sustainability and sustainable development is the most perennial issue to contemplate. Further, how it is playing in the lives of the people across the globe, especially for the marginalised one, whether it is beneficial and just or contrarily proving detrimental to social justice and hampering the possibility of equity and a just social order. Here, the Indian experience of neo-liberal globalisation holds immense relevance and significance due to the country being home for a large number of marginal and excluded people living below the poverty line.

Against this backdrop, the current volume is initiated with a view to comprehend the process of globalisation and to assess the interlinkages between globalisation, environment and social justice by putting the Indian experience at centre stage. However, in order to capture a comparative picture, some articles depicting the experiences of Brazil, Kenya, China, the European Union and so forth are also included in the volume. The chapters in this volume are crafted with the intent to examine and comprehend the perspectives, issues and concerns enveloping the process of 'Globalisation vis-à-vis Environment and Social Justice' which has caught the attention of the intelligentsia all over the world. For convenience and thematic understanding, the chapters of the volume are divided into three sub-parts apart from one introductory chapter in the beginning. Each part covers one important facet of globalisation, namely, 'Globalisation, Environmental Sustainability and Social Justice: Perspectives and Issues', 'Globalisation, Marginalised Sections and Social Justice: Problems and Challenges', and 'Globalisation and Questions of Equity and Social Justice: Issues from Various Sectors'. The first part of the volume comprises eight chapters, and five papers are included in each of the second and third parts of the volume. Chapters are organised to address the sub-themes to which they particularly pertain and are contributed by academicians and experts hailing from renowned universities and institutes of the world.

Due to having a broader canvas and interdisciplinary nature of issues covered, the book will be of immense significance for academicians, researchers, post-graduate and graduate level students of social sciences and development studies, policymakers and NGOs working in the area of globalisation, environment, development and social justice.

Lastly, it is time to extend gratitude and acknowledge all those who stood by me for the completion of the edited volume. At the outset, I owe a deep sense of gratitude to all the contributors of the volume. Without their novel contributions, dedicated hard work and support, the edited volume *Globalisation, Environment and Social Justice: Perspectives, Issues and Concerns* would have been a distant dream. They have extended their full support, cooperation and forbearance at every stage of the completion of the book and shown intense willingness to help me in the editing work to make the volume a reality.

I am thankful to Prof. R. C. Sobti, the vice chancellor of the Babasaheb Bhimrao Ambedkar University, Lucknow, for sparing me from the university affairs which enabled me to pen down the volume in a focused way. The motivation and support of Prof. Kameshwar Choudhary, my senior colleague in the Department of Sociology, needs special mention here. He not only prepared me mentally to work for this volume but also provided all kinds of support and assistance in formulation, sketching and editing of the book. The meticulous discussions held with him to streamline the format of the book proved extremely helpful in shaping the volume in a presentable form. I also express my deep sense of gratitude to Prof. N.M.P. Verma, my senior in the university, whose support and guidance proved extremely valuable. I am equally thankful to the office assistant of the Department of Sociology, Mr. Ajay Kumar, for providing secretarial assistance. The contribution of my research scholars, Mr. Narendra Kumar and Mr. Raju Shah, is quite appreciative in this regard.

It is high time to show my sincere gratitude towards my teachers. First of all I extend a deep sense of gratitude to the eminent sociologist, extremely noble man and most fortunately my revered teacher, the legendary Prof. Yogendra Singh, who always stood by me and showered his blessings despite all odds. Along the same line, Prof. K. L. Sharma, Prof. T. K. Oommen, Prof. Nandu Ram, Prof. Anand Kumar and Prof. Ehshanul Haque are foremost among my notable teachers. It is their teaching and blessings which strengthened me at every moment of my life.

It will go without saying if I don't mention the contribution of my family members whose encouragement, cooperation and forbearance enormously helped me to complete the volume. It is with the inspiration and blessings of my late grandfather and grandmother that I am in this position to fulfil their dreams. Even from their heavenly abode, their blessings are encouraging and motivating me to work diligently to come up to their expectations. I take this opportunity to thank my parents, brother and sisters, in-laws and other relatives for their love and cooperation extended to me at every moment of my life. The cooperation, help and assistance extended by my wife Runu and the patience of my beloved son Aradhya Dev is highly appreciable for the completion of this endeavour. After all, it is their encouragement, mental support and sacrifice which strengthened me to work on this volume. I must admit that my thorough academic engagement for the timely completion of the volume undermined and took away their share of time and space which they would have certainly spent and enjoyed with me. Therefore, without their help, cooperation and forbearance, this work would not have taken a proper shape.

Finally, I owe a deep sense of gratitude to Mr. Robert Langham, Mr. Shashank Shekhar Sinha, Ms. Antara Ray Chaudhary, Ms. Avneet Kaur and their entire team at Routledge, Taylor & Francis Group for taking a personal interest in getting this volume out of press with a high level of efficiency and the least amount of aberrations and errors.

At the last, I must admit that I have benefitted greatly from the suggestions of many colleagues in the process of writing and editing this volume. However, the entire responsibility about the content and form of the edited volume is mine, and if there are shortcomings I alone am to be blamed.

Introduction

Manish K. Verma

Perhaps no other term has received as much scholarly attention as globalisation in the last couple of decades due to its all-pervasive dynamics and impact on society across the world. The spurt in globalising processes has led to a compression of the world; as a result, the whole world, it is opined, has turned into a 'global village' (McLuhan 1960), diminishing the boundaries of time and space. Globalisation has been viewed differently in different academic disciplines. However, there is broad agreement among scholars that it is a multidimensional phenomenon with social, economic, political, cultural and environmental dimensions engulfing different countries and sections of society globally, including India. Its ramifications are experienced in both material and non-material domains of society all over the world. So recent years have drawn considerable attention worldwide to understand and find ways to deal with the multifarious issues emerging from the rapid pace of transformation brought about by neo-liberal globalisation, which is propelled by the policies of liberalisation and privatisation affecting both environment and society. However, there is no agreement among scholars in the matter. Generally, it is held that a symmetrical and close linkage exists between globalisation, environment and society. Globalisation is affecting environment and society and at the same time its nature and direction are getting determined by environment and society. However, it is important to consider whether the nexus between globalisation, environment and society is benign and a blessing or a curse.

It is observed that the shift in paradigm of development due to incessant globalisation has affected different countries and different sections of society differently – the dominant trend being major benefits of economic growth accruing to the resourceful privileged people and stagnation or increased exclusion and marginalisation of the resource-poor and resourceless sections. It is held that the currently dominant neo-liberal globalisation has replaced the state-centred welfarist development model with a market-driven, economic growth and profit-maximising paradigm at the core of development. Hence, some scholars consider the globalisation process as a fit case of 'crisis of success', wherein the powerful and hegemonic sections expropriate its benefits leaving the marginal and deprived sections excluded from its ambit. However, on the other hand, 'for most of its proponents, it is an irresistible and desirable force sweeping away frontiers, liberating individuals and enriching all it touches' (Ghuman et al. 2010: 1). Like many other countries, India, the second largest populated country in the world, has also embraced the neo-liberal path of development since the 1990s onwards through adopting the policies of liberalisation, privatisation and globalisation (popularly known as LPG reforms) and emerged as one of the fastest developing countries in the world. Eventually, being part of the global village and carried by the wave of globalisation, India also embraced all the major symptoms which emerged due to the intricate processes. Therefore, it is important here to deliberate upon how the benefits and the costs of globalisation processes can be shared fairly between different countries and among different sections of society within a country to ensure social justice. It becomes interesting, on a micro level, to ponder over the pattern and dynamics of interaction between neo-liberal globalisation, environment and social justice in India.

In order to delve deep into the issue and ascertain answers to the queries generated by the surge in globalisation and its impact on environment and society, it would be prudent to first introspect into the nuances of perspectives and issues related to globalisation, environment and social justice.

Perspectives and issues

Undoubtedly globalisation, as a concept and a process of social change, has become a buzzword in the last couple of decades in the world and mesmerised most people living on this planet. However, what exactly globalisation connotes, the nature of changes it is driving and its effect on environment and society especially from a social justice point of view is highly debated and contested issue in contemporary times. Globalisation can mean many things and accordingly scholars and disciplines vary in their opinion and perception. While economists view globalisation as the creation of a world economic market by removal of free trade barriers and the closer integration of national economies; sociologists put emphasis on mitigation of time and space boundaries, migration, communication, cultural diffusion, social relations and creation of a 'reflex society' (Giddens 1990), whereas political scientists view it in the way power dynamics and relations operate internationally to foster international relations, new systems of governance and global regulations. Despite varied perspectives and diverse viewpoints expressed by different scholars about the nature, magnitude, direction and impact of globalisation, it is almost agreeable that it 'has ushered a new vista of life for the mankind living on this earth' (Verma 2015: 1).

While going beyond perspective lenses held by different schools of thought, globalisation corroborates a policy of access to global resources and market; having two kinds of stakeholders: those who gain and contrarily another group of people that loses out. Another way to perceive globalisation is as a process of social, economic, political, cultural, ecological and technological interconnectedness for bringing prosperity through economic efficiency and the use of global resources. Yet another but contrasting perspective is that of a process over-emphasising economic efficiency and failing to reduce economic disparity or social exclusion. Ironically, it exacerbates both, apart from accentuating human misery through induced plunder of natural resources. In this context, Bhagwati has opined critically by stating that 'globalization is the cause of several social ills today, such as poverty in poor countries and deterioration of the environment worldwide' (Bhagwati 2008: 4). In an overview of globalisation, Sen express his contention with a word of caution for fairness and equity, which is a hallmark of his scholarly work. Sen states that

> the rich in the world are getting richer and the poor poorer. This is by no means uniformly so but the crucial issue is whether this is the right way to understand the central issue of fairness and equity in the global economy today.
>
> (Sen 2007: 132)

The challenge is to strive for an ideal condition of a win-win situation for all the participants. The moot question is, whether such an ideal situation is possible?

Another perennial issue which confronts humanity is the limits of environment vis-à-vis scarce availability of natural resources. Even though markets are getting integrated, technologies are improving day by day in the wake of globalisation and industrialisation, and the environment has limitations to supply natural resources to cater industrial requirements of a rapidly expanding consumer society. The main mantras of globalisation today are that the market believes in consumption of commodities and the capitalist *suo motu* is to expropriate profit even if it comes at the cost of compromising environment and sustainability: both social and ecological. The powerful capitalist capitalises the situation by advertently manipulating the situation for personal gains, which triggers an irreversible chain of deprivation, exploitation and exclusion of the marginalised on the one hand and environmental catastrophe on the other. Hence, in this sense environmental problems and social pathologies cannot be seen as separate entity but are two facets of the same coin. Bell has rightly summarised the situation by stating that

> Environmental problems are not only problems of technology and industry, of ecology and biology, of pollution control and of pollution prevention. Environmental problems are also social problems. Environmental problems are problems for society – problems that threaten our existing pattern of social organization and social thought. Environmental problems are as well problems of society – problems that challenge us to change those patterns of organization and thought.
>
> (Bell 2012: 2)

By further taking the issue to a much higher level of assessment, correspondingly Bookchin (1985) accentuated in his major work *The Ecology of Freedom*, 'current ecological problems are embedded in deep-seated social problems, and particularly in the hierarchical forms taken by political and social systems' (Ballet et al. 2013: 31). Bookchin's notion of assessment considers a natural craving among humans to dominate nature as they dominate fellow human beings.

Having established symmetrical linkages between environmental catastrophe, social problems and human beings as intentional perpetrators and offenders, Bell highlights the asymmetrical nature and trends of mounting problems:

> not only are the effects of the environmental problems distributed unequally across the human community, but social inequality is deeply involved in causing those problems. Social inequality is both a product and a producer of global warming, pollution, overconsumption, resource depletion, habitat loss, risky technology and rapid population growth. As well, social inequality influences how we envision what our environmental problems are. And most fundamentally, it can influence how we envision nature

itself, for inequality shapes our social experiences and our social experiences shape all our knowledge.

(Bell 2012: 3)

Hence, in the opinion of Bell, an all-encompassing globalisation has not only intensely accelerated the process of social change which has a deep impact on environment and society per se but also shaping up the idea and thought of the contemporary era. It is also proving to be a prime source of distributive social justice by ensuing who will benefit and who will face exclusionary injustice due to the intricate process emerged out of globalisation. Therefore, the deep embedded nexus between globalisation, environment and social justice urgently necessitates cautious approach to get rid of the environmental and social problems. In this backdrop, Dunlap has rightly remarked, 'the noted trends underline the current emphasis being given to the notions of "sustainability" and "sustainable development", for these trends call into question the long-term sustainability of modern industrial societies' (Dunlap and Michelson 2008: 11).

Among the pioneer scholars who addressed the issue of current trends of market-oriented ecological pandemonium and environmental destruction was the scholarly work of Catton and Dunlap, popularly acknowledged as 'three competing functions of the environment' depicted in Figure 0.1.

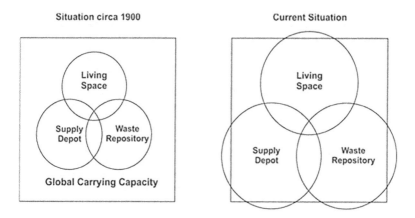

Figure 0.1 Competing functions of the environment

Source: Dunlap, Riley E. and Michelson, William (ed.). 2008. *Handbook of Environmental Sociology*. Indian Reprint. New Delhi and Jaipur: Rawat, p. 2.

The model of Catton and Dunlap identifies three of the most apt roles that the environment performs for human beings in terms of supply depot, living space and waste repository. Supply depot connotes the ability of the environment to serve as a source of renewable natural resources (air, water, forests, fossil fuels) that are most crucial for living species for survival. Excessive use of these precious resources results in scarcities and shortfalls. Living space or habitat bestows housing, a system of transportation and other day-to-day necessary requirements for sustenance. Excessive use and burden on these resources leads to congestion, overcrowding, jamming and the devastation of habitats for other species. Lastly, environment serves as a 'sink' for garbage, sewage, industrial pollution and other by-products with the aid of a waste repository function. Exceeding the threshold level of ecosystems to absorb wastes inevitably leads to health tribulations from contaminated pollutants and eventually ecosystem disruption. Moreover, each of these functions contends for space and often encroaches upon the others, namely:

> placing garbage landfill in a rural location near to a city both make that site unsuitable as a living space and destroy the ability of the land to function as a supply depot for food. Similarly, urban sprawl reduces the amount of arable land that can be put into production while intensive logging threatens the living space of native (aboriginal) peoples.
>
> (Hannigan 2006: 19)

Dunlap and Michelson, therefore, put it as the by-product of globalisation:

> in so far as the supply of space in communities, regions, nations and even the entire globe is becoming increasingly limited relative to the size and distribution of human populations and their socio-economic activities, interactions and potential conflicts among environmental uses will likely occur with increasing frequency and at larger geographical scales, creating shortages, contamination, crowding, conflicts and other negative outcomes.
>
> (Dunlap and Michelson 2008: 14)

Hannigan further adds to the apprehensive statement of Dunlap by accentuating that 'in recent years, the overlap and therefore conflict, among these three competing functions of the environment has grown considerably. Newer problems such as global warming are said to stem from competition among all three functions simultane-ously' (Hannigan 2006: 19). It is important here to note the appended fear that the emergent tribulations are often difficult to recognise by human beings through direct sensory perception. Therefore, in order to make us aware of them essentially requires scientific expertise. These environmental predicaments often impinge on enormous geo-graphical regions and may even capture the globe comprehensively. Their devastating effects are potentially capable of affecting future generations as well. The potential catastrophic consequences of such tribulations undoubtedly exceed our capability to alleviate their impacts and in cases we even feel helpless to adequately compensate the victims. Hence

> we are in danger, as we seem increasingly to fear, of losing con-trol of our own technological creations. We are as well losing the technological and rationalist confidence we once enjoyed, perhaps chastened by normal accidents, new species of trouble, risks that now seem less than voluntary and other inadequacies of rational risk assessment.
>
> (Bell 2012: 245)

Hence, it is widely recognised now that environmental and techno-logical risks have become more endemic to modern industrial socie-ties with the emergence of new set of 'mega-hazards'. The risks they pose have major implications for environment and society. Therefore, modern industrialised societies being described as 'risk societies' (Beck 1992) by Beck.

> Beck argues that Western societies are headed this way and it is leading to a major reconfiguring of the basis of social conflict. For-merly, the central conflicts in the society were class-based struggles over money and other resources. But in the risk society, conflict shifts to non-class-based struggles over pollution and other social and environmental bads. In short, we in the West are moving, says Beck, from conflicts over the distribution of goods to conflicts over the distribution of bads.
>
> (Bell 2012: 245)

Even though Beck captures the picture of modern Western industrial societies, however, the same is true in cases of other parts of the world including India which are widely integrated now due to globalisation processes. Subsequently, the whole globe is finding hard to escape many of the bads of modern society – pollution, congestion, techno-logical hazards, dreadful and haphazard development. The perverted phenomenon has evolved a new form of equality among all the citi-zenry of the world which Beck calls an 'equality of risk'.

> In Beck's words, 'the driving force in the class society can be sum-marized in the phrase, *I am hungry!* The movement set in motion by the risk society, on the other hand, is expressed in the state-ment, *I am afraid*'.
>
> (Bell 2012: 245)

Beck envisions complete restructuring in patterns and dynamics of society through a radical shift in focus from 'goods' to 'bads'. This reflects a restructuring of social organisation as well.

> In the words of Beck, in class society, 'being determines conscious-ness', and in risk society, 'consciousness (knowledge) determines being'. What he means is that in class society, your material position – your income, your employment, your place of residence and upbringing – dominated your sense of who you were. In risk society, it is your ideas and beliefs that matter most, including worries you may have about the trustworthiness of the social and technological world. We are thus moving from a risky life to a life of risk.
>
> (Bell 2012: 245)

Pieterse, a severe critique of modern developmentalism which the world is experiencing at the moment, writes in contention,

> the crisis of developmentalism as a paradigm manifests itself as a crisis of modernism in the West and the crisis of development in South. The awareness in ecological limits to growth is a significant part of modernism. Modernity is viewed increasingly as a theory and practice that is more exclusive than inclusive. The charmed circle of achievement and success, which is glamorized in media and advertisements, exacts a high toll excludes and marginal-izes many. The United States, the post war epitome of modernity, claims the largest underclass of any Western country and a grow-ing number of homeless people. East Asian 'tiger' economies, the newest arrivals to modernity, do not serve as examples either in terms of democracy or ecological management.
>
> (Pieterse 2006: 27)

Hence, in the opinion of Pieterse, 'modernity no longer seems so attractive in ecological problems, the consequences of technological change and many other problems' (Pieterse 2006: 1). He further asserts by taking an extreme viewpoint, 'development discourse in its ahistorical and apolitical character is incapable of coming to terms with the realities of world power and global interests' (Pieterse 2006: 27). Kothari has seen modern developmentalism as a portrayal of new hegemonic mechanism adopted by the West by stating that, 'Development is also a neocolonial discourse – "where colonialism left off, development took over" ' (Kothari 1988: 143). Therefore, Stiglitz strongly contends that 'the critics of globalization accuse Western countries of hypocrisy, and the critics are right' (Stiglitz 2012: 6).

Sen perceives two endemic problems with regard to the process and outcome of globalisation.

> The first is the need to recognize that given the global facilities that exist today, including the problems of omission as well commission, many people find it hard to enter to global economy at all. The concentration on those who are gainfully engaged in trade leaves out millions who remain excluded – and effectively unwelcome – from the activities of the privileged. Exclusion is as important problem here as unequal inclusion. The remedying of such exclusion would demand radical departures in domestic economic policies (such as greater facilities for basic education, health care and microcredit at home), but they also call for changed international policies of other, particularly richer, countries.
>
> (Sen 2007: 133)

The second issue, according to Sen, is more complex and demands far more clearer understanding. He underlines,

> even if the poor who are engaged in globalized economy were becoming just a little richer, this need not imply that the poor are getting a fair share of the benefits of economic interrelations and of its vast potential. Nor is it adequate to ask whether international inequality is getting marginally larger or smaller. To rebel against the appalling poverty and staggering inequalities that characterize the contemporary world, or to protest against unfair sharing of the benefits of global cooperation, it is not necessary to claim that the inequality not only is terribly large, but is also getting marginally larger.
>
> (Sen 2007: 134)

Bhagwati rightly remarked in this perspective that

> the chief task before those who consider globalization favourably, then, is to confront the fears that while globalization may be economically benign (in the sense of increasing the pie), it is socially malign. These fears relate to several areas, among them accentuation of poverty in both rich and poor countries, erosion of unionization and other labour rights, creation of a democratic deficit, harming of women, imperiling of local mainstream and indigenous cultures and damage to the environment.
>
> (Bhagwati 2008: 30)

Therefore

> the consideration on which many of the debates on globalization have concentrated, to wit, whether the poor too benefits from the established economic order, is an entirely inadequate focus for assessing what has to be assessed. What must be asked instead is whether they can feasibly get a better (and fairer) deal, with less disparities of economic, social and political opportunities and if so, through what international and domestic rearrangements this could be brought about. That is where the real engagement lies.
>
> (Sen 2007: 136)

Scholars have perceived the endemic crisis of globalisation induced modern developmentalism differently and accordingly taken varied position. One extreme viewpoint advocates that, 'development is in crisis, let's close the shop and think of something entirely different – "beyond development"'. This is the position associated with post-development thinking. A different reaction is to qualify the crisis, acknowledging the failures of the development record but also its achievements, avoiding simplistic, one – sided assessment. Another reaction is to acknowledge crisis and to argue that crisis is intrinsic to development, that development knowledge is crisis knowledge. Development then is a field in flux, with rapid change and turnover of alternatives (Pieterse 2006: 1). Sen views the issue from a different perspective by stating that

> widespread interest in global inequalities and asymmetries, of which antiglobalization protests are a part, can be seen as embodiment of closer economic relations that bring distant people within the reach of 'the gradual enlargement of our regard to justice'.

This fits in with the claim, that the voices of global protest are part of the newly developing ethics of globalization in the contemporary world.

(Sen 2007: 148)

Globalisation, environment and social justice interface

On the basis of the preceding discussion it is clear by now that globalisation, environment and social justice is obstinately interconnected: the relationship is intuitively straightforward yet somewhat complex. Change and movement in one component symmetrically leads to impact and alteration on others. However, a harmonious interaction between all the three connotes homogeneous world along the matrix of sustainable development with equality and equity as the main spirit and goal for the global society. It essentially necessitates swift relation and interaction between local to global wherein manifestation lies on cordial and supportive dialogue between bottom and top rungs of society and nations.

The famous phrase 'think global, act local' helps us along in seeing these connections. But relationship should be just as much the other way around. We should think local when we act global, considering the local effects of global decisions.

(Bell 2012: 301)

However, divergence is experienced between the expected juxtaposition between the three very important components sweeping the world in their wave and the actual reality which is transfiguring. The diagram denotes that globalisation, environment and social justice are forming a triangular axis like a tripod on which the global world is resting for stability and sustainability. All the three are intrinsically interconnected and supporting each other. However, they shape up like quadrilaterals having sharp edges on all four sides through which they are penetrating, threatening and endangering the global spirit of homogeneity, sustainability, equity and equality on the one hand, and on the other, human beings and society are exposed to manifold risks, uncertainties and vulnerabilities. Even within society as a whole, the most susceptible part which remains under the constant threat of globalisation and environmental catastrophe are from marginalised and powerless communities. It comprises Scheduled Castes (SC), Scheduled Tribes (ST), women, the aged and the disabled which form the most exposed external layer of society that always remains under threat of getting punitively penetrated and suppressed and as a result struggle earnestly to quest social justice.

Now let us take each component separately for a better understanding that how they are propelling and threatening the serene existence of human beings on the earth. For a better and comprehensive understanding, the illustrative figure (Figure 0.2) of globalisation, environment and social justice interface can be much helpful. To begin with, globalisation has augmented the channels of information, communication, transportation (ICT) which helped improved scientific and technological understanding and enhanced the surveillance capacity of the state. It also helped in creating a homogenous world by diminishing the national boundaries and integrating the society, culture, polity, economy and market. But at the same time it is also blamed for environmental degradation. However, the main contention here

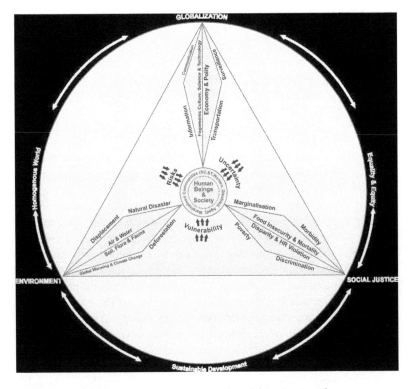

Figure 0.2 Globalisation, environment and social justice interface

Source: Prepared by the author

is that whether globalisation is able to provide access to all, including the marginalised communities, the basic rights of life and sustenance: food, shelter, clothing, water, health, sanitation, quality education, livelihood, social security and most importantly, human dignity and social justice. It is strongly advocated that nations and societies which are more equipped to face global competition and challenges are better placed to gain from globalisation, as compared to nations and societies who have lagged in this respect. As a result, the dominant, hegemonic and powerful nations, societies, communities, class and caste could not only be able to gain from globalisation but also be denied and excluded the marginalised nations and communities from its fruits by the clever use of their vigour and clout.

Environment, both biotic and abiotic, is under constant turmoil due to the hasty pace of globalisation which not only undermines the sustainability and equitable access of the present generation over natural resources but also creates serious doubt about the rights of the forthcoming generations. To meet mammoth industrial and urban needs, continuous plunder of natural resources is currently underway. As a direct outcome, deforestation, climate change and global warming is emerging as the most common ailment which is threatening society. Since we are discussing the interlink between globalisation, environment and social justice here, it may be prudent to agree with those who equate deforestation, an environmental hazard, as social injustice. Deforestation is an expression of social injustice because it has serious social ramifications – disturbing livelihoods and socio-cultural traditions of communities dependent on forests. In a similar fashion, incessant expropriation of nature and forest is hazarding the quality of air and water, degrading the fertility of soil and affecting flora and fauna. On an abiotic part, as an offshoot of globalisation, migration and involuntary displacement is shaping up as the biggest disaster in the 21st century, more fatal than war and famine, undermining social justice and human rights of the displaced and migrants. Recent statistics of UNHCR (UNHCR The UN Refugee Agency 2017) are eyeopening. They emphasise that in a world where nearly 34,000 people are forcibly displaced every day, the present century has witnessed an unprecedented 65.3 million people being forced from home. Among them are 21.3 million refugees, and more ironically, more than half of these are under the age of 18. Alarmingly, there are also 10 million stateless people who have been denied a nationality and access to basic rights such as education, healthcare, employment and freedom of movement. India, being the second-largest populated and fastest growing economy in the world, holds a sizeable representation in the above figures. Similarly, due to insatiable demand for land to meet globalisation, privatisation and industrialisation prerequisites, 'some 60 million people have been displaced in India since independence' (Dubey 2008: xv) according to one estimate causing widespread concern for development induced displacement. Paradoxically, 40% of such displaced represent STs and 20% hail from SCs – the most marginalised and vulnerable sections in India.

While interrogating social justice in such a globalised world which is not at all sensitive and critical for the environment, we see that recent years have seen a steep rise in disparity between the rich and poor, and the graph of poverty is mounting day-by-day as more and more people are falling in its ambit.

> A growing divide between the haves and have-nots has left increasing numbers in the Third World in dire poverty, living on less than a dollar per day. Despite repeated promises of poverty reduction made over the last decade of the 20th century, the actual number of people living in poverty has actually increased by almost 100 million. This occurred at the same time that the total world income actually increased by an average of 2.5 percent annually.
>
> (Stiglitz 2012: 5)

Similarly, a recently published Oxfam report titled 'An Economy for the 99 Per Cent' underlines that

> in signs of rising income inequality, India's richest 1 per cent now hold a huge 58 per cent of the country's total wealth – higher than the global figure of about 50 per cent. On the other hand, the poorest 10 per cent have seen their share of income fall by more than 15 percent.
>
> (*The Hindu* 2017)

Eventually, discrimination and exclusion found a conducive environment to be strongly rooted in the social and economic matrix. Food insecurity, morbidity and mortality are accentuating human misery through induced plunder of natural resources and often violating the human rights of the masses. Therefore, globalisation to be universally accepted necessitates reassurance against endemic fears and risks – in order to be more just. Even those who concede globalisation as 'benign' and consider it as a potential force to benefit and enrich everyone homogeneously in the world, especially the poor, deprived and marginalised, add caution and alarm to the debate, and don't hesitate to admit, as Stiglitz did, that

> Globalization today is not working for many of the world's poor. It is not working for much of the environment. It is not working for the stability of the global economy . . . poverty has soared as incomes have plummeted.
>
> (Stiglitz 2012: 214)

Beck, being highly critical about the nature of globalisation, warns against the fears by stressing that we are slipping on the ladder: risk society is about more than the materially risky, it is also about the ideas of the risk. According to him, globalisation not only trapped and imprisoned ourselves and the artefacts which we created but also made captive of our ideas under invariable risks.

The hope of a tranquil, sustainable and just world

Despite the hegemonic, asymmetrical, hazardous, risky and crisis-oriented path of development adopted by humanity in the age of globalisation, hope is not lost as a silver lining in the dark cloud still exists. Scholars see potential signs of hope in despair. Beck perceives it by stating that

> if ideas and beliefs now matter most, then maybe we can regain control over where science and technology are taking us. May be we can move from the modernization that was associated with class society to a new modernization, a 'second modernization' that Beck terms 'reflexive modernization' – a form of modernization in which we think critically and engaged in democratic debate about science and technology. In Beck's words the goal of reflexive modernization is 'to break the dictatorship of laboratory science. . . . by giving the public a say in science and publicly raising questions'. By reflexive, then, Beck does not mean 'reflexes' or a mirror's 'reflections', but 'self confrontation' in which we collectively reflect on the meanings of modernity, science and rationality.
>
> (Bell 2012: 246)

Similarly, Pieterse argues for critical globalisation, which refers to the

> critical engagement with globalization processes, neither blocking them out nor celebrating them. The keynote of globalization is the

nation state can no longer be taken for granted as the unit of development; cross border transactions and micro or macro regionalization may become major avenues of development. As a global agenda, critical globalism means posing the central question of global inequality in its new manifestations. It entails, among other things, the identification of the social forces that carry different transnational processes and examining the varying conceptualizations of the global environment and globalizing momentum; an analysis of global babble and whose interests are being served.

(Pieterse 2006: 47)

Accordingly scholars may pledge to fulfil the pursuit of a just, harmonious and environmentally sound globe.

Further, population explosion in recent decades has immensely augmented the requirement of commodities and therefore, a mad race is seen among capitalists and industrialists to supply goods to cater market requirements. It is happening even at the cost of the plunder of nature and environment and has created a paradoxical situation that increasingly challenges the quest for sustainable development. Therefore

in view of the need to take into account the concerns of the poorest, in terms of access to the resources necessary for a dignified life and a healthy environment for all, environmental justice constitutes a new paradigm that articulates social justice with environmental concerns.

(Ballet et al. 2013: 31)

The true spirit of the approach on environmental justice strongly advocates that the relationship between human beings and nature are above all relationships between human beings concerning nature. It also refers people back to their own responsibilities towards social and environmental justice.

Following a similar pattern of thought, Dunlap strongly advocates the path of an ecologically sound and balanced society by underlining that 'moving toward a more sustainable society will require using natural resources far more efficiently in order to minimize both resources withdrawals and pollution resulting from resources extraction, use and disposal' (Dunlap and Michelson 2008: 11). In order to accomplish the goals of a sustainable society, environmental sociology therefore has gone through two distinct phases to meet the endemic crisis and risks as a discrete discipline.

In the first stage, the major theoretical task was to identify a key factor (or a closely related set of factors) that created an enduring 'crisis' of environmental degradation and destruction. More recently, there has been a significant shift towards another task: discovering the most effective mechanism of environmental reform or improvement which will help 'chart the way forward to more socially secure and environmentally friendly arrangements'.

(Hannigan 2006: 16)

Despite the endemic crisis of developmentalism and environmental challenges facing the world at contemporary time due to global processes, Sen has not lost hope of a just society. Sen perceives the situation from a more pragmatic and optimistic point of view in his most celebrated volume on *The Idea of Justice*. He asserts that 'what moves us, reasonably enough, is not the realization that the world falls short of being completely just – which few of us expect – but that there are clearly remediable injustices around us which we want to eliminate' (Sen 2010: vii). For making justice more instrumental and accessible, he further advocates the prudent means. He stresses:

First, a theory of justice that can serve as the basis of practical reasoning must include ways of judging how to reduce injustice and advance justice, rather than aiming only at the characterization of perfectly just societies – an exercise that is such a dominant feature of many theories of justice in political philosophy today.

(Sen 2010: ix)

Therefore, even though the steep and risky path of globalisation which we are following today doesn't seem to provide a suitable world ahead from the point of view of sustainable development, environmental sustainability, ecological harmony and a just social order with equity and equality; but everything is not lost. We still have hope: the hope of a tranquil, sustainable and just world, a place where we can live peacefully in perfect harmony with nature, environment and our fellow human beings.

Structure of the present volume

At such a time when the galaxy of intelligentsia is grappling with the symmetrical nexus between globalisation and environment, its impact on the marginalised sections and concern for promoting social justice, the present volume is contoured to ascertain answers to paramount riddles by situating Indian experiences at centre stage. However, to have a broader view on the subject and to develop a comparative insight, it also includes some chapters dealing with other countries. Under the given backdrop, the volume is titled *Globalisation, Environment and Social Justice: Perspectives, Issues and Concerns*. It begins with a foreword followed by an introduction, which unfolds the theme of the book by emphasising the perspectives, issues and concerns related to globalisation, environment and social justice, their interlinkages and significance by taking into account the views and standpoint of various scholars. Further, it bestows an analytical portrayal of various papers covered in the edited book vis-à-vis their respective sub-themes by assessing impact on environment and concomitant social justice.

Now let me briefly provide a synoptic view of the volume, which is divided into three parts. Part I is captioned 'Globalisation, Environmental Sustainability and Social Justice: Perspectives and Issues' and has a broad canvas. In consonance of the sub-theme title, this section is specifically devoted to examine various perspectives and issues concerning globalisation, environmental sustainability and social justice, especially by taking into consideration the Indian experience. However, to deduce a comparative global picture, some chapters covering the international issues are also covered in the section. Part I comprises eight chapters in toto.

In the first chapter of the section, 'Globalisation, Environment and Social Justice: A Theoretical Insight', B.K. Nagla applies the world system theory to comprehend the contemporary discourse on globalisation, environment and social justice. He argues that globalisation is pervasive and affects all aspects of human life. Evidence shows that it operates in a lopsided and haphazard manner further widening inequality and stratification embedded in the society. As a consequence, the hegemonic minority holds a maximum chunk of resources and the majority suffers in acute poverty. In a world system framework, globalisation and neo-liberal policies practiced by the core dominant countries through ecological unequal exchange to serve their interest and greed have produced hazardous wastes of industrial production exported to peripheral countries. It has endangered health, induced safety concerns and environmental risks to the residents of the peripherals. Therefore, environmental justice needs to be ensured regardless of race, colour, national origin, or income with respect to the development, implementation, and enforcement of environmental laws, regulations and policies. Social justice enshrined in the policies of the welfare state is marred by globalisation. In the contemporary context, the social justice agenda is hijacked by non-state organisations, which is quite critical. The older theories of social justice are not able to compete with new challenges of developments in the era of globalisation and therefore they necessitate critical review, specifically in the Indian context. In this background, the chapter explores the intricate nexus that has emerged as a result of globalisation, inextricably linking issues of environment and social justice. It highlights three very important aspects: first, the analysis of invasive currents of globalisation which swept environment and impinged social justice; second, by coalescing perspectives and debates of scholars on environment and social justice, it explores the links that exists between the two and the effect of globalisation on them; third, it accentuates the discourse on common concerns related to the predicament.

Marco Grasso and Venkatesh Dutta focus on 'A Comparative Assessment of Climate Policies of Top Global Emitters and Evolution of an Effective Climate Regime', wherein their concerns include issues of environmental effectiveness, economic efficiency, equity and political feasibility. They observe that top emitters of the world are unwilling to do anything substantial to meaningfully mitigate climate change risks, and they continue to disagree over the extent of each other's responsibilities. They also seem to deter action on their commitment of common but differentiated responsibilities. The first commitment period of the Kyoto Protocol expired in 2012, and the protocol failed because it prescribed an uneven burden sharing and missed including all major emitters in a meaningful way. In the current climate policy landscape, the prospects for a rational climate policy are exceedingly vague. Several negotiations, agreements and policies have failed consistently for the last several decades. This chapter evaluates the climate policies of top emitting countries by using four broad criteria, namely, environmental effectiveness, economic efficiency, equity and political feasibility. The chapter first delineates the rationale and general evaluative framework of the analysis and then investigates top emitters' climate policies according to the four perspectives indicated. On the basis of the analysis, top emitters are clustered according to their performances in the determinants of climate policy into three main actors: laggards, average and pushers. The chapter shows that political feasibility is the weakest component in top emitters' current climate policies, followed by equity concerns, while environmental effectiveness appears to be the most successful constituent and much progress is still required in the domain of economic efficiency. Finally, the chapter points out some common threads in, and emerging issues from, top emitters' climate policies. The chapter concludes that the politics of climate change, energy policy and environmental justice might be reoriented in ways that could result in more robust and sustainable political consensus for action.

Sheetal Sharma deals with the 'Politics of Environment' with a focus on green parties in Europe as a model for India. She notes that modernity and its concomitant processes of development, industrialisation and urbanisation ushered advancement of humanity to such a level which had never been seen in the history of mankind. However, such development has an intrinsic cost which humanity has to pay. The process of development has had its set of negative impact and consequences as much as it had a positive impact seen in terms of the material enrichment of humanity. One most critical effect of such development has been the environment. The relentless pursuit of growth and material accumulation has led to the abuse of natural resources beyond replacement and repair. Environmental movements that emerged at different points of time in the last century have in varying degrees and capacities drawn attention towards the destruction of the fragile ecological balance and ensuing natural disasters. The Western countries have also seen the green ideology shaping up in the policies of political parties. However, developing countries like India essentially necessitate the green ideology in politics to endow an equilibrium between industrialisation, economic growth and conservation of nature and natural resources for future generations. Ironically, India does not have political groups that can push the green agenda forward emphatically. Hence, the chapter draws attention to the issues involving deficient embodiment of the green ideology in Indian politics. To deduce a comprehensive portrait, it emphasises three focal aspects. It begins with the discussion about modernity, its consequences and the idea of environmentalism. The concomitant part highlights the ideology of the greens and the European green parties. Finally, in the background of earlier discussion and on a comparative note, the last section critically underscores the missing green ideology in Indian politics.

In her chapter, 'Globalisation and Political Economy of Protected Areas', Sudeshna Mukherjee holds that the omnipresent process of globalisation, despite manifold affirmative outcomes, often takes a toll on the environment. Globalisation and synchronised privatisation and liberalisation under the ambit of structural adjustment is corroborating an upsurge of poverty, unemployment, discrimination, injustice, and inequality besides environmental degradation. The vicious situation demands a desperate search for alternatives to comprehend the interests of conservation and people's livelihood rights together. It accentuates a conservation policy which essentially requires economically viable protected areas. It has its genesis in the 1992 Earth Summit, when a bold new Convention on Biological Diversity (CBD) evolved which, inter alia, calls on governments to establish systems of protected areas and to administer them for conservation, sustainable use and equitable benefit sharing. The governments' recognition of protected areas as economic institutions have a key role to play for alleviation of poverty and maintenance of critical life-support systems of global communities. The emergent perception for protected areas entails comprehensive awareness and understanding towards economic values generated by them. However, global conventions and programs alone are not sufficient to ensure continued existence of, and sufficient funding for, protected areas. In times of fiscal austerity and tightening government budgets – especially in developing countries which are home for immense global biodiversity – traditional funding sources for protected areas are increasingly under threat. Innovative alternatives to these traditional sources are needed in order to secure enduring viability of protected areas. It is through indigenous development which calls for social, economic and cultural transformations of societies based on revitalisations of traditions, respect for environment and equitable relations of production; hitherto excluded communities can be organised to develop the potential of every region. In this background, the chapter explores the impact of globalisation on conservation policies of India and economic viability of protected areas.

Edgard Leite Ferreira Neto in his chapter discusses 'Environmental Challenges in Brazil, Local and Global'. He rightly notes that Brazil has immense mineral resources, a mild and usually humid climate, fertile land and the largest rainforest. A traditional exporter of commodities, Brazil has a progressive framework of depletion of its natural resources. This process has its own cultural and historical variables, whose interruption presents itself as a very difficult proposition. Brazil has at least five major moments of environmental depletion: first, connected to the start of the Portuguese colonisation process, in the 16th century, that led to the depletion of coastal forests; second, related to the expansion of cultural mining, which is the source of the great ecological and economic crisis of the 18th century; third, the expansion of sugar, cotton and coffee cultures, which culminated in a relative resource depletion in the South Central regions, throughout the 19th and early 20th centuries, when for the first time the issue of water resources has become politically obvious; fourth, derived from the expansion process to the Central Highlands, which began in the mid-20th century with the construction of Brasilia and finished in the 1970s, when large-scale Amazon predatory processes began; and fifth, due to the expansion policy of agricultural business and extensive mining related to the economic growth cycle of the late 20th and early 21st centuries, whose results have global implications today. The nature and reason for this historical environmental predation are related to peculiarities of Brazil: among them the most prominent are (1) the predominance of an expansionist model that seeks the conquest and expansion of borders, and (2) the social belief in a divine, not organic or mechanical, organisation of the natural world. Hence, the chapter examines the historical causes and inter-related local and global aspects for environmental challenges in Brazil in contemporary times.

Benson M. O. Agaya delves into the issue of 'Globalisation, Environment and Sustainable Development' with a focus on the challenges and opportunities in the conservation of water catchments in South Eastern Kenya. He opines that globalisation presents a complex set of dynamics that not only offers many opportunities to better the human condition but also involves significant potential threats. The central argument of the chapter holds that globalisation introduces business and environmental standards that are vital for strengthening the competitiveness of communities that have historically been on the margins of formal economies. On the other hand, liberalisation of trade, an inevitable companion of globalisation, is known to intensify the demand and exploitation of environmental resources leading to depletion or degradation of vital livelihood-supporting resources. Considering the importance of creating symmetry between the benefits and costs of globalisation, especially with respect to sustainable environmental and natural resource management, the chapter seeks to fulfil two objectives: first, to identify appropriate interventions that could be applied to realise sustainable management and conservation of natural resources in valuable water catchments and wildlife habitats in South Eastern Kenya; second, to examine the ways in which micro and small enterprise development can be utilised to strengthen local community links with the world through entrepreneurship and tourism. The chapter concludes that the development of conservation-oriented enterprises is an important means of reducing direct reliance of local communities on extracted natural resources from the environment while securing sustainable livelihoods in a globally competitive business environment that has traditionally disadvantaged the poor. It further observes that technology diffusion is a crucial tool to spur entrepreneurship and promote environmental sustainability and equitable human development in low-income communities living in fragile ecosystems of South Eastern Kenya.

Aditya Raj and Papia Raj discuss 'The Glocal Paradox: Waste Production in Patna'. In this chapter, the authors examine the local impact of global influences with a specific focus on waste production, which is as old as human civilisation though the nature of waste has changed substantially. The rapidly mounting waste production in developing countries today is caused by three interrelated factors: the soaring rates of population intensification, hasty urbanisation, and inception of a more sophisticated form of consumerism. However, the sources as well as composition of these wastes are varied. Evidences show that it is becoming an ever-growing challenge to manage waste, especially for low-income cities and countries. Patna, the capital city of Bihar (India), is an ideal instance as it has been declared by the State High Court as the 'Garbage City' of the country. Even though the city is the dearth of industries, households and growing businesses generate a huge chunk of wastes. The streets of Patna are strewn with garbage, which not only is a displeasing sight but also has several environmental and health effects. The findings suggest that Patna is the most populated and urbanised district of Bihar. It is habitual for large-scale in- and out-migration within as well as outside the state and even overseas. Migration brings in diverse consumption patterns and behavioural practices. Traditional norms and values along with the sense of ownership and practices of social spaces are vanishing while emergent patterns are facing difficulties in getting established. The horizontal and vertical transformations have thrown challenges, and waste production in Patna represents an instance of the growing glocal paradox that calls for integrated thinking for informed policy decisions.

B. N. Prasad deals with 'Neo-liberal Development, Environmental Sustainability and Social Justice: Contextualising the Mahatma Gandhi National Rural Employment Guarantee Scheme' in the last chapter of the section. He finds that the practice of development has undergone a change during the last eight and a half decades. Evolved from economic growth, it culminated into sustainable development; hence, the approach has changed from income to capability building. In convergence to the latest development paradigm, MNREGS (Mahatma Gandhi National Rural Employment Guarantee Scheme, 2005) was started by the Government of India with much fanfare with the purpose to guarantee sustained employment, ensure minimum wages and ultimately capacity building of the rural masses. However, the scheme was not free of criticism, as eminent economists have dubbed

MNREGS as the 'dole' of the UPA (United Progressive Alliance) government. Criticism of this sort has serious implications on concept, theory and practice of development, especially in a developing country like India. In this backdrop, the chapter is a modest attempt to explore the relationship between market-led development, the issue of social justice and the potential of MNREGS within the sustainable development paradigm by keeping at centre stage three critical components of sustainable development: social, economic and environmental. The findings underline that MNREGS brings economic sustainability by guaranteeing a minimum 100 days of employment to rural households, thus ensuring acritical minimum economic security to the labouring poor. The issue of social sustainability is also ensured through the mandatory provisions of the act to convene Gram Sabha meetings at least twice a year for choice of works and site selection, social audit, crèche facility, drinking water, village vigilance committee, right to check muster rolls and unemployment allowance, medical treatment in case of injury and ex gratia payment for disability or death. These measures are meant to increase people's participation and bring transparency in the program, thereby creating social sustainability through development. Finally, the act is a major source of environmental sustainability in terms of the symbiotic relationship between the environment and rural social structure. The foremost permissible works under its aegis are water conservation and harvesting, irrigation, renovation of traditional water bodies, flood control, drought proofing and rural connectivity. Hence the central endeavour of such development programs is to improve the resource base of the rural economy, thereby promoting environmental sustainability. On the basis of the above exposition, a rosy picture of the program emerges, but the scheme is not free from bottlenecks and misuse of public finance. The scheme has been attacked on grounds of corruption, executive apathy, quality of created assets, inclusivity, lack of awareness and so forth. These criticisms are valid to a great extent. But it can never be ignored that the scheme is the world's largest experiment in contemporary times in the quest for sustainable development. Hence the tremendous potential of MNREGS to improve the socio-economic status of the labouring poor cannot be ignored and stands merit.

Part II of the volume focuses on 'Globalisation, Marginalised Sections and Social Justice: Problems and Challenges'. It has become a cause of serious concern and debate nowadays, that globalisation has further widened and amplified the existing disparities in the society and the marginalised sections of the population, especially the SCs, STs and women, are the greatest losers. The prevailing circumstance hampers the possibility of ensuring social justice unto the last. Hence the section is devoted to analysing the impact of globalisation on marginalised sections from the point of view of social justice. The section possesses five chapters submitted by scholars from India and abroad. In their chapter, 'Institutional Challenges of CPR Management', Amlendu Jyotishi, R. Parthasarthy and Sajiv Madhavan discuss insights from the Tawa Reservoir Fisheries Cooperative. They find that in the context of growing concerns over tribal rights and amid continual contention between government and people's cooperatives for the safeguard of tribal livelihoods, there are many supporters of a decentralised people's cooperative management for natural resources. Based on this premise, however, this chapter looks into micro realities to unearth the foundation of cooperative management to explore causes which induce cooperation or conflict. In what way does the decision to constitute cooperatives affect daily operations? What needs to be done to ensure the relevance of the institution with changing circumstances? With the case study of Tawa Matsya Sangh, the chapter explores the internal and external dynamics of cooperatives and their effects on the livelihood of the people. The conclusion drawn emphasises that the cooperative system works very well when equity among the members is ensured, even when the composition of the group is heterogeneous. Further it concludes that all the potential members who can benefit from the resource system must be included in the cooperative. It reiterates the age-old conflict between equality and efficiency and suggests that pursuing one at the expense of the other is not a wise decision.

In her chapter, Jan Marie Fritz focuses on 'Social Justice for Women and Girls: Global Pacts, Unmet Goals, Environmental Issues'. The chapter examines the tribulations encountered by women and girls in a world that is increasingly connected but also is more asymmetrical and has profound issues of sustainability. While people are discussing and/or intervening to address the world's daunting problems, there are increasing calls for these interventions to be based on social justice (inclusion and fairness) principles. The first section of the chapter discusses the global situation of women and girls and analyses the extent by which their world is inclusive and fair. The second section exemplify the goals outlined in three very imperative international documents concerning human rights for women: the UN Convention on the Elimination of All Forms of Discrimination Against Women, the Beijing Declaration and Platform for Action, and UN Security Council Resolution 1325: Women, Peace and Security. Analysis is done particularly with reference to environmental issues. The third section of the chapter examines some glaring initiatives recently embarked to progress the society towards accomplishing the goals noted in the human rights documents pertaining to women and the environment. Finally, the concluding section argues and underscores the role of human rights documents in meeting the goals of ensuring justice to women and girls and embarks on the future blueprint of expectations to improve their situation further.

S. N. Chaudhary deliberates upon 'Globalisation, Environmental Degradation and Tribal Identity: With Particular Reference to Central India'. He affirms that environment is historically related to tribes in a symbiotic manner. Elements and traits of culture – both material and non-material – are constructed in consonance of the local environment which in turn protects and promotes the environment. Tribes develop their language, religion, food habit, dress pattern, dispute management mechanism and rituals related to vital demographic events in the light of their specific environmental setting to ensure peaceful living. Therefore elements of environment provide a basic foundation for the construction and sustenance of their identity. Analogous states of affairs, with nominal changes, continue for generations without harming the core identity of tribes. Low population pressure, insignificant and ad-hoc interaction with outside world and limited requirements retain and perpetuate their symbiotic relations. But over a period of time, under global influences, appropriation of different constituents of environment is done by external forces which in turn have proved detrimental to the composition of environment and tribal identity. Gradually, with growing unregulated interaction with the exterior world, the process of environmental degradation has become hasty. No successful effort in a tenable manner is able to retard environmental degradation; rather, it has accelerated since the year 1991 with the commencement of globalisation in India. By taking into consideration the glaring instances of Central Indian states like Madhya Pradesh, Chhattisgarh, Jharkhand, Odisha and Rajasthan, where large number of tribes of different categories are residing, the chapter comprehensively examines the state of tribes by integrating both 'bookview' and 'fieldview'. The findings suggest that environmental degradation has caused serious harm to a majority of these tribes, their material and non-material culture including livelihood and identity. The relentless pursuit of resources failed them miserably to associate with the so-called mainstream process and help them to form new identity. Many of them have failed to retain their traditional identity either, due to environmental degradation, decreasing carrying capacity and access to these resources. Hence pervasive environmental squalor has converted them rootless in social, psychological and economic terms. It has brought them in a paradoxical situation to what Michael Cernea calls 'impoverishment risks' in terms of landlessness, joblessness, homelessness, marginalisation, food insecurity, high morbidity, loss of access to common property resources (CPRs) and community disarticulation. Gomati Bodra Hembrom discusses the issue of 'Sacred Landscape, Modes of Subsistence and Adivasi Rights in the Globalised World'. She observes that the world over the indigenous population has shared a symbiotic relationship with environment and natural resources. They have developed cultural traditions, economy, social-control mechanism, religious institutions and production techniques to retain these relationships. Their cultural system ensured a sustainable use of resources and it continued their means of livelihood for several generations. It is a fact that indigenous and tribal communities, even though inhabited in different regions of the globe, have been playing a vital role in preservation and management of natural resources within the framework of their indigenous knowledge. Their identity as a community is closely linked to these natural resources. Indigenous spiritual and cultural practices depend upon access to their traditional land, including historically and spiritually significant sites. Recent years have seen indigenous territories being used on a larger scale by the state, for expropriation of iron, uranium, coal, copper and other metals by mining; to build mega dams, urban cities, infrastructural developments and so forth. These developments are essential for industrialisation but have adversely affected Adivasis. It crumbled their traditional economy as well as the ecological base. Loss of natural resources also brought exceeding calamities such as climate change, global warming, pollution, floods, droughts and intense storms, epidemics, depletion of forests and loss of biodiversity. Today indigenous communities are finding it difficult to maintain sustainable economic systems, to practice their traditional ceremonies, and to preserve their hunting, gathering and fishing cultures. Industrialisation, urbanisation and national development objectives have seriously affected tribal profoundly embedded spiritual and cultural relationship with the ecosystem. In this backdrop, the chapter draws upon the sociological perspectives for an understanding of environment, modes of subsistence and adivasi life (i.e. the inter-relations of human beings, flora and fauna as well as the elements of the physical and natural environment). These interrelations are explored by putting special emphasis on issues of livelihood, sustainability and survival, conservation of biodiversity, and assessing significance of sacred landscape which are deeply inherent in their culture. The chapter also focuses upon the interface between environment, the role of the state, globalisation initiatives and identity struggles among Adivasis. Further, it tries to trace the issues of rights and social justice related to policy framework, with special focus on PESA (Panchayat [Extension to Scheduled Areas]) Act 1996 and Tribal and Forest Dwellers Right Act 2006.

In their chapter, 'Re(caste-ing) Justice: Globalisation and Dalits in India', Antara Ray and Ramanuj Ganguly observe that in the last two and half decades, India has restructured in the direction of a wider open market economy. Thereby borderless exports and imports of all types of goods and services are working as a central apparatus of development leading to unfettered and extraordinary changes in the society. The justification forwarded for liberalisation and globalisation largely argues that structural reforms would bring even-handed competition and optimal efficiency in the economy resulting in engagement of labour, a surge in income and inclusive affluence. It is also expected that the impact of globalisation would extend to touch such facets of the life situation that are not only restricted to the economic sphere. It will proliferate into the key elements of social living, environmental usage, social identity and delimiting the role of the state. However, it has been observed that globalisation has differential impact from country to country, from region to region and from community to community. Thus it becomes difficult to identify the beneficiaries, measure the scale and direction of development, or assign value of the overall growth. Studies conducted on the Indian panorama during the last 25 years substantiate that the concomitant political and economic transformation enveloped inequity and unsustainability which deprived the masses from sharing the riches and in achieving social justice. Furthermore, there are varying perceptions of development and social justice. Though upholders of globalisation would like us to believe that we may perceive egalitarian growth within and beyond our country, nevertheless a differentiated measurement frequently exposes that perception about development and justice is actually an amalgamation of divergent variables socially constructed by community sub-dimensions dependent on the cultural context and their historical experience. Under these arguments, the present chapter engages with the question, can we have a uniform idea at all, construction and application of social justice where a multiple reality of Dalits (as we have various categories of Dalits with respect to class, gender, region, religion, language, aim, status, occupation and so on) exists in the contemporary globalised world and within a democratic-capitalised Indian state? It further examines that how globalisation has changed (if it has changed at all) the status of Dalits and the idea of social justice with respect to them? In doing so, the chapter attempts to examine the importance and need of social justice in caste-ridden, contemporary India, with specific reference to Dalit conceptualisation and the changing idea and construction of social justice from the pre-independence to the post-independence period.

Part III is captioned 'Globalisation and Questions of Equity and Social Justice: Issues from Various Sectors'. Globalisation, being a multifaceted and highly dynamic process of change, has affected almost all the aspects and sections of human beings living on this planet including their society and environment. However, there are many grey areas which have never been considered worthy for serious scrutiny and analysis. Hence the unit is an attempt to bring into consideration some very important yet neglected issues which needs proper attention for the convenience of understanding the issues comprehensively. It would be interesting to note, through the five chapters of the unit, the response of these sectors in the wave of globalisation for the accomplishment of equity and social justice.

Here, Ravi S. Singh and Dipankar Roy deliberates upon the issue of 'Service-Level Benchmarking: Some Emerging Global Lessons for Indian Water Governance'. They observe that accessibility to water is traditionally subjected to multi-level social exclusions in the name of social (caste) and economic (class) identities in India. Paradoxically, the Global Water Partnership (GWP 1996) regime is overwhelmingly vociferous over issues of efficiency, and particularly silent on questions of equity in water accessibility. The recently introduced Service-Level Bench Marking (SLBM) program by the Ministry of Urban Development for the urban water supply and sanitation (WSS) sector is a flagship drive towards GWP. It has two key components, namely, full cost recovery and loss minimisation in terms of unaccounted water. Ironically, here the definition of efficiency is understood only in monetary terms and the parameters of access-equity are hardly given any consideration. There is a strong possibility that such biased measurement of efficiency would further augment the destitute of the already excluded communities. To support this argument, few debatable features of SLBM have been discussed in this chapter with the aid of number of secondary data sources. In this vein, rationalities of the much-hyped link between increasing private sector participation and efficiency enhancements have been analysed. An attempt has also been made to evaluate the weak aspects of SLBM and outline some suggestive measures to ameliorate the situation.

Purba Chattopadhyay's chapter deliberates upon 'Shifting Food Production and Consumption Patterns in Globalised India: Issues of Sustainability, Security and Justice'. In her opinion, food production, consumption and choices are determined by society, economy and culture which remain under flux due to continuous interactive processes. It reflects upon a complex, dynamic process of development, distribution and social justice in any economy at a given point of time. Globalisation has a distinct impact on all three aspects of food. Economic growth is typically embodied by improvements in a country's food supply, both quantitative and qualitative, and a gradual reduction in nutritional deficiencies. It also brings out changes in the production, processing, distribution and marketing of food. Diets evolve over time and are influenced by income, prices, individual preferences and beliefs, cultural traditions and geographical, environmental, social and economic aspects. The growth rate of agriculture has declined during the reform period and subsequently food grain production has shown a significant decline. A vexing issue is the mismatch between the steadily declining productivity of inferior goods and the malnourished masses that live below the poverty line. In this background, the aim of this chapter is to ascertain food productivity and evince its supply in the Indian context, to determine ways by which production intricacies gets affected by multinational companies (MNCs) under the realities of globalisation and its consequent repercussions. Further, it examines linkages between globalisation and nutritional trends by taking into consideration food demand. It also focuses on the economic costs and consequences of the increased demand of unhealthy foods and how it is proving detrimental. In addition, while analysing the demand supply interface, the chapter examines the cultural transition of India reflected in terms of food choices and tries to see how social justice is ensured to all in the domain of globalisation. The findings highlight that the world is witnessing drastic changes in consumption patterns. The consumption of edible oils and sugar has increased drastically from what they were a few decades ago. India too is not an exception to this process and is witnessing what may be termed as nutrition transition. As a direct consequence of such consumption there is a steep rise in non-communicable diseases like diabetes, obesity and cardiovascular diseases. Thus, India showcases the worst of both: severely undernourished as well as over-fed masses.

Siri Gamage, in his chapter 'Transnational Higher Education (TNHE) Trends in India and China: Comparison of Euro-American and Chinese Models', offers observations on international trends on education in India and China. According to him, it is a commonly held knowledge and understanding that the European – particularly British – used education at schools and university level to establish their colonial hegemony, supremacy and power in the Asian region during the colonial period. To accomplish this endeavour, religion along with educational institutions and print media played a significant role. Now the central issue is whether the same is happening in the post-colonial era of globalisation. In this context, the chapter examines five inter-related aspects: (1) the way higher education has been internationalised by the Anglophone countries to the extent of it becoming a massive income earning industry; (2) the promotion of English as an international language for the above purpose; (3) the way international schools are promoted in less developed countries to compete with national schools; (4) the undermining of local languages and knowledge in the process; and (5) the need to re-articulate and re-invigorate indigenous knowledge systems in social sciences by way of *Southern* Theory as articulated by Raewyn Connell and other scholars located in the global south.

Siddhartha Mukerji deals with 'Globalisation, IT and Governance: Implications for Social Justice and Inclusivity' by evaluating the inter-linkage between globalisation, IT and governance through the lens of social justice and inclusivity. The chapter asserts that globalisation contains within its womb both benefits and challenges. The expansion and integration of economies have led to rapid growth on one hand, while on the other it has resulted in new forms of marginalisation and exclusion. The story of India's information technology (IT) industry is the best illustration of this thesis. It is widely known and acknowledged that India has taken a global lead in the service industry. The skilfulness and proficiency of its software professionals are unparalleled. The recent decade has witnessed rapid growth in the IT industry. Though state incentives have contributed extensively for its grand success, however, due to export orientation its benefits have not flown towards local development. Lately, the inclusive agenda of e-governance has provided a new impetus aligned on novel perspective to technology and communication sector. It seeks to bring technology to grassroots level and minimises the digital divide embedded in the society. It can be seen as one of the major breakthroughs in IT policies in recent years. But the recent development is not harmonious. A closer look at the IT industry portrays new forms of exclusion and marginalisation that have cropped up recently. The above debate provides a wider platform to probe into emergent questions: (1) How did IT emerge as an export-oriented sector? What were the political motivations? (2) What led to a shift in orientation towards e-governance, and how was it achieved? (3) How does e-governance act as a tool for empowerment and inclusive development? (4) What are the internal facets of marginalisation and labour rights violations within the industry?

In the last chapter of the unit and the volume, Manisha Tripathy Pandey focuses on 'Risk and Vulnerability in the Neo-liberal Order: Assessing Social Security in India'. She notes that the discourse of risk society describes the stresses and strains characteristics of contemporary social life. Risks are result of the process of modernisation which gets heightened in the neo-liberal age where market is a deciding factor. This chapter differentiates between risk and social vulnerability. Vulnerability is the outcome of the neo-liberal order and refers to the incapacity and failure of the state and society to withstand the consequences of an aggressive market. Whereas risks can be managed, vulnerability persists as threats and problems to the state and society at large. The chapter reviews and analyses the National Pension Scheme, 2004 for the organised sector and the Unorganised Workers' Social Security Act, 2008 for the unorganised sector to understand India's social security system. The vulnerability due to market forces makes the society insecure, uncertain and catastrophic. The catastrophe could be rise in insurgencies, riots, conflict and anxiety. Thus, socially vulnerable society is the result of inevitable structural form of the neo-liberal order. The neo-liberal market develops crisis-related safety nets, but these are not permanent, redistributive and sustainable.

References

Ballet, Jerome et al. 2013. 'Environment, Justice and the Capability Approach', *Ecological Economics*, 85: 28–34, January, www.sciencedirect.com/science/article/pii/S0921800912004144, accessed on 28/11/2016.

Beck, Ulrich. 1992. *Risk Society: Toward a New Modernity*. New Delhi: Sage.

Bell, Michael Mayerfeld. 2012. *An Invitation to Environmental Sociology*. New Delhi: Sage India.

Bhagwati, Jagdish. 2008. *In Defense of Globalization*. New Delhi: Oxford University Press.

Bookchin, Murray. 1985. The Ecology of Freedom: The Emergence and Dissolution of Hierarchy. California: Cheshire Books

Dubey, Muchkund. 2008. 'Preface', in *India Social Development Report 2008: Development and Displacement*. Council for Social Development. New Delhi: Oxford University Press.

Dunlap, Riley E. and Michelson, William. (eds.) 2008. *Handbook of Environmental Sociology*. Indian Reprint. New Delhi: Rawat.

Ghuman, R. S., Singh, Surjit and Brar, Jaswinder Singh. 2010. *Globalization and Change*. Jaipur: Rawat.

Giddens, Anthony. 1990. *The Consequence of Modernity*. Cambridge: Polity Press.

Hannigan, John. 2006. *Environmental Sociology*. New York: Routledge.

The Hindu. 2017. 'Richest 1% Owns 58% of Total Wealth of India: Oxfam', www.thehindu.com/business/Economy/Richest-1-own-58-of-total-wealth-in-India-Oxfam/article17044486.ece, accessed on 5/3/2017.

Kothari, Rajni. 1988. *Rethinking Development: In Search of Human Alternatives*. University of Michigan and New Horizons Press.

McLuhan, M. 1960. 'Exploration in Communication', in E. Carpenter and M. McLuhan (eds.), *Exploration in Communication*. Boston: Bedon Press.

Pieterse, Jan Nederveen. 2006. *Development Theory: Deconstruction/Reconstruction*. New Delhi: Sage India.

Sen, Amartya. 2007. *Identity & Violence: The Illusion of Destiny*. New Delhi: Penguin India.

Sen, Amartya. 2010. *The Idea of Justice*. New Delhi: Penguin India.

Stiglitz, Joseph. 2012. *Globalization and Its Discontents*. New Delhi: Penguin India.

UNHCR The UN Refugee Agency. 2017. 'Figures at a Glance', www.unhcr.org/figures-at-a-glance.html, accessed on 5/3/2017.

Verma, Manish K. 2015. *Globalization and Environment: Discourse, Policies and Practices*. New Delhi: Rawat.

Part I

Globalisation, environmental sustainability and social justice

Perspectives and issues

1   Globalisation, environment and social justice

A theoretical insight

B. K. Nagla

Globalisation is the process by which all peoples and communities come to experience an increasingly common economic, social and cultural environment. Globalisation has not only affected all aspects of human life but also influenced the social institutions to a great extent. It operates in an uneven and unequal manner. The neo-liberal economy (i.e. liberalisation, privatisation and globalisation) has further compounded the unevenness and inequality in society. The small minority of world's population holds maximum resources and a majority of people are grappled in poverty. Hence, the globalised world sweeps away regulation and undermines local and national politics, just as the consolidation of the nation state swept away local economies, dialects, cultures and political forms. Globalisation creates new markets and wealth even as it causes widespread suffering, disorder, and unrest. It is both a source of repression and a catalyst for global movements of social justice and emancipation. The great financial crisis of 2008–09 has revealed the dangers of an unstable, deregulated, global economy but it has also given rise to important global initiatives for change (Global Policy Forum 2005–2015).[1]

In this context, local and global environmental problems are increasingly demanding our attention, as threats to our quality of life and even our physical survival become more apparent. The environmental agenda has largely been driven by understandable concern for the increasing pressure placed on the natural world by human behaviour. Therefore, it may be argued that the globalisation of hazards puts the health of people in peripheral countries at risk in order to benefit those living in the core countries. Contextualising the export of hazardous products, industrial production processes, and wastes in a world systems framework, it discusses how ecological unequal exchange, the treadmill of production and metabolic rift have contributed to the globalisation of health, safety and environmental risks.

Environmental justice is the fair treatment and meaningful involvement of all people regardless of race, colour, national origin or income with respect to the development, implementation, and enforcement of environmental laws, regulations and policies. The state, as an institution, guarantees social welfare and social justice to the marginalised groups but globalisation has not only threatened it but also made it weak. It has now retreated back from its welfare role. In the contemporary context, the social justice agenda is taken over by non-state organisations that are critical. The older theories of social justice, which are either inadequate or inapplicable, today cannot cover the new developments that have taken place in the era of globalisation and therefore they have to be reviewed, specifically in the Indian context.

The present chapter is an exploration of the intricate nexus that emerges as a result of globalisation, inextricably linking together issues of environmental and social justice. The chapter deals with three main things: (1) to analyse the main currents of globalisation which have an impact on environment and social justice; (2) to bring together views of different scholars, the chapter focuses on the area of environment and social justice, and explores the links that exists between the two and the effect of globalisation on these areas; and (3) to discourse upon the common concerns related to the problem.

Global context

The last 20 years have demonstrated as never before the interdependence of life on the globe. The whole global environment is affected by changes in weather and land use, which in turn have direct implications for individuals and communities. Economic developments on one continent can have almost simultaneous consequences on another. Conflicts in one area can provoke actions and reactions on the other side of the world which can be watched simultaneously on television or the internet by the whole world. Broadly, we may refer here to four types of environment, namely, the natural environment, the war and peace environment, the economic environment and the social environment. We shall discuss here briefly about these entire environments but our emphasis will be on the natural environment.

The natural environment

People share a common need for and a right to a fair share of the Earth's resources, including a clean, safe and healthy environment. These basic requirements are under threat from climate change and environmental degradation. These challenges are widely recognised as presenting the greatest priority for global cooperation. The degradation of the global environment has observable social and economic consequences and therefore has an impact on the ability of people and communities to achieve their potential as human beings and to give expression to their human rights.

The war and peace environment

Some have argued that one reaction to the process of globalisation has been an escalation of tension and in particular the development of conflicts between religious and ethnic groups.

The economic environment

From 1945 until the 1970s, conventional economic wisdom saw the improvement of living conditions for all as an economic, social, and moral imperative, built upon the lessons of US President Franklin D. Roosevelt's New Deal and 'Keynesian' economic theories. Improvement in living and economic conditions was considered fundamental to the promotion and maintenance of social stability, order, peace and prosperity. The construction of social welfare protection was an important component of building social harmony and integration. Programs of public works and public investment were considered to be important ways to tackle the problems of unemployment.

These global movements and economic policies also affect the natural environment as has been described in the section on the physical environment above. Structural impoverishment, environmental degradation, pauperisation, and social and economic exclusion are contrary to basic, universal human rights and social work values, are economically unsound, and ignore the interdependence between the various sectors of society nationally and internationally. Social work cannot avoid confronting these realities and searching for solutions.

Social environment

Our communities have been rediscovering that a positive social environment is not possible without a sustainable natural environment. It is generally accepted that our natural environment not only influences but also is crucial for our social lives now and in the future.

The world's resources are limited and threatened by pollution and consumption patterns all over the world. Pollution does not respect national boundaries, but is rapidly spreading its effects from one country or region to another. The critical condition of the physical environment demands a more holistic approach (Hoff 1997). The rapid global changes in the environment are complex and of a magnitude that significantly affect the planet and how it functions. The degradation of the natural environment calls for effective multilateral cooperation and policy measures which humanity needs to work on together. We are all exposed to environmental degradation, but some more than others. There is evidence that poor neighbourhoods, communities and countries are more affected than others (Rogge and Darkwave 1996). Lack of political and social power and limited access to economic alternatives increase the exposure of people to the dangers of environmental degradation. Children are more exposed than others because toxins concentrate more rapidly in smaller bodies; child workers are especially exposed. Large groups of the population in more fortunate circumstances are affected by multiple chemical sensitivity (MCS) due to exposure to chemicals found in personal care products, building material, processed food, pharmaceuticals and plastics.

The very future existence of some communities and nations is affected by anticipated changes in sea levels, itself a product of increasing industrialisation brought about by globalisation.

Globalisation

There are few topics as controversial as globalisation. It is meant to bring economic growth and solve a range of social, cultural and humanitarian problems. However, there are significant debates in relation to the extent that the reality of globalisation reflects this idealised vision. In particular, globalisation has produced a highly interdependent world, rendering state boundaries meaningless and challenging the ideology and limits of certain areas of international law. Alma et al. (2010) provide the opportunity to address some of the multifaceted issues provoked by the issue of globalisation.

In the 40 years since the publication of Rachel Carson's *Silent Spring* first drew attention to the consequences of human activity on natural systems, the scale of the problem has grown inexorably. The human population has more than doubled, economic activity has quadrupled and carbon dioxide emissions have increased tenfold.

In their exploration of the intricate nexus that emerges as a result of globalisation, they inextricably link together issues of international law, human rights, environmental law and international trade law.

Bringing together a number of experts in the field, the book of Alma et al. focuses on the areas of social justice and environmental justice and explores the links that exists between the two and the effect of globalisation on these areas. A variety of topics are addressed throughout the chapters of this book – including biodiversity, the law of the sea, biotechnology, child labour, the rights of women, corporate social responsibility, terrorism and counter-terrorism, water resources, intellectual property rights and the role of non-government organisations. As globalisation has many facets and actors, the contributions to the book engage with interdisciplinary research to deal with the various challenges identified, and critically explore both the potential of globalisation as a vehicle of sustainable and equitable development.

Over many centuries, human societies across the globe have established progressively closer contacts. Recently, the pace of global integration has dramatically increased. Unprecedented changes in communications, transportation, and computer technology have given the process new impetus and made the world more interdependent than ever. Multinational corporations manufacture products in many countries and sell to consumers around the world. Money, technology and raw materials move ever more swiftly across national borders. Along with products and finances, ideas and cultures circulate more freely. As a result, laws, economies and social movements are forming at the international level.

The term globalisation encompasses a range of social, political and economic changes. Within the section defining globalisation, we provide an introduction to the key debates. The materials ask what is new, what drives the process, how it changes politics, and how it affects global institutions like the UN.

Globalisation expands and accelerates the exchange of ideas and commodities over vast distances. It is common to discuss the phenomenon in highly generalised terms, but globalisation's impacts are often best understood at the local level. Cases of globalisation explore the various manifestations of interconnectedness in the world, noting how globalisation affects real people and places.

Globalisation often appears to be a force of nature, a phenomenon without bounds or alternatives. But peoples' movements have shown that it is neither unalterable nor inevitable. Citizens all over the world – ordinary people from the global north and south – can work together to shape alternate futures, to build a globalisation of cooperation, solidarity and respect for our common planetary environment.

Issues of globalisation and social justice

This special issue of the *Journal of Sociology and Social Welfare* (1 June 2007) presents a number of articles that address aspects of the way the issues of globalisation, social justice and social welfare have been addressed in social work, social policy and social welfare. Although much of the existing literature has focused on the social problems that may be attributed to globalisation, an attempt has been made here to focus on issues of mainstream social welfare concern in the context of globalisation.

A major problem is the way the effects of globalisation on social welfare have been reduced to simplistic, rhetorical statements that either condemn all aspects of globalisation or uncritically extol its benefits. In reality, however, globalisation has complex and paradoxical consequences for human well-being. For example, international trade is widely viewed by many progressive observers as being exploitative and unequal and many are appropriately critical of the way neo-liberal writers wax lyrical about its purportedly positive impact. On the other hand, it cannot be denied that some countries have benefitted from export-led development, and that incomes and standards of living for many of their citizens have improved as a result of the increased rate of employment generated through trade.

However, arguments about the social consequences of globalisation cannot be reduced to a simple dichotomy in which globalisation is viewed either as having disastrous consequences of otherwise as bringing untold benefits. The issues are far more complex. While employment opportunities and incomes have indeed increased for many people in low income countries that have adopted export-led industrialisation strategies, improvements in incomes and standards of living have come at a cost for many of these countries. Rapid urbanisation, congestion, heightened inequalities, the decline of traditional values, emotional stress and other negative manifestations of prosperity now characterise many newly industrialising developing countries.

Globalisation has also fostered the diffusion of Western cultural beliefs and practices to other parts of the world which many traditionalists abhor. This has resulted in the resurgence of fundamentalist religious and cultural movements that have in some cases used violence to resist the spread of secularism, individualism and consumerism. On the other hand, rapid advances in communication technologies and more the frequent exchanges between people of different cultures through these technologies and travel have produced results that cosmopolitans view as highly desirable. As these examples suggest, a proper analysis of the impact of globalisation requires a nuanced understanding of the complexities and paradoxes of the globalisation process.

Environment and social justice

In this section, we would like to discuss the views of different scholars in the area of environment and social justice, and explore the links that exist between the two and the effect of globalisation on these areas.

The special issue begins with an article by James Midgley, one of the special editors. Midgley views that the phenomena of globalisation forms more than a Western view in order to permit the formulations of interventions to promote social justice and social welfare that are culturally congruent and socially compatible. Pamela Anne Quiroz argues that privatisation has increasingly dominated our world and disparities between countries have grown.

Charles Fiki presents an exploratory study of alcohol and drug use in two rural communities in Plateau State, Nigeria, with the aim of raising awareness to the rural alcohol and drug problem. This article examines the patterns of alcohol consumption and drug use, and their perceived functions for substance use among rural farmers in Nigeria. He discusses the common use of marijuana and alcohol in addition to prescription drugs as well as multiple or combinational drug use. Pleasure and relaxation emerged as the major reasons for drug and alcohol use. Fiki concludes that the factors influencing alcohol and drug use are the relative neglect of rural communities and the activities of hawkers, quacks and other untrained individuals pervading the rural health sectors. He calls for further research to adequately capture the reality of alcohol and drug use in rural communities in Nigeria.

Gregg M. Olsen argues that as a result of domestic pressures and strains and/or the impact of globalisation, welfare states were declining in tandem. Loring Jones, David W. Engstrom, Tricia Hilliard and Mariel Diaz argue that globalisation demands more than just local and national perspectives; in this context one has to adopt an international viewpoint as well. This reflects an understanding of the relationship between globalisation and localisation. Therefore, globalisation should be appropriately applied contextually in a hermeneutic manner.

Vanna Gonzales argues that our understanding of the relationship between globalisation and contemporary social welfare systems is heavily influenced by three conventional approaches to studying welfare reform: the political economy, moral economy and mixed economy approaches. In addition to analysing the strengths and weaknesses of each of these approaches, she introduces the social economy approach as an emergent alternative. Gonzales argues that the social economy approach makes a valuable contribution to understanding the role of welfare networks in reconfiguring globalisation's impact on the character and quality of social welfare so as to better reconcile social efficacy with social justice.

Qingweh Xu examines the issue of globalisation and immigration to focus not only on whether and how much globalisation has caused international immigration but also how to promote and sustain a just global system for the growing number of immigrants. His article selects three developed countries with different welfare state philosophies and traditions – Australia, Sweden and the United States – and compares how they cope with the growing number of immigrants and their various needs. This article reflects thinking about states' ability to redistribute resources, about the ability to agree upon a unified theory of welfare rights in a diverse society and the feasibility of opening nations' welfare systems to all immigrants in the globalisation context to reinforce the value of immigrant.

Howard Karger, Christian Iyiani and Pat Shannon examine how and why five major stakeholders – international financial organisations, NGOs, governmental entities, multinational corporations and community development projects – have failed to significantly and uniformly reduce aggregate global poverty. This article uses the results of a case study of HIV/AIDS prevention in a low-income Nigerian city to argue that effective action must involve local and global stakeholders in collaborative partnerships. It concludes by discussing the critical role of facilitators in such partnerships.

Ernie Lightman, Andrew Mitchell and Dean Herd explore whether people are better off working in the precarious employment associated with a neo-liberal globalised economy. Their research shows the impacts of globalisation on the composition of food bank users in Toronto, Canada. They then compare two groups of food bank users, one with at least one household member working, the other without. The findings demonstrate that the life experiences of the two groups remain depressingly similar: those employed remained mired in poverty and continued to lead marginalised, precarious lives.

The lack of investment in education or training characteristic of 'work-first' welfare reforms leads to unstable, low-paid work for the vast majority of those leaving welfare. The authors call for a rejection of the narrow work-first models and the continued development of broader mixed models offering pre- and post-employment services and financial supports necessary to make work both realistic and sustainable, challenging the assumption that any work is the route out of poverty for all groups within society.

Karen Smith Rotabi, Denise Gammonley, Dorothy N. Gamble and Marie O. Weil define social work as a global profession. The authors encourage a broadening of social work education, moving beyond the traditional conception of 'internationalised' to a 'globalised' social work curriculum which embraces a world systems perspective. They emphasise practical teaching strategies for a globalised perspective specifically applied to human behaviour in the social environment, and sustainable development which also includes macro scale ethical considerations in a neo-liberal economic system.

An analysis of this kind not only challenges scholars to understand the complexities of globalisation but to explore a socially just system of global exchange that explicitly incorporates social welfare and social justice ideals. The goal of creating a socially just global system is now more frequently discussed in both the media and the academic literature. The issue today is not whether globalisation should be welcomed or rejected but how globalisation can be regulated in terms of principles that promote social justice.

These articles demonstrate the wide range of areas and content that can help provide a better understanding of globalisation and social justice issues facing policymakers, educators, social workers, and the diverse groups of people impacted by the changing international context.

Discourse on environmental justice

Environmental justice is an important part of the struggle to improve and maintain a clean and healthful environment, especially for those who have traditionally lived, worked and played closest to the sources of pollution. This emerged as a concept in the United States in the early 1980s. The term has two distinct uses. The first and more common usage describes a social movement in the United States whose focus is on the fair distribution of environmental benefits and burdens. Second, it is an interdisciplinary body of social science literature that includes (but is not limited to) theories of the environment, theories of justice, environmental law and governance, environmental policy and planning, development, sustainability and political ecology (Schlosberg 2007; Miller 2003).

The US Environmental Protection Agency (EPA)[2] defines environmental justice as follows:

> As we have mentioned in the preceding section that *environmental justice is the fair treatment and meaningful involvement of all people regardless of race, color, national origin, or income with*

respect to the development, implementation, and enforcement of environmental laws, regulations, and policies. EPA has this goal for all communities and persons across the Nation. It will be achieved when everyone enjoys the same degree of protection from environmental and health hazards and equal access to the decision-making process to have a healthy environment in which to live, learn, and work.

(Taylor 2000: 555–565)

Other definitions include equitable distribution of environmental risks and benefits; fair and meaningful participation in environmental decision-making; recognition of community ways of life, local knowledge, and cultural difference; and the capability of communities and individuals to function and flourish in society (Schlosberg 2007).

Environmental discrimination

One issue that environmental justice seeks to address is that of environmental discrimination. Discrimination against minorities centres on a socially dominant group's belief in its superiority, often resulting in (a) privilege for the dominant group and (b) the mistreatment of non-dominant minorities. The combined impact of these privileges and prejudices is just one of the potential reasons that waste management and highly polluting sites tend to be located in minority-dominated areas. A disproportionate quantity of minority communities (for example in Warren County, North Carolina) play host to landfills, incinerators, and other potentially toxic facilities (Skelton 2011).

Environmental discrimination has historically been evident in the process of selecting and building environmentally hazardous sites, including wasteful disposal, manufacturing, and energy production facilities. The location of transportation infrastructures, including highways, ports, and airports, has also been viewed as a source of environmental injustice. Among the earliest documentation of environmental racism was a study of the distribution of toxic waste sites across the United States (Chavis et al. 1987). Similarly India has problem of casteism and weaker section of the society. The waste of developed world has been sent to the underdeveloped or developing countries. India is also victim of such things in the name of the cheaper goods which become useless for the developed world. Due to the results of that study, waste dumps and waste incinerators have been the target of environmental justice lawsuits and protests (Cole and Sheila 2001).

Law is an instrument of environmental justice. Some environmental justice lawsuits are based on violations of civil rights laws (Skelton 2011). The Civil Rights Act is often used in lawsuits that claim environmental inequality. The Act prohibits discrimination based on race, caste, colour, or national origin by any government agency receiving federal assistance. In fact, it also depends upon proper implementation of the rule or regulation in question had a discriminatory impact. Equal protection was used many times to defend minority rights during the 1960s and has also been used in numerous environmental justice cases (Roberts 1998). The only problem is with the minority participation that fears to go against the dominant groups.

When environmentalism first became popular during the first half of the 20th century, the focus was wilderness protection and wildlife preservation. These goals reflected the interests of the movements of initial supporters. The actions of many mainstream environmental organisations still reflect these early principles (Sandler and Phaedra 2007). Many low-income minorities felt isolated or even negatively impacted by the movement.

The environmental movement is so concerned about cleaning up and preserving nature that it ignored the negative side effects that doing so caused communities nearby, namely less job growth (Sandler and Phaedra 2007). In addition, the movement has transferred locally unwanted land uses from middle-class neighbourhoods to poor communities with large minority populations. Therefore, vulnerable communities with fewer political opportunities are more often exposed to hazardous waste and toxins (Gerrard 1993–94). As a result, some minorities have viewed the environmental movement as elitist. Environmental elitism manifested itself in three different forms (Morrison 1986):

1 *Compositional* – Environmentalists are from the middle and upper class.
2 *Ideological* – The reforms benefit the movement's supporters but impose costs on non participants.
3 *Impact* – The reforms have 'regressive social impacts'. They disproportionately benefit environmentalists and harm underrepresented populations.

Supporters of economic growth have taken advantage of environmentalists' neglect of minorities. They have convinced minority leaders looking to improve their communities that the economic benefits of industrial facility and the increase in the number of jobs are worth the health risks. In fact, both politicians and businesses have even threatened imminent job loss if communities do not accept hazardous industries and facilities. Although in many cases local residents do not actually receive these benefits, the argument is used to decrease resistance in the communities as well as avoid expenditures used to clean up pollutants and create safer workplace environments (Sussman 1982).

One of the major initial barriers to minority participation in environmental justice is the initial costs of trying to change the system and prevent companies from dumping their toxic waste and other pollutants in areas with high numbers of minorities living in them.

During the African American Civil Rights Movement in the 1960s, activists participated in a social movement that created a unified atmosphere and advocated goals of social justice and equality. The community organisation and the social values of the era have translated to the environmental justice movement (Roberts 1998). Civil rights are often claimed environmental inequality which prohibits discrimination based on race, colour, or national origin by any government agency receiving federal assistance.

The *environmental justice movement* and the *civil rights movement* have many commonalities. At their core, the goals of movements are the same: 'social justice, equal protection, and an end to institutional discrimination'. By stressing the similarities of the two movements, it emphasises that environmental equity is a right for all citizens. Because the two movements have parallel goals, it is useful to employ similar tactics that often emerge at the grassroots level. Common confrontational strategies include protests, neighbourhood demonstrations, picketing, political pressure and demonstration (Bullard 1992).

Among the affected groups of environmental justice, those in high-poverty and racial minority groups have the most propensities to receive the harm of environmental injustice. Poor people account for more than 20% of the human health impacts from industrial toxic air releases, compared to 12.9% of the population nationwide (racial/ ethnic inequality: Los Angeles). This does not account for the inequity found among individual minority groups. Some studies that test statistically for effects of race and ethnicity, while controlling for income and other factors, suggest racial gaps in exposure that persist across all bands of income (Bullard 1992; Ash et al. 2009).

Indigenous groups are often the victims of environmental injustices. Native Americans have suffered abuses related to uranium mining in the American West. The most common example of environmental injustice among Latinos is the exposure to pesticides faced by farmworkers

(Shrader-Frechette 2002). Exposure to chemical pesticides in the cotton industry also affects farmers in India and Uzbekistan.

Maquiladoras use cheap Mexican labour to assemble imported components and raw material and then transport finished products back to the United States. Much of the waste ends up being illegally dumped in sewers, ditches, or in the desert. Along the Lower Rio Grande Valley, Maquiladoras dump their toxic wastes into the river from which 95% of residents obtain their drinking water. In the border cities of Brownsville, Texas, and Matamoros, Mexico, the rate of anencephaly (babies born without brains) is four times the national average (Bullard, 1992). Steel works, blast furnaces, rolling and finishing mills, and iron and steel foundries are responsible for more than 57% of the total human health risks from industrial pollution (Sandler and Phaedra 2007: 57–83).

This means that if the government wanted to make major reformative legislation for environmental justice, they could easily do so by targeting these industries.

Right to know movement

A new movement, bent on educating the people, was born after the Bhopal disaster, called the 'right-to-know' movement. A series of laws and reports was created, all built to inform the people of the pollutants being dumped into our neighbourhoods and atmosphere, and exactly how much of each chemical is being exposed and dumped. The theory behind 'right-to-know' is that once people are informed on what is polluting their neighbourhood, then they will begin to take action in both bringing down their own emissions, as well as begin to make the companies causing the most pollution, through means such as protests, to take into account their actions.

Globalisation, environmental health and social justice description

As we have discussed above, countries in the West regularly export their environmental harms – dumping heavy metals and greenhouse gases, for instance – to countries with (often fast) developing economies. These practices may seem beneficial to both the core and the periphery, providing jobs and investment in the latter, while outsourcing expensive health and safety commitments in the former. But given the lack of infrastructure and regulation necessary to assess and manage these hazards, is it safe?

In his book entitled *Globalisation, Environmental Health and Social Justice*, Frey (2016) argues that the globalisation of hazards puts the health of people in peripheral countries at risk in order to benefit those living in the core countries. Contextualising the export of hazardous products, industrial production processes, and wastes in a world systems framework, it discusses how ecological unequal exchange, the treadmill of production and metabolic rift have contributed to the globalisation of health, safety and environmental risks. Three case study chapters explore the forces driving these transfers and the adverse socio-economic consequences associated with them. Including examples from Mexico, China and Bangladesh, they present empirical research on hazardous products and processes from pesticides, cigarettes, and leaded gasoline, to ship-breaking, e-waste and specialist export processing zones. Frey discusses the need for an alternative political strategy of globalisation from below, arguing that conventional solutions fail to take into account a world system based on unequal relationships between the core and the periphery.

Emergency Planning and Right to Know Act of 1986

After the Bhopal disaster, where a Union Carbide plant released 40 tons of methyl isocyanate into the atmosphere in a village just south of Bhopal, India, the US government passed the Emergency Planning and Right to Know Act of 1986 (EPCRA)[3] introduced by Henry Waxman. The act required all corporations to report their toxic chemical pollution annually, which was then gathered into a report known as the Toxics Release Inventory (TRI 2015). By collecting this data, the government was able to make sure that companies were no longer releasing excessive amounts of deadly toxins into populated areas, so as to prevent another incident like that of the thousands of people killed and the tens of thousands of people injured in the Bhopal disaster.

Between northern and southern countries

Environmental discrimination in a global perspective is also an important factor when examining the environmental justice movement. Even though the environmental justice movement began in the United States, the United States also contributes to expanding the amount of environmental injustice that takes place in less-developed countries (Clap, 2002). Some companies in the United States and in other developed nations around the world contribute to the injustice by shipping the toxic waste and by-products of factories to less developed countries for disposal. This act increases the amount of waste in third world countries, most of which do not have proper sanitation for their own waste much less the waste of another country. Often the people of the less developed countries are exposed to toxins from this waste and do not even realise what kind of waste they are encountering or the health problems that could come with it (Pellow 2007).

The reason that this transporting of waste from northern countries to southern countries takes place is because it is cheaper to transport waste to another country and dump it there, than to pay to dump the waste in the producing country because the third world countries do not have the same strict industry regulations as the more developed countries. The countries that the waste is taken to be usually impoverished and the governments have little or no control over the happenings in the country or do not care about the people (Basel Action Network).[4]

Environmental justice

The Indian people are multi-religious ethnic minorities whose culture and castes differ from the rest of the countries in the world by their culture, language, and history. The environmental discrimination that they experience ranges from the unequal distribution of environmental harms as well as the unequal distribution of education, health services and employment.

The European Union is trying to strive towards environmental justice by putting into effect declarations that state that all people have a right to a healthy environment.

In the United Kingdom

While the predominant agenda of the environmental justice movement in the United States has been tackling issues of race, inequality and the environment, environmental justice campaigns around the world have developed and shifted in focus. For example, the environmental justice movement in the United Kingdom is quite different. It focuses on issues of poverty and the environment but also tackles issues of health inequalities and social exclusion as reported in *ESRC Global Environmental Change Programme* (Stephens et al. 2001).

Building of alternatives to climate change

In France, numerous alternate events, or villages of alternatives, are providing hundreds of alternatives to climate change and lack of environmental justice, both in order to raise people's awareness and to stimulate behaviour change. They have been or will be organised in over 60 different French and European cities, such as Bilbao, Brussels, Geneva, Lyon and Paris.

The African National Congress (ANC 1994) noted 'poverty and environmental degradation have been closely linked' in South Africa. The new South African Constitution, finalised in 1996, includes a bill of rights that grants South Africans the right to an 'environment that is not harmful to their health or well-being' and

> to have the environment protected, for the benefit of present and future generations through reasonable legislative and other measures that
>
> 1   prevent pollution and ecological degradation;
> 2   promote conservation; and
> 3   secure ecologically sustainable development and use of natural resources while promoting justifiable economic and social development.
>
> (McDonald 2002)

Globalisation and environmental social movements

Environmental social movements include protest movements and lobbying groups, generally started by ordinary citizens that work to preserve and protect the natural environment in local communities, and at national and international levels. Such groups have a history dating back to the conservation and preservation societies (such as the Audubon Society) of the late 19th century. Many more environmental social movements, such as Greenpeace, were founded in the 1960s and 1970s. Many analysts argue that environmental groups like Greenpeace represent a new, 'globalised' form of politics (e.g. Wapner 1996). Globalisation has indeed altered the landscape in which environmental social movements operate. Thus the purpose of this section is to briefly summarise major perspectives on how globalisation – including economic, political, and cultural globalisation – has shaped environmental social movements in countries around the world as discussed by Ignatow (2007) and cited from Hite (2007).

Economic dependency

Beginning with the pioneering work of Wallerstein (e.g. 1974), social scientists have argued that social and political issues within nations must be understood in the context of a global economic system. Dependency theory is premised on the idea that less developed countries are exploited by over-consumptive countries who seek to enhance economic growth. In an effort for exploited nations (whose economies are generally less commodified) to enhance their own economic growth, exploited nations offer natural resources and labour at prices much lower than those available in the markets of the exploiting countries. In turn, the exploiting countries support policies that maintain an economy based on exploitation of natural resources and the local labour market. Within this paradigm, environmental activism within a nation is seen as a response to the ecological damages brought about by global economic liberalisation and industrialisation. In dependency arguments, environmental movements in developing countries are seen as opposed to the encroaches of multinational corporations abetted by national governments into local, communitarian settings.

Cultural diffusion

Cultural diffusion is generally known as the process by which ideas, values and courses of action are spread from one society to another. Globalisation generally promotes indirect diffusion, which results in cultural changes that become embedded within societies even when two cultures do not have direct geographical contact. From a cultural diffusion perspective, environmental social movements, especially those in developing countries, are thought to mimic environmental movements in more developed countries, while at the same time the issues raised as a priority in developed countries may originate in developing nations. This is partly because public awareness of environmental problems is in large measure a product of global communications technology. Images of environmental damage reflect from disaster in the Ukraine, the ecological and social costs of the Three Gorges Dam project and the loss of tropical biodiversity. In this way, global environmentalism is a result of the 'cultural power' of both the global media and international non-governmental organisations. Cultural arguments tend to treat instances of 'indigenous' anti-globalisation environmental activism with scepticism. Instead, instances of environmental activism in developing countries are argued to result from flows of information radiating from the global centre to the periphery. Through the global media, global networks of non-governmental organisations, and even multinational corporations, environmental politics in the developing world is seen as being influenced by the politics of the developed world as much as by local grievances and interests.

Globalisation as hybridisation

Hybridisation is premised on the idea that when cultures mix, ideas and values are shared to result in the evolution of a new culture, which is often some form of a synthesis of the ideas and values of the originating cultures. This hybridisation perspective sees globalisation as leading not only to economic and cultural uniformity, but as creating new opportunities for identity politics within nations. This perspective focuses on how globalisation weakens traditional state power as new social and political infrastructure appears, often via the following processes:

1   Economic globalisation erodes states' sovereignty over economic policy.
2   Media liberalisation and global communications technology erodes states' media hegemony.
3   Media globalisation weakens public faith in large state-sponsored development projects, because faults with such projects are given immediate national and global exposure (e.g. the Chernobyl episode).
4   Accelerating flows of people (such as migrants and tourists) and capital across national borders creates new resources and opportunities for identity politics within nations.
5   Global civil society works to protect minority rights within nations.

These five processes have weakened states' power and hegemony, have created opportunities for sub-state actors and have led to new, 'hybrid' forms of environmental politics. Examples include environmental justice groups, religious environmental groups and highly organised local and regional groups that combine indigenous cultural traditions with environmental causes and concerns. Groups such as these are organised more at local and global levels than at the level of the nation state.

Transnational movement networks

Many of the environmental justice networks that began in the United States expanded their horizons to include many other countries and became transnational networks for environmental justice. These networks work to bring environmental justice to all parts of the world and protect all citizens of the world to reduce the environmental injustice happening all over the world. Listed below are some of the major transnational social movement organisations (Pellow 2007).

- Basel Action Network (1989) – works to end toxic waste dumping in poor undeveloped countries from the rich developed countries.
- GAIA (Global Anti-Incinerator Alliance) – works to find different ways to dispose of waste other than incineration. This company has people working in over 77 countries throughout the world.
- GR (Global Response) – works to educate activists and the upper working class how to protect human rights and the ecosystem.
- Greenpeace International – was the first organisation to become the global name of environmental justice. Greenpeace works to raise the global consciousness of transnational trade of toxic waste.
- Health Care without Harm – works to improve the public health by reducing the environmental impacts of the health care industry.
- International Campaign for Responsible Technology – works to promote corporate and government accountability with electronics and how the disposal of technology affects the environment.
- International POPs Elimination Network – works to reduce and eventually end the use of persistent organic pollutants (POPs) which are harmful to the environment.
- PAN (Pesticide Action Network) – works to replace the use of hazardous pesticides with alternatives that are safe for the environment.

Notes

1 Global Policy Forum (GPF) is an independent policy watchdog that monitors the work of the United Nations and scrutinises global policymaking. It promotes accountability and citizen participation in decisions on peace and security, social justice and international law. GPF uses a holistic approach, linking peace and security with economic justice and human development. GPF was founded in New York in December 1993 by a group of 14 progressive scholars and activists, among them James Paul, Erskine Childers and Joel Krieger. GPF is a non-profit, tax-exempt organisation with consultative status at the UN. In September 2004, Global Policy Forum Europe (GPF Europe) was founded as the sister organisation of GPF. GPF Europe's primary aim has been to monitor and analyse German and European policymaking relating to and within the UN. The office of GPF Europe is located in Bonn, Germany. GPF's main programs cover currently environment and development concepts and politics, financing for development, tax justice, UN reform, global governance, corporate accountability, peace and security.

2 Epa.gov: The US Environment Protection Agency is an agency of the US federal government that was created for the purpose of protecting human health and the environment.
3 EPCRA: The Emergency Planning and Community Right-to-Know Act (EPCRA) of 1986 was created to help communities plan for chemical emergencies. It also requires industry to report on the storage, use and releases of hazardous substances to federal state, and local governments. In November 1986, the US Congress passed EPCRA to help America's communities 'deal safely and effectively with the many hazardous substances that are used throughout our society'.
4 Basel Action Network (BAN), BAN's namesake is the 1989 United Nations Basel Convention, which restricts the trade of hazardous waste between more developed countries and less developed countries.

References

ANC (African National Congress). 1994. *The Reconstruction and Development Programme*. Johannesburg: Umyanyano Publications.

Alam, Shawkat, Klein, Natalie and Overland, Juliette (eds.) 2010. *Globalisation and the Quest for Social and Environmental Justice: The Relevance of International Law in an Evolving World Order*. New York: Routledge.

Bullard, Robert D. 1992. *'The Quest for Environmental Equity: Mobilizing the African-American Community for Social Change'. American Environmentalism: the U.S. Environmental Movement, 1970–1990*. New York: Taylor & Francis.

Bullard, Robert D. and Johnson, Glenn S. 2000. 'Environmental Justice: Grassroots Activism and Its Impact on Public Policy Decision Making', *Journal of Social Issues*, 56(3).

Chavis, Benjamin F., Goldman, Benjamin A. and Lee, Charles. 1987. 'Toxic Wastes and Race in the United States: A National Report on the Racial and Socio-economic Characteristics of Communities with Hazardous Waste Sites', Commission for Racial Justice, United Church of Christ.

Clapp, Jennifer. 2002. 'The Distancing of Waste: Overconsumption in a Global Economy' in the *Journal on Confronting Consumption*, June, pp. 27–44, Cambridge, MA: MIT Press.

Cole, Luke and Foster, Sheila R. 2001. *From the Ground Up: Environmental Racism and the Rise of the Environmental Justice Movement*. New York: New York University Press.

Frey, R. Scott. 2016. *Globalisation, Environmental Health and Social Justice*. London: Routledge.

Gerrard, Michael B. 1993–1994. 'The Victims of NIMBY', *Fordham Urban Law Journal*, 21(3), 495–521.

Global Policy Forum (GPF). 2005–2015. *Global Policy Forum Organization*. New York: UN Plaza, 866.

Hite, Kristen (ed.). 2007. 'Globalisation: International Environmental Issues', *The Encyclopaedia of the Earth*, November 9.

Hoff, M.D. 1997. 'Social Work, the Environment and Sustainable Growth', in M.C. Hokenstad and J. Midgley (eds.), *Issues in International Social Work: Global Challenges for a New Century*. Washington, DC: NASW, 27–44.

Ignatow, G. 2007. 'Transnational Identity Politics and the Environment', *Journal of the Theory of Social Behaviour*, 37(2): 115–135.

McDonald, David A. 2002. *Environmental Justice in South Africa*. Cape Town: Ohio University Press.

Miller, Jr., G. Tyler. 2003. *Environmental Science: Working with the Earth* (9th ed.). Pacific Grove, CA: Brooks and Cole.

Morrison, Denton. 1986. 'Environmentalism and Elitism: A Conceptual and Empirical Analysis', *Environmental Management*, New York, September, 10: 581–589.

Pellow, David Naguib. 2007. *Resisting Global Toxics*. Cambridge, MA: MIT Press.

Roberts, R. Gregory. 1998. 'Environmental Justice and Community Empowerment: Learning from the Civil Rights Movement', (PDF). *American University Law Review*, October issue, Washington, DC.

Rogge, M.E. and Darkwa, O.K. 1996. 'Poverty and the Environment: An International Perspective for Social Work', *International Social Work*, 39: 395–409.

Sandler, R. and Phaedra, P. 2007. *Environmental Justice and Environmentalism*. London: MIT Press, 27–55.

Schlosberg, David. 2007. *Defining Environmental Justice: Theories, Movements, and Nature*. New York: Oxford University Press.

Shrader-Frechette, Kristin. 2002. *Environmental Justice Creating Equality, Reclaiming Democracy*. New York: Oxford University Press.

Skelton, Renee. 2011. 'Environmental Racism', U.S. Environmental Protection Agency (EPA), Cleveland, OH.

Stephens, C., Bullock, S. and Scott, J.U. 2001. *Environmental Justice: Rights and Means to a Healthy Environment for All: ESRC Global Environmental Change Programme* (Special briefing No. 7). Brighton: University of Sussex.

Sussman, Paul. 1982. "Job blackmail' Used to Avoid Pollution, Safety Rules', *Pittsburgh Post-Gazette*, November 4.

Taylor, Dorceta E. 2000. 'Environmental Racism – United States, Industrial, Toxic, Human, Power, Use', *Pollution Issues*, 555–565.

'Toxics Release Inventory (TRI) Program' 2015. EPA gov. U.S. *Environmental Protection Agency*, Boston, MA, 02109.

Wapner, Paul. 1996. *Environmental Activism and World Civic Politics*. Albany: State University of New York Press.

2 A comparative assessment of climate policies of top global emitters and evolution of an effective climate regime

Issues of environmental effectiveness, economic efficiency, equity and political feasibility

Marco Grasso and Venkatesh Dutta

Introduction

Climate change exists, despite its deniers, and it is extremely likely that, since the mid-20th century, human activity has been its major determinant (IPCC 2013). Altered climate dynamics are causing an array of negative impacts on our planet's natural and socio-economic systems directly or indirectly harmful to all of humankind and potentially catastrophic for many of the poorest people in the world. In their scientifically ascertained anthropogenic determinants, such impacts are largely the consequence of conduct that people have adopted in the past and/or adopt now that harms other people living both now and in the future. Sustained economic growth with increasing levels of human well-being and comfort has also resulted in accelerations of anthropogenic climate change (Jorgenson 2014).

The scientific evidence makes it clear, in fact, that climate-related harm would be to a large extent avoidable if behaviours and actions more attentive to protecting nature from anthropogenic emissions were adopted. Consequently, the climate crisis can be blamed on humans, and people harmed by climate change are subject to wrongs that exist per se, independently from, and prior to, considerations of justice, that is they are victims of injustice (Wolgast 1987; Shklar 1990). On this understanding, climate change is therefore a moral wrong that unjustly harms individuals and societies – especially the most deprived ones – through the adverse, yet greatly regionally differentiated, impacts on freshwater resources, ecosystems, food, fibre and forest products, coastal systems and low-lying areas, industry, settlement and society, and human health (IPCC 2007: chs. 1, 3–8); and its anthropogenic component is, in fact, largely produced by the harmful conducts pointed out above.

Global efforts to check carbon emissions commenced in earnest almost three decades back, yet there has been no plausible indication that both international agreements and national commitments have done much good to cap and reduce greenhouse gas (GHG) emissions. Fair and effective climate policy has always seemed daunting in a highly heterogeneous world. The global community has attempted to tackle the challenge of climate change through international negotiations encompassing some 195 countries under the auspices of the 1992 United Nations Framework Convention on Climate Change (UNFCCC). UNFCCC provided a framework for the principle of 'common but differentiated responsibilities', in which countries have a common accountability in reducing GHG emissions, but due to differences in their historic emissions and current development levels, countries have adopted different levels of emissions reduction obligations. There are also enormous differences in income, population, resources, technologies and capacity across countries. To date, this process has yielded only partial results (Gupta 2010; Laviña et al. 2012; Fischer and Geden 2015). Both of the previous IPCC Assessment Reports have accepted the widespread inequity in the causes and effects of climate change even though operationalising the principle has proved complex (IPCC 2014, 2007).

The Paris Agreement makes a reference to equity principles and the differentiation is in practice left up to each country to decide for itself. The countries are required to submit new intended national determined contributions (INDCs) every five years without any international negotiation over the contributions.[1] The INDCs, as part of the Paris Agreement, albeit testifying an unprecedented global breadth of climate initiative, do not set sufficient emissions cuts for achieving the goal of limiting the global temperature increase 'well below' 2°C above pre-industrial level, the safety level reported at article 2 (Allen 2015). Global emissions of GHGs must follow a reduction path that reaches zero from 2060 to 2080 in order to limit global warming to less than 2°C (IPCC 2014). Although these NDCs together lead to a significant reduction compared to scenarios in the absence of credible climate policy, assessments have also shown that their impact falls short of the necessary emission reduction targets to be consistent with 2°C and 1.5°C (Rogelj et al. 2016).

At any rate, there is a lack of operational details as well as significant commitments and institutional mechanisms to stabilise the climate system (Robins 2016; Bulkeley 2015). It is also very likely that considerations of distributive fairness will continue to play a key role, but that it will do so increasingly in a national setting (Robiou du Pont et al. 2017). The US and the EU were the key drivers of the Paris Agreement in 2015, however, after the Trump administration, the prospect of climate cooperation with other top emitter such as China, and other emerging and developing countries seems dim. The US plans to reverse the climate policy legislation that will subdue US emission targets. This will weaken the international efforts that have been growing to put the US as a likely climate policy partner that is serious about tackling global climate risks.

At the same time the current climate crisis requires significant action and obliges a rethinking of the approaches and strategies that may contribute to effective policy design. To this end, it is first necessary to emphasise that the international relations literature (e.g. Keohane and Nye 2000), and in particular that focused on global climate change (e.g. Victor 2006; Keohane and Victor 2011; Sælen 2015), makes it clear that climate regimes are shaped by, and to some extent cater to, the interests of the most powerful countries or groupings of countries. Accordingly, it seems meaningful to evaluate the key climate policy strategies of such actors. This chapter attempts, in fact, to evaluate top emitting countries' climate policies according to their environmental, economic, ethical and political dimensions. It should be specified that the evaluative exercise carried out does not provide a single index of the overall goodness of climate policies, like, for instance, those calculated by Steves et al. (2011) and Bernauer and Böhmelt (2013). It seems, in fact, preferable to keep the different perspectives of climate policy evaluation separate, so as to bring out the complexity and multidimensionality of current climate policy, represented in Figure 2.1.

Climate change is an intricate issue that entails distinct cooperation challenges, among which '[t]he hardest and most central problem is *coordination of emission regulations*' (Keohane and Victor 2011: 13, emphasis in the original). Therefore, given the sensitivity of emissions abatement in the climate policy debate, a measure of the significance of countries in the climate context is their contribution to the build-up of cumulative emissions. Consistently, the evaluative exercise carried out should focus on largest emitters' climate policies, if it is to envision the likely evolution of global climate policies and ultimately of the future climate regime(s). Top emitters are, in fact, the ultimate agents of international climate policy (Prins and Rayner 2007), a group small

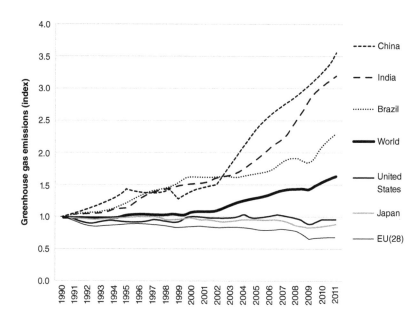

Figure 2.1 Index of global industrial direct GHG emissions. The data are normalised to 1990, when UNFCCC accounting started.

Source: Data are from (WRI 2015 WRI. (2015). CAIT 2.0. 2014. retrieved 20 February 2016, from http://cait2.wri.org).

enough to avoid the unworkability of global agreements and at the same time sufficiently broad to exert leverage on the global situation (Victor et al. 2005: 1821). A second rationale for focusing on the largest emitters is that they are the most powerful and influential countries because the group consists of the G8 member countries plus China and the European Union (EU). Third, top emitters also capture the extreme complexity of climate politics and political economy, as made clear later. These countries, in fact, belong to different UNFCCC categories (Annex I and non-Annex I), and they have diverse economic structures, industrial systems and institutional capacities, as evinced in Figure 2.2.

All in all, the objective of the chapter is to carry out an evaluative analysis of top emitters' climate policies according to four broad benchmarks, namely environmental effectiveness, economic efficiency, equity and political feasibility. To this end, the chapter first delineates the rationale and general evaluative framework of the analysis carried

Top greenhouse gas emitters

70% of all carbon emissions come from just 10 sources

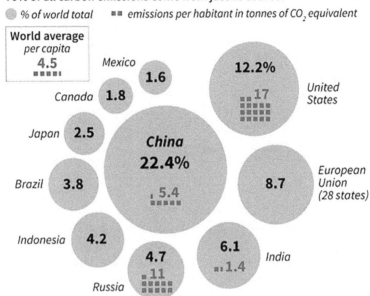

Figure 2.2 Per capita carbon emission – from top GHG emitters, accounting for 70% of the total carbon emissions

Source: World Resources Institute (percentage for 2012 including land use change and forestry – LUCF); Climate Analysis (per capita emissions for 2010 excluding LUCF)

out, and then investigates the largest emitters' climate policies according to the four perspectives indicated. Finally, the chapter briefly points out some common threads in and emerging issues from such policies.

Emerging climate politics and climate policy evaluation

It is often debated that the top emitters are not always vulnerable to the same extent as they cause GHG emissions. Dutta et al. (2016) empirically determined the relationship between countries' GHG emissions and their vulnerability to negative effects of climate change. They find an enormous global inequality where 20 of the 36 top emitters are among the least vulnerable to negative impacts of future climate change. The finding is in line with the results of other earlier studies. The study conversely presents that 11 of the 17 countries with low or moderate GHG emissions are highly vulnerable to negative impacts of climate change.

The post-Copenhagen climate policy no longer formally distinguishes between a North and a South (i.e. between Annex I and non-Annex I countries), as patently reaffirmed by the 2015 Paris Agreement. This opens the way to inclusive bilateral and regional agreements, also potentially focused only on single critical areas of climate policy, that is to a multi-track approach (Laviña et al. 2012). As anticipated, smaller groups of key countries can cooperate better on climate change issues because such regime complexes are more flexible across issues and adaptable over time (Keohane and Victor 2011). As for mitigation, the top 10 emitters account for 80% of the world's 1990–2008 cumulative CO_2 emissions (Table 2.1).[2] Therefore the Kyoto-like inclusion of additional countries would be of scant significance in terms of contributing to solution of the problem, yet extremely onerous in terms of transaction costs and negotiation complexity (Prins and Rayner 2007).

In general, climate policy is understood here as a set of actions, plans, projects, instruments, and initiatives with the ultimate purpose of stabilising, and later reducing, the concentrations of greenhouse gases (GHGs) in the atmosphere 'at a level that would prevent dangerous anthropogenic interference with the climate system', consistently with the main objective of the UNFCCC as set out in article 2.[3]

Table 2.1 Top 10 global emitters' cumulative 1990–2008 CO_2 emissions: million metric tons ($MtCO_2$) and percentage of world's cumulative emissions (%)

Top emitters	*$MtCO_2$*	*%*
USA	103,700	22.1
China	75,341	16.0
EU 27	76,717	16.3
Russia	31,371	6.7
Japan	23,914	5.1
India	21,701	4.6
Germany	16,459	3.5
UK	10,652	2.3
Canada	9,587	2.0
Italy	8,458	1.8
Total	377,900	80.5

Source: Elaboration on Peters et al. (2011) dataset

Before defining the yardsticks against which climate policy should be evaluated, it is necessary to clarify some fundamental issues concerning the evaluation process. Taking account of the usual standpoints of policy evaluation analyses – that is prospective or ex ante and retrospective or ex post (Crabbè and Leroy 2008) – there are three complementary dimensions along which current climate policy should be ex post evaluated: environmental effectiveness, economic efficiency and equity. Furthermore, because of the intrinsic long-term, intergenerational nature of the climate crisis, also a fourth prospective dimension, the political feasibility of climate policies not yet implemented, can offer a valuable ex ante contribution to an overall evaluation of climate governance systems. A brief outline of these four yardsticks, the ones most employed in the relevant literature (Verbruggen 2011; Pickering et al. 2012), is provided below.

Environmental effectiveness involves consistency with the objective of global climate policy, that is the stabilisation of GHG in the atmosphere at a non-dangerous level. On theoretical grounds, it is therefore necessary to investigate the extent of effectiveness against climate change of actions/initiatives/projects in terms of mitigation strategies, that is with regard to their emissions abatement potential.

Economic efficiency demands optimal climate policies, that is climate policies that achieve their goals at the least possible cost for society. Such policies require the minimisation of the costs borne by all subjects involved (regulators, the industry, the public sector, individuals), through, in theory, equalisation of their marginal abatement costs.

Equity plays a major role as a unifying principle that facilitates collective actions against climate change: the more climate policies are informed by ethical considerations, the more they are likely to succeed. Equity, in fact, can persuade parties with conflicting interests to cooperate more closely on collective actions.

Perceptions of the political feasibility of climate policy affect the choice of actions, plans, projects, instruments and initiatives, and they depend on the relationships among ideas, power and resources. All in all, it seems that inclusion of considerations of political feasibility demands investigation of the political economy on climate change of top emitters, that is a brief analysis of the political, institutional, economic, cultural and scientific factors that affect climate policymaking.

In the following sections the article conducts a systematic evaluation of top emitters' climate policies according to these four yardsticks.

Environmental effectiveness

Three sub-criteria are used to evaluate the environmental effectiveness of top emitters' climate policies: (1) share of renewable energies (RE) in gross electrical consumption, (2) change in the energy intensity of the economy during 1990–2010, and (3) consistency with climate science (2°C pledges).

Share of renewable energies in gross electrical consumption

The share of RE in gross final energy consumption is identified as a key indicator with which to measure progress in abating carbon emissions while satisfying the energy needs for economic growth. It is defined as the ratio between electricity produced from renewable energy sources and gross national electricity consumption. RE includes wind power, solar power (thermal, photovoltaic and concentrated), hydroelectric power, tidal power, geothermal energy and biomass. A greater deployment of RE has a positive effect on economic growth through reducing the negative effects of oil prices volatility as well as contributing to the energy supply security (Awerbuch and Sauter 2006). An increased share of renewable energy sources in final energy consumption is thus likely to reduce pressures on the environment and human health resulting from energy production (see Table 2.2).

The share of renewables in gross electricity consumption increased by 7.4%/yr in Germany between 1990 and 2010, the highest among the major emitters, followed by UK (6.2%/yr), Italy (2.9%/yr) and China (1%/yr). In general, EU countries are progressing well in RE deployment. However, the share of renewables in gross electricity consumption has decreased in the US by 0.7%/yr since 1990. Other countries which exhibit slighter decreases in renewables in gross electricity consumption are Japan (–1%/yr), and Canada (-0.1%/yr).

Change in the energy intensity of the economy (kg of oil equivalent – KgOE/US$, ppp)

Taking a long-term perspective, change in the primary energy intensity of the economy reflects progress in the country's output of goods and services, as measured by inflation-adjusted gross domestic product (GDP). High-energy intensities like those of Russia, China and Canada indicate a high price or cost of converting energy into GDP. Major emitters have shown a decline in primary energy intensity since

Table 2.2 Share of renewable energies in gross electrical consumption and average annual change during 1990–2010

Top emitters	Per capita share of RE (kwh/capita) [a]	Per capita electricity consumption (kwh/capita) [b]	Ratio of RE to the total electricity consumption [a/b]	Average annual change in share of RE in gross electricity consumption during 1990–2010, % [c]
Canada	10,336	15,471	0.67	–0.1
China	567	2631	0.22	1.0
EU 27	1,171	6,403	0.18	2.6
Germany	1,273	6,779	0.19	7.4
India	109	571	0.19	0.7
Italy	1,264	5,271	0.24	2.9
Japan	806	7819	0.10	–1.0
Russia	1,170	6,133	0.19	0.0
UK	422	5,692	0.07	6.2
USA	1,391	12,914	0.11	–0.7

Source: [a] US Energy Information Administration (EIA), International Energy Statistics, 2010 data; [b] World Bank, Electric power consumption (kWh per capita), 2009 database; [c] World Energy Council database.

1990, the highest being in China (–4.6%/yr). India is also gradually decreasing its energy intensity.

Table 2.3 shows that the emission intensity of the economy has improved to a great extent for most of the top emitters during the last two decades. For some emitters such as China, India and the UK, the improvement in emission intensity is more than for others, mainly due to improvement in energy efficiency, and partly because economic growth has been faster in relatively cleaner sectors such as IT and services.

Consistency with climate science

Consistency with climate science is measured as pledges and the remaining gap in achievement of global climate change mitigation goals. Pledges reflect acknowledgment of the precautionary principle on reducing climatic risk associated with carbon emissions leading to a temperature rise beyond the 2°C limit. In order to have a good chance of keeping within the 2°C limit this century – a limit that has recently assumed a normative role in understanding what constitutes

Table 2.3 Change in the primary energy intensity of the economy at purchasing power parity during 1990–2010 (%/yr)

Top emitters	1990 (kgOE/US$, ppp)	2010 (kgOE/US$, ppp)	Change in primary energy intensity during 1990–2010 (%/yr), ppp
Canada	0.278	0.213	−1.3
China	0.722	0.279	−4.6
EU – 27	0.170	0.124	−1.6
Germany	0.174	0.123	−1.7
India	0.305	0.196	−2.2
Italy	0.112	0.105	−0.6
Japan	0.137	0.128	−0.3
Russia	0.471	0.352	−1.4
UK	0.152	0.100	−2.1
USA	0.240	0.173	−1.6

Source: European Environmental Agency database (2012) and IEA (2011)

dangerous climate change (Grasso 2012) – emissions in 2020 should not be higher than 44 Gt of CO_2 equivalents (UNEP 2011).

Most Annex I countries (see Table 2.4) have submitted an unconditional pledge (lower end of the pledge) and a more ambitious pledge that is mainly conditional on other countries pledging comparable reductions (higher end of the pledge).[4] The unconditional pledges would result in a total Annex I emission reduction target of 4 to 18% below 1990 levels by 2020. The conditional pledges amount to a higher reduction target of 9 to 21%.

In China, for instance, owing to faster than expected economic growth, the pledge would result in emissions of about 13 $GtCO_2e$ by 2020. In India, the National Action Plan on Climate Change (NAPCC) provides eight national missions in key areas, not yet properly quantified, but more ambitious than the official pledge to the Copenhagen Accord. The US pledges are not yet sufficiently ambitious: with still inadequate legal and political processes at the national level, it is very unlikely that comprehensive climate and energy legislation will be considered in the near future. For EU 27, the high end of the pledge is conditional upon a global agreement post-2012. Similarly, Japan's targets may be optimistic as they are conditional on an effective international framework in which all major economies participate. Canada is also least likely to meet its pledges, having ratified late with a decade of strong emission growth and unproductive domestic consultations on

Table 2.4 National mitigation pledges and their impact on GHG emissions in 2020

Top emitters	Pledges	MtCO$_2$e in 2020 Low pledges strict rules	High pledges strict rules	Capability of pledges	Likelihood of meeting the pledges
Canada	17%, to be aligned with the final economy-wide emissions target of the US in enacted legislation	0	200	Inadequate – pledge does not lead to emission reductions below the 1990 level	Unlikely to be met
China	CO_2 emissions reduction of GDP by 40–45% by 2020 relative to the 2005 level	1,010	1,730	Inadequate – emissions to reach about 14 GtCO$_2$e in 2020 according to China's second National Communication	Likely that pledge will be met
EU 27	20 to 30% relative to 1990 by 2020 and by 80 to 95% below 1990 by 2050	972	1,529	Inadequate	Likely to meet its unconditional pledge of 20% below 1990
India	Emission intensity reduction of GDP by 20 to 25% by 2020 relative to 2005 level	523	523	Reasonably sufficient	Likely to be met with current policy actions
Japan	25% relative to 1990 emissions by 2020 and by –60 to –80% relative to 2005 by 2050.	0	358	Sufficient	Currently not clear if pledges will be met
Russia	15 to 25% relative to 1990 emissions by 2020	0	0	Inadequate	Likely to be met
USA	17% relative to 2005 emissions by 2020	0	1407	Inadequate – only 3% reduction below 1990 level	Unlikely that pledge will be met with currently implemented policies

Germany, Italy and UK have been clubbed under EU-27.
Based on UNEP (2011) and Climate Action Tracker (Source: http://climateactiontracker.org/countries.html).

mitigation. In general, it appears that the climate action being taken by the major emitters is highly unlikely to shrink the gap between real emissions and what is needed to keep the rise in global temperature to 2°C, though they represent a significant departure from the BAU trends (for details, see UNEP 2011). All in all, the analysis indicates that pledges are not enough, and that there is a gap between pledges and domestic policies. Targets may be also optimistic because they are conditional on an effective international framework in which all major economies participate. It is also evident from the top emitters' pledges that the aggregated emissions level is still likely to induce warming exceeding 2°C by a wide margin, unless pledges are improved and more policies are implemented on a national level. There are notable differences in the environmental effectiveness of climate policy across top emitters. Tougher environmental policy regulations lead to investment in cleaner technologies and reallocation of export activities away from energy-intensive sectors. While most of the top emitters have adopted comprehensive policy frameworks to deploy and sustain RE, the US has not adopted any consistent and stable policy at the national level to encourage wider RE installation. EU and UK regulations on energy efficiency appear to have been remarkably effective in lowering emissions (Hills 2012: 43). Similarly, China, Germany and India have also developed robust policies for the deployment of renewable energy. The EU seems to be doing far better than other emitters in terms of deployment of renewable energies and offsetting emissions. The EU's climate policy has relevance well beyond European borders, both in terms of its role as a driver of international policy and as a source of successful policy lessons for other emitters. Major emitters have recorded declines in primary energy intensity since 1990 – most of all China (-4.6%/yr) and India (-2.2%/yr) – which explains top emitters' efforts on energy conservation and CO_2 emissions mitigation. However, a considerable part of the capital stock in the energy sector needs to be replaced by the growing and emerging economies of China and India.

Economic efficiency

The efficiency of climate policies depends upon their interactions with already-existing sources of distortion in the economy which are driven by market forces. By all accounts, investment in low carbon technologies (LCT) is essential if emitters are to reach 2020 targets and set themselves on an effective decarbonisation path beyond 2020. However, without a clear carbon price signal, market forces fail to determine whether investing in LCT will be a profitable strategy. Basic economic efficiency concerns call for measures like carbon taxes, pricing and emission trading systems. Economic inefficiency commits emitters to high carbon investments, significantly increasing mitigation costs in the future. According to Baranzini et al. (2017), 'there is still much misunderstanding about the many reasons to implement a global carbon price, ideological resistance against it prospers'. The most important reason to use carbon pricing is environmental effectiveness achieved at a relatively lower cost, which contributes to enhancing social and political acceptability of climate policy. Both carbon pricing and low-carbon technology policies are harmonising and are both needed for effective climate policy.

It is widely recognised that an adequate and stable long-term carbon price is required to induce an abatement of emissions and to encourage investments in LCT, which otherwise would fail to penetrate the market spontaneously (IEA 2011; Martin et al. 2011; Battles et al. 2013). Spurring innovation in LCT would require a price of carbon higher than the price set by current initiatives. Efficient markets can raise the carbon price and stimulate LCT investments. However, the allocation of public and private capital to LCT deployment at scale has been constrained by the low price prevailing in the short term and the absence of a price signal in the long term, which is further compounded by the global financial crisis that favours less risky assets and markets (Neuhoff and Weber 2010).

Carbon tax

Policy interventions such as carbon taxes with revenues substituting for the increase in tax that would otherwise be required to finance the government's budget have been suggested as promising means to abate carbon emissions and reduce energy use, improve energy efficiency and simultaneously promote the development of renewable energy (Andersen 2004; Parry and Williams 2010). However, there has been a great deal of resistance against implementing a carbon tax, with debate on its possible implications for social welfare (Boccanfuso et al. 2011), despite the possible double dividend that it would provide (Goulder 1995; Bovenberg and Goulder 2002). Several EU member states, including the UK and Germany, have established their own domestic carbon taxes, as reported in Table 2.5, while some emitters like China, Russia and Japan have yet to introduce carbon taxes.

Despite general consensus on carbon tax intervention among the top emitters, and the adoption of short-term, ad hoc measures to sustain

Table 2.5 Summary of carbon tax among top emitters

Top emitters	Carbon tax
Canada	No federal carbon tax; some Canadian provinces – Alberta, British Columbia, Quebec – have carbon taxes
China	Not yet
EU-27	Tax on pollution permits purchased under the EU Emissions Trading System (EU ETS) in which the tax is calculated in terms of carbon content rather than volume
Germany	Began taxation reform in 1999 and raised the 'ecological tax' rate of fossil fuel consumption; part of the tax revenue is used to promote the energy substitution and renovation of low-carbon buildings.
India	Introduced a nationwide carbon tax of 50 rupees per tonne ($1.07/t) of coal both produced and imported into India since 2010
Italy	Energy tax reform in 1998 implemented, revised in 1999, then suspended
Japan	Withdrew an earlier planned carbon tax in 2012
Russia	Not high on the political agenda
UK	Fuel duty escalator (FDE), an environmental tax on retail petroleum products to reduce carbon emission introduced in 1993, but later withdrawn; implemented a climate change levy in 2001 that adds about 15% to the cost of electricity; a carbon floor price under consideration
USA	No nationwide carbon tax, few states – California, Colorado, Maryland – have introduced carbon taxes

Source: Compiled from several country-specific sources

confidence in the market, long-term tax reforms are required for large-scale low-carbon investment.

Emission trading systems and market barriers

The EU-Emission Trading Scheme (EU-ETS) is the world's largest emissions trading system and has to a great extent led the way in building an international carbon market. In the past 10 years, almost all Annex I parties have either established or strengthened existing trading schemes and are in some way participating in either national or international carbon markets. There is growing experimentation with carbon trading among large emitters such as China, South Korea and Australia, but some major emitters, like the US, are still not part of a globally linked carbon market, although national and regional carbon trading strategies are under way in such countries. The EU has agreed to link its ETS with Australia's scheme by 2018 and has struck a deal with China to help with the design and implementation of its emissions trading schemes. Carbon prices fell drastically with the global financial crisis as well as increased volumes within existing carbon markets. The oversupply drove down the price of carbon, weakening the incentive to cut emissions for those included in the scheme. Table 2.6 synthesizes critical evidence on carbon trade.

Policy uncertainty and competitiveness have a huge effect on price because investors are unsure that they will be able to have an adequate return on investments. The experience in the EU ETS, with repeated over-allocation and crashing prices, calls for market efficiency and intervention through adoption of tighter caps beyond 2020 and mandating EU emission allowance (EUA) price floors and ceilings. Market efficiency, good governance with a sound legal and administrative framework, macroeconomic stability and the overall institutional environment have strong bearings on emission reduction strategies. It is widely understood that a global agreement is a prerequisite for a global carbon market, which is in turn the prerequisite for setting a price on carbon. Since the launch of the ETS in 2005, the actual carbon price has continuously dipped below the level required to promote actual abatement of emissions. It is much easier for top emitters to agree on a set of climate actions, in particular harmonised carbon taxes, than on quantitative national emission reduction targets.

Equity

Equity plays a crucial role in the climate crisis. Climate change is, in fact, still characterised by a condition of 'structural' (Okereke 2011: 131) injustice that by and large penalises the vital interests of poor people and countries in favour of the (often) trivial ones of the affluent world. Therefore, current climate policies necessarily need to include issues of justice in order to favour new architectures (Grasso 2011). In regard to emissions abatement, a major stumbling block for future climate agreements relates to the developed world's recognition of its carbon debt, that is the portion of the ecological debt ascribable to carbon-emitting activities towards developing countries, as made clear by Davis and Caldeira (2010). Indeed, the developed world is offshoring its emissions to poorer countries (Roberts and Parks 2009). In fact, the relative decarbonisation of wealthy countries is largely due to their emission transfers via international trade to poorer countries (Peters et al. 2011), whose emissions, conversely, have roughly doubled in the past 20 years (Hertwich and Peters 2009).

Table 2.6 Global competitiveness and barriers in carbon trade

Top emitters	Market stages	GCI* rating	Emission trading scheme	Barriers in carbon trade
Canada	Innovation driven	5.33	A number of Canadian provinces, including Ontario, Quebec, Manitoba and British Columbia, have begun implementing the regulations necessary to join a regional carbon market known as the Western Climate Initiative (WCI)	Lacks aggressive and effective innovation strategy, internal barriers to trade and labour mobility
China	Efficiency driven	4.90	Carbon trading schemes (planned)	Lacks regulatory flexibility and transparency
EU-27	Innovation driven		European Union Emission Trading Scheme (2005)	
Germany	Innovation driven	5.41	EU ETS	Rigid labour markets
India	Factor driven	4.30	Energy efficiency trading scheme (planned)	Transport, ICT, and energy infrastructure Still largely insufficient and ill-suited to the market's needs
Italy	Innovation driven	4.43	EU ETS	Labour market remains extremely rigid, financial markets are not sufficiently developed
Japan	Innovation driven	5.40	Tokyo metropolitan trading scheme (2010), Japanese National Trading System (planned)	High budget deficits and increasing public debt
Russia	Factor driven	4.21	Internal carbon caps and a trading system (planned)	Lacks quality institutions, lower levels of labour market efficiency, business sophistication, and innovation, market structures dominated by a few large firms, inefficient anti-monopoly policies, and restrictions on trade and foreign ownership
UK	Innovation driven	5.39	UK ETS, UK Carbon Reduction Commitment (CRC) Energy Efficiency Scheme (2010)	Low national saving rate and increasing public debt
US	Innovation driven	5.43	The Regional Greenhouse Gas Initiative (RGGI) in the northeast of the US (2009); The Western Climate Initiative (WCI), and California cap-and-trade program (planned)	Fiscal deficits, public debt

Note: *GCI (Global Competitive Index) captures the national competitiveness of countries, which can be improved through an array of reforms that affect longer-term productivity, including low-carbon development and mitigation strategies. It is also agreed that fiscal pressures may lead to a reduction of R&D investments and innovation in markets for low-carbon growth.

Source: World Economic Forum (2011) and various studies

The climate equity Lorenz curve with Gini and Robin Hood indices as presented in Figure 2.3 shows that the current distribution of GHG emissions is highly inequitable. The graph shows the equity of the distribution of GHG emissions data for the year 2010. The straight line represents the hypothetical line of equality where countries would reside if GHG emissions were divided with perfect equity between all countries. The curved line represents the Lorenz curve and denotes actual GHG emissions equity for the year 2010. The distance between the lines represents GHG emissions inequity and is quantified by the Gini (80.9) and Robin Hood indices (64). The climate equity Lorenz curve and both indices show that the current distribution of GHG emissions is highly inequitable.

The interpretative frame of carbon debt is, in our opinion, particular useful for understanding the ethical nature of climate change in the context of this article, since it moves the discourse from the abstract dimension of distributive justice to the pragmatic one of political justice. In practical terms, the article adopts a notion of carbon debt/credit based on the difference between territorial- and consumption-based emissions inventories: those countries with consumption-based emissions larger than territorial-based ones have a carbon debt, and vice versa, as shown for top-emitters in Table 2.7.[5]

In terms of climate policy evaluation, the chapter therefore abandons the exclusive national focus of previous effectiveness and efficiency

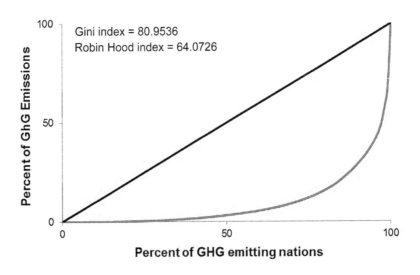

Figure 2.3 Climate equity Lorenz curve

Source: Elaborations of the authors

Table 2.7 Top 10 emitters: carbon-exporting (E), carbon-importing (I) countries, the carbon credit/debt based on cumulative 1990–2008 territorial (T), consumption (C) emissions [carbon credit/debt = T – C], percentage of the carbon credit (+) debt (–) in relation to territorial cumulative emissions, and climate funding

Top emitter	T Cum emissions $MtCO_2$	C Cum emissions $MtCO_2$	Carbon credit (+) and debt (–) $MtCO_2$	% Carbon credit/debt on total emissions	Funding pledged (Mln. US$)
China (E)	75,341	63,335	12,006	0.16	8.2
Russia (E)	31,371	27,916	3,455	0.11	3.5
India (E)	21,701	20,182	1,519	0.07	6.4
Japan (E)	23,914	23,239	675	0.03	15,277.3
Canada (I)	9,587	10,720	–1,133	–0.12	479.5
UK (I)	10,652	12,281	–1,629	–0.15	4,872.2
Italy (I)	8,458	9,917	–1,459	–0.17	60.0
Germany (I)	16,459	19,913	–3,454	–0.21	2,204.6
USA (I)	103,700	109,385	–5,685	–0.05	2,398.8
EU 27* (I)	76,717	92,310	–15,593	–0.20	8,759.7

Note: * We could not include six EU member countries owing to a lack of data: Bulgaria, Estonia, Latvia, Lithuania, Malta and Poland (whose contributions to climate funding are, however, very likely non-significant in absolute value).

Source: Elaboration on Peters et al. 2011; for funding pledged, Climate Funds Update (www.climatefundsupdate.org)

yardsticks: the deeply global nature of climate injustice demands, in fact, that the equity of national climate policy be weighed internationally. Furthermore, again differently from the two previous evaluative perspectives, the dimension of equity intrinsic to the carbon debt can be usefully captured by a single indicator of multilateral and bilateral funding for adaptation, mitigation and REDD. This is, in fact, an excellent proxy for the willingness of the developed world to recognise its carbon debt. In particular, equity demands that carbon debtors (Canada, UK, Italy, Germany, USA and EU 27, the 'debt emitters') should contribute to multilateral and bilateral climate funding in proportion to the relative sizes of their carbon debts. Therefore, in order to evaluate the ethical contents of climate policy, the chapter checks the consistency of this provision with the real politik of climate finance for every debt emitter. It ultimately looks for an acceptable degree of consistency between the emitter's contribution and the relative size of its carbon debt: the greater the consistency, the closer the adherence of the country's climate policy to equity.

More specifically, acknowledgement of the carbon debt is measured by the weight of climate funding on the monetised amount of the carbon debt. The monetisation of the carbon budget is given by multiplying it by the average price of a ton of carbon as specified by the prices of two Kyoto flexibility mechanisms allowances implemented by the EU, the EUA and the CER (Certified Emission Reduction). Accordingly, the UK is the only subject among debt-emitters acknowledging its climate debt, with pledges to climate finance that are more than two times the average pledges of the other top emitters. By contrast, Italy has the lowest contribution to climate finance, with pledges 95% less than the debt emitters' average. The two North American countries' pledges are half the average; those of the EU and Germany are respectively 34% and 25% below the average (see Table 2.8).

It should be noted that the notion of carbon debt adopted, as outlined above, determines the exclusive focus on the relative equity status of debt emitters. It is, in fact, a notion of relative equity calculated only on the basis of the specific situation of debt emitters that highlights their carbon debts acknowledgments. The outcomes of the application of this perspective may indeed be counterintuitive, since in absolute terms the contribution of every debt emitter (and of other richer countries, also those not included among top emitters) is still largely insufficient (Grasso 2010: 71–88). However, the purpose of the article is simply to assess the equity of the climate policy of a particular category of subjects – debt emitters – as expressed by their contribution to climate funding, the purpose being, as anticipated, to point out their attitude toward equity. This standpoint, furthermore, implies the

Table 2.8 Equity of debt emitters' climate funding

Top emitter	Carbon debt (MtCO₂)	Monetised carbon debt (billion US$)	Current pledges (million US$)	Acknowledgment of carbon debt (% of pledges on monetised carbon budget compared to the average of debt-emitters)
UK	1,629	11,110	4,872.2	253.4
Germany	3,454	23,556	2,204.6	–24.6
EU 27	15,593	106,344	8,759.7	–33.6
USA	5,685	38,772	2,398.8	–50.1
Canada	1,133	7,727	479.5	–50.0
Italy	1,459	9,950	60.0	–95.1

Source: Elaboration on Peters's et al. (2011) dataset; for funding figures, elaboration from Climate Funds Update (www.climatefundsupdate.org)

non-consideration as equity yardsticks of both the historical responsibility of debt emitters and their ability to pay as determined by their GDPs.[6]

Overall, the UK shows greater acknowledgment of its carbon debts – as captured by a single indicator of multilateral and bilateral funding for adaptation, mitigation and REDD – than the remaining debt emitters (Canada, Italy, Germany, the US and the EU). This ultimately reveals a high level of relative equity, understood as climate debt acknowledgment, among debt emitters. By contrast, Italy, which almost completely disregards climate finance, has the most unjust climate policy. Among other debt emitters, Germany and the EU show a relatively acceptable degree of equity in their climate policies, whereas North American countries still need to improve their carbon debt recognition, so that the equity of their climate policies is still inadequate.

It is also important to mention here that what is considered fair and equitable in India may be widely different from what is considered fair in the China and USA. Therefore, interpretations of fairness concepts are likely to differ, and this difference will tend to reflect conflicts of interest of various emitters (Kallbekken et al. 2014). Any attempts to find a single convincing and acceptable formula are therefore unlikely to be of broad interest (Skeie et al. 2017). If equity principles are successfully applied, they can form a major driver to bridge the gap between the currently predicted and the optimum reduction targets in international climate policy (Bretschger 2015).

After establishment of a binding global carbon budget, the first, largest part of it should be freely distributed to top emitting countries through a cap-and-trade system consistent with the welfare utilitarian moral perspective and the International Paretianism feasibility constraint. The second part should be auctioned off to top emitters mainly for raising revenues against extreme poverty, whereas the third and final portion should be earmarked for business-as-usual emission pathways in all other countries.

Political feasibility

The evaluation of the political feasibility of top emitters' climate policies requires, as said, the adoption of a prospective stance. This boils down to the following blunt question: why do some countries have ambitious climate policies, and others do not? The ex-ante evaluation dimension of political feasibility concerns the concrete possibility of national climate policy to achieve the necessary support among policymakers, civil society, and industry so that it can be implemented

(Brandt and Svendsen 2004). This is indeed a very broad evaluation category that focuses on the relationships among ideas, power and resources (Tanner and Allouche 2011) and involves national cultures and sensitivities, the role of science, as well as political, institutional and economic systems. It is therefore extremely difficult to reduce and dissolve the complexity and breadth of this soft evaluation perspective into a single hard yardstick. Consequently, a realistic and useful approach for assessing the political feasibility of national climate policies consists in scrutinising how related ideas, power and resources are conceptualised, negotiated and agreed (i.e. in investigating the political economy of climate change). More specifically, the article provides a concise overview of the major factors that are likely to drive top emitters' climate policies.

According to the emerging literature on the political economy of climate change (e.g. de Serres et al. 2011; Steves et al. 2011), which largely draws on experiences of structural reforms around the world, such factors can be synthesised into the following main categories: (1) burdens; (2) public awareness; (3) democracy and institutional capacity; and (4) interest groups.

As regards the first category, it can be claimed, as also the literature on political science unambiguously points out (e.g. Dahl 1998: 145–165), that the lower the burden of a policy, the more it is likely to succeed in the long term, at least in democratic societies. To this end the article assumes, consistently with its focus, that the main burden of climate policy relates to the associated mitigation cost (Nemet 2010). It should be noted that climate policy acceptability has been further weakened in the past few years by the global economic crisis, by the post-Copenhagen sense of disillusion and by a certain loss of credibility of climate science. Therefore, the political feasibility of future mitigation policies by and large depends on the projected marginal cost of emission abatements (MAC) contextualised to the country's average welfare level. To this end, we parameterised the absolute MACs to countries' 2011 per capita GDP. In particular, the article assumes, in line with the relevant literature, that the higher the marginal abatement cost, the proportionally lower is the political feasibility of future mitigations (Goulder and Parry 2008; Bosetti and Frankel 2009). Table 2.9 reports the absolute and parameterised MACs for top emitters aggregated on a regional basis.

According to this evidence, India and China are the least willing to abate carbon emissions, whereas Russia and, to a lesser extent, the EU and its members are the most favourable to mitigation initiatives. Canada, the US and Japan lie somewhere in between, so that their

Table 2.9 Marginal abatement costs (MAC)

Top emitter	MAC (2005 USD per ton CO_2)	Parameterised MAC
India	28.5	160.7
China	20.6	38.5
North America	40.7	18.5
Japan	45.0	13.4
EU 27 and Members	29.6	7.8
Russia	15.7	2.1

Source: Elaboration on Morris et al. 2008. Calculated as average of 2010 MAC for the 7 (1, 5, 10, 20, 30, 40, 50%) levels of abatement

incentive to emissions abatement cannot be clearly understood according to this category.

Public awareness of the threat posed by climate change is expected to be an influential driver of stronger climate policies, given the extent to which governments, at least in democratic societies, respond to public pressure. The correlation between public knowledge and better climate policy is indeed complex, however with a crude simplification, the article assumes that the greater the awareness of the dangerousness of climate change, the stronger the climate policy. In particular, the World Values Survey provides important insights into the perception of the threat posed by climate change.[7] It makes it possible to identify three groups of top emitters with high, medium and low awareness of the climate crisis: 1-High: Canada, EU 27, Italy, and Japan; 2-Medium: Germany, India, USA; 3-Low: China, Russia, UK. Consistently with our assumption, we argue that group 1-High would be most likely to implement courageous climate policies, followed by the other groups with decreasing likelihoods of introducing meaningful climate policies.

Also the level of democracy and institutional capacity can have an ambivalent effect on climate policy (Steves et al. 2011). However, the article assumes, in line with most of the relevant literature, that democracies are more likely to provide environmental public goods like climate stability (Burnell 2012; Bernauer and Böhmelt 2013) empirically found that democracy has a positive effect on the performances of climate policy), and that democracies, also by virtue of their greater institutional capacity, can better participate in international environmental regime-making (e.g. Ward 2008; Bernauer et al. 2010; Neumayer (2002) empirically proved this claim). There are several indexes that measure the state of democracy at country level: they by and large establish very similar rankings. The article uses the Economist Intelligence Unit Democracy Index, since it includes both indicators on the quality of democratic processes and on the institutional capacity to implement policies.[8] According to this index, Canada, Germany, the UK, the US and Japan are *full democracies*. Consequently, even if not expressly calculated by the index, also the EU can be considered as belonging substantially in this category, similarly to the majority of its most influential members. India and Italy are instead *flawed democracies*, whereas Russia and China are considered *authoritarian regimes*. In the current analysis, full democracies are the ones most likely to implement effective climate policies, as opposed to authoritarian regimes, whose climate policies are expected to be the least incisive.

The strength of interest groups, and in particular the power of the carbon-intensive industry lobby, is probably the most important single determinant of climate policy. If the role of the carbon lobby is theoretically uncontroversial, in practice it is also the most difficult factor to circumscribe, let alone to measure. In other words, the role of the carbon-intensive industry lobby can be only roughly captured: to this end, consistently with what suggested by Steves et al. (2011), the article calculates the share of carbon-intensive industries – manufacturing, mining and utilities – in top emitters' GDPs (Table 2.10). The larger the share, the greater the importance and weight of the carbon lobby in contrasting actions against carbon-intensive activities, and the lower the eventual possibility of effective climate policy. It should be noted

Table 2.10 Shares of carbon-intensive industry in total GDP 2010 in US$ current price

Top emitter	Shares	% in comparison to average share
China	0.407	+78
Russia	0.310	+36
Germany	0.237	+4
Canada	0.218	−5
Japan	0.214	−6
EU 27	0.203	−11
Italy	0.193	−15
India	0.181	−21
US	0.163	−29
UK	0.157	−31

Source: Elaboration on UN Statistics, National Accounts Main Aggregates Database (http://unstats.un.org/unsd/snaama/introduction.asp)

Table 2.11 Political feasibility of climate policies in top emitters according to categories of factors

Top emitter	Burdens	Public awareness	Democracy	Interest groups
Canada	Medium	High	High	Medium
China	Low	Low	Low	Low
EU 27	High	High	High	Medium
Germany	High	Medium	High	Medium
India	Low	Medium	Medium	High
Italy	High	High	Medium	Medium
Japan	Medium	High	High	Medium
Russia	High	Low	Low	Low
UK	High	Low	High	High
US	Medium	Medium	High	High

Source: Elaborations on tables and information related to the four categories of political feasibility

that this insight into top emitters' GDP compositions also shows the nature of their industrial structures, which is indeed another possible determinant of climate policy. However, this we do not explore, in order not to extend the scope of our investigation excessively.

All in all, it seems possible to divide top-emitters into three groupings, with diminishing likelihoods of implementing effective climate policies: (1) high carbon-intensive industry: China and Russia; (2) medium carbon-intensive industry: Germany, Canada, Japan, EU 27 and Italy; and (3) low carbon-intensive industry: India, the US and the UK.

In light of these considerations to answer the question posed at the beginning of this section it is useful to refer to the synoptic Table 2.11, where indicated for each top emitter is the relevance (low, medium, high) of the category of factors for favouring the implementation of climate policies.

First of all, it seems evident that in both China and Russia the political feasibility of climate policies is rather problematic, and that the scope for climate-incisive action is rather limited. On the other hand, the EU 27 and to a lesser extent the UK are, according to our analysis, the most proactive subjects in terms of climate policy. The situation of the other top emitters is more nuanced. Canada, Germany, Japan, Italy and the US seem ready for more forceful climate policies, even if they are still encumbered by some specific resistances, while India's climate policy is instead characterised by an apparently lower politically feasibility.

Conclusions: common threads and emerging issues

By way of conclusion it is worth synthesising the outcomes of the four evaluation exercises carried out on top-emitters' climate policies into a synoptic table (see Table 2.12) which highlights some common threads in, and emerging issues from, top emitters' climate policies.

First and foremost, it seems possible to cluster top emitters on the basis of their performances in the determinants of climate policy, into three main groups. In fact Russia and China, the first group, share a certain degree of laggardness: China's and, especially, Russia's attitudes, coupled with their absolute and growing relevance in climate negotiations, are rather worrisome for the paucity and inertia of their climate policy. As emerges from the current analysis, they could be major stumbling blocks for the development of the international climate regime(s). As for the second group, the climate policies of Canada, India, Italy and the US can be considered more proactive, even if the North American countries and Italy seem nonetheless to disregard ethical issues, and India's economic efficiency is still apparently inadequate. The remaining top emitters, namely EU, Germany, Japan and the UK, the third group, instead seem to have a well-articulated climate policy and a supportive political context – especially so the UK, which, in fact, performs admirably on every determinant. Climate policy, furthermore, has emerged as a vital area of EU governance.

Second, to be stressed are the emerging climate policy issues of top-emitters based on the relevance of the determinants highlighted in Table 2.12. In this regard, it seems possible to argue that political

Table 2.12 Performance of top global emitters in regard to determinants of climate policy: laggards (L), average (A), pushers (P)

Top emitter	Environmental effectiveness	Economic efficiency	Equity	Political feasibility
Canada	A	P	L	A
China	A	L	P	L
EU 27	P	P	A	P
Germany	P	P	P	A
India	P	L	P	L
Italy	P	A	L	A
Japan	P	P	P	A
Russia	L	L	L	L
UK	P	P	P	P
US	A	P	L	A

Source: Authors' conceptual elaboration from Tables 2.2–2.11.

feasibility is the weakest component of the climate policy architecture, followed by equity concerns. While environmental effectiveness appears to be the most successful constituent of current top emitters' climate policies, much progress is required in the domain of economic efficiency. In this regard, it seems that any future climate regime(s) should pay extremely close attention to the political economy of climate change in order to prompt fairer and more effective and efficient solutions to the climate crisis.

Third, if a coalition of the top emitters assumes significantly stronger mitigation goals, this may give competitive advantage to reduce global emissions and may create incentives for other emitters to join them. For example, the EU can increase partnerships with other top emitters such as China and US and their emissions schemes as part of efforts to improve its own ETS. The cost of meeting the emissions reduction commitments of the top emitters can be substantially reduced by engaging in meaningful global carbon trading.

There exist significant reduction possibilities in GHG emissions under the policy regimes of global carbon tax and emission trading permits. Since most of the world's emissions come from a relatively small number of countries, the international effort must firmly commit top emitters to mitigation. It is clear that the top emitters of the world have to entirely decarbonise the power sector as well as other key sectors such as transportation, industry and agriculture. In the short term, it appears to be difficult agenda, however, given the technological developments in near future, options for decarbonisation may be more open than the current conventional nuclear, wind and solar alternatives. Also, the CBDR principle highlights the potential policy conflict between economic efficiency and equity, therefore, the global carbon policy will have to strike a balance between economic efficiency and equity or fairness among world's top emitters.

A new policy approach must seek agreement on what may constitute fair and acceptable among the global emitters. In brief, if humanity is to address climate-related harm meaningfully, it must undertake a complicated and costly collective effort to reduce carbon emissions drastically and rapidly. It should also be noted that since climate change is, especially in the more destitute southern countries, a major cause of poverty – another serious global plague (Pogge 2010)[9] – the solutions to these two problems necessarily interact: it makes little sense to deal with the harm brought about by climate change while neglecting and/ or worsening poverty, and vice versa. Therefore, in order to reduce climate-induced injustice further, a purposefully designed framework for abating emissions should also combat poverty (Shue 2013). It is also observed that many top emitters need clear policy on carbon regulation and a climate adaptation strategy.

Notes

1 Many parties formulated and submitted INDCs that outline the post-2020 climate action plans they intend to take under the Paris Agreement (UNF-CCC 2015). After the Agreement entered into force on 4 November 2016, the INDCs for those countries that have ratified the Agreement, turned into Nationally Determined Contributions (NDCs). By relying on voluntary contributions and respecting national circumstances, do not ensure efficient and equitable country policies. According to Bretschger (2017: 1), 'concrete climate policy measures are not implemented on a global level but formulated in terms of independent country contributions, which may be called the "bottom-up" approach to climate policy'.

2 The data presented in this article, unless otherwise specified, are authors' elaborations on Peters' et al. (2011) dataset, which is in turn based on the primary data on the annual fossil fuel, cement, and gas-flaring emissions between 1990 and 2008 reported by the Carbon Dioxide Information Analysis Center (CDIAC).

3 Therefore, the article analyses only the so-called mitigation policy, and not the increasingly important adaptation one. It does so for the sake of consistency with acknowledgment of both the urgency of emission abatement and the consequent selection of the largest emitters as key-players in climate change, and with the spirit of article 2 of the UNFCCC, which states that the stabilisation of GHG concentrations produced by emissions abatement should ease adaptation to climate change.

4 Forty-two Annex I countries have pledged quantified economy-wide emissions targets for 2020, and 36 non-Annex I countries have pledged mitigation actions under the Copenhagen Accord.

5 To be noted is that other schools of thought, especially from the developing world, put forward a different notion of carbon debt that refers to the overuse of the atmospheric capacity of absorbing GHG, i.e. to the greater historical contribution of the developed countries (for a thorough investigation of the ethical arguments backing the notion of carbon debt see Pickering and Barry 2012: 671–677). The current choice of the more prudent account of the carbon debt is based on the non-dependency of the latter on any a priori ethical assumptions that artificially split (top) emitters into developed and developing countries with consequent a priori different moral duties and rights.

6 Having specified thus, however, extremely noteworthy is the conduct of Japan, which, though belonging among the 'credit emitters', has by far the largest absolute contribution to climate finance with US$15,277 million pledged (and US$12,777 million deposited). By contrast, Russia, the other Annex I credit emitter, has never shown any real interest in equity, let alone advanced any ethical argument in the realm of negotiations, so that it seems possible to envisage a nonchalant attitude towards this dimension of climate policy.

7 www.worldvaluessurvey.org. The data used are from the fifth wave of the World Values Survey (WVS 5), in particular from question V111,

'Environmental problems in the world: Global warming or the greenhouse effect'. The percentages of respondents in top emitters that believe that climate change is a very serious issue are the following: Canada, 66.7%; China, 38.0%; EU 27, 61.2%; Germany, 49.9%; India, 51.1%; Italy, 71.4%; Japan, 71.3%; Russia, 41.2%; UK, 36.8%; US, 48.5%.

8 Economist Intelligence Unit: https://www.eiu.com/topic/democracy-index
9 World Bank data (Chen and Ravallion 2012) show that 43% (2.47 billion) of the population of the developing world lived on less than $2 a day in 2008. The financial (and technological) transfers to the developing world in order to prevent climate harm and the related injustice are widely held to be primary strategies in combating poverty in the global south.

References

Allen, M. 2015. 'Paris Emissions Cuts Aren't Enough – We'll Have to Put Carbon Back in the Ground', *The Conversation*, 14 December 2015, https://theconversation.com/paris-emissions-cuts-arent-enough-well-have-to-put-carbon-back-in-the-ground-52175.

Andersen, M.S. 2004. 'Vikings and Virtues – A Decade of CO_2 Taxation', *Climate Policy*, 4: 13–24.

Awerbuch, S. and Sauter, R. 2006. 'Exploiting the Oil-GDP Effect to Support Renewables Deployment', *Energy Policy*, 34 (17): 2805–2819.

Baranzini, A., Bergh, J.C., Carattini, S., Howarth, R.B., Padilla, E. and Roca, J. 2017. 'Carbon Pricing in Climate Policy: Seven Reasons, Complementary Instruments, and Political Economy Considerations', Wiley Interdisciplinary Reviews: Climate Change.

Battles, S., Clò, S. and Zoppoli, P. 2013. 'Policy Options to Support the Carbon Price Within the European Emissions Trading System: Framework for a Comparative Analysis', Working Paper No. 1, January 2013, Ministry of Economy and Finance, Italy.

Bernauer, T. and Böhmelt, T. 2013. 'National Climate Policies in International Comparison: The Climate Change Cooperation Index', *Environmental Science & Policy*, 25: 196–206.

Bernauer, T., Kalbhenn, A., Koubi, V. and Spilker, G. 2010. 'A Comparison of International and Domestic Sources of Global Governance Dynamics', *British Journal of Political Science*, 40 (3): 509–538.

Boccanfuso, D., Estache, A. and Savard, L. 2011. 'The Intra-Country Distributional Impact of Policies to Fight Climate Change: A Survey', *Journal of Development Studies*, 47 (1): 97–117.

Bosetti, V. and Frankel, J. 2009. 'Global Climate Policy Architecture and Political Feasibility: Specific Formulas and Emission Targets to Attain 460 PPM CO_2 Concentrations', The Harvard Project on International Climate Agreements, Discussion Paper 09–30.

Bovenberg, A.L. and Goulder, L.H. 2002. 'Environmental Taxation and Regulation', in A. Auerbach and M. Feldstein (eds.), *Handbook of Public Economics* (1471–1545). New York: Elsevier.

Brandt, U.S. and Svendsen, G.T. 2004. 'Fighting Windmills: The Coalition of Industrialists and Environmentalists in the Climate Change Issue', *International Environmental Agreements: Politics, Law and Economics*, 4 (4): 327–337.

Bretschger, L. 2015. *Greening Economy, Graying Society*. Zurich: CER-ETH Press.

Bretschger, L. 2017. 'Equity and the Convergence of Nationally Determined Climate Policies', *Environmental Economics and Policy Studies*, 19 (1): 1–14.

Bulkeley, H. 2015. 'Can Cities Realise Their Climate Potential? Reflections on COP21 Paris and Beyond', *Local Environment*, 20 (11): 1405–1409.

Burnell, P. 2012. 'Democracy, Democratization and Climate Change: Complex Relationships', *Democratization*, 19 (5): 813–842.

Chen, S. and Ravallion, M. 2012. 'An Update to the World Bank's Estimates of Consumption Poverty in the Developing World', Washington, DC: Development Research Group, World Bank.

Crabbè, A. and Leroy, P. 2008. *The Handbook of Environmental Policy Evaluation*. London: Earthscan.

Dahl, R. 1998. *On Democracy*. New Haven, CT: Yale University Press.

Davis, S. and Caldeira, K. 2010. 'Consumption-Based Accounting of CO_2 Emissions', *PNAS*, 107 (12): 5687–5692.

de Serres, A., Llewellyn, J. and Llewellyn, P. 2011. 'The Political Economy of Climate Change Mitigation Policies: How to Build a Constituency to Address Global Warming?' Paris, OECD, Economics Department Working Papers No. 887.

Dutta, V., Dasgupta, P., Hultman, N. and Gadag, G. 2016. 'Evaluating Expert Opinion on India's Climate Policy: Opportunities and Barriers to Low-Carbon Inclusive Growth', *Climate and Development*, 8 (4): 336–350. doi:10.1080/17565529.2015.1067181

Fischer, S. and Geden, O. 2015. 'The Changing Role of International Negotiations in EU Climate Policy', *International Spectator*, 50 (1): 1–7.

Goulder, L.H. 1995. 'Environmental Taxation and the 'double dividend': A Reader's Guide', *International Tax and Public Finance*, 2 (2): 157–183.

Goulder, L.H. and Parry, W.H. 2008. 'Instruments Choice in Environmental Policy', *Review of Environmental Economics and Policy*, 2 (2): 152–174.

Grasso, M. 2010. *Justice in Funding Adaptation Under the International Climate Change Regime*. Dordrecht: Springer.

Grasso, M. 2011. 'The Role of Justice in the North-South Conflict in Climate Change: The Case of Negotiations on the Adaptation Fund', *International Environmental Agreements: Politics, Law and Economics*, 11: 361–377.

Grasso, M. 2012. 'Sharing the Emission Budget', *Political Studies*, 60: 668–686.

Gupta, J. 2010. 'A History of International Climate Change Policy', *Wiley Interdisciplinary Reviews: Climate Change*, 1 (5): 636–653.

Hertwich, E.G. and Peters, G.P. 2009. 'Carbon Footprint of Nations: A Global, Trade-Linked Analysis', *Environmental Science & Technology*, 43: 6414–6420.

Hills, J. 2012. *Getting the Measure of Fuel Poverty: Final Report of the Fuel Poverty Review.* CASE Report 72, Centre for the Analysis of Social Exclusion. London: London School of Economics.

Intergovernmental Panel on Climate Change (IPCC). 2013. *Working Group I Contribution to the IPCC Fifth Assessment Report Climate Change 2013: The Physical Science Basis, Summary for Policymakers.* Geneva: IPCC.

International Energy Agency. 2011. *World Energy Outlook 2010.* Paris: IEA.

IPCC. 2007. *Climate Change 2007: Impacts, Adaptation and Vulnerability: Working Group ii Contribution to the Fourth Assessment Report of the IPCC* [Parry, M. L., Canziani, O. F., Palutikof, J. P., Van Der Linden, P. J. and Hanson, C. E. (Eds)]. Cambridge: Cambridge University Press.

IPCC. 2014. 'Climate Change 2014: Impacts, Adaptation, and Vulnerability. Part A: Global and Sectoral Aspects. Contribution of Working Group II to the Fifth Assessment Report of the Intergovernmental Panel on Climate Change' [Field C. B., Barros V. R., Dokken D. J., Mach K. J., Mastrandrea M. D., Bilir T. E., Chatterjee M., Ebi K. L., Estrada Y. O., Genova R. C., Girma B., Kissel E. S., Levy A. N., MacCracken S., Mastrandrea P. R., and White L. L. (eds.)]. Cambridge: Cambridge University Press.

Jorgenson, A. K. 2014. 'Economic Development and the Carbon Intensity of Human Well-Being', *Nature Climate Change*, 4: 186–189.

Kallbekken, S., Sælen, H. & Underdal, A. 2014. *Equity and Spectrum of Mitigation Commitments in the 2015 Agreement.* Nordic Council of Ministers.

Keohane, R. O. and Nye, J. S. Jr. 2000. 'Introduction', In J. S. Nye Jr. and J. D. Donahue (eds.), *Governance in a Globalizing World.* Washington, DC: Brookings Institution Press.

Keohane, R. O. and Victor, D. G. 2011. 'The Regime Complex for Climate Change', *Perspectives on Politics*, 9 (1): 7–23.

Laviña, A.G.M., Ang, L. G., De Leon, A. and Roxas, M. 2012. *The UNFCCC After Durban: Recognizing Limitations and Calling for a Multi-Track Approach to Climate Multilateralism and Action.* London: FIELD Working Paper.

Martin, R., Muuls, M. and Wagner, U. 2011. *Climate Change, Investment and Carbon Markets and Prices – Evidence from Manager Interviews.* London: Climate Policy Initiative.

Morris, J., Paltsev, S. and Reilly, J. 2008. *Marginal Abatement Costs and Marginal Welfare Costs for Greenhouse Gas Emissions Reductions: Results from the EPPA Model.* Cambridge, MA: MIT Joint Program on the Science and Policy of Global Change, Report No. 164.

Nemet, G. F. 2010. 'Cost Containment in Climate Policy and Incentives for Technology Development', *Climatic Change*, 103: 423–443.

Neuhoff, K. and Weber, T. A. 2010. 'Carbon Markets and Technological Innovation', *Journal of Environmental Economics and Management*, 60: 115–132.

Neumayer, E. 2002. 'Do Democracies Exhibit Stronger International Environmental Commitment? A Cross-Country Analysis', *Journal of Peace Research*, 39 (2): 139–164.

Okereke, C. 2011. 'Moral Foundations for Global Environmental and Climate Justice', *Royal Institute of Philosophy*, Supplement 69: 117–135.

Parry, Ian W.H. and Williams, R. 2010. 'What Are the Costs of Meeting Distributional Objectives for Climate Policy?' *B.E. Journal of Economic Analysis & Policy*, Berkeley Electronic Press, 10 (2), 9.

Peters, G.P., Minx, J.C., Weber, C.L. and Edenhofer, O. 2011. 'Growth in Emission Transfers via International Trade from 1990 to 2008', *PNAS*, 108 (21): 8903–8908.

Pickering, J. and Barry, C. 2012. 'On the Concept of Climate Debts: Its Moral and Political Value', *Critical Review of International Social and Political Philosophy*, 15 (5): 667–685.

Pickering, J., Vanderheiden, S. and Miller, S. 2012. "If Equity's in, we're out': Scope for Fairness in the Next Climate Agreement', *Ethics & International Affairs*, 26 (4): 423–443.

Pogge, T. 2010. *Politics as Usual: What Lies Behind the Pro-Poor Rhetoric.* Malde: Polity Press.

Prins, G. and Rayner, S. 2007. 'Time to Ditch Kyoto', *Nature*, 449: 973–975.

Robbins, A. 2016. 'How to Understand the Results of the Climate Change Summit: Conference of Parties 21 (COP21) Paris 2015', *Journal of Public Health Policy*, 37 (2): 129–132.

Roberts, J.T. and Parks, B.C. 2009. 'Ecologically Unequal Exchange, Ecological Debt, and Climate Justice: The History and Implications of Three Related Ideas for a New Social Movement', *International Journal of Comparative Sociology*, 50 (3–4): 385–409.

Robiou du Pont, Y., Jeffery, M.L., Gutschow, J., Rogelj, J., Christoff, P. and Meinshausen, M. 2017. 'Equitable Mitigation to Achieve the Paris Agreement Goals', *Nature Climate Change*, 7: 38–43.

Rogelj, J., Den Elzen, M., Höhne, N., Fransen, T., Fekete, H., Winkler, H. and Meinshausen, M. 2016. 'Paris Agreement Climate Proposals Need a Boost to Keep Warming Well Below 2 C', *Nature*, 534 (7609): 631–639.

Sælen, H. 2015. 'Side-Payments: An Effective Instrument for Building Climate Clubs?' *International Environmental Agreements: Politics, Law and Economics*, 16 (6): 909–932. https://doi.org/10.1007/s10784-015-9311-8

Shklar, J.N. 1990. *The Faces of Injustice.* New Haven, CT: Yale University Press.

Shue, H. 2013. 'Climate Hope: Implementing the Exit Strategy', *Chicago Journal of International Law*, 13: 381–401.

Skeie, R.B., Fuglestvedt, J., Berntsen, T., Peters, G.P., Andrew, R., Allen, M. and Kallbekken, S. 2017. 'Perspective Has a Strong Effect on the Calculation of Historical Contributions to Global Warming', *Environmental Research Letters*, 12 (2): 024022.

Steves, F., Treisman, D. and Teytelboym, A. 2011. 'Political Economy of Climate Change Policy in the Transition Region', in A. Chirmiciu and S. Fankhauser (eds.), *The Low Carbon Transition*, Chapter 4. London: European Bank for Reconstruction and Development (EBRD).

Tanner, T. and Allouche, J. 2011. 'Towards a New Political Economy of Climate Change and Development', *IDS Bulletin*, 42 (3): 1–14.

UNEP. 2011. *Bridging the Emissions Gap Report – A UNEP Synthesis Report*. Nairobi: United Nations Environment Programme.

UNFCCC. 2015. 'UNFCCC, Intended Nationally Determined Contributions (INDCs)', www4.unfccc.int/submissions/indc/Submission%20Pages/submissions.aspx.

Verbruggen, A. 2011. 'Preparing the Design of Robust Climate Policy Architectures', *International Environmental Agreements: Politics, Law and Economics*, 11 (4): 275–295.

Victor, D. G. 2006. 'Toward Effective International Cooperation on Climate Change: Numbers, Interests and Institutions', *Global Environmental Politics*, 6 (3): 90–103.

Victor, D. G., House, J. C. and Joy, S. 2005. 'A Madisonian Approach to Climate Policy', *Science*, 309: 1820–1821.

Ward, H. 2008. 'Liberal Democracy and Sustainability', *Environmental Politics*, 17 (3): 386–409.

Wolgast, E. H. 1987. *The Grammar of Justice*. Ithaca, NY: Cornell University Press.

World Economic Forum. 2011. *The Global Competitiveness Report 2011–2012*. Geneva: World Economic Forum.

3 Politics of environment

Green parties in Europe as a model for India

Sheetal Sharma

Human beings are different from other species by virtue of being capable of empathy, reflexivity, and spirituality. This is possible because of the faculties human beings are endowed with such as cognition, reasoning, language, introspection, and problem solving, among others. These capacities/faculties are unique in the sense that they help human beings make sense of their knowledge and experience, the present as well as the past. These faculties also invest human beings with the ability to visualise, comprehend, forecast, and plan for the future and aspire for living in culturally organised ways. This they do for a variety of cultural and psychological reasons, of which 'ego/self-aggrandisement', self-preservation/procreation, greed and narcissism can arguably be attributed to be the main reasons. Thinking-planning-organising traits, obsession with the self to the disregard of others and the 'cultural' ways of living have led to evolution and flourishing of institutions like that of science and technology, governance, communication and transport and so forth by human beings. Impetus on science and technology enabled humans to further create material products and institutions that have come to dominate nature and landscape on an unprecedented scale. Material accumulation accompanied by invention of (the idea of) money and means of communication and transport transformed human societies from simple living to complex lifestyles and associated social practices and institutional structures. Interestingly these very tendencies/capacities and faculties have also led to a range of problems, bringing humanity to the verge of local and global 'disasters' in the form of environmental pollution/degradation. Humanity is grappling with these issues on a day-to-day basis. Not only is the earth losing its carrying capacity but according to certain estimates at least one species is being lost/going extinct every day from the face of earth. The very survival of life and a variety of species, in various parts of the earth, is at stake. The gravity and negative impact of environmental degradation and pollution on life and living standards have, kind of, impelled thinkers, philosophers and most well-meaning individuals to pose basic critical questions of survival. Humankind for its survival depends upon existence of healthy environment, yet it is humankind through its activities that is threatening the environment and has pushed it to the threshold of collapse and irreparable damage and destruction.

The present state of environmental degradation and pollution is an instance of human disregard for the nature in conception, production and utilisation of art and artefacts, products and processes of modern industrial societies. The urban settlements in form of modern cities and towns are verily a result of human faculties and capacities and the institutions borne out of them. The structures of urban agglomerations, aided by science and technology-based products, services, and processes, continued to grow bigger and complex. The urban settlements and agglomerations had their concomitant enabling institutions like municipalities, transport and energy structures, governance institutions, lobbying and civil society groups, and so forth. The continually waxing size and complexities of these urban agglomerations gave rise to problems of health and hygiene basically emerging from the womb of environmental degradation and pollution. Thus the environmental and health related problems of mega cities can be said to be culturally generated as they are products of modern lifestyles (Beck, U. 1994).

The state of environmental crises necessitates viewing of nature and culture as manifestations of same reality; just a pair of vantage points looking at the same phenomenon; or more clichédly – two sides of the same coin. Depletion of ozone layer, global warming, air and water pollution, ecological degradation, or extinction of species all emanate from exploitation of nature by humans for greed and not just need; more for instrumental reasons rather than substantive ones – in the words of critical theorists. Thus it can be argued safely that the environment is immensely impacted by a way of life that is characteristic of industrial societies, dictated by not only fulfilment of basic necessities but ruthless exploitation of resources for accumulation as well (Andersen, M. S. and Massa, I. 2000). Radiation from nuclear plants, hormonal dysfunction, falling-out of the protective ozone layer by irresponsible use of chlorofluorocarbons, pollution from the burning of fossil fuels, and motorised transport are just a few examples that illustrate that what can be the unintended and unforeseen consequences of industrial and technological development (Barman, Himadari 2014). As a threat to our very existence, these industrial advancements bring us face-to-face with the fundamental reality that we are rooted in and dependent upon nature. As two sides of the same coin – the success and excess, need and greed – have brought us full circle to confront the basis of our existence and present us now with the opportunity to rethink the meaning of modernity, science, and technological development. The situation necessitates breaking down and restructuring of the boundaries of the nature-culture divide. Whereas the early human being confronted nature for his basic survival, the modern being has to now preserve nature for his very survival. In the journey from being 'helpless' in front of nature to being a ruthless 'exploiter' of nature, the issue of survival of mankind remains central. But what has changed over centuries is the way man has been able to relate to nature. This shifting ground of conception and knowledge presents an opening for seeking fresh answers to the question, 'how shall we live?' (Adam 2005: 24). Modernity brought development along with a plethora of problems: social, economic, psychological, and ecological. Modernity is characterised by its belief in 'progress' associated with the explosion in scientific knowledge and the promises of technology. It is a crucible for the development of major unifying theories and the search for major organising principles such as democracy, communism, and capitalism which convey universal values (Mol, A.P.J. and Spaargaren, G. 2000).

Environmentalism

The modern-day environmental movement grew largely in the last quarter of the 20th century. It reflected upon the popular and academic concerns about the local and global degradation of the natural environment which was increasingly and primarily being studied by natural scientists from a hard-core scientific perspective. However it soon became clear that arresting environmental degradation was not merely a technical and managerial task: merely knowing about environmental problems did not in itself guarantee that enterprises, institutions, governments, businesses, or individuals would start caring about them (Benford, Robert D. and Snow, David A. 2000). It is now acknowledged that a critical understanding of socio-economic, political, and cultural processes and structures of particular society and given context is absolutely essential in understanding environmental problems and establishing environmentally sustainable development. Hence the maturing of idea of environmentalism has been marked by growing scholarship in the social sciences and humanities, exploring the complexity and dynamics of society-environment relationships

(Gold 2004). The growing salience of environmental problems over the past decade stemmed not only from increased attention accorded to them by scientists, media, and policymakers, but also from discernible changes in the way natural phenomenon are changing, weather patterns are being disturbed, and a whole set of the problems pertaining to environment [United Nations Conference on Environment and Development (UNCED) 2013].

It is difficult to identify a precise date to establish the beginning of the contemporary environment movement. The rise of environmentalism can be classified in different phases and eras. A number of periods have been identified by the scholars (Lowe and Goyder 1983). The period between the late 1800s and the early 1900s can be considered as the most significant, as it started with a concern of degrading environment as a consequence of industrialisation. This period, also known as the Resource Conservation period, arose from the ideas of the era of the Enlightenment and a corresponding utilitarian position which called for the sensible use of natural resources. The Enlightenment was an era where it was thought that man was capable of controlling, manipulating and improving nature and it was possible through exercises of rationality and reason and by use of means of science and technology. It was believed that *Homo sapiens* were the sole species to have the unique characteristics of intellectual capacity, language, organisation and culture. By virtue of possessing these qualities, humans were then able to adapt nature to human ends rather than having to adapt humans to the natural environment.[1]

However some philosophers and intellectuals were weary of the optimism of use of scientific rationality, economic liberalism and its pronouncement of social and economic advancement through laissez-faire capitalism. They criticised ruthless exploitation of natural resources in the name of development and progress of humankind. What was to become known as Romanticism developed during this period in opposition to this popular and powerful line of thought. They condemned the materialist society and the conformist obsession with technology and were alarmed with the destructive capacity of post-Newtonian science.[2] The mindless exploitation of resources was also a consequence of expanding imperialism and a quest for raw material and natural resources. Particularly related to the environment was the threat generated by the rise of industry and machinery that aided further destruction of environment, and led to disastrous consequences. An environmental utopianism arose with the formation of such groups as the Sierra Club,[3] formed in 1892 in the United States. Henry David Thoreau[4] advocated a back-to-nature way of life, and

Peter Kropotkin[5] proposed an anarchist solution of a communitarian existence (Pepper 1990). This was the rise of idea of preservation of the wilderness which involved slightly less practical commitment to the environment, but advocated for a more spiritual attitude towards nature and ecology. But this view was still dominated by anthropocentric perspective because it regarded the spiritual utility in relation to human beings only, in other words it is only humans who were entitled to moral consideration. Milbrath (1983) also placed the roots of the modern-day movement in the conservation movement of the late 19th and early 20th centuries in the US. During this period, the country was being developed and there was a plentiful supply of land. This often led to exploitation of nature when individuals sought to maximise their profit in the development of land and resources. In reaction to this, and from the interest of individuals who wished to preserve land for public use, such as parks, a conservation movement emerged. One of the primary aims of the movement was the preservation of nature, ecological balance, and conservation of natural resources. The movement also aimed to end the waste and despoliation and instead develop efficiently, as there was a perception that this exploitation would reduce the capacity to create wealth. The same situation was developing in Britain (O'Riordan 1995). A large number of the members of the environmental movement at this time were supportive of industrialisation, and, of market economy and capitalism. Till then the conflict between conservation of nature and economic growth was not clearly evident. The conservation movement grew and it started to attract people from all walks of life, including intellectuals, academicians, scientists, researchers, policymakers, and so forth, and interestingly it eventually attracted those participants of sport, such as hunters and fishers, and recreationists as well. These events laid the foundations for the re-emergence of an environmental movement with greater intensity. Although there are differences of opinion and various strands within the movement and among the activists, all of them agree with the fact that something needs to be done to arrest environmental degradation, but how this is to be done is a matter of debate among them. Thus the causes and effects of modernity, industrialisation, and urbanisation have been identified as factors inducing environmental problems and how to solve these problems are the big questions at the centre of the environmental debate (Mol, A.P.J. and Spaargaren, G. 2000).

It is generally accepted that the current phase of the environmental movement started in the late 1960s with the first wave, followed by a second wave in the late 1980s. During the first wave, a general sense began to emerge regarding the connection between growth of population growth and rising levels of pollution. Up until the mid-1970s, there was a lack of willingness to accept the idea of potential resource shortage as it would have indicated a limit to the process of economic growth. Along with it there were other factors identified as well that were underlying the rise of this first wave of environmentalism, such as the existence of a growing disillusionment among affluent and educated middle classes with the materialistic philosophy that supported their affluence; the effects of technological advancements; the widespread concern about a plethora of issues, not just those strictly of an environmental nature, such as the fear of the nuclear threat in the use of nuclear power and weapons, with a growing realisation of the mass nature of the threats to society; and the development of a mass movement where environmental concerns entered the mass consciousness of the public through the media and large demonstrations (McCormick, John. 1995). Along with the environmental movement a wide variety of other social movements can be identified that were occurring at this point of time, such as the civil rights movement and the peace movement. Interestingly all these movements shared some common elements, whether it was the actual members or the philosophies and values that formed their foundation. In particular, the youth of the 'hippie' movement were withdrawing from society, rejecting the dominant set of values and connecting with the values of the Romantic and wilderness movements of the late 19th and early 20th centuries.[6] These movements defined the 'anti-establishment' attitude among the masses all over the world.

It is significant to note that the phases identified so far have all followed periods of rapid and continuous economic expansion, for example during the 1950s and 1960s social progress, social stability and upward mobility were secure dreams for Western populations, and the dream was to be supported by material existence. Interestingly the decline in the popular support of the environmental movement is seen when the economy was on the path of contraction (Hall, S. and Gieben, B. 1992). But on the contrary, the recession of the late 1980s and early 1990s did not produce the degree of decline of popular support evident in past periods of high concern for the environment. This could be attributed to the growing evidence of the development of a new worldview, a new ecological paradigm (McCormick, John. 1995). The values espoused by the constituents of the environmental movement may be having a far reaching and sustained impact, with environmental concerns becoming ingrained in more people's consciousness as the status of the environment as a topic of interest grew in the eyes of the public, the media and the educational institutions.[7]

There was a growing awareness and acceptance within the movement that environmental problems could not be solved by technological measures primarily. A conclusion was being drawn that saw a necessity for society to undergo fundamental changes; the foundations of the modern industrial society had to be challenged and an alternative to technological mess-up needs to be developed. 'The environmentalist movement has been forced to change . . . from a concern with reform within a framework of consensual values to a radical challenge to societal values. This was a change from a norm-oriented to a value-oriented movement' (Cotgrove 1982: 10).

The environment movement subsequently entered the political arena, although not without debate, apprehension, and related concerns. The dilemma was how to be a movement and be a political party simultaneously. There were some who believed that no interaction should occur with the existing institutional structures in order to affect change, while others stressed that conventional means of influence should be broached. According to Milbrath (1984), environmental organisations were not organised into political parties, they did not have a leader or organised leadership cadre, they did not have a doctrine, and they did not have an identifiable enemy. Some organisations within the movement had their own bureaucracies and lobbyists, thereby having a significant impact upon policy decisions. The new politics these environmentalists advocated was consultative and participatory. Some other generalisations Milbrath arrived at were that the movement was value-oriented and reformist in nature; that there was a very strong emotional component; that it was viewed sympathetically by the public; and that it was un-institutionalised and generated opposition, although no anti-movements existed. The latter two observations no longer apply in the 1990s as there are sectors of the population which vehemently oppose the movement's ideals and activities, and there now exists anti-movement organisations.[8]

The ideology of the Greens

The green ideology is a critique of the relentless growth of the capitalist economy. The Green parties are based on the philosophy that

> A system based on inequality and exploitation is threatening the future of the planet on which we depend, and encouraging reckless and environmentally damaging consumerism. A world based

on cooperation and democracy would prioritise the many, not the few, and would not risk the planet's future with environmental destruction and unsustainable consumption.[9]

The Greens purport that 'Conventional political and economic policies are destroying the very foundations of the wellbeing of humans and other animals. Our culture is in the grip of a value system and a way of understanding the world which is fundamentally flawed'.[10] The Greens hold the 'left'-wing ideology in the political spectrum offering a criticism of unmindful growth of the capitalist economy at the cost of social justice, equality and environment. According to Caroline Lucas, the

infinitely growing capitalist economy is destroying nature, fuelling injustice and leading to an alienated way of life. Since we threaten our future if we try to live beyond what the Earth can provide, we must build a sustainable society that guarantees our long-term survival. Everyone should be entitled to basic material security. In Green politics, basic needs are classed as not only the physiological needs of food, water, and shelter, but also the need for love, respect, autonomy, security, and meaningful activity within communities. The fact that many people's basic needs are not met has far-reaching consequences, expressed as anxiety, insecurity, and aggressive behaviour towards others, and exploitation of the environment. These personal factors give rise to, and are perpetuated by, social institutions which actively encourage oppression, pollution, resource depletion, poverty and military conflict.

According to the Greens' philosophy,

Traditional politics divides humans from nature and the individual from society. The rejection of this way of seeing the world is fundamental to Green philosophy. Rather than set them against each other, the Green Party seeks healthy interdependence of individual, nature and society.[11]

Understanding the significance and complexity of social, political, economic and personal factors and actors in bringing about the change, the Green philosophy

places both personal and political change at the heart of its response to the ecological crisis and is committed to creating a society in which individuals, through their ability to satisfy their basic needs more fully, are then able better to contribute to future sustainability. This principle is reflected in the radical Green agenda both for changes in values and lifestyles, and for reformed social, economic and political structures.[12]

With such philosophy at its core, the first Green parties were founded during the early 1970s. The Values Party of New Zealand was the world's first countrywide Green party to contest parliamentary seats nationally in 1972. In 1973 Europe's first Green party, the UK's Ecology Party, was established. The German Green Party has been an example of electoral success as one of the most significant parties winning 27 seats in the Bundestag in the 1983 federal elections in Germany. There have been more than 80 parties the world over constituted around the ideology of the Greens. The last two decades have seen the emergence of global greens.[13] The Charter of the Greens is the foundational document. It draws upon the charters and constitutions of Green parties around the world, as well as some ideas from the Earth Charter and from the global gathering of Greens at Rio in 1992 (Global Greens Charter. 2012). Many European countries also developed 'Green' parties which constitute a good percentage of the total number of seats in the European parliament. The European Greens have always been committed to basic tenets of Green politics, such as environmental responsibility, individual freedom, inclusive democracy, diversity, social justice, gender equality, global sustainable development, and non-violence (European Union, http://european greens.eu, 2015). In the 1970s and 1980s the European Greens were generally sceptical of European political and economic integration, which was seen as contrary to environmental and social interests. In its 1984 program, the European Greens advocated the formation of an alternative Europe, which would be neutral and decentralised (Mol, A.P.J., Lauber, V. and Liefferink, J. 2000). In 1989, some member parties adopted a more parliamentary course and became more supportive of European integration. The program advocates the democratisation of Europe's institutions. In their 1994 program, the Greens abandoned their principled opposition of European integration and began to propose pragmatic alternatives for the European Union's policies and institutions.[14] The most successful of these is probably the Germany's Green Party (founded in 1979); by the end of the century Germany's Greens had become the nation's third largest party. In 1998 they became part of a coalition government together with the Social

Democrats, and were rewarded when the government agreed to phase out nuclear power. Green parties also joined coalitions in France, Finland, New Zealand, and elsewhere. In the last two decades around 7% of votes in the European parliamentary elections went in favour of Greens/Green parties committed to the ideology of green politics. Despite being criticised for a number of factors, in the last parliamentary elections the European Green Party won 42 seats, which is so far the best performance by the party in the European parliamentary elections although, as experience from the West indicates, the Green parties may find it difficult to garner substantial share of votes or a majority on the issue of environmentalism alone. Even though the ideology of the Greens encompasses or combines philosophies of social equality, justice, equal distribution, and peaceful coexistence, prima facie it is known for its association with issues pertaining to nature alone. No matter what is at the core of the philosophy of the Greens, environmental issues are a subject of common concern.

European Green parties

The European Green Party was founded on 22 February 2004 at the Fourth Congress of the European Federation of Green Parties (EFGP) in Rome attended by over 1,000 delegates. Thirty-four Green parties from all over Europe have joined this new pan-European party. The Greens were the first to form a political party at European level. The other European political federations followed suit in the period 2004–06. For the Greens, this was the culmination of a process which had started with the formation of a loose coordination 1979–93 and the EFGP 1993–2004. The coalition of Greens/European Free Alliance won 50 seats in the elections held in 2014 for 751 members of the European Parliament. Although it was slightly less than the election results of 2009 when the Greens had won 57 seats out of the total 766 for which elections were held. Nevertheless, one can observe the Greens gaining 6%–8% of seats consistently in the European Parliament since the beginning of the new century. The first goal of the re-organised European Greens was the 2004 European Parliament election campaign. The EGP ran the first election campaign in Europe that featured common motifs and slogans in all EU countries.[15] Its members are 45 national Green parties from across Europe – both within the EU and beyond – supporting each other to strengthen Green politics across the continent.[16] The representatives of the EGP's member parties within the European Union came out with a lengthy common manifesto for the European elections in the year 2014. The manifesto begins with the following paragraph:

> We Greens believe that Europe is our common home and our future. Yet, that future is under threat. If the EU's achievements are to be preserved and enhanced, now is the time for a fundamental political reorientation and for a democratic renewal of the European Union. To safeguard our common future we want to change Europe to strengthen it. That is why we stand for more solidarity, sustainability and justice. If we give room for populism, nationalism or economic chauvinism, then no region, no country, no part of Europe will remain or become prosperous on its own. In a globalised world, it is only by acting together that we stand a chance of meeting the daunting social, environmental, economic and security challenges ahead. We need fair economic cooperation that respects our ecological responsibilities. We need solidarity within and between our nations. We need a strong democracy. We must live our values, upholding freedom and liberties domestically and internationally.[17]

The introduction sums it up that how the EGP has integrated a range of social, economic, political, and environmental issues in its vision of creating a better, secure Europe.

The European Greens proudly stand for the sustainable development of humanity on planet Earth, a mode of development respectful of human rights and built upon the values of environmental responsibility, freedom, justice, diversity, and non-violence.[18] The origin of the Green political party can be traced back to many other social movements. Some of these movements are environmental movements, anti-nuclear activists, and their concerns with growing threat to planet from radiation, non-violent peace activists promoting alternative ways to resolve conflicts among communities struggling to gain control over resources; feminists, struggling for real equality between women and men in terms of access and control of natural resources; freedom and human rights movements fighting against dictatorial and authoritarian regimes; third-world solidarity movements supporting the end of colonisation and more economically balanced relations between the North and the South of our planet; and activists campaigning against poverty and for social justice within our own societies.

According to the Green parties, in contemporary times economic growth and industrialisation are supported by relentless consumption or one may say devouring of both finite and infinite resources equally.

However even the renewable energy sources can be consumed to a limit. The Greens realise that there are limits to consumption of even infinite resources. The current pace and pattern of growth is leading to depletion of natural resources. The Greens advocate for developing new processes of production, new technologies and research in the field of manufacturing. Often the onslaught of natural resources is justified in the wake of the logic that 'we can't stop progress'. But technological development is not a given and is not the only path to development. It is a choice, the most convenient that the society has adopted. The Greens purport that the humanity should choose technology and process of development that is good to both the humans and the nature rather that developing at the cost of nature first and then ultimately harming humans in the process. The Greens do acknowledge that there is no one way to transform society, nor do they have answers to all the problems or solutions ready for many of the current problems. However they seek to be part of wider green movements all over the world that seek to challenge the human-centric notion of existence. The Greens claim that

> Our beliefs will bring us into conflict with those committed to material affluence, the accumulation of power and the unsustainable exploitation of the Earth. We are always ready to negotiate with those who oppose us, and seek fair settlements that respect their needs for security, self-esteem and freedom of choice.[19]

Missing Greens in Indian politics

Almost seven decades after independence, politics in India is still based on retrograde ideas of caste and identity. Campaigning during elections in India usually looks more like a drama to woo voters rather than a serious effort to sensitise the masses about the issues that impact their lives and livelihood. The largest democracy of the world and the nation with the second largest population is just not rising above the level of caste and communal politics. Besides the never-fulfilled promise for *bijli-paani-sadak* corruption has become an important issue in the elections in the last couple of years, such as Delhi State Assembly elections of 2014. Among the cacophony of created and irrelevant issues, some of the important and urgent issues are never debated, discussed, or even raised. One such concern is environmentalism. India faces some of the serious ecological crises which are on the verge of turning into disaster and have already become so. Some of the important environmental challenges that India faces include land degradation, declining soil fertility, over-utilisation of underground water sources, air pollution, and deforestation. According to the India State of Forest Report 2013, released by the Forest Survey of India (FSI), India has lost 627 km² of forest cover in the past two years. As per the estimates, the total forest cover in the country is now at 697,898 km². This accounts for 24.01% of the total geographical area of India. The report also mentions that the north-eastern states and tribal districts particularly have witnessed unprecedented loss of forest which happens to be their prime source of livelihood and sustenance. The threat has almost reached the tipping point, and already crossed the danger mark in some cases.

The example of the Kedarnath disaster in 2013 cannot be ignored or forgotten without learning appropriate lessons. Apart from the tragedy in the hills we can take the example of the holy river Ganga turning into a drain in its journey from the holy city of Haridwar (where it enters Uttar Pradesh) to Birpur (where it leaves Uttar Pradesh). Yamuna and many other main rivers too meet the same fate. The industrial effluents discharged into these rivers pose a threat to plant and animal species in and around the river. Ganga dolphins are on the verge of extinction. At Varanasi, the condition of the river becomes unimaginable with semi-burnt bodies of people cremated at *ghats* flowing in the dying river. According to the statistics released by Water.org, a non-profit organisation working in the field of water and sanitation worldwide, approximately 97 million people lack safe drinking water and 814 million have no sanitation facility in India. But none of the political parties or groups will take up the issue of fighting for one of the most basic needs for human survival, that is, water. What Arvind Kejriwal of the Aam Admi Party (AAP) fought for was reducing the water (and electricity) bill not for the issue of continuous supply of usable drinking water. Almost all the states and regions in India have specific problems related to environment that cannot be ignored. We cannot remain immune to environmental issues as they pose a serious challenge to the economic development of our nation. The struggle for survival and fight over finite resources is also leading to extreme conflict and violence in certain parts of the country. Some immediate steps are required to address the basic issues related to people's survival and management of environment, and find sustainable solutions to the problems (Chatterjee, P. 1997).

In representative democracies like India, people are represented through political parties. Political parties are organised groups of citizens who profess to share the same political views and who by acting as a political unit are oriented towards achieving legitimate control of the government through an electoral process. Political parties are based on certain understanding of society, how it ought to be structured and raise issues of national, local or global concern; they serve as a link between the people and government. However, members of different political parties in India – those who aspire to win seats of power and become legislators – are least interested in the issues that affect the people's lives indeed, such as the one discussed above: of the basic needs of access to and availability of safe drinking water.

National or regional parties in developing countries like India can incorporate the fundamental agenda of the Greens along with other equally important agendas like caste, community, or secularism and make it a mainstream concern. There is a need that parties or people take cognisance of environmental issues and environmentally sustainable development and sensitise the people about the impending environmental threats. In fact, more than the West it is the developing countries like India that need Green parties to represent voices pertaining to conservation of ecology and environment. If this sounds uncontestable in the context of how elections are contested in India, then the masses must be assured of access to basic minimum resources required for survival that are derived from nature. Amid blue, saffron, tricolour and other hues, politics in India misses the Greens. Successive governments and political parties have barely taken interest in the ideology of greens or environmental concerns. It is desirable that politics in India should mature and move at least to a level where parties represent ideologies concerning issues that are related to the basic existence of the people and their struggle for survival on a daily basis.

Conclusion

To conclude, human society has started to respond to environmental concerns, and taking stock of the situation has resulted in attempts to design remedial mechanisms and institutions. The sensitivity to tackle these issues too can therefore also said to be continually building along with the increasing 'pathology' of the modernity; after all, whatever be the unintended consequences of modernisation and science-based transformation, human enterprise for self-aggrandisement can be said to be at the core of it all, more so after the fate of comparatively altruistically pronounced structures of communism/socialism. At least, arguably so. Since the etiology of these problems take us to the domain of culture and psychology, I believe the way out/solution also lies in the same domains of culture and human psychology. The same cultural institutions of science and technology, ideology, governance, bureaucracy, and civil society that have led us here may also inhere the way out.

If the fundamental issue for any society is the growth and development of its people, then we cannot achieve sustainable development independent of environment. Economic growth and social development are dependent upon the nature of environment and availability of natural resources. At the same time growth and development also have an impact upon the environment in terms of how we use/abuse our resources, and/or how sustainable our growth is. The Indian polity needs to address issues pertaining to people's survival and their relationship with the environment. At the most, environmental issues appear in a line in glossy manifestos printed by the parties. It is high time to realise that, being one of the growing economies in the world, sooner or later we will have to address the issues that affect the people's actual living conditions and livelihood rather than socio-cultural identity and religion (Sharma 2013). There is a need for the ideology of the Greens in a substantive way to enter Indian politics rather than as a cosmetic presence.

As the major hopes of modernity, its principal symbols are gradually crumbling. As Pathak has averred in his words, 'Modernity does not mean well-fed/well-clothed individuals – politically indifferent and culturally insensitive – living in their own worlds. It should mean a vibrant public sphere in which people participate and reflect on the world' (Pathak 2006: 20). That is, modernity should be able to bear individuals, institutions and processes that are continually creating and recreating culture that is not self-consuming; and not known by just consumption of the mass-produced culture – and its symbols, products and processes – in the factories and production houses of individuals, societies and nation states that happen to bequeath/appropriate/own the 'means and forces of production' through various but equally arbitrary political economy and history, through processes and instruments of law, market and hegemony (Bandyopadhyay, J. 2002). The failures and challenges of modernity, till now, of course do not undermine the legitimacy of the hopes that underlay the ideals vested in human spirit to wrest the loss back and infuse, what Gandhi had referred to as enlightened self-interest in all individuals, institutions, and their modus vivendi/operandi (Das, Debmalya. 2010). That of course is now contingent upon what has become of the initial 'projects' of modernity, globalisation, and materialistically oriented societies and cultures over the course of time, and is likely to be conditioned by them (Bhushan, Nalini and Garfield, Jay L. 2007). The social and environmental destruction rendered by the monoscopic assault of opportunistic 'rationalism' is capable of being slowed, stationed, and even reversed by the same cultural institutions of science, governance, law, and the market if conditioned by the emergent ethos of environmentalism as it comes to inhere itself in ideology, psychology, imagination, and in sum, apperception.

Notes

1 E. W. Ven der Veen, 2001, Environment Movements, available at www. people.okanagan.bc.ca/wvdveen/WILMA%20WEBPAGE/environment/ environment_movement.htm, accessed on 17 October 2014.
2 E. W. Ven der Veen, 2001, Environment Movements, available at www. people.okanagan.bc.ca/wvdveen/WILMA%20WEBPAGE/environment/ environment_movement.htm, accessed on 17 October 2014.
3 The Sierra Club is an environmental organisation in the United States. It was founded on 28 May 1892 in San Francisco, California, by the Scottish-American preservationist John Muir, who became its first president.
4 Henry David Thoreau (12 July 1817–6 May 1862) was an American author, poet, philosopher, abolitionist, naturalist, tax resister, development critic, surveyor, historian, and leading transcendentalist. He is best known for his book *Walden*, a reflection upon simple living in natural surroundings, and his essay 'Civil Disobedience', an argument for individual resistance to civil government in moral opposition to an unjust state. (Source: Biography available on internet and Wikipedia.)
5 Prince Pyotr Alexeyevich Kropotkin (9 December 1842–8 February 1921) was a Russian zoologist, evolutionary theorist, philosopher, scientist, revolutionary, economist, activist, geographer, writer, and one of the world's foremost anarcho-communists. Kropotkin advocated a communist society free from central government and based on voluntary associations between workers. He wrote many books, pamphlets and articles, the most prominent being *The Conquest of Bread* and *Fields, Factories and Workshops*, and his principal scientific offering, *Mutual Aid: A Factor of Evolution*. He also contributed the article on anarchism to the *Encyclopaedia Britannica Eleventh Edition* (Source: Biography available on internet and Wikipedia).
6 E. W. Ven der Veen, 2001, Environment Movements, available at www. people.okanagan.bc.ca/wvdveen/WILMA%20WEBPAGE/environment/ environment_movement.htm, accessed on 17 October 2014.
7 E. W. Ven der Veen, 2001, Environment Movements, available at www. people.okanagan.bc.ca/wvdveen/WILMA%20WEBPAGE/environment/ environment_movement.htm, accessed on 17 October 2014.
8 E. W. Ven der Veen, 2001, Environment Movements, available at www. people.okanagan.bc.ca/wvdveen/WILMA%20WEBPAGE/environment/ environment_movement.htm, accessed on 17 October 2014.
9 Philosophical Basis of the Green Party available at https://policy.green party.org.uk/philosophical-basis.html, accessed on 16 October 2014.
10 Philosophical Basis of the Green Party available at https://policy.green party.org.uk/philosophical-basis.html, accessed on 16 October 2014.

11 Philosophical Basis of the Green Party available at https://policy.green party.org.uk/philosophical-basis.html, accessed on 16 October 2014.
12 Philosophical Basis of the Green Party available at https://policy.green party.org.uk/philosophical-basis.html, accessed on 16 October 2014.
13 The Global Greens Charter was adopted by consensus at the first Global Greens Congress in Canberra in 2001. The core of the document sets out the principles that bind together Greens from around the world: ecological wisdom, social justice, participatory democracy, nonviolence, sustainability and respect for diversity. The second section is a 'political action' plan covering some of the most pressing problems facing the world.
14 European Greens, available at http://europeangreens.eu, accessed on 23 November 2013.
15 European Greens, available at https://europeangreens.eu/organisation# history, accessed on 23 November 2013.
16 The European Green Party's member parties (full members, associate members and candidate members) within the European Union as of March 2014 are: Die Grünen (Austria), Ecolo (Belgium), Groen (Belgium), Zelena Partija (Bulgaria), Zelenite (Bulgaria), Cyprus Green Party (Cyprus), Strana Zelených (Czech Republic), Socialistisk Folkeparti/SF (Denmark), Eestimaa Rohelised (Estonia), Vihreät – De Gröna (Finland), Europe Ecologie – Les Verts (France), Bündnis 90/Die Grünen (Germany), Ecologoi Prasinoi (Greece), Lehet Más a Politika / LMP (Hungary), Zöld Baloldal (Hungary), Comhaontas Glas (Ireland), Federazionedei Verdi (Italy), Latvijas Zala Partija/LZP (Latvia), Déigréng (Luxemburg), Alternattiva Demokratika – the Green Party (Malta), Groen Links (The Netherlands), De Groenen (The Netherlands), Zieloni (Poland), Partido Ecologista – Os Verdes (Portugal), Partidul Verde (Romania), Strana Zelených (Slovakia), Strankamladih – Zeleni Evrope (Slovenia), Iniciativa per Catalunya Verds/ICV (Spain), EQUO (Spain), Miljöpartiet de gröna (Sweden), Green Party of England and Wales (United Kingdom), Scottish Green Party (United Kingdom). (Source: Manifesto of the EGP), available at http://europeangreens.eu/sites/europeangreens.eu/files/2014%20Mani festo.pdf, p. 8, accessed on 23 November 2013.
17 European Greens, available at http://europeangreens.eu/sites/european greens.eu/files/2014%20Manifesto.pdf, p. 8, accessed on 23 November 2013.
18 European Greens, available at http://europeangreens.eu/content/charter-european-greens, accessed on 23 November 2013.
19 Philosophical Basis of the Green Party available at https://policy.green party.org.uk/philosophical-basis.html, accessed on 16 October 2014.

References

Adam, Barbara. 2005. *Timescapes of Modernity: The Environment and Invisible Hazards*. London: Routledge.
Andersen, M. S. and Massa, I. 2000. 'Ecological Modernisation: Origins, Dilemmas, and Future Directions', *Journal of Environmental Policy and Planning*, 2(4): 337–345.

Bandyopadhyay, J. 2002. 'Between Local and Global Responsibilities', *Seminar*, (51), August.

Barman, Himadari. Industrialisation and Environmental Pollution', himadri. cmsdu.org/ . . . /Industrialisation_and_Environmental_Pollution, accessed on 23/8/2014.

Beck, U. 1994. 'The Reinvention of Politics: Towards a Theory of Reflexive Modernisation', in U. Beck, A. Giddens and S. Lash (eds.), *Reflexive Modernization: Politics, Tradition and Aesthetics in the Modern Social Order*. Oxford: Polity Press.

Benford, Robert D. and Snow, David A. 2000. 'Framing Processes and Social Movements: An Overview and Assessment', *Annual Review of Sociology*, 26: 611–639.

Bhushan, Nalini and Garfield, Jay L. 2007. 'Swaraj and Swadeshi: Gandhi and Tagore on Ethics, Development and Freedom', www.smith.edu/philosophy/docs/garfield_swaraj.pdf, accessed on 12/9/2014.

Chatterjee, P. 1997. 'Development Planning and the Indian State in Chatterjee', in C. Partha (ed.), *State and Politics in India* (9271–9298). New Delhi: Oxford University Press.

Cotgrove, S. 1982. *Catastrophe or Cornucopia: The Environment, Politics and the Future*. Chichester: John Wiley & Sons.

Das, Debmalya. 2010. 'Challenging Enlightenment Paradigms: Responses of Benjamin and Tagore', *Rupkatha Journal on Interdisciplinary Studies in Humanities*, 2(4).

'Forest Survey of India, India State of Forest, Report 2013', http://fsi.nic.in/cover_2013/executive_summary.pdf, accessed on 23/7/2015.

European Union, http://europeangreens.eu, accessed on 15/7/2015.

Global Greens Charter. 2012. www.globalgreens.org/globalcharter-english, accessed on 12/10/2013.

Gold, John. 2004. *Representing the Environment*. London: Routledge.

Hall, S. and Gieben, B. (ed.). 1992. *Formations of Modernity*. Cambridge: Polity Press, https://policy.greenparty.org.uk, accessed on 22/7/2015.

Lowe, P. and Goyder, J. 1983. *Environmental Groups and Politics*. London: George Allen and Unwin.

Lucas, Caroline. 2013. 'Green Politics', www.ethicalpolitics.net/index.php/Green_Politics, accessed on 16/7/2013.

McCormick, John. 1995. *The Global Environmental Movement*. London: John Wiley & Sons.

Milbrath, L. 1984. *Environmentalists: Vanguard for a New Society*. New York: New York Press.

Mol, A.P.J., Lauber, V. and Liefferink, J. (eds.) 2000. *The Voluntary Approach to Environmental Policy: Joint Environmental Policy-making in Europe*. Oxford: Oxford University Press.

Mol, A.P.J. and Spaargaren, G. 2000. 'Ecological Modernisation Theory in Debate: A Review', *Environmental Politics*, 9(1): 17–49.

O'Riordan, Timothy. 1995. *Environmental Science for Environmental Management*. Longman: London.

Pathak, Avijit. 2006. *Modernity, Globalization and Identity: Towards a Reflexive Quest*. New Delhi: Aakar Books.

Pepper, D. 1990. *The Roots of Modern Environmentalism*. London: Routledge.

Sharma, S. 2013. 'Missing Greens the European Way: Ideology – based Politics', *Mainstream*, 51(34), August 10.

United Nations Conference on Environment and Development (UNCED), Rio de Janeiro, 3–14 June 1992, www.un.org/geninfo/bp/enviro.html, accessed on 4/11/2013.

4 Globalisation and political economy of protected areas

Sudeshna Mukherjee

In India, as in many other developing and developed countries, the conservation policies have been centred upon the creation of protected areas. According to the definition of Moscovici, this reactive conservationism of the 19th century, in which the natural world is attributed all the virtues and society all the vices, was a reaction to 'culturalism', which sees in nature the infirmity of man, a threat of return to savagery to which culture must be opposed. At the 1992 Earth Summit, a bold new Convention on Biological Diversity (CBD) was developed which, inter alia, calls on governments to establish systems of protected areas and to manage these in support of conservation, sustainable use, and equitable benefit sharing. In the globalised world order, the governments' recognition of protected areas as economic institutions have a key role to play in the alleviation of poverty and the maintenance of the global community's critical life-support systems. This new vision for protected areas requires an awareness and understanding of the economic values generated by protected areas. Global conventions and programs alone are not enough to ensure the continued existence of, and sufficient funding for, protected areas. In times of fiscal austerity and tightening government budgets – especially in developing countries which are home to much of the world's biodiversity – traditional funding sources for protected areas are increasingly under threat. Innovative alternatives to these traditional sources are needed in order to secure the long-term viability of protected areas. It is through endogenous development which calls for social, economic, and cultural transformations of societies based on the revitalisations of traditions, respect for environment and equitable relations of production; hitherto excluded communities can be organised to develop the potential of every region. In this light, my chapter, following descriptive diagnostic research designs, based on secondary data, would like to explore following objectives:

- Globalisation and its impact on the environment
- Emergence of protected areas
- Social construction of nature versus the material nature of the environment
- Genesis of India's conservation policy and locating protected areas within it
- Globalisation and bourgeois environmentalism versus the 'environmentalism of the poor'
- Economic viability of protected areas and need for innovative, hermeneutic, endogenous alternative approaches for development.

Globalisation and its impact on environment

Globalisation is the process of extending social relations across world space. Such extensions arise from the movements of people, things and ideas. In spite of the taller claim of economists' globalisation cannot be defined in terms of internationalisation or integration. These developments might be an outcome of globalisation. Globalisation describes interplay across cultures of macro-social forces including religion, politics, and economics. Globalisation can erode and universalise the characteristics of a local group through advances in transportation and telecommunications infrastructure, including the rise of the internet (Guyford 1972). Though several scholars place the origins of globalisation in modern times, others trace its history long before the European age and voyages to the New World. Some even trace the origins to the third millennium BCE (Frank 1998). Since the beginning of the 20th century, the pace of globalisation has intensified at a rapid rate.

Capitalist market-driven economic development and globalisation share a symbiotic relationship. The development debate, especially after the 1970s, and more particularly after the 1980s, offered strong critique of all those models of development which emerged supreme following the industrial revolution after the Second World War. A new scenario for development began with the new phase of economic integration during the late 1980s; when the growth models inspired by the fundamentalism of capital were no longer useful. Easterly (2001) pointed out that this has happened not only due the breakdown of the Soviet Union and the fall of the Berlin Wall which proved the superiority of the market economy over a planned economy, but also because of the failures of the policies carried out in many developing countries and implemented by international aid programs and international organisations (Pieterse 1998). These models of development have emphasised industrialisation, colonisation, increasing reliance on science and technology, ruthless exploitation of environment, natural resources, and free run of the capitalistic market. Initially these growth-oriented Western development models sold the dream of prosperity to the third world developing countries, but its hollowness and neo-colonialist nature was soon exposed.

The term globalisation has been in increasing use since the mid-1980s and especially since the mid-1990s. In 2000, the International Monetary Fund (IMF) identified four basic aspects of globalisation: trade and transactions, capital and investment movements, migration and movement of people and the dissemination of knowledge (International Monetary Fund 2000). Further, environmental challenges such as climate change, cross-boundary water and air pollution, and over-fishing of the ocean are linked with globalisation. Globalising processes affect and are affected by business and work organisation, economics, socio-cultural resources, and the natural environment. Globalisation and its concurrent avatars of privatisation and liberalisation under the aegis of structural adjustment program is giving rise to an upsurge in poverty, unemployment, discrimination, injustice, and inequality besides environmental degradation (Pieterse 1998). The whole global environment is affected by changes in weather and land use which in turn have direct implications for individuals and communities. Economic developments on one continent can have almost simultaneous consequences on another. Conflicts in one area can provoke actions and reactions on the other side of the world which can be watched simultaneously on television or the internet by the whole world. People share a common need for and a right to a fair share of the Earth's resources, including a clean, safe and healthy environment. These basic requirements are under threat from climate change and environmental degradation. These challenges are widely recognised as presenting the greatest priority for global cooperation. The degradation of the global environment has observable social and economic consequences and therefore has an impact on the ability of people and communities to achieve their potential as human beings and to give expression to their human rights. These demand a conservation policy which creates economically viable protected areas. There is a desperate search for alternative ways to bring the interests of conservation and people's livelihood rights together.

Emergence of protected areas

In North America, the myth of 'wilderness' as an uninhabited space has fuelled the move to create protected restricted-use areas. By the end of the 19th century, after the conquest and widespread massacre of the native peoples, and the westward expansion of the frontier by European settlers, the land was perceived to be uninhabited. With the movement of human settlements to the west, the mid-19th century saw natural areas being degraded by mining and forestry companies. This raised protests from the nature lovers who had been influenced by the ideas of Henry David Thoreau and George Perkins Marsh. In 1864, in his widely read book *Man and Nature*, Marsh argued that the preservation of virgin areas was justified as much for artistic and poetic reasons as it was for economic reasons and held that the destruction of the natural world threatened the very existence of humans on earth. On 1 March 1872, when the decision was made to create Yellowstone National Park, the US Congress decided that the region could not be colonised, occupied, or sold, but would be separated as a public park or recreation area for the benefit and enjoyment of the people (Diegues 2000: 2–3). Any person who occupied any part of this park would be breaking the law and would be removed. A North American model of conservationism, which dichotomises 'people' and 'parks', has spread rapidly throughout the world. Because this approach has been adopted rather uncritically by the countries of the third world, its effects have been devastating for the traditional populations – extractivists, fisherfolk, and indigenous peoples. This model was transposed from industrialised countries with temperate climates to the third world, whose remaining forests have been, and continue to be, inhabited by traditional populations (Diegues 2000: 2–3).

By definition, a protected area is 'an area of land and/or sea especially dedicated to the protection and maintenance of biological diversity, and of natural and associated cultural resources, and managed through legal or other effective means' (IUCN 1994: 3) A protected area may be a wetland, a tropical or deciduous forest, a cultivated landscape of value, an alpine region, a savannah, a marine area, or any number of other types of natural or partially modified ecosystems – or indeed any combination of types of ecosystems. In addition to covering an array of ecosystem types, protected areas are defined in a number of different ways relevant to the objectives and values for which they are managed (Phillips 1998).

Six categories of protected areas defined by IUCN

> *Category I*: An area of land and/or sea possessing some outstanding or representative ecosystems, geological or physiological features and/or species available primarily for research and/or environmental monitoring. A wilderness area is a large area of unmodified or slightly modified land and/or sea retaining its natural character and influence without permanent or significant habitation which is protected and managed so as to preserve its natural condition.

> *Category II*: A natural area of land and/or sea designated to (a) protect the ecological integrity of one or more ecosystems for present and future generations; (b) exclude exploitation or occupation inimical to the purposes of the area; and (c) provide foundation for spiritual, scientific, educational, recreational, and visitor opportunities all of which must be environmentally and culturally compatible.

> *Category III*: An area containing one or more specific natural or natural/cultural feature which is of outstanding or unique value because of its inherent rarity, representative or aesthetic qualities or cultural significance.

> *Category IV*: An area of land and/or sea subject to active intervention for management purposes so as to ensure the maintenance of habitats and/or to meet the requirements of specific species.

> *Category V*: An area with coast and sea, as appropriate, where the interaction of people and nature over time has produced an area with significant aesthetic, ecological and/or cultural value and often with high biological diversity. Safeguarding the integrity of this traditional interaction is vital to the protection, maintenance and evolution of such an area.

> *Category VI*: An area containing predominantly unmodified natural systems managed to ensure long term protection and maintenance of biological diversity while providing at the same time a sustainable flow of natural products and services to meet community needs (IUCN 1994).

Social construction of nature versus the material nature of the environment

We, as human beings, have material, intellectual, and symbolic access to our surroundings and we work to alter and make sense of it through

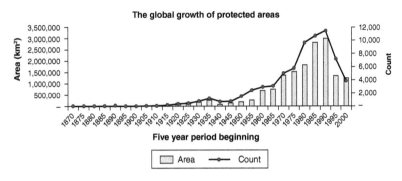

Figure 4.1 The global growth of protected areas
Source: West et al. (2006: 251–277)

our daily actions. The world is out there, and we interact with it in ways that reproduce it, often altering it in the process (Smith 1990), yet the world only has meaning for us as language-using and symbol-making animals owing to how we intellectually apprehend it. Our contention is that protected areas matter because they are a way of seeing, understanding, and (re)producing the world. As such, they are rich sites of social production and social interaction. Contemporary protected areas not only affect the people living in them, adjacent to them, and displaced by them, but also the people working for the non-governmental organisations (NGOs) and government agencies that create and manage the protected areas. They also change the face of the earth by renaming places, drawing boundaries around areas, and erasing boundaries between states. IUCN's (International Union for Conservation of Nature) attempt to create a worldwide category system compels national governments to fit their protected lands into these international categories that separate people from their surroundings (West et al. 2006: 251–277).

Anthropologically speaking, these separations mirror Western imaginaries of nature and culture and impose them on much of the world. NGOs rely heavily on the 'western division between nature and culture'. NGO publications frequently present nature as a static object, separate from human beings. By extension, they present the ecological effects of human activities – as part of culture – as unnatural. In other cases, they may present indigenous peoples as ecologically noble savages, whose cultures are somehow closer to nature. Whether indigenous peoples are imagined, or project themselves, as inside or outside nature however, the imposition of putative nature/culture dichotomy, (Moscovici, 1974) has had significant material and social impacts, either by forcefully excluding people from their land or holding them to discursive standards that are nearly impossible to live up to in practice (West et al. 2006: 251–277). This model of preserving wilderness has been criticised both inside and outside the US (the place of origin of protected areas), as governments rarely assess the environmental and social impact that the creation of parks will have on the local inhabitants, whose land-use practices often have preserved these natural areas over the years. They are transferred from regions where their ancestors lived to regions that are ecologically and culturally different. The hunters, fisherfolk, and other resource users who have developed a symbiosis with the forests, rivers, and coastal areas, once relocated to other areas, have great difficulty surviving due to the accompanying prohibition of their traditional activities.

These populations have difficulty comprehending how their traditional activities could be considered detrimental to nature, when hotels and tourism infrastructure are created for the use of people from outside the area. Very little of the budget for protected areas is allocated for improving the living conditions of the traditional populations, who, if encouraged, could make a positive contribution. When they have organised and become vocal about defending their historical right to remain on ancestral land, they are accused of being against conservation. In most cases, these are people who are illiterate, without political power or legal ownership of the land, and are therefore not compensated when their land is expropriated (Diegues 2000: 3–4).

Genesis of India's forest and conservation policies and evolution of protected areas

According to noted environmental historian Ramchandra Guha, among the different agencies of the Indian government the Forest Department is distinctive in having been exempted from the scrutiny of scholars for most of its long history.

> When analyzing policy or law, it is inevitable, especially in a plural society, that any policy will involve some ad-hoc resolution of conflicting interests; the question is which side has the relative advantage, and the extent to which a policy generates further conflict.
>
> (Sundar in Guha et al. 2012: 13)

The First Forest Act of 1865 was the first attempt in the direction of regulation of collection of forest produce by the forest dwellers. In the process, the socially regulated practices of the local people were restrained by law. The First Forest Policy was envisaged in 1894 and forest officials seriously appeared on the scene and claimed the authority to limit and regulate the traditional tribal rights over forests. The Indian Forest Act 1927 was in continuation of the measures already taken to regulate further people's rights over forest land and forest produce. Forest offences were defined as offences punishable under the Act. This Act created an extremely powerful and adequately protected executive consisting of forest officers of the Indian forest service, State Forest Service, rangers, foresters, and forest guards. These officers enjoyed legal powers. Forest was transferred to the state list according to the Government of India Act 1935 (Hussain 1996: 211–217).

The Forest Department in India was founded in 1864, but it was not until the 1980s, more than a century later, that scientists and social scientists began to systematically examine its policies and programs. The new National Forest Policy 1980 states that the principle aim of the forest policy must be to ensure environmental stability and the maintenance of ecological balance including atmospheric equilibrium, vital to the sustenance of all life forms: human, animal, and plant. The derivation of the economic benefit must be subordinated to the principle aim (Hussain1996: 211–217).

Successive forest policies have evolved in part as a response to conflict. The 1990 Joint Forest Management (JFM) resolution, for example, was pitched as a way of reversing the long history of conflict between forest staff and villagers. By placing the onus of forest protection on villagers, the forest department hoped to reduce some of the conflict over access; while the villagers saw JFM as a way of gaining incremental benefits – wage labour, some money for village development, and also a backing from the state in protecting their own forests (Sundar 2001). However, because of its limited mandate, JFM not only had failed to address the livelihood needs of villagers to the extent required, but also outsourced some of the conflict to villagers themselves, making them responsible for protecting forests against people from other villages or against disadvantaged users from within the village (head loaders, women, etc.; Sundar et al. 2001: 183–187).

Within a decade, the excitement around JFM gave way to two other processes – the judicialisation of competing claims to the forest, and second, the mobilisation around the enactment of what was eventually passed as the Scheduled Tribes and Other Traditional Forest Dwellers (Recognition of Forest Rights) Act 2006 (Sundar in Guha et al. 2012).

The Forest Rights Act aims to redress the 'historical injustice to the forest dwelling Scheduled Tribes' by recognising their property rights to land, as well as non-timber forest produce, and the community right of control and management which was appropriated by the Forest Department. The United Progressive Alliance (UPA) government propelled by the growing visibility of the Naxalite[1] activities, especially in the tribal-dominated forest areas of the country, seeing secure tenure rights as a way of countering the growing discontent among Adivasis, tabled the bill in the parliament. The bill soon ran into trouble, both from wildlife conservationists and the Ministry of Environment and Forests. Conservationists pitched it as a conflict between 'tigers and tribals', predicting the end of all forest covers and wildlife as tribal and vested interests carved up the forests between themselves. The Ministry of Environment and Forests feared loss of control over its domain to the Ministry of Tribal Affairs (Sundar in Guha et al. 2012).

As initially drafted, the bill gave the primary power to determine forest rights to the Gram Sabha or village assembly, invoking for the first time the use of oral evidence as proof of occupation – doing away with the tyranny of incomplete forest and land records maintained by a rent seeking bureaucracy. The bill was referred to a Parliamentary Committee, many of whose members were adivasi ministers, and here a combination of successful lobbying by the campaign and several other adivasi or forest dwellers organisations, with help from the parliamentary left, ensured that the bill went through and was enacted at the very end of December 2006 (ibid.: 26–27).

Thus we see, in India, as in many other developing and developed countries, the conservation policies have been centred upon the creation of protected areas. Protected areas, especially those that involve very restricted use, are more than a government strategy of conservation: they are emblematic of a particular relation between humans and nature. The expansion of the US mid-19th-century idea of uninhabited national parks is based, first, on the myth of an untouched natural paradise. This reactive conservationism of the 19th century, according to the definition of Moscovici, in which the natural world is attributed all the virtues and society all the vices, was a reaction to 'culturalism', which sees in nature the infirmity of man, a threat of return to savagery to which culture must be opposed (Torri 2011).

The modern environmental movements that become popular in the United States and in Europe during the 1960s create in India a strong international pressure for the adoption of the North American conservation model. In the international context, India attracts attention for its species threatened by extinction, such as the Asiatic lion, the elephant and the tiger. Constituted around the 1960s, the World Wildlife Federation (WWF) represents the most important catalyst of government action in India. Protected areas have been designed on the basis of a particular set of scientific principles that focus on standard criteria such as the requisite size and shape of the area; landscape fragmentation; the creation of 'breeding nuclei' within 'inviolate' core zones; and the assigning of ecological values to large mammals, described as 'umbrella' species, against which human actions are to be judged (Torri 2011).

The growth rate of protected areas has been steady over the past decades, with faster growth in the 1990s (Naughton Treves et al. 2005). Until 2002, the Wild Life Protection Act provided for two kinds of protected areas (PAs), wildlife sanctuaries (WLS) and national parks (NP). While by law certain human uses can be allowed in a WLS, no human use is allowed in a NP. At present, India has a network of 670 PAs (102 NPs, 517 WLS, 47 conservation reserves and 4 community reserves). During the 12th Five Year Plan, the total outlay for the scheme is 800 crore, of which 74.62 crore was spent in 2012–13 and another 55.17 crore during 2013–14 by 31 December 2013 (Annual Report, Ministry of Environment and Forests 2013).

Most PAs in India have a core zone with national park status and a peripheral buffer zone, which can be either a wildlife sanctuary or a reserve forest. Resource use has been restricted to the buffer zones, where it has been regulated, while core areas are completely closed. A 1991 amendment to the Wildlife Protection Act specifies that, in wildlife sanctuaries, the chief wildlife warden must certify that any manipulation does not harm wildlife, and that the manipulation be approved by the state government.

The basic approach to management of PAs has been isolationist, based on the questionable assumption that certain areas are pristine or primary and that management must protect the park from people living in surrounding areas and shield wildlife and other natural resources from exploitation. This is achieved through the strict enforcement of legislation, patrols to prevent illegal activities and infrastructure maintenance. In this scenario, attempts to protect PAs from human intervention by coercion have often led to hostile attitudes of local people towards wildlife management and forestry staff, and sometimes to open conflict.

The need to exclude people from protected areas is in itself debatable. Numerous ecological studies have shown that not all human use is detrimental to wildlife conservation interests. Throughout the world, present-day forest quality and biodiversity patterns reflect the influence of past land use practices (Gomez-Pompa and Kaus 1992). In fact, in some cases, excluding human activities from ecosystems can actually reduce biodiversity and lead to habitat deterioration (Hussain 1996), while certain habitats have improved following human use/habitation (Ramakrishnan 1992).

Globalisation and bourgeois environmentalism versus the 'environmentalism of the poor'

Globalisation and its concomitant economic liberalisation of India post-1990s has been characterised by the empowerment of the 'middle class' and its sense of entitlement vis-à-vis other social classes and created a particular orientation to the environment that may be described as 'bourgeois environmentalism' (Baviskar 2007). Unlike the 'environmentalism of the poor' (Guha and Martinez 1998), which brought a social justice lens to bear upon issues of resource distribution and ecological sustainability, bourgeois environmentalism is preoccupied with ecological anxieties primarily perceived as 'quality of life' issues. Among these, concerns about health and safety, order, and aesthetics predominate over the question of livelihoods and social justice (Baviskar 2012).

Bourgeois environmentalists see themselves as 'ecological nationalists' (Cederlof and Sivaramakrishnan 2006), upholding the public interest by protecting 'pristine' environments and flagship species such as the tiger. This conservationist attitude is generally accompanied by support for forest management policies that exclude local populations. This class also tends to value techno-managerial expertise over more democratic decision-making. Thus it endorses 'professional management' – a euphemism for authoritarian conservation at the expense of poor forest-users. It must be noted that bourgeois environmentalism receives widespread support from the courts and media, creating an atmosphere of tacit tolerance for the eviction of forest-dwellers (Baviskar 2012) while supporting mining activities in the name of development.

At the 1992 Earth Summit, a bold new Convention on Biological Diversity (CBD) was developed which, inter alia, calls on governments to establish systems of protected areas and to manage these in support of conservation, sustainable use and equitable benefit sharing. The government's recognition of protected areas as economic institutions has a key role to play in the alleviation of poverty and the maintenance of the global community's critical life-support systems. This new vision for protected areas requires an awareness and understanding of the economic values generated by protected areas. Global conventions and programs alone are not enough to ensure the continued existence of, and sufficient funding for, protected areas.

In times of fiscal austerity and tightening government budgets – especially in developing countries which are home to much of the world's biodiversity – traditional funding sources for protected areas are increasingly under threat. Innovative alternatives to these traditional sources are needed in order to secure the long-term viability of protected areas. It is through endogenous development which calls for social, economic and cultural transformations of societies based on the revitalisations of traditions, respect for environment, and equitable relations of production; hitherto excluded communities can be organised to develop the potential of every region.

Economic valuation of the protected area

The process of valuation provides protected area managers with information about the protected area's goods and services, the values which people (potential supporters or customers) place on those, which values are being captured and which are not, and which groups could derive more benefits through alternative uses of the protected area and are therefore inclined to be a 'threat' to the protected area (Phillips 1998: 11–13). In this way, valuation provides useful information for management and financing decisions regarding protected areas. This information is likely to expose those who are not contributing to the protected area but derive benefits from it (and are therefore potential sources of funding), as well as those who are excluded from deriving benefits from the protected area but are being asked to 'pay' for the protected area, e.g. through taxes, property loss or foregone opportunities. The concept of total economic value (TEV) is now a well-established and useful framework for identifying the various values associated with protected areas (Phillips 1998: 13).

- The total economic value of a protected area consists of its use values and non-use values.
- A protected area's use values are in turn made up of its direct use values, indirect use values, and option values.
- Non-use values include bequest values and existence values.

The *direct use values* of a protected area are values derived from the direct use of the protected area for activities such as recreation, tourism, natural resource harvesting, hunting, gene pool services, education, and research. These activities can be commercial, meaning they

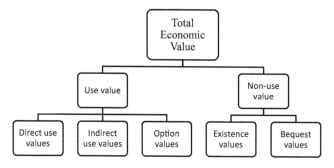

Figure 4.2 Economic values of protected areas

Sources: Phillips 1998: 11 (Phillips, Adrian. 1998. *Economic Values of Protected Areas Guidelines for Protected Area Managers.* World Commission on Protected Areas (WCPA), Cardiff: Cardiff University)

are traded on a market (resource harvesting, tourism, and research), or non-commercial, meaning there is no formal or regular market on which they are traded, fuel-wood collection, and informal grazing (Phillips 1998: 12).

The *indirect use values* of a protected area are values derived from the indirect uses of the protected area. Indirect uses are largely comprised of the protected area's ecological functions such as watershed protection, breeding habitat for migratory species, climatic stabilisation, and carbon sequestration. Protected areas also provide natural services, such as habitat for insects which pollinate local crops or for raptors which control rodent populations. Indirect use values are often widely dispersed and thus go unmeasured by markets. Alternative valuation techniques discussed later are necessary for measuring them (Phillips 1998: 12).

The *option values* of a protected area are values derived from the option of using the protected area sometime in the future. These future uses may be either direct or indirect and may include the future value of information derived from the protected area. Future information is often cited as particularly important for biodiversity as untested genes may provide future inputs into agricultural, pharmaceutical or cosmetic products. *Non-use values* are values which humans hold for a protected area which are in no way linked to the use of the protected area. Two common examples of non-use values are bequest values and existence values. *Bequest values* relate to the benefit of knowing that others benefit or will benefit from the protected area. *Existence*

Table 4.1 Total economic values of protected area

Use values			Non-use values	
Direct use value	*Indirect use value*	*Option value*	*Bequest values*	*Existences values*
Recreation	Ecosystem services	Future information	Use and non-use values for legacy	Biodiversity
Sustainable harvesting	Climate stabilisation	Future uses (indirect or direct)		Ritual or spiritual values
Wildlife harvesting	Flood control			Culture, heritage
Fuel wood	Ground water recharge			Community values
Grazing	Carbon sequestration			Landscape
Agriculture	Habitat			
Gene harvesting	Nutrient retention			
Education	Natural disaster prevention			
Research	Watershed protection natural services			

1 Phillips 1998: 18 (Sources: Phillips 1998: 11 (Phillips, Adrian. 1998. *Economic Values of Protected Areas Guidelines for Protected Area Mangers.* World Commission on Protected Areas (WCPA), Cardiff: Cardiff University)

2 Barbier, E., Acreman, M. and Knowler, D. (1997) (Barbier, E., Acreman, M. and Knowler, D. 1997. *Economic Valuation of Wetlands.* IUCN, Cambridge, UK.

values reflect the benefit of knowing that the protected area exists even though one is unlikely to visit it or use it in any other way. Non-use values are particularly difficult to measure.

An array of methods for eliciting both market and non-market values from people for environmental goods and services have been developed over the last few decades. Though still a developing field, some of the more common and widely used methods include (Phillips 1998:19–22).

1 *Contingent valuation method* (CVM) uses a direct approach to valuing an environmental good or service in that it asks people of their willingness to pay for the good or willing to accept for the loss of the good. Contingent valuation is particularly attractive

because it can estimate values where markets do not exist or where market substitutes cannot be found. For these reasons, CVM is widely used to measure existence values, option values, indirect use values and non-use values.

2   *Hedonic pricing* uses existing markets – such as the housing or labour markets – to determine the value of an environmental good. The assumption is that property values or wages reflect a stream of benefits, some of which are attributable to the environmental good. The analyst's task is to isolate that value which is attributable to the good. Hedonic pricing can be used to establish some of the more aesthetic values of protected areas as residential property. Adjoining place of a protected area is likely to hold a higher value for environmental (clean air, temperate climate) and aesthetic benefit. On the other hand, hedonic pricing can be used to value environmental damages, and their effects on property values or wages. Hedonic pricing becomes problematic where alternative markets are distorted or where information about environmental products is not widespread and data are scarce.

3   *Travel cost method* also uses existing markets, determining a person's value of an environmental good from what they spend on travelling in terms of time, travel expenditures and entry fees. Travel cost methods are particularly useful for assessing the non-commercial tourism, recreation and leisure values of a protected area.

4   *Change in productivity methods* values the goods and services of a protected area by estimating the change in the value of production of a good or service that occurs as a result of the change in land of the protected area. Measuring the change in productivity is particularly useful when trying to discover the ecological values of a protected area. To take an example, the forest provides a service to farmers downstream by keeping the river from silting up.

5   *Loss (or gain) of earnings methods* evaluate the change in productivity of humans resulting from environmental deterioration (or improvement). Such methods may be useful in determining some of the more concrete effects of a change in the regulatory functions of protected areas. These regulatory functions include watershed protection, storage and recycling of organic matter, nutrients, human waste, and climate regulation. For example, if water quality improvements reduce the levels of disease resulting from poor water quality, then the loss of earnings approach can be used to estimate benefits of clean water.

6   The *opportunity cost approach* provides an estimate of the value of a protected area based on the foregone income of the best

alternative use of the area. Measuring the opportunity cost of the protected area can give the manager an idea of the competitive threats to the area. In the case of potential threats from people living adjacent to a protected area, the relevant opportunity costs will be the value of alternative land uses they may prefer, such as farming or ranching. Other interest in the area may come from pressures for industrial or urban development, mining or intensely modified recreation uses.

7   The *replacement cost approach* can be used to measure the cost of damage done to the protected area by looking at how much it would cost to replace the assets that are damaged. For example, the cost of restoring a protected area could be used as an estimate of the cost of environmental damage to the protected area. These costs are then compared to the costs of preventing the damage in the first place. If the replacement costs exceed the prevention costs, then the damage should be avoided.

Possible sources of income and employment in protected areas

Capitalist market economy commodifies every product (including environment) and globalisation creates global market for those commodities. A Category V or VI protected area has the potential to accommodate a wide range of uses by zoning the resources within the area. A Category I area offers a much more limited array of use options such as research. Tourism, especially ecotourism and recreation values are particularly attractive because they are relatively easy to capture and they can be a source of significant funds. But some areas may not have the ability to draw tourists. An economic valuation study conducted at a national level can indicate which areas are most able to obtain funding from tourists and which are not. A system of cross-subsidisation, or a separate funding strategy, can then be used to support wildlife which may be biologically important, but with little appeal to tourists (West et al. 2006).

Utilisation of services and domain knowledge of the local indigenous people in tourism can push local employment. Ecotourism can make protected areas, and experience and interaction with them, into things that have an economic value on the basis of visitors' consumption of them. Rural peoples' previous interactions with plants and animals were unique social ways of relating to their surroundings but instillation of these plants and animals' into economic valuation erases local ways of seeing and being.

Identifying a protected area's goods and services, determining who values those goods and services, and measuring these values are not always a straightforward process. The goods and services include plant and wildlife habitat, genetic resources, water supply, protection against natural disasters, carbon sequencing, and so on. Many of these goods and services are not traded on commercial markets and therefore have no evident market value. The values of non-market goods and services need to be measured and expressed in monetary terms, where possible, so that they can be weighed on the same scale as commercially traded components. Commercial sales of timber and non-timber products, including medicinal and ornamental plants, honey, bush, meat, and so on (Phillips 1998) need to be measured in terms of their economic return. From Table 4.2, it is evident that how diverse economic benefits can be reaped out of protective areas.

If the protected area serves as a watershed, it provides benefits to downstream water users including farmers, miners, manufacturers, and villagers. If it is an area visited by people from cities nearby, then it offers a range of benefits (recreational, educational, etc.) to urban dwellers. These groups have a stake in conserving the protected area, but they should have means to express that interest.

We need to adopt measures which will encourage and enable them to support the protected area and fiscal measures need to be used

Table 4.2 Markets and some means of capturing direct use values

Benefit	Market	Capturing the values
Sustainable harvest	Income from sales, market prices for similar goods, proportion of income from final products	User fees, access charges
Recreation	Tourism expenditure	Gate fees, concession, rent, tax
Education	Price of alternative courses on offer elsewhere	User fees, interpreter fees, gate fees
Scientific	Proportion of income from final research products	access charges
National ecosystem services	Price of alternative services	Tax, user fees

Source: Adrian Phillips 1998: 13 (Phillips, Adrian. 1998. *Economic Values of Protected Areas Guidelines for Protected Area Mangers*. World Commission on Protected Areas (WCPA), Cardiff: Cardiff University)

to collect revenues from these downstream customers. Consider the global customers of this protected area. Within the mandates of global environmental agreements, the protected area may provide several global benefits (Shahabuddin 2015). These could include biodiversity conservation, carbon sequestration, habitat for endangered species and migratory species, replenishing fish stock for traditional and commercial fisheries, mitigation of natural disasters and impacts related to climate change, and so on (Badola, NA) We need to adopt measures which will enable the global community to support the protected area. The Global Environmental Facility (GEF) can be used as a means of finance in such cases. Indeed, integrated conservation and development projects (referred to as ICDPs or ICADs) are premised on the idea that people living in and around protected areas can come to value their surroundings as 'in situ biological diversity' if they intellectually connect it to markets and cash income. But they rarely take local systems of evaluation into account.

Even without ecotourism, protected areas at times provide employment for rural peoples although in some instances protected areas turn people into labour in ways that create new sorts of subjectivities employment for expatriates (Peters 1998) and employment for in-country elites. Protected areas also provide some in-country scientific capacity building. When animals are turned into commodities in local peoples' minds, they retaliate against national parks because of the financial burdens imposed on them through the killing of wildlife. Certain species have gone from being little known or valued by local people to being highly valued commodities. The commodification of plants may erase their social value and lead to overproduction within protected areas. Local people and their image can also be turned into commodities, as can their intellectual property (ethno-medicine, handicrafts, etc.) that is concerned with their surroundings.

Protected areas and conservation efforts have profound effects on gender relationships worldwide (Agarwal 1997), while conservation practices initially virtually ignored the women, but when it responded to gender need it disrupted local power structures and gender relations, thereby creating spaces for new forms of environmental activism and political alliances. Because they were ignored, women began to build alliances and work outside of their immediate family. This allowed women new ways of constituting themselves as persons. Instead of making themselves only through family interactions, women broadened their social networks and their networks of self. Similarly, women's participation in handicraft production projects aimed at tourist markets has given them economic power that they did not have in the past.

Finally, the creation of wilderness spaces has often also resulted in the creation of liminal spaces, beyond the control of the state. Parks in Africa and Latin America and in India as well have served as staging grounds for anti-state guerrilla movements; for drug trafficking and marijuana plantations; as a preferred route for people seeking to enter the country illegally, and so on. Parks sometimes offer indigenous communities' opportunities to elude state control and other incursions onto their land. Thus security, protection, and military importance of protected areas are immense, and local indigenous people's expertise can be utilised positively by providing them gainful employment as forest guards and security personnel.

Conclusion

Clean environment and sustainable environmental policy hold the key for the future of human progress and development. Globalisation is like a double-edged sword. In one way it calls for death and destruction of environment for its ruthless expansion, and in the other it promotes creation of protected areas. While rate of environmental destruction is high in developing countries like India; globalisation induced structural adjustment policies made availability of local governmental support inadequate. Many PAs continue to be ineffective and remain 'paper parks' with insufficient financing and inappropriate management. One of the main reasons is that PAs still remain largely marginal to the economic planning of developing countries and the economic potential of many PAs remains either underutilised or appropriated. Primarily this happens due to lack of recognition of economic potentials of PAs. Total economic value analysis of PAs will make them attractive before the globalised market and private investments and will led to creation of more such places by maintaining the critical balance between environmental sustainability and issues of local indigenous people's livelihood in more hermeneutic ways. There is no doubt that we have made significant strides in improving PA management conceptually, but this knowledge needs to be actively percolated into the implementation level.

Note

1 Maoist revolutionaries in India are commonly known as Naxalites.

References

Agarwal, B. 1997. Environmental Action, Gender Equity and Women's Participation. *Development and Change*, 28(1): 1–44.

Barbier, E., Acreman, M. and Knowler, D. 1997. *Economic Valuation of Wetlands*. Cambridge: IUCN.

Baviskar, Amita. 2007. *Cows, Cars and Cycle-rickshaws: Bourgeois Environmentalists and the Battle for Delhi's Streets*, Paper presented at the workshop on *The Middle Classes in India: Identity, Citizenship and the Public Sphere*. New Delhi: At the Institute of Economic Growth, March.

Baviskar, Amita. 2012. 'India's Changing Political Economy and its Implications for Forest, Users', in Guha Ramchandra, Sundar Nandini et al. (eds.), *Deeper Roots of Historical Injustice: Trends and Challenges in the Forests of India* (33–46). Washington, DC: Rights and Resources Initiative.

Cederlof, Gunnel and Sivaramakrishnan, K. 2006. *Ecological Nationalisms: Nature, Livelihoods, and Identities in South Asia*. Seattle: University of Washington Press.

Diegues Antonio Carlos. 2000. 'Commons and Protected Areas in Brazil', The Eight Conference of The International Association for the Study of Common Property Constituting the Commons; Crafting Commons in the New Millennium, Bloomington, IN.

Easterly, William. 2001. *The Elusive Quest for Growth: Economists' Adventures and Misadventures in the Tropics*. Cambridge, MA: MIT Press.

Frank, Andre Gunder. 1998. *Reorient: Global Economy in the Asian Age*. Berkeley: University of California Press.

Gomez-Pompa, A. and Kaus, A. 1992. 'Taming the Wilderness Myth', *Bioscience*, 42(4): 271–279.

Guha, Ramachandra and Martinez-Alier, Juan. 1998. *Varieties of Environmentalism: Essays North and South*. New Delhi: Oxford University Press.

Guha, Ramachandra et al. 2012. *Deeper Roots of Historical Injustice: Trends and Challenges in the Forests of India*. Washington, DC: Rights and Resources Initiative, 1–12.

Guyford Stever, H. (1972). Science, Systems, and Society Journal of Cybernetics. 2 (3): 1–3. doi: 10.1080/01969727208542909.

Hussain, S. A. 1996. *A Case Study on Effective Wetland Management*, Dehradun, India, Wildlife Institute of India. (Unpublished mimeo).

International Monetary Fund. 2000. *Globalization: Threats or Opportunity*. IMF Publications, 12 April 2000.

IUCN. 1994. 'Guidelines for Protected Area Management Categories', IUCN, Gland, Switzerland and Cambridge.

Jan Nederveen Pieterse. 1998. 'My Paradigm or Yours? Alternative Development, Post-Development, Reflexive Development and Change', *Institute of Social Studies*, 29, Oxford Blackwell.

Ministry of Environment and Forests. 2013. *Annual Report 2012–13, Ministry of Environment and Forests*. New Delhi: Government of India.

Moscovici, Serge. 1974. *Hommes domestiques, Hommes sauvages.* Paris: Unión Géneralled Editions.

Nadeem, Hasnain. 1996. *Tribal India.* New Delhi: Palaka Prakashan, 211–217.

Naughton Treves, L., Holland, M. and Brandon, K. 2005. 'The Role of Protected Areas in Conserving Biodiversity and Sustaining Local Livelihoods', *Annual Review of Environment and Resources*, 3(1): 219–252.

Peters, J. 1998. Transforming the integrated conservation and development approach: observations from the Ranomafana National Park Project. *Journal of Agricultural and Environmental Ethics* 11: 17–47.

Phillips, Adrian. 1998. *Economic Values of Protected Areas Guidelines for Protected Area Mangers.* World Commission on Protected Areas (WCPA) and Cardiff University.

Ramakrishnan, P. S. 1992. *Shifting Agriculture and Sustainable Development,* Man and the Biosphere Series No. 10. Paris: UNESCO/Parthenon Publishing Group.

Shahabuddin, Ghazala. 'Emerging Trends in Protected Area Management', Occasional Paper, Environmental Studies Group, Council for Social Development, New Delhi, www.fao.org/, accessed on 20/12/2015.

Smith, N. 1990. *Uneven Development: Nature, Capital and the Production of Space.* Oxford: Basil Blackwell.

Stever, Guy H. 1972. 'Science, Systems, and Society', *Journal of Cybernetics,* 2 (3): 1–3.

Sundar, Nandini, Roger, Jeffery and Neil, Thin. 2001. *Branching Out: Joint Forest Management in India.* New Delhi: Oxford University Press.

Torri, Maria Costanza. 2011. 'Conservation Approaches and Development of Local Communities in India: Debates, Challenges and Future Perspectives', *International Journal of Environmental Sciences,* 1 (5): 871–883.

West, Paige, Igoe, James and Brockington, Dan. 2006. 'Parks and Peoples: The Social Impact of Protected Areas', *Annual Review of Anthropology,* 35: 251–277.

5 Environmental challenges in Brazil, local and global

Edgard Leite Ferreira Neto

Three distinct paradigms are used in order to understand nature: that of nature as a deity, as an organism and as a machine. Western religious tradition overcomes the divinisation of natural world and orbits between those of organism and machine. However, both, mainly the one involving the organism, do not present any significant resistance to human beings' deliberate and predatory actions. Such movement that transforms the natural world and extracts resources for society's development presents in many cultures and historical moments the same irresponsible profile as refers to the environment. Such movement in turn derives permanent human need to cross the borders between the orderly human universe and the natural state world and is driven mainly by their needs. Brazil is a privileged country in what refers to wealth of natural resources and faces the same environmental challenges of other societies and times. The collapse of its biomes follows the expansion of Brazil's and the world's borders. In Amazon's specific case, the process of deforestation is linked to internal expansionist movements and to global economy's expansion – which exports their ecological borders to peripheral areas in the world, mainly Brazil's. A disorderly transformation process of the environment, however, apparently cannot be made to stop, except by controlling individual needs (hard to be accomplished) or by cooling down economic demands.

Western intellectual tradition

Western intellectual tradition has come up with at least three models to understand nature. These three paradigms have different conceptual structures and date back to distinct time origins, and, as such, they are still present in contemporary thinking. Those concerned with various issues involving the relationship between man and the environment orbit around these concepts. In so doing, they depart from efficient theoretical bases for solving or managing several issues related to the relationship between man and nature, such as environmental problems.

In these distinct paradigms, nature appears as either endowed with the attributes of a divinity or as an organism, or, still, as a machine.

The notion that nature is a divinity is as old as the first signs of some religious movement. This probably emerged from the perception of the existence of some regularity, order or cyclical profile in the functioning of the cosmos. Such perception implies both the recognition of human submission to greater forces, and perceived divine powers in the functioning of nature, and in the integration of man in some kind of sacred universe that mixes itself with the divine.

The approach towards understanding nature as an organism, at least as a theoretical construct, comes from intellectual elaborations typical of Greek philosophy. Collingwood defends that such notion originates itself from an analogy between the world and the nature of the individual being (Collingwood 1949: 8). Since Plato, mainly in the *Timaeus*, the world has been understood as 'an animal', *zôon*, and though Aristotle never used such formulation to define the cosmos, he sees the whole as a connection of parts that carry with themselves the idea of good order (Furley 2005: 31; Nederman 2005: 1673) and seeks the common good in their components.

The machine idea derives from the great importance given to mathematics on the understanding of the world. As such, it became clear on the threshold of modernity when, following Collingwood, nature was considered as 'deprived of both intelligence and life' of its own (Collingwood 1949: 5). However, it was thought to be governed by laws that placed it in motion, or in a mathematically predictable development, as a mechanism. In a society where the machine experience was becoming increasingly commonplace, this model became highly understandable.

The organism or machine models have never been alien to Western religious tradition for, in both, the presence of a first movement or a greater architect could be evoked as a root or source.

Thus, on the one hand Saint Francis of Assisi became familiarised in his *Canticle of the Creatures* with an organic perspective, a tendency that led, for example, to the current pope's encyclical, *Laudato Si*, and on the other, a long tradition beginning with Copernicus and leading up to Descartes got closer to mechanism, and considered its understanding as a divine vocation (Russell 2000: 46). In the latter dimension, the theory that affirmed the existence of natural laws never ceased to have advocates and followers in medieval Christian philosophy, beginning with Saint Thomas of Aquino. From both perspectives, the being, as part of an organism or a machine, bows himself before a superior power: God.

Christianity has always denied the divinisation of nature, for the divine, within Christian tradition, is free before the natural world, that is, it does not submit to it. The thesis, typical of a consistent biblical interpretation, that God created nature and gave it to man is deeply rooted in Western consciousness.

In the non-religious inflections of the paradigms, developed in modernity, both the organism and the machine developed the thesis that man must bow himself not before God but before a totality – which prescinds from personal interests to a greater or smaller extent. Actually, such modern perspectives equate the human being to other agents, either because they see it as just another nature's organ or because it considers him as just a part of the engine, thus reducing or eliminating his singularity.

In fact, in this sense, the traditional religious perspective has somehow preserved personal interest or the individual's singularity in that it establishes individual redemption as a goal and submits it to a will and reason that transcends both the organism and the machine.

Issue of environmental balance

In the 1960s the environmental balance issue was placed in evidence during a period of strong rebellion against social values and norms. Historian Lynn White then defended that Christianity had a great deal of guilt for the environmental problems existing at the time because, as a consequence of the belief in the power conceded to human being by God, man believed that nature should be freely governed by him without greater concerns than the attainment of their very human goals and interests (White 1967).

At the time, many suggested White should be cautious. In fact, it does not appear that the predatory nature eventually attributed to human action in the environment is an exclusive phenomenon of Western culture, or of a specific religious strengthening of individual action or human personal interests. In fact, as Gondon Childe long noted, the sedentarisation process that characterises the so-called Neolithic revolution and involves taming plants and animals has implied the building of a differentiated human space that is, by definition, destructive to the local environment, as it installs an energy drain in the nearby environment and thus damages the environment's balance.

Studies that developed, for example, in the analysis of the disappearance of the Indus Valley Civilisation in the second millennium BC point at the probability of its being caused by an environmental imbalance of great proportions. Such crisis might have partly derived from uncontrollable tectonic events (the physical disappearance of the river Sarasvati, for example; Allchin 1995) or of events stemming from an incapacity to manage and control an environment changed by agriculture and urbanisation, or, still, from the impossibility of dealing with increasingly limited resources in a society unconcerned with the greater ecological effects of its urban and population growth (Dales 1965; Raikes 1965). Similar ecologically based evaluations have also been made, for example, of the understanding of the collapse of the Mayan civilisation (McKillop 2004).

Thus, the environmental disaggregation issue does not appear to be the sole responsibility of a given perspective towards the understanding of the world, but comes from an attitude that emerges as a solution to problems that came with the growth of human civilisation space.

The need to clear fields for cultivation, domesticate animals or establish a sedentary community always imposes itself as a primary solution that creates a controlled world, a safe space, which is a permanent source of food. However, the subordination of such space to nature, though evident, is not always considered in all its outcomes and dynamics, among them the one that refers to the need for a continuous and growing drain of surrounding resources. That often occurs without the immediate perception of the signs of depletion of the environment or of eminent environmental collapses.

In 1662, John Evelyn published his pioneering *A Discourse of Forest Trees and the Propagation of Timber in His Majesty's Dominions*, in which he reveals his concerns on the maintenance of natural resources in the United Kingdom. In this founding paper, Evelyn departed from the principle that, yes, the human being is, by God's will, the manager of nature and responsible for the preservation of its mechanism (Livingstone 2000: 492). Instead, he defends that, yes, man also has the power to influence decisively on the environmental conditions by means of reason. Thus by controlling the necessary process of intervention on the environment, he can avoid or manage the environmental collapses that may threat the existence of societies.

Throughout the 19th century the perception developed that the human being could think of such process from an active perspective. The concept of ecology was then pioneeringly built, initially by Ernst Haeckel in his *General Morphology*, from 1866, with a view to consolidating a field of knowledge that allowed the development of reflections pertaining to studies of the relationship between organic forms and the environment. In other words, it allowed the theorisation of the relations between organisms and their environment, thus seeking to understand, for instance, the necessary logic to keep the balance of conflict relations, as those between men and the environment.

That occurred to a large extent because in a society with growing associations between distinct cultures within a global scale, the use of natural resources reached levels so far unknown. The problems in this area, which originally occurred at local level, had greater implications that knowledge, reason and science could equate, whether nature was a clock, of which the human being would be the clockmaker, by replacing or fixing parts, or an organism on which man would act as a physician capable of intervening in favour of the whole.

In the West, the process of secularisation of the state had impacts on all sciences. In the specific area of studies of environmental relations, as already noted, as it prescinds of a divinised nature or of a God external to it, this thinking ended up stimulating an exclusive appreciation of the role played by the constituent components of the organism, or machine, within the process of good functioning of the natural world. Such perspective strengthened non-religious dimensions in which the human being became an agent endowed with powers similar, from a qualitative point of view, to the other agents, like earthquakes, for instance.

An influential proposal, for instance, was made by James Lovelock in his remarkable and influential *Gaia, a New Look at Life on Earth*. Lovelock considers it reasonable to suppose that human beings can even act against asteroids that threaten the balance of the environment by eliminating chance and can thus face, with great chances of success, the making of procedures to cope with any possible return of an ice age. Thus, science not only plays the role of an element capable of managing the sustainability of human expansion over the natural world, but can also act as an instrument for the preservation of the planet, as part of the intelligence of the cosmos (Lovelock 1979: 139).

Similar contemporary digressions and speculations, however, were not always completely successful in dealing with the fact that the expansion of man over nature is usually an expansion of frontiers, and the ones involved in the process are mainly driven by need, and not by some given perception or general theory of the logic underlying the relation between man and the environment.

This aspect was raised by Lewis Moncrief (Moncrief 1970) in his controversial debate with Lynn White, when referring specifically to the role of the 'frontier' in American history, from which he shows the dynamics driving man to conquer the space to be colonised. The border experience can be generalised to every human experience involving the relationship with the environment, and Leroi-Gourhan notes this when he points out that the passage to the civilisation implies the building of a radiant space, marked by a border between the human and the natural, a border whose barriers are destined to be continually overcome (Leroi-Gourhan 1979: 136). The expansion over nature has to do with an act of survival driven by vital demands on the surrounding environment in order to stabilise sources of food and personal and collective satisfaction, extracting energy from nature by means of different materials and mechanisms.

Such process that secularising rationalism attempted to control or manage in a balanced way has a similar dynamics, whether in the ancient cultures of the Indo valley, in England's forests, in the American border or in Brazil. Human beings act driven by demands that call for such expansion for inescapable economic reasons. As such, they are, above all, agents pressed by personal or local realities in which the expansion of a productive space can only occur by means of the destruction of the ecosystems established beyond the borders of orderly areas.

The extent reached by such destruction is always complex and is hard or impossible to manage by those who benefit from it, as the variables involved in such process are peculiar and often involve different aspects, which usually surprising associations and reality. The exponential increase of demands for natural resources thus generates increasingly bigger problems as a result of the growing expansion of border areas. Moreover, because of the growing scale of borders that occur worldwide (without taking into account the fact that the moon and Mars are nowadays also potential frontiers), the problems that take on eminently local dimensions become also problems of a global scale.

Brazil, as a frontier

The participation of a territory, which is now Brazil, in a worldwide network for raw material extraction and agricultural production, as well as its establishment as a 'frontier' of a production vector initially located in Europe, took place in the first years of the Portuguese colonisation, beginning in 1500. The first local inhabitants, the native indigenous peoples had their own borders, adequate to their reality, but these were assimilated by the great global border of the European economic system. If one takes into consideration that the pioneering expansion process was mainly driven by the extraction of the tree called paubrasilia (*Caesalpinia echinata*) for dyes, paint and carpentry (hence the name of the country), the expansion borderline was located in the biome, in the biological community, nowadays known as 'Mata Atlântica' (Atlantic Forest).

In this same area, other transforming and production activities took place later on. Still during colonial times, sugarcane cultivation began and, later on, coffee cultivation took place. This region ended up concentrating the biggest part of Brazilian urban centres and, as a consequence, the biggest industrial areas. Such process irreversibly destroyed the original biome. In 2014, there was only 8.5% left of the forest original coverage. It is worth noting that, by then, 72.2% of the Brazilian population, or around 145 million of a total of 200 million inhabitants lived in the area (SOS Mata Atlântica 2015; Brasil, Ministério do Meio Ambiente 2015 (a)).

The collapse of the 'Mata Atlântica' was already evident by the beginning of the 19th century. One of the first Brazilian administrators to deal with the subject was José Bonifácio, who was one of the mentors of the political emancipation process. In his *Representaçãoà Assembléia Geral Constituinte do Império do Brasilsobrea Escravatura* (Representation, on Slavery, to the General Assembly of the Empire of Brazil), Bonifácio criticised the social model based on slavery, which in his opinion was predatory, and warned against the growing deforestation and disappearance of aquifer sources:

> Our precious forests are disappearing, victimized by fire and by the destructive axe of ignorance and selfishness. Our mountains and hillsides are daily balding, and in time there will be a shortage of the fertile rains that appease the vegetation and feed our watersheds and rivers, without which our beautiful land of Brazil will be reduced, in less than two centuries, to the condition of the empty plains and the arid deserts of Libya. The day (a terrible and fatal day) will then come when scorned nature will have completed its revenge against so many mistakes and crimes committed against it.
>
> (Bonifácio 1825: 40)

Bonifácio's thesis is part of a tradition based on an organic approach to nature, for it attributes certain subjective qualities, as 'vengeance', which is not present in a mechanistic discourse. However, what is crucial is that his defence of rational cultivation methods and more harmonious social rules (his text aims to attack African slavery) emphasises the emergence of a 'healthier' society which could, by means of its intrinsic characteristics, generate ecological events favourable to everybody. The pursuit of harmony presupposes the existence of an organic understanding of the cosmos that must guide human attitude towards the environment.

It does not seem that Jose Bonifácio's view of the world had any significant impact on the policies for territory occupation. To a great extent because his belief in the therapeutic role played by human beings and in his power went against the traditional thesis according to which nature belongs to man for his exclusive use. Such thesis was broadly disseminated, and necessary, as it is focused on the demands for survival in the bordering regions and in society itself. As a matter of fact, it relied on similar productive activities. Thus it proved infeasible the establishment of a policy to make the management of the expansion of human frontier in the natural world a sustainable or ecologically harmonious process.

In fact, the needs of consuming countries and local producing groups established throughout the 19th and 20th centuries an economic expansion process that was marked by a necessary lack of control. Such process spread in areas of biodiversity wealth by means of agents who could only implement such progress through low cost, without significant aggregation of either cultural or technological capital. The uncontrolled clearing of land for agriculture and livestock and predatory extraction of biodiversity materials or minerals made it possible to implement profitable activities in Brazil's frontier.

Such actions, which began during colonial times, can be seen as a consequence of the expansion of agricultural and livestock economic borders, from Europe, and from Portugal in principle, and, more directly, from Brazil. These events initially caused local damages. However, as the expansion process involving greater or circumstantial economic interests spread, both because of the increase of the global and local population and the increase of the demands, human intervention spread over other biomes existing in Brazil, namely: the Caatinga (north-eastern arid land) and the Cerrado (central and northern regions in Brazil), the Amazon (northern region), the Pampa (southern region) and the Pantanal (western region) (Figure 5.1). However, it is worth mentioning the sea coast biome, which has been under predatory intervention since colonial times and currently goes through a significant process of disaggregation.

Brazil occupies 47.7% of South America territory and 20% of the continental American territory as a whole. Besides, its territory is wide (37 degrees latitude and 38 degrees longitude), and it holds the largest

Figure 5.1 Brazilian biomes
Source: Map prepared by the author

tropical forest in the world and incalculable fresh water reserves. The Amazon basin alone holds 20% of all freshwater on the planet and has the biggest tropical forest in the world, with 4.5 million km², in Brazilian territory, (India has 3.3 million km²) and 10% of all vegetation species in the planet, which has a fundamental impact on the South American climate.

The amount of unused land in Brazil is immense and the tropical and subtropical climates are highly recommended for almost all types of agricultural cultivation. The country's mineral reserves are equally enormous and not completely known (Krech 2003: 200–204). Thus, every process of productive expansion in this universe yet to be explored goes beyond local sphere and transforms itself in an event of global dimension.

Currently, Brazil is the fourth biggest exporter of pork in the world, the third biggest exporter of agricultural produce, the second biggest exporter of soy and ethanol, and the world's biggest exporter of sugar, coffee, orange juice, tobacco, beef and chicken. Besides, the country currently has the second biggest cattle stock in the world (US Department of Agriculture 2015). If we take into account its enormous biodiversity, Brazil also accounts for 15% of international wild animal trafficking (Ambiente Brasil 2015).

Therefore, possible ecological imbalance and infeasibilities caused by the expansion of the frontier that originally caused only local impacts can currently occur and generate global imbalance. Thus, a problem that used to be originally circumstantial, like the ones involving the water sources in the 'Mata Atlântica' region, can have impacts on other neighbouring biomes and cause imbalances that may affect in a greater or smaller extent greater balances, with consequences for both the world's economy and the global environment.

The Amazon

The Amazon case is revealing as it currently constitutes the main Brazilian internal frontier area and an open space for expansion, mainly after the deliberated action in the Cerrado biome in the 1950s, which opened the path to the Amazon basin. The inauguration of Brasília in 1960 was the symbol of this expansion in the Cerrado. During General Emílio Médici's term of office (1969–74), several government projects were implemented to open the frontier in the Amazon biome, among them the building of the Transamazonica, a highway that was meant to link different zones in the region with the Cerrado and the Mata Atlântica, in addition to incentives given to rural settlements for populations coming from the South of the country.

Currently, Amazon is an open space for agricultural and extensive livestock production in lands understood as abandoned that have often been inhabited by indigenous peoples for centuries. The massacre of native populations in the 1960s and 1970s was interrupted after the democratisation process in the 1980s. However, land conflicts are still frequent, both in Amazon and in the borders of the Cerrado expansion. In the Amazon specific case, the agricultural and livestock frontier is marked by intense deforestation.

As a response to pressure from several social groups, both internal and external, the Brazilian government has been making some efforts against the destruction process of the Amazon biome. Between 2012 and 2015, within the scope of the Plano de Açãopara Prevenção e Controle do Desmatamentona Amazônia Legal (Action Plan for Prevention and Control of Deforestation in the Legal Amazon; PPCDAm), experts from different ministries identified 112 causes for deforestation (Brazil, Ministry of Environment 2015 (b)). Among the main reasons are:

1   From the perspective of productive activities:

   a   Poor feasibility of the productive chains that constitute alternatives for deforestation
   b   Disorderly expansion of agricultural and livestock activities
   c   Poor production of sustainable timber
   d   Settlers' productive activities that are not compatible with the environmental legislation
   e   Forest and soil degradation.

2   From the perspective of land and territorial organisation:

   a   Irregular occupation of public land
   b   Disorderly expansion of occupation of forest areas
   c   Poor management of the land network.

3   From the perspective of monitoring and control:

   a   Delayed processes of licensing of deforestation and management plans
   b   Poor supervision and control
   c   Poor presence of the state in the Amazon
   d   Administrative and penal impunity related to illegal deforestation
   e   Low level of environmental accountability
   f   Poor efficiency of the monitoring of the progressive degradation and selective deforestation.

It seems clear that 'from the perspective of productive activities', all the aforementioned reasons are related to the high costs of a non-predatory agriculture and the corresponding superior profitability of predatory practices, in addition to the inescapable processes of ecological disaggregation. These, when they occur, make it inevitable for people to move on to preserved areas. 'From the perspective of land and territorial organisation', the reasons are linked to problems involving land, settlement, feasibility that affect rural populations that are led to seek a solution by moving to forest areas. 'From the perspective of monitoring and control', the reasons point at an institutionalised complicity between supervising institutions and monitoring of predatory practices, as well as a lack of responsible attitudes towards the environment by the agents involved.

We can conclude that the process of disaggregation affecting Amazon is a response to human, economic, financial and commercial demands that can only be controlled by the constitution of a society significantly different from the one that currently exists. In such a society, the different social agents would act in a conservative way seeking to adjust their various economic and financial demands to a harmonious and limited social and ecological context.

That would be, for instance, the case of extractive communities in the state of Acre, located in the extreme north of Brazil, who are contented with the subsidies they receive to have low-tech production with low return, based on extraction of chestnut and rubber, thus preserving the forest against deforestation. As this is not a general expectation, at least for the great majority, added to the fact that such policy usually implies subsidies, deforestation is part of the reality in the frontier and reveals the existence of serious and profound social demands.

This means that the government and, thus, society, runs a disaster that is unfortunately both necessary and interesting for the development of the commercial activities themselves and also represents a disruption of a previous crisis or stagnation situation. Among the social agents involved, such reality also points to the lack of any theoretical understanding of an organic or mechanistic basis, as well as the predominance of 'interested actions' or 'personal interest' revealed in attitudes or probably in the mere belief that God gave man land for him to draw his livelihood out of it.

Notwithstanding this, another reality comes up when an analysis is made of the historical trends involving deforestation since 1988 (Figure 5.2).

At this point, we can see that, though the government attributes a progressive decrease of deforestation to the PPCDAm, significant decreases in the level of deforestation can be observed in 1991, 1997, and, progressively, as from 2008. When we look at the growth indicators of the world's and Brazilian economies in the same period, we can see that the smallest deforestation rates correspond to the 1989–91 (Japan and the US), 1997 (Asian crisis) and mainly the 2008 world crises, whose enormous impacts on the world's economy affected the process of deforestation, which is, as previously mentioned, a frontier

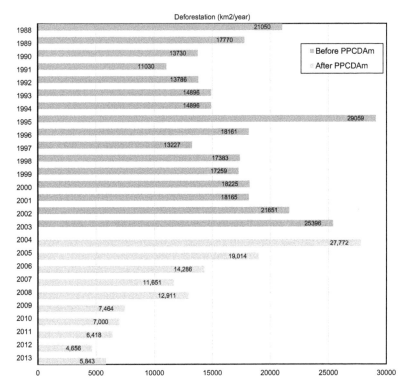

Figure 5.2 Deforestation, 1988–2013
Source: PRODES/ INPE/ MCTI. Note: The figure is the author's own creation.

activity. Therefore, even if the PPCDAm has some impact, this derives, to a large extent, from consumers market retraction and an economic stagnation that does not give the necessary stimulus to expansion on unexplored areas in order to allow new foci of raw material production.

The local problem, however, cannot be seen solely in terms of its local but in its global dimension as well. In fact, the Amazon frontier is equally a world's economy frontier. In other words, though central countries may stabilise their frontiers with nature by formulating sustainable preservation policies, this is to a large extent implemented by means of export of their demands to peripheral countries like Brazil. In fact, the contraction of central economies leads to a corresponding reduction in timber extraction.

Besides, it is not just Brazil's issue, but humanity's as well. The transformation of this process presents a series of difficulties. In fact, in addition to controls and subsidies, or change of economic paradigms, this also demands a substantial change in terms of man's attitude towards the place he occupies in nature. In other words, it demands a shift of perspective of a mere user, as held in the traditional view, to that of a manager or accomplice of the environment. Such change is above all hard to accomplish because, for human beings using the environment is a crucial demand of his condition. Such use implies variable degrees of approaches and dissociations from surrounding nature.

Conclusion

Concerns on environmental imbalance are precedent and do not seem to be exclusive of our time. The amount of civilisations that perished as a consequence of ecological disasters points at the reoccurrence of inescapable events. Other communities faced insurmountable environmental limitations. It is evident that the degree of the seriousness of the collapses increases as they involve a growing number of people and territorial extensions, which aggravates concerns.

The problem nowadays is the dynamics of the solutions. Is it possible, for instance, to renounce personal interests or disqualify 'acting upon interests'? This aspect of the issue is easy to understand, and it comes as no surprise for Western religious thinking, for example, which reveals Lynn White's mistake. If God gave man earth, He did not give it so man could manage it as if he were God himself. Individuals are not infinitely powerful. Thus, the topic is part of a broader criticism against individualism in Western culture, if seen as one of the driving forces that aggravate the world's environmental situation.

Demands for an exponential growth of agricultural and livestock production, the growing eagerness for the most varied types of metals and the insistence on the use of energy sources that are potentially dangerous to the environment is deeply rooted in a process that many identify with the first signs of an environmental collapse of great proportions. Besides, one cannot deny that certain regions in the world are already experiencing the impacts of irresponsible management of these demands.

Such irresponsibility is, to a large extent, natural, for it is personal interests that are placed before commitments in any type of entrepreneurship. Besides, the process of transformation of the environment presents a conflict between the need for satisfaction and the often incomprehensible and surprising complex profile of nature. Therefore, the criticism against an individual-centred society and its demands, for they seem to be one the main causes of greed in the process of environmental transformation. Thus, certain models are suggested or imposed upon, notably organic ones, which restrict or eliminate such individuality.

What makes it even more complex is that, to a greater or smaller extent of this individuality, there is a demand or expectation of a submission to models that disregard the challenge reality of the ecological frontiers, as well as the role played by the 'acting upon interests' view in its administration. It must be taken into account that society lies in the threshold of the frontier of the environment. If this were not the case, we would not be permanently in conflict with viruses and bacteria – and frequent infeasibilities involving sanitation in the urban world. It is in the space of the frontier that we continuously broaden the basis of our existence. Besides, this frontier is both local and global, internal and external, individual and collective, before which the human being is permanently placed. Moreover, we do not do so without interest.

Is it possible to live in a world where disorderly growth imposed by industrialisation can be restrained? Can we live in a world where extensive plantations can coexist harmoniously with the small family farm? Can we live in a world where new sources of energy, at least, initially more expensive, can replace other that is more dangerous to the environment? Can we submit personal interests? There does not seem to be easy answers to the above mentioned questions.

Harmonising immediate personal interests and collective and strategic concerns is the right path. In any of the existing models of nature, preservation of individual interests, either from a religious or financial perspective, or still from the viewpoint of its challenging power, can establish the parameters of good policies for ecological balance. It can only be achieved though if combined with responsibility for collectivity.

Balancing the eagerness to transform with that of preserving, finding a continuous balance between the need to cross the frontier between the orderly human world and the disorderly world that surrounds us and change it according to our demands, equating our personal ambitions with those of the collectivity are important human challenges. Avoiding the catastrophe should not mean ruling out our success. The frontier experience is crucial for the human being. We must not fear crossing it, but should rather do it in a responsible way by recognising the need to take care of the human aspect and respect surrounding nature.

Adopting such policy is a permanent challenge for societies: Brazil and other countries. It calls for our humility before nature. That is, it demands an understanding of it as an organism, as machine, as a gift from God or as a deity, but it hardly involves a utopia that demands renouncing the impetus to transform the environment. In fact, there does not seem to be any significant initiative to stop man's dangerous actions on nature, unless when one manages to stagnate needs by means of subsidies, or when frontiers are transferred to distant zones, with a corresponding transfer of needs, as seems to be the case in Brazil. Such reality is, in fact, a greater challenge for our survival – that of Brazil and the global society.

Indian philosophical tradition, however, offers some important insights into the dimensions of this process. Swami Vivekananda once said that

> the ideal man is he who, in the midst of the greatest silence and solitude, finds the intensest activity, and in the midst of the intensest activity finds the silence and solitude of the desert. He has learnt the secret of restraint, he has controlled himself.
>
> (Vivekananda 2013: 2692)

Such attitude, which is neither brought about by policies nor pressed by needs, translates into an inner mutation that is capable of transforming the relationship with the environment. In his study of the Karma Yoga, Vivekananda says that 'we think that man "lives to eat" and not "eats to live". We are continually making this mistake' and 'makes us work not from freedom, but like slaves' (Vivekananda 2013: 2993). The balance with the environment begins, thus, by balancing our interior environment. Our slavery, or ruin, is largely grounded in an excessive clinging to fleeting values and principles. Our freedom is thus largely based in the possibility of ascending to a higher plane in terms of understanding the world and the being. What we must know is whether we will really be capable of thus dealing with our deep anxieties.

References

Allchin, J. R. 1995. 'The End of Harappan Urbanism and It's Legacy', in F. R. Allchin (ed.), *The Archaeology of Early Historic South Asia: The Emergence of Cities and States* (26–40). Cambridge: Cambridge University Press.

Ambiente Brasil. 2015, http://ambientes.ambientebrasil.com.br/fauna/trafico_de_animais_silvestres/trafico_de_animais_silvestres.html.

Andrada e Silva, José Bonifácio. 1825. *Representação àAssembléia Geral Constituinte do Império do Brasil sobre a Escravatura*. Paris: Firmin Didot.

Brasil, Ministério do Meio Ambiente. 2015a. www.mma.gov.br/biomas/mata-atlantica.

Brasil, Ministério do Meio Ambiente. 2015b. www.mma.gov.br/images/arquivo/80120/PPCDAm/MODELO%20LOGICO%20PPCDAM%20 2012%20-%20site.png.

Collingwood, R. G. 1949. *The Idea of Nature*. London: Clarendon Press.

Dales, G. F. 1965. 'Civilization and Floods in the Indus Valley', *Expedition*, 7 (2): 10–19.

Furley, David. 2005. 'Aristotle the Philosopher of Nature', in David Furley (ed.), *Routledge History of Philosophy*, vol. 2 (9–39). London: Routledge.

Krech III, Shepard (ed.) 2003. *Encyclopedia of World Environmental History*, vol. 1. London: Routledge.

Leroi-Gourhan, André. 1979. *O Gesto e a Palavra 2 – Memórias e Ritmo*. Lisboa: Edicões 70.

Livingstone, David. 2000. 'Ecology and the Environment', in Gary Ferngren (ed.), *The History of Science and Religion in the Western Tradition: An Encyclopedia* (491–497). New York: Garland.

Lovelock, James. 1979. *Gaia: A New Look at Life on Earth*. Oxford: Oxford University Press.

McKillop, Heather. 2004. *The Ancient Maya: New Perspectives*. Santa Barbara: ABC Clio.

Moncrief, Lewis W. 1970. 'The Cultural Basis of Our Environmental Crisis', *Science*, 170: 508–512.

Nederman, Cary J. 2005. 'Organicism', in Maryanne Horowitz (ed.), *New Dictionary of the History of Ideas* (1672–1674). Farmington Hills, MI: Thomson Gale.

Raikes, R. L. 1965. 'The Mohenjo-Daro Floods', *Antiquity*, 39: 196–203.

Russell, Colin. 2000. 'Views of Nature', in Gary Ferngren (ed.), *The History of Science and Religion in the Western Tradition: An Encyclopedia* (43–50). New York: Garland.

SOS Mata Atlântica. 2015, www.sosma.org.br/nossa-causa/a-mata-atlantica/.

United States Department of Agriculture, 2015. www.ers.usda.gov/topics/international-markets-trade/countries-regions/brazil/trade.aspx.

Vivekananda, Swami. 2013. *The Complete Works of Swami Vivekananda*. Vol. 1–9. Advaita Asharama.

White, Lynn. 1967. 'The Historic Roots of Our Ecologic Crisis', *Science*, 155: 1203–1207.

6 Globalisation, environment and sustainable development

Challenges and opportunities in the conservation of water catchments in south-eastern Kenya

Benson M. O. Agaya

Kenya's forest cover is estimated at 6% of the total land area with primary (natural) forest accounting for 1.2% of land area and yet goods and services derived directly or indirectly from forests account for a significant proportion of the national economy (FAO 2010). According to the United Nations Environment Programme (UNEP 2009: 4), about 70% of Kenya's domestic energy comes from wood and 95% is collected from forests and rangelands. In addition to providing a variety of wood and non-timber products, Kenya's forests provide a range of ecosystem services. These include trapping and storing rainwater, regulating river flows and preventing flooding, helping recharge groundwater tables, improving soil fertility, and reducing soil erosion and sediment loads in river waters (ibid.). In addition, forests not only provide essential wildlife habitats but also serve as sites of important traditionally cultural ceremonies as well as sacred sites to local communities.

Apart from forests, it is estimated that roughly 42% of the country's gross domestic product (GDP) is derived from natural resource sectors, such as agriculture, mining, forestry, fishing and tourism, while 42% of the total employment comes from small-scale agriculture and pastoralism (UNEP 2014: 2). In particular, the United Nations Environmental Programme (UNEP 2012) reports that Kenya's water catchments or 'water towers' and forests contribute more than 3.6% of national GDP. Thus, the economic benefits of forest ecosystem services are more than four times higher than the short-term gains of deforestation. Sustainable forest management and utilisation is important not only for local community livelihoods, water security, energy security and food security but also for regional peace and stability in the larger East Africa region. This is because many of these ecosystems transcend international boundaries. Since Kenya shares borders with five other East African countries (Ethiopia, South Sudan, Uganda, United Republic of Tanzania, and Somalia), many of its ecosystems and natural resources are trans-boundary (UNEP 2009). For instance, Kenya shares one main protected area with Uganda, Mount Elgon National Park; and two with Tanzania, the Maasai Mara and Tsavo West (see Figure 6.2). In particular, the ecology of the 1,510 km² Maasai Mara Game Reserve that is one of the greatest regions of migrating wildlife in the world is supported by the Mau forest and water catchments known also as the 'Mau complex' located in Kenya.

Global and regional importance of Kenya's forests

The United States Agency for International Development (USAID 2014) observes that Kenya's rich biodiversity attracts hundreds of thousands of tourists each year. The agency further recognises that tourism is the second highest revenue earner, accounting for 12% of gross domestic product. It therefore notes that conservation and sustainable management of this natural capital is an important strategy for Kenya's economic growth. The protection of Kenya's water catchments or water towers thus forms a crucial component of this strategy. This is because the watersheds feed hydropower, support wildlife and tourism destinations, irrigate both export and smallholder farms, and nurture grazing areas (UNEP 2009). The environment thus underpins economic vitality, including future tourism growth. South-eastern Kenya, for example, is home to the largest wildlife park in the country, Tsavo National Park. This ecological zone consisting mainly of the Chyulu, Taita and Shimba Hills forests and water catchments supports the vital beach and wildlife tourism in south-eastern Kenya including the key port city of Mombasa.

According to Woodley (2008), the entire Tsavo ecosystem comprising the Tsavo National Park that is divided into Tsavo East and Tsavo West by the main Mombasa-Nairobi road and also includes the South Kitui National Reserve and Chyulu Hills National Park makes it one of the largest coherent conservation areas in Africa. UNEP (2009: 70) further reports that Tsavo West Park covers 7,065 km², which represents about 30% of Kenya's total area under parks. Tsavo West joins Tanzania's Mkomazi Game Reserve (MGR), which lies in north-eastern Tanzania between the coast and Mount Kilimanjaro, and forms the southern limit of the Tsavo ecosystem. The springs at the foot of Mount Kilimanjaro, especially the Mzima Springs, feed the Tsavo River that flows through Tsavo West (ibid.). On their part, Deeble and Stone (2001) describe Mzima Springs as a series of four natural springs in Tsavo National Park whose source is a natural reservoir under the Chyulu Hills to the north.

According to UNEP (2009: 70) Kenya's border with Tanzania bisects the 30 km^2 Lake Jipe, at the south-west corner of Tsavo West. It is a trans-boundary water body of global and local significance for a number of reasons: it is a Ramsar wetland of international importance; it is an essential permanent water reservoir for wildlife in the two national parks; it supports a thriving fishing and water transport businesses; and it is the only place in the world where the *Oreochromis jipe* fish, now on the verge of extinction, lives. The UNEP analysis, however, reveals that the lake has been drying up, threatening people's livelihoods and the health and survival of dependent wildlife. The assessment shows that the lake lost about half of its water mass between 1996 and 2006 and siltation and salinity levels rose dramatically (ibid.). The UNEP assessment further reveals that its water catchment continues to be degraded by farmlands and water diversions from the River Lumi, and it suffers from the proliferation of the typha weed, which at one point covered 65% to 80% of the lake.

Challenges to ecological diversity and water catchments in Kenya

Despite the importance of the national resource base for large proportions of the Kenyan population, its neighbours, and the global community as shown above, the environment is under threat from a variety of sources. Among the challenges are encroachment into the forested areas that make up Kenya's main watersheds and seriously degrading these catchments as neighbouring local populations fell trees for fuel, expand into new farming areas, and create settlements and pastures (UNEP 2009: 107). Hsu et al. (2014: 79) observe that in many nations the high rates of forest loss is attributed to economic development goals that tend to override social and environmental concerns associated with deforestation and other human land use activities. They further note that given the global importance of forests, it is imperative that countries strive to curb deforestation and bolster protection of these valuable ecosystems. They also emphasise that it is only through a widespread and concerted global effort to reduce the loss of these ecosystems that the future of forests can be ensured (ibid.: 80).

A report by the International Fund for Animal Welfare (IFAW 2009: 16) indicates that according to officials at Tsavo West National Park, the volume of water discharged daily at the Mzima Springs has been declining over the years due to illegal logging, charcoal burning and other destructive activities on the nearby Chyulu Hills. According to IFAW, most of the areas adjoining the Tsavo Parks lack adequate rainfall for arable farming and as a consequence, poverty levels are high and standards of living low. Many people turn to charcoal burning, bush meat and even armed poaching to make ends meet, placing great pressure on biodiversity and if this trend continues unabated, the consequences would be dire for Tsavo East and West National Parks and Kenya's coastal region which mainly depend on water from the Mzima Springs (ibid.: 14).

According to USAID (2000: 20), even though forests of high cultural and subsistence significance to the Kenyan people such as the Kaya forests of the coast are now protected by local custom for sacred ceremonies of nearby villages, this cultural protection does not guarantee their safety, however. Tree poaching and clear-cutting are commonly reported even from culturally protected forests. The agency notes that this is hardly surprising considering such extremes of poverty among the local populations. Citing Kamweti (1999), USAID (2000: 21) identifies four common constraints to the conservation of forest resources in Kenya. They include high population pressure that puts enormous strains on limited resources; inadequate involvement of local communities, including lack of incentives for local people to conserve indigenous forests; limited alternative resources to offset pressure on forest resources; and low agricultural yields as a result of which forest land is encroached (i.e. excision to make room for food production).

One of the most common threats to sustainable forest and water catchments management is fuel wood and charcoal use. Charcoal for instance remains one of the most popular fuels among urban residents in Kenya providing ready market for rural manufacturers of this product. Another common threat to forest management in Kenya is degazetting and encroachment. In some instances political interests tend to motivate public officials to abet or ignore groups that encroach into protected areas and water catchments in return for votes or political support. However, in most situations the encroachments are illegal and involve harvesting of timber for construction and other uses, crop farming and creation of human settlements.

Theorising globalisation

The forgoing analysis of the importance and challenges to the environment and natural resources particularly in the south east of Kenya therefore calls attention to need to theorise on globalisation and explore its links to ecological resources in Kenya. There are many conflicting perspectives on environment and economic life in the developing countries especially with respect to globalisation. One of the most common approaches to this subject draws on the Marxist tradition and broadly perceives globalisation from the 'loser perspective' suggesting that globalisation does not hold any benefits for the third world. For instance critics question the argument that the rapid expansion of the neo-liberal market economy to the remotest parts of the world necessarily supports the mobility of goods and access to information, science and technology for the benefit of developing countries.

Wangari et al. (2005) argue that although proponents of globalisation see it as a means of expanding market economy with tremendous benefits such as investments, employment and incomes to developing economies, submerged in this rhetoric of economic growth, are unequal social relations between the first and the third world. According to them, developing economies do not benefit from globalisation due to unequal competition from goods produced in technologically advanced economies, exploitation of cheap labour and resources by transnational corporations originating from the developed societies, and imposition of non-tariff barriers on trade with the latter economies (ibid.: 292).

Robinson (2008: 125) points out that there is nearly no field of knowledge or human experience that has not been touched by globalisation. He observes that the ubiquity of the effects of globalisation and the expansive breadth and depth of research on the phenomenon present enormous challenges in theorising about globalisation. Robinson nevertheless identifies two patterns of theorising and interpretations of the meaning and impact of globalisation on human societies. The first he observes is the set of theories that associate globalisation with expanding worldwide inequalities, new modes of exploitation and domination, displacement, marginalisation, ecological holocaust and anti-globalisation movements (ibid.: 126). The alternative theories on the other hand are those that relate globalisation with the process that creates prosperity, freedom, emancipation and democracy.

The ontological assumptions based on the first category of theories is that globalisation is essentially an instrument of hegemony, division, exploitation and impoverishment particularly to the less dominant, low-income and less technologically advanced societies. The converse is that globalisation is liberating, integrating, empowering and enriching to all societies that embrace it. From the epistemological standpoint, there are theories that interpret globalisation on the basis of ideational or subjective determinacy and those that interpret it on the basis of material determinacy. Depending on whether they are materially or ideationally oriented, these theories emphasise different domains of economics, politics and culture as constituting the core of the process of globalisation. Whatever their ontological and epistemological claims, these theories of globalisation are largely grounded in the broader theoretical traditions such as Marxism, Weberianism and functionalism. However, considering the multifaceted and multidisciplinary nature of globalisation, it would not be useful to attempt a classification of theories but rather to select appropriate theoretical discourses that would apply to the subject of environment and natural resource management in Kenya.

Manuel Castells's network society theory as cited by Robinson (2008: 132) suggest itself as one of the most appropriate frameworks for explaining environmental change and its impacts in the early 21st century. The thrust of Castells's theory is that developments in information technology in the late 20th century not only fostered a new 'mode of development' otherwise known as 'informationalism' but also reshaped capitalism thereby ushering in a new system of 'information capitalism' also referred to as the 'new economy'. This new economy has three dimensions: (1) informational, knowledge-based; (2) global, in that production is organised on a global scale; and (3) networked, in that productivity is generated through global networks of interaction (ibid.: 132).

Another important theoretical perspective on globalisation is that which is advanced by Kellner (2002). Kellner identifies two dominant although contrasting perspectives on the concept of globalisation in the literature. According to him, the first perspective is that globalisation represents the continuation of modernisation as fostered throughout the industrial capitalism period but intensifying capturing attention of researchers from the 1990s. From this perspective globalisation is presented as a force of progress, increased wealth, freedom, democracy, and happiness. The contrary view is that globalisation is a cover concept for global capitalism and imperialism, implying that it is a channel for the imposition of the logic of capital and the market on ever more regions of the world and spheres of life (ibid.). Critics therefore view globalisation not only as negative due to its tendency to perpetuate domination and control of the wealthier developed nations over the poor developing countries but also for encouraging increased destruction of natural species and the environment.

These contestations notwithstanding, Kellner (2002: 286) advances the critical theory of globalisation and adopts a dialectical framework that distinguishes between its progressive and emancipatory features and oppressive and negative attributes. He therefore rejects technological and economic determinism and all one-sided optics of globalisation that have tended to dominate explanations of the phenomenon. Kellner thus argues that the key to understanding globalisation critically is theorising it at once as a product of technological revolution and the global restructuring of capitalism in which economic, technological, political and cultural features are intertwined. The central arguments of this theory is that technology is not the sole organising principle of society but rather the synthesis of technology and capital is the organising principle of globalisation. Kellner employs the concept of techno-capitalism to emphasise that critical theory of globalisation grounds globalisation in a theory of capitalist restructuring and technological revolution (ibid.: 289). The emphasis therefore are on both the increasingly important role of technology and the enduring primacy of capitalist relations of production.

It is evident from the forgoing analysis that Castells's and Kellner's are not mutually opposed theories of globalisation but Kellner's is a variant of Castells's theoretical approach. The network society theory therefore provides a sound basis for harnessing information technology within the framework of community action plans to realise resilient, equitable and pro-poor development though investments that reduce natural resources dependency, lessen environmental degradation and promote Kenya's global competitiveness (UNEP 2015). One of the ways to achieve these goals is to develop a robust system of regulations and standards. This would involve eco-labelling and embracing technical standards related to product standards and labelling. It would also involve providing support to assist producers, especially small and medium enterprises (SMEs), achieve these standards and to increase their competitiveness in international trade where such standards are increasingly being applied.

Globalisation and environment

According to Huwart and Loïc (2013: 112) globalisation, which is partly synonymous with rising international trade, has fostered the rapid production, trade and consumption of material goods in unprecedented quantities. This, they argue, has resulted in a huge eco-logical footprint of human activities around the world. In environment conservation and natural resource management terms, ecological footprint is the measure of human demand on the Earth's ecosystems. Although many of these challenges including loss of biodiversity may only have an indirect link with globalisation, Huwart and Loïc (2013: 115) point out that globalisation implies the multiplication of distribution channels, creating new needs and new demand for products that are used around the world. They observe that it accentuates industrialisation and the quest for and exploitation of new lands and natural resources, thereby weakening many ecosystems. For example popular taste for exotic wood furniture and other utensils has pushed some kinds of wood, like teak, into the threatened species category. Likewise sandalwood is threatened by the global expansion of the cosmetic and pharmaceutical industry.

One of the main environmental problems emerging alongside globalisation is climate change. Climate change is a problem mostly associated with the greenhouse effect – meaning the excessive retention of solar energy in the atmosphere due to an accumulation of certain gases, particularly carbon dioxide. Apart from industrial production and transportation, carbon dioxide emissions are also indirectly linked to deforestation. Deforestation, for example, is not only associated with reduced volume of carbon dioxide that trees convert into oxygen but also with declining farm yields due to resultant unreliable rain patterns as well as flooding (Huwart and Loïc 2013: 114). These problems, they observe, tend to disproportionately affect the poor and vulnerable populations.

Although many of the environmental challenges enumerated above can be associated with the globalisation process, it is also important to recognise that globalisation has some clear benefits for environment conservation. For instance, it increases awareness of the need to conserve biodiversity, hence the growing number of protected natural areas worldwide since the last century. Huwart and Loïc (2013: 119) have in this respect pointed out that globalisation can also help lessen and prevent environmental damage by, for example, utilising international trade to help spread the most sophisticated environmental solutions far and wide. They emphasise that globalised research and innovation can help promote sources of 'green growth' and are particularly effective instruments to fight environmental degradation. It therefore requires the combined efforts of national political decision makers, researchers and academics, private entrepreneurs and communities to take pro-environmental measures to prevent or repair the environmental damage arising, in part, from globalisation.

The latter arguments resonate with Frankel's (2003) observations that fears that globalisation necessarily hurts the environment are not well-founded. He points out that arguments that openness to international trade undermines national attempts at environmental regulation are not backed by any empirical observations or statistics. He stresses that people care about both the environment and the economy and that as real incomes rise, their demand for environmental quality rises. This translates into environmental progress under the right conditions – democracy, effective regulation and externalities such as pollution and environment degradation that are largely confined within national borders and are therefore amenable to national regulation.

Frankel points out that whereas it is widely accepted that the direct effects of globalisation on the economy are positive, as measured by GDP, concerns rise more with regard to 'noneconomic' effects of globalisation. He observes that the question that often triggers this debate is whether globalisation helps or hurts in achieving the best trade-off between environmental and economic goals. Noting that globalisation is a complex trend, encompassing many forces and many effects, it would be surprising if all of them were always unfavourable to the environment, or all of them favourable (Frankel 2003: 4). Further, he questions the argument of the anti-globalisation movements that seem to suggest that the capacity of individual states to defend national sovereignty and to protect the environment would be enhanced without the intrusion of globalisation. He emphasises that it is an illusion to think that environmental issues could be effectively addressed if each country were insulated against incursions into its national sovereignty at the hands of international trade or the WTO (ibid.: 4). He contrasts this argument with the observation that increasingly, people living in one country want to protect the air, water, forests and animals not just in their own countries, but also in other countries as well. For such efforts to succeed, he argues, international cooperation is required. He further suggests that in such circumstances national sovereignty is the obstacle to such efforts, not the ally. Likewise multilateral institutions are a potential ally, not the obstacle.

Frankel thus suggests that the highest priority should be to determine ways in which globalisation can be successfully harnessed to promote protection of the environment, along with other shared objectives, as opposed to degradation of the environment. He identifies three practical ways in which globalisation could be used to support environment conservation and natural resource management. The first step is to strengthen the exercise of consumer power. This strategy accords with the growing worldwide trend toward labelling, codes of corporate conduct, and other ways that environmentally conscious consumers can use their purchasing power to give expression and weight to their wishes. In his view these tools would not be effective without international trade. The second mechanism would be use multilateral rules to govern international cooperation on environment issues. These negotiated multilateral environmental management and monitoring systems would be employed reasonably to balance both economic and environmental objectives. The third objective would be to encourage countries to learn from others' experiences. This strategy would draw on the cross-country accumulated statistical evidence that demonstrate how globalisation and growth would affect environmental objectives on average, even without multilateral institutions (ibid.: 5). They would for instance leverage on environmentally sound processes and production methods (PPM) to gain international competitive advantage.

Green growth strategy to water catchments management in Kenya

Since a large percentage of Kenya's total land area (approximately 80%) is semi-arid or arid, the country relies heavily on its forests as the only protector of its critical water catchment areas (UNEP 2015: 6). Conservation International, for instance, has designated the Eastern Arc Mountains, including Kenya's Taita Hills forests, a part of the South Eastern Kenya ecological zone, among its top 25 global 'hotspots' for urgently needed protection. The Taita Hills is a major water catchment area and high source of plant endemism, surrounded on all sides by plains, and its richly diverse resources are just beginning to be recognised within Kenya as being in need of monitoring and protection. The term 'biodiversity hotspot' is attributed to the British biologist Norman Myers who coined it in 1988 to refer to a bio-geographic region characterised both by exceptional levels of plant endemism and by serious levels of habitat loss associated with human activities (Conservation International 2007).

The conservation of the vital ecological resources described in part two of this chapter has taken the green economy approach. The thrust of this strategy according to Gakuru and Khainga (2013: 8) is to align economic growth with socioeconomic and environmental challenges related to climate change, natural resource depletion, inequality, and loss of biodiversity and ecosystem services. The strategy is to not only ensure that social and economic programs confirm to national laws and policies but also fulfil the country's international obligations on sustainable exploitation, utilisation, management and conservation of the environment and natural resources.

In order to secure broad based support for effective management of forests and water catchments, World Wildlife Fund, Eastern Africa Regional Program Office (WWF EARPO 2006: 2) recognises the need to involve communities and the private sector especially with respect to overcoming barriers to sustainable forest management and decreasing pressure on natural forest ecosystem.

The model for sustainable forests and water catchments is graphically illustrated in Figure 6.1. It incorporates internationally recognised and agreed standards and practices as shown with appropriate modifications and adaptations to local contexts.

The objectives to be realised through this model include creating consultation forums with key stakeholders to develop and build consensus concerning strategies to establish diversified and sustainable local economies in the south-eastern Kenya ecological zone. The model also provides the basis for development of projects in agriculture, bio enterprises, and SMEs that support the realisation of sustainable forests and water catchments management, conservation and utilisation. Further, the model establishes an economic strategy to implement

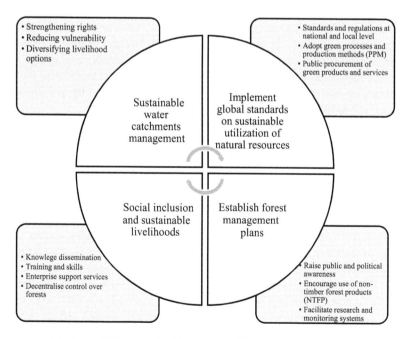

Figure 6.1 A model for sustainable forest and biodiversity management

Source: Prepared by the author

selected projects in conformity with international standards and regulations as well as green processes and production methods.

Results of sustainable forest and water catchments management strategies

Some of the key achievements of the sustainable forest and water catchments management strategy in south-eastern Kenya are in the areas of agro-forestry, agriculture (in particular, beekeeping and goat rearing), and non-timber forest products (NTFPs) and services which the Millennium Ecosystem Assessment estimates accounts for up to 96% of the value of forests (Convention on Biodiversity {CBD} 2009: 23). It is also widely recognised that this sustainability model taps into the vast resources of traditional knowledge of uses of forests for medicine and food that rests with women to achieve gender inclusivity in natural resource utilisation and conservation.

Agro-forestry for instance involves a wide range of trees grown on farms and in rural landscapes. These trees include fertiliser trees for land regeneration, soil health and food security, fruit trees for nutrition, and fodder trees that improve smallholder livestock production (CBD 2009: 17). The convention further describes the benefits of agro-forestry to humans as providing additional income, increasing food security through a higher diversity of agricultural products (e.g. fruits, nuts, medicinal plants and edible oils), providing fuel wood and construction material and thus reducing deforestation, and by stabilising soil and water tables.

Apart from agro-forestry, another area of achievement is in the utilisation of NTFP that significantly contributes to a reduction in exploitation and destruction of forests. This approach generates products such as hats, mats, baskets, brooms and roof thatch for homes in addition to providing alternative sources of income to households that would otherwise turn to destructive practices like charcoal and firewood production and sales.

USAID (2014) has similarly reported tremendous achievement in the promotion of local and long-term resource management that helps Kenyans who live in or around Kenya's national forests and parks to establish nature-based enterprises that preserve, rather than deplete, natural resources. The agency reports that in 2013, 65,000 men and women participating in biodiversity programs earned up to KSh 224.4 million ($2.54 million) in income from a variety of conservation enterprises – ecotourism, women's butterfly farming and crafts exports, sale of seedlings and honey, livestock business, and payment for environmental services. Nature-based enterprises are also known to provide employment to an estimated 13% of residents of south-eastern Kenya who surveys previously showed had no defined employment or source of income (Kenya Water Towers Agency (KWTA) 2015).

The inclusion of local communities in the forest resource management and conservation trusts are also critical to monitoring threats to forests and water catchments by undertaking prompt intervention measures especially with respect to deforestation. Other important outcomes of these initiatives are the development of ecotourism facilities and in particular the production of wood carvings for sale to local and international tourists. They also include the development of bird watching sites and nature walk facilities both for recreation and income generation.

Summary

One of the critical debates on the subject of globalisation is the question of its impacts on natural resources and environment. The analysis affirms that the environment is intrinsically linked to economic development, providing natural resources that fuel growth and ecosystem services that underpin both life and livelihoods. Further considering that the economy of most societies are increasingly globalised, it is not in doubt that globalisation has relevance to the environment and economy of the societies in south-eastern Kenya. With regard to the question as to whether globalisation holds any tangible benefits for the poor and marginal groups in developing countries, the finding is that it does help reduce direct reliance on natural resource by the poor and offering alternatives through value chain development. The third and final finding is that micro and small enterprise development supported by appropriate technologies are instrumental in opening up international markets and employment opportunities for communities occupying critical environmental zones such as the water catchments of south-eastern Kenya.

Conclusion

As our analysis has shown, it is possible not only to reconcile globalisation and conservation of the environment, but also to act so that globalisation becomes a vector of green growth. This analysis demonstrates, for example, that globalisation can be successfully harnessed to promote protection of the environment especially by utilising the

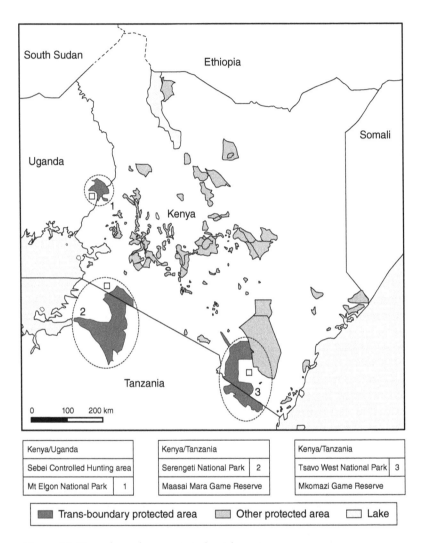

Figure 6.2 Trans-boundary protected catchment area
Source: Map prepared by the author

globally negotiated and set standards and regulations and monitoring frameworks. In addition, the national plans on natural resource management and nature-based enterprises also provide useful avenues for using the thrust of globalisation to the advantage of the poor communities in developing countries.

References

Conservation International. 2007. 'Biodiversity Hotspots', *The Encyclopaedia of Earth*, www.eoearth.org/view/article/150569/, accessed on 28/11/2015.

Convention on Biodiversity (CBD). 2009. *Sustainable Forest Management: Biodiversity and Livelihoods – A Good Practice Guide*. CBD/IUCN.

Deeble, M. and Stone, V. 2001. *Kenya's Mzima Spring Comes Alive*. New York: National Geographic, http://ngm.nationalgeographic.com/ngm/data/2001/11/01, accessed on 28/11/2015.

Frankel, J. A. 2003. *The Environment and Globalisation, Working Paper 10090*. Cambridge, MA: National Bureau of Economic Research.

Gakuru, R. and Khainga, D. 2013. 'A Green Growth Path for Kenya: Opportunities, Challenges and Risks', *Policy Monitor*, 5 (2): 8–10.

Hsu, A., Emerson, J., Levy, M., de Sherbinin, A., Johnson, L., Malik, O., Schwartz, J. and Jaiteh, M. 2014. *The 2014 Environmental Performance Index*. New Haven, CT: Yale Center for Environmental Law & Policy.

Huwart, J. and Loïc, V. 2013. 'What Is the Impact of Globalisation on the Environment?' in *Economic Globalisation: Origins and Consequences* (108–125). OECD Publishing.

International Fund for Animal Welfare (IFAW). 2009. *Tsavo: Small Steps, Big Impacts July 2007–June 2008*. Nairobi: IFAW.

Kellner, Douglas. 2002. Theorizing Globalization, *Sociological Theory*, 20 (3): 285–305.

Kenya Water Towers Agency. 2015. 'Community Development Action Plan for Chyulu Hills Water Tower', KWTA Report.

Robinson, William I. 2008. 'Theories of Globalization', in George Ritzer (ed.), *The Blackwell Companion to Globalization* (125–143). John Wiley & Sons.

United Nations Food and Agriculture Organization. 2010. *Kenya Forest Information and Data*. Rome: FAO.

United Nations Environment Programme. 2009. *Kenya: Atlas of Our Changing Environment*. Nairobi: UNEP.

United Nations Environment Programme. 2012. *Water Towers, Forests and Green Economy: Outcome of the First High Level National Dialogue in Kenya*. UNEP: Nairobi, 5–7 November 2012.

United Nations Environment Programme. 2014. *Green Economy Assessment Report – Kenya*. Nairobi: UNEP.

United Nations Environment Programme. 2015. *Green Economy Scoping Study: Kenya*. Nairobi: UNEP.

United States Agency for International Development. 2000. *USAID/Kenya Strategic Plan: Environmental Threats and Opportunities Assessment*. Washington, DC: USAID.

United States Agency for International Development/Kenya. 2014. *Environment and Natural Resources Management*. Washington, DC: USAID.

Wangari, E., Kamau, W. and Kinyau, A. M. 2005. 'Globalization in the Third World: Impact on Women's Land Rights and Education', *Kenya Forum on Public Policy*, 1 (3): 290–304.

Woodley, D. 2008. *Tsavo Trilogy – The Nature & Landscape Book*. Vienna: Severin.

World Wildlife Fund. 2006. *Poverty and Environment Issues: Governance Institutions, Institutional Frameworks and Opportunities for Communities*. Nairobi: WWF Eastern African Region Program Office (EARPO) & Broadcast Solutions International Ltd (*BSI*).

7 The glocal paradox
Waste production in Patna

Aditya Raj and Papia Raj

While waste production is as old as human society, the nature of waste produced has changed with time. Earlier waste materials were from the natural habitat or body parts of species. These wastes were mostly biodegradable. With time, the waste generated in our society has become more complex. Now, waste production is guided more by materialistic needs of people than subsistence livelihood practices. Industrial revolution has led to a spurt of production and consumption that has been the key factor influencing an exponential rise in waste. The problem is accentuated in developing country like India. Here, the rapidly rising waste production is due to three interrelated factors: high rates of population growth, rapid urbanisation, and a more sophisticated form of consumerism. On an average a resident in developing countries produce up to 0.79 kg of waste per day (Hoornweg et al. 2012). The sources of these wastes include industrial, construction, biomedical, as well as municipal solid waste from households, hotels, resorts, restaurants, and other businesses. The waste, therefore, is composed of both organic and inorganic materials such as paper, soil, metal, plastics, glass, stone, wood, cardboard, textiles, and tires. Projections show that over the coming decades both per capita waste production rates and population size will increase, leading to even bigger challenges for relatively low income cities and countries, which currently contribute up to 35% of the total waste production in the world (ibid.).

The study

This chapter draws from the fieldwork which was conducted as part of the project, Waste Management Training to Reduce Health Hazards of Solid Wastes in Patna, funded by the Centre for Energy and Environment, Indian Institute of Technology Patna. Patna, being the capital city of Bihar, has experienced a very high rate of population growth coupled with rapid urbanisation and increased consumption – all these factors together are responsible for making it the 'Garbage City'. As a consequence, Patna faces the dual problem of extreme waste generation and poor quality of management of these wastes. For a nuanced understanding of the situation, a survey was conducted in New Capital/ Nutan Anchal region of Patna. It covers more than half of the total area of the city and has the highest population thus generating maximum amount of solid waste. It is also this milieu which has the most unplanned waste disposal. The fieldwork was conducted between 2014 and 2015. A stratified random sampling method was used to choose respondents for the study, ensuring it was most representative of the region. Though both quantitative as well as qualitative methods were used to generate information for the project, in this chapter we specifically focus on information gathered from in-depth interviews, focus group discussions, and participant observations focusing on the behavioural practices of the community responsible for waste production.

It is pertinent to define that in this article we focus only on solid waste, which is defined as the unwanted or useless solid materials generated from combined residential, industrial, and commercial activities in a given area. It may be categorised according to its origin (domestic, industrial, commercial, construction, or institutional); according to its contents (organic material, glass, metal, plastic, paper, etc.) or according to hazard potential (toxic, non-toxic, flammable, radioactive, infectious, etc.). Within various solid wastes, we specifically focus on municipal solid waste (MSW), which is commercial and residential waste generated in municipal or municipal notified areas in either solid or semi-solid form, excluding industrial hazardous wastes but including treatable bio-medical waste (Municipal Solid Wastes Management and Handling Rules 2000).

We situate this study within the broader framework that locates the interplay between globalisation processes and local culture generating waste production in a specific geographic locale. It is certainly necessary and, complementary, to the focus on production and consumption that have been central to sociology. Emphasis on waste, as Fagan (2003) indicates, is urgently needed as it is vital for understanding the relationship between social and environmental change induced by globalisation.

Contextualising the study

'Globalisation' is a key buzzword in today's world. It is used by journalists, politicians, business executives, academics, and others to signify that the world is changing rapidly, giving rise to a new world order in terms of economics, politics, and culture. In academic circles, however, it was not recognised as a significant concept until the 1980s (Robertson 1992). Hoogvelt (1997) states that in the mid-1980s 'globalisation' began to replace terms such as 'internationalisation' and 'transnationalisation' as a more suitable concept for describing the ever-intensifying networks of cross-border human interactions. Since then, it has become one of the most discussed and debated concepts in the social sciences and, not surprisingly, is frequently defined differently across disciplines. Typically, globalisation is described as increased economic, cultural, environmental, and social interdependencies, along with new transnational financial and political formations, arising out of the increasing mobility of capital, labour, and information, with both homogenising and differentiating tendencies (Yeung 1998; Kellner 2000; Mittelman 2001). Giddens (1990) summarises globalisation aptly when he suggests that globalisation can be defined as the intensification of worldwide social relations that link distant localities in such a way that local happenings are shaped by distant events, occurring many kilometres away and vice versa.

Other notable definitions of globalisation can be found in the works of sociologist Ronald Robertson (1992) and geographer David Harvey (1989). McGrew (1992) provides another balanced, but different, view of globalisation. He describes globalisation as the multiplicity of linkages and interconnections between the states and societies that make up the modern world system. Thus, globalisation describes the process by which events, decisions, and activities in one part of the world can come to have significant consequences for individuals and communities in quite distant other parts of the world. He states that the two distinct dimensions of globalisation are scope (or stretching) and intensity (or deepening). Based on these dimensions, on the one hand globalisation defines a set of processes that operate worldwide and thereby he assigns a spatial connotation to the concept. On the other hand, globalisation also implies intensification in the levels of interaction, interconnectedness or interdependence between states and societies that constitute the world community. Accordingly, stretching and deepening of global processes occurs simultaneously.

While numerous debates have emerged with respect to globalisation, central to many nowadays is the question of the nation state's role in the contemporary global world. According to one school of thought the power of the state has declined and that in the globalised world, there is a common consumer culture that unifies all people (Appadurai 1999; Valentine 2001; Grant and Short 2002), while few others believe that globalisation is a 'myth' (Dicken 1994; Hirst and Thompson 1996; Newman 2006). Yet another school of thought takes a more moderate 'middle path' and suggests that globalisation transforms the power relations between the nation state and international powers but that the state remains an important agent (Luke 1994; Dicken 1998; Yeung 1998; Kelly 1999; Held 2000). They argue that globalisation is a contradictory process that will proceed hand in hand with uneven spatial development and that these processes will be realised in institutionally, historically, and geographically specific sites. Based on these arguments, they tend to favour the concept of *glocalisation*. Robertson (1995: 28) has defined glocalisation as 'the processes that telescope the global and local (scales) to make a blend'. This idea acknowledges the dominance of large, powerful corporations acting on the global scale, as well as the characteristics of particular communities and regions (Luke 1994; Peck and Tickell 1994; Cox 1997; Mittelman 2001). Glocalisation is hence the double movement of globalisation processes on the one hand and localisation processes on the other. Cox (1997) and Mittelman (2001) argue that geographical differences in the character of the market prevail despite the supposedly homogenising influence of globalisation due to local cultural variations or regulatory discontinuities. Hannerz (1996) strengthens the argument by stating that in cultural life one experiences the development of cultural ecumene resulting in multiple hybrid cultures and identities. It is our contention that the ongoing global processes of consumption are a major cause resulting in increased volume of waste generation in Patna (read local).

Patna is the capital city of Bihar which, according to Das (1992), is the land of paradoxes. Das, in his book the *Republic of Bihar*, recognises that here wealth exists but there is no investment because of lawlessness. In Bihar, plenty also takes a back seat to the comfort of middlemen and landlords. This is about the land, we ponder, which has been renowned in the past for good education, good governance, and worthy ways of life. The history of ancient India is the history of ancient Bihar (Thapar 1966). But unfortunately, all these significant achievements appear to have left no living legacy for contemporary Bihar. If there are few millimetres of rain in the state capital, Patna, residents are fearful that the city will soon resemble a flooded locale, as the drainage system of the city is in abysmal state. To reiterate, there is filth and stink everywhere, including the New Capital/*Nutan Anchal* region (the study area) where the relatively rich and the affluent reside. Several bureaucrats and political leaders live in this area.

Many national and international non-governmental organisations have their regional offices in this part of the city.

Analysing the current situation

Various studies (Huntley 2010) have noted that MSW is the most difficult source of solid waste to manage because of its diverse range of composite materials. A considerable portion of these wastes consists of organic matter resulting from the preparation and consumption of food, including vegetable peelings and leftover food. It also consists of plastics, paper, glass, textiles, cellophane, metals, and some hazardous waste from household products such as paint, garden pesticides, pharmaceuticals, fluorescent tubes, personal care products, batteries containing heavy metals, and discarded wood treated with dangerous substances such as anti-fungal and anti-termite chemicals. In the recent past there has been an increased focus to address issues related to solid waste management in developing countries, especially in terms of methods of disposal, recycling, and treatment of waste. However, none of the studies till date have accounted for the factors that lead to production of waste as practices of everyday lifestyle within a specific socio-cultural milieu.

Our research affirms that MSW generations are result of practices of everyday life. Therefore, MSW management is a complex issue due to changing lifestyle of people, rapid urbanisation, and under-estimated contributors and stakeholders (Jha et al. 2011). Our research illustrates that the rate of generation of solid waste is more a functional result of our social activities. As noted earlier, one of the major sources of MSW generation is households. Here the family is the primary unit of socialisation where individuals develop their understanding of 'what are wastes'. Learning and formation of basic habits forms the kernel of our social practices. This includes daily dietary practices including preparation and consumption of food. They also include leisure activities, customs, rituals, hobbies, and other lifestyle choices. These everyday practices are co-related with our environmental practices as their manifest or latent functions effect our environment. Hoornweg et al. (2012) indicate that waste composition and production are related to factors such as culture, climate, and state of development.

Like other cities of developing countries, waste production in Patna is also affected by these three interconnected factors of population growth, urbanisation, and increased consumption. Patna is the most populated districts in Bihar, with the decadal growth rate of population

(2001–11) being 22.34%, and population density of 1,102 persons per square kilometre (Census of India 2011). The increase in population growth rate in Patna is attributed to dual causes of natural increase, due to high fertility rate, as well as a high rate of rural to urban migration. Patna is also the most urbanised district in Bihar, with an urbanisation rate of 43.5%, much higher than the national average (ibid.). Patna ranks very high in terms of solid waste generation in India, and in Patna (2011) 52% of the waste generated is organic in nature and only 13% of the total waste is recyclable. Due to lack of industries in Patna, a large proportion of the waste is generated from households, hotels, resorts, restaurants, and other businesses.

Consumption: the engine of waste production

Consumption is a multi-dimensional concept. Its definitions vary according to the academic discipline by which it is perceived. For example, sociologists have focused on consumption as a social activity rather than as a pure economic activity (Bocock 1993). Once people are influenced by the social and cultural practices associated with the ideology of current-day consumerism stemming from westoxicated values, then even if they cannot afford to buy the goods portrayed in films, advertising, and in the media, they still desire them. Consumption is, therefore, seen as being based increasingly upon desires, not simply upon need (Baudrillard 1998). This sows the seed for analysing an exceptional form of consumer behaviour termed *conspicuous consumption*. Mason (1983: 3) distinguishes it as 'being motivated by a desire to impress others with the ability to pay particular high prices for prestige products'. He, further, asserts that it is a form of consumption which is inspired by social rather than by the economic or physiological utility of products. Conspicuous consumption is not a recent phenomenon although it may be in a new avatar in Patna. This concept surfaced as early as 1899 when Veblen (1992), in his seminal work *The Theory of the Leisure Class*, mentioned such consumption behaviour. Veblen contends that wealthy individuals often consume conspicuous goods and services in order to advertise their wealth and thereby achieve greater status. Hence, in conspicuous consumption the commodities consumed are not necessities. They are 'status goods' or 'positional goods'. According to Baudrillard (1998) such goods are 'signs' or 'sign values' as well as images or messages rather than commodities that are consumed. The purposes of these goods are as means of communication to express identity and mark status (Stillman 2003). Thus, conspicuous consumption feeds off a status system

(Mason 1981). Categories of waste produced in Patna, and as discussed in the section above, justify this pattern of consumption.

When Veblen proposed his theory of conspicuous consumption, it was designed as a concept applicable only to the rich and wealthy class, but in the postmodern society, often termed the 'consumer society' (Clarke 2003), conspicuous consumption is one of the most dominant features of the new middle class. As Mason (1981: 150) states, 'conspicuous consumption may well be confirmed in future as an exclusively middle-class form of behaviour'. Ger and Belk (1996: 272) have added 'consumptionscape' to Appadurai's initial five scapes (ethnoscapes, mediascapes, technoscapes, financescapes, and ideoscapes) that have defined global cultural flows and disjunctures (Appadurai 2003) and have tried to explain recent global flows of consumption. They state that the global consumptionscape adds to the resources available to people and becomes part of how consumers draw from all available global and local, new and old sources, as they use products to position themselves in local age, gender, social class, religion and ethnic hierarchies. Based on this, Kjeldgaard (2003), situates consumption behaviour within the broader perspective of the global-local nexus, and explains how relations of a particular 'local' with the global cultural economy affect consumption behaviour. Being cool and hanging out may signify global flow, but consuming *litti* (a popular food in Bihar) at a street corner gives a local flavour.

Bocock (1993) asserts that modern patterns of consumption for urban dwellers are, in part, a result of living in the metropolis, the city and its suburbs. The processes involved of living in an urban location increase the awareness of style, of the need to consume within a repertory which is both distinctive to a social group and expressive of individual preferences. Ger (1999) states that in transitional societies they also face tensions in their attempt to face the future (modernity, progress) rather than the past (poor, rural, backwards, traditional) while maintaining their roots and habits. Day in, day out, practices reflect the negotiation of what it is to be modern, to be sensible and thrifty while demonstrating success and respectability, and so on. Their argument can be supported by the patterns of conspicuous consumption among the urban middle class in Patna. Easy availability and accessibility of materials to the middle-class population in cities like Patna allows this group of people to imitate the consumerist values of the West disregarding their traditional behaviour. This, we believe, is a noteworthy cause of increasing waste generation.

The meaning of an object, like a car or organic foods, or a practice such as biking, reflects perceptions and judgements about how and in what ways it differs from or is similar to alternatives, and where, when, how, and by whom it is owned, consumed, or engaged in. Desire gets introduced into thought, discourse, and then into action. Against this background the waste produced in Patna can be classified under the following heads.

Food is the first category. It is one of the most common items of consumption that is directly related to waste production. Apart from what we eat, food involves various other aspects that acquire meaning and significance when examined from the perspectives of waste generation. To start with common sense, rationality influences the selection of different foods. For example, many of our respondents pointed that would prefer to buy the vegetables from a specific outlets that sells the vegetables in plastic bags properly labelled with price and weight rather than common vendors where one needs to bargain and where even the vegetables are not properly packed.

Most of the families surveyed are nuclear and often have double income. In such a situation they lead a very busy life. Also due to the availability of large amount of disposable incomes, these families tend to engage in eating out more often. Events of eating out in Patna does not necessarily mean dining at restaurants; rather people also prefer to buy fast food from street vendors and small eating joints at the roadside. Foods at these joints are served either in aluminium or thermocal plates, which are easily disposable after use but not degradable. Large portions of MSW that are littered on roads in Patna are composed of such items. Interestingly, almost all the small restaurants in Patna offer 'free home delivery services' which have become very popular, as one gets to enjoy restaurant food at home without having to physically travel. All these foods are served in aluminium foiled packets in a plastic bag and accompanied by a latest menu card of the restaurant along with paper napkins, plastic spoon or forks, and pouches of sauce or salad. This practice is not environmental friendly and becomes a big part of the daily waste production at household level.

More than 70% of the respondents stated that on average the intake of non-homemade food is approximately three times a week. Most residents have a competition with those who live in other apartments of the building or with those in the neighbourhood about their cool lifestyle including the practice of eating out. This is quite an alarming rate of consumption generating a huge amount of waste. As Baudrillard (1998) depicts these are consumptions of 'signs' to reinforce a specific social status. Respondents were given option as to whether they would prefer food to be served in steel or other metal utensils which could be washed and re-used. All of them replied they would not prefer such arrangements as they feel it might not be hygienic. They also gave examples, why they choose certain restaurants over other for home delivery mainly because of their 'hygienic packaging'. Then respondents were asked whether they are aware of the environmental effects of using such products, all of them gave an affirmative reply, but when they were asked as to what could be done to minimise production of waste, none replied that they should check their levels of consumption. Rather everyone blamed the municipal authority for not implementing better pickup and transport facilities of solid waste.

Waste generation from food consumption is not only limited at household level but also at the source where food is sold. Here, the roads are infested with numerous eating joints and vendors selling various types of fast food at different price ranges affordable by people of all income groups. Based on participant observation, it was noticed that in the evening time the sale of such fast food items increases and the consumers are mostly young adults. There is an increasing trend in Patna for young people to attend academic coaching classes. Most of such classes are held after school or college hours in the evening. This provides a specific type of socialisation among young adults, who hang out after the classes at the roadside eating joints. These eating vendors provide a particular space for interaction among young people where along with food they also enjoy the company of their friends. Under these circumstances, consumption of food is more an act to establish a social identity among a peer group. However, such consumption practices are a major cause of generating huge amount of solid waste in the region, characterised by 'use and throw' plates, cups, glasses, spoons, and napkins.

Consumption pattern of food and the kind of waste generated around it leads us to situate the behaviour as hedonism. Packaged food points to an experience of enjoyment. It means that you eat exactly what you want and when you want it. Hedonism can also take an environmental form, as when consumers view the consumption of packaged food as a sensual treat and take pleasure in the experience or at least the association of better quality, taste, and texture. This might be a case that women who spent more time in kitchen preparing food are now busy. *Being busy* is a sign of having an active and time-scheduled daily life. This is a context where shopping and cooking are designed not to take up too much time. Hence, semi-manufactured goods seem to be necessary. The proliferation of processed foods promises *emancipation from household chores*, especially for women. Media and advertising reinforce these symbolic meanings. Moreover, *signs of being modern and Western* are important especially in Patna.

Processed foods are associated with a sense of decency and self-respect that comes from not depriving ones family of the good life as seen on TV or as lived by ones more affluent neighbours. All such foods are available at the supermarkets in plastic, tin, or aluminium packets. Though it is easy to prepare and consume these food items but unfortunately their packaging materials are neither bio-degradable nor recyclable. As per the Municipal Solid Waste Handling Rule (2000), the minimum time taken for tin and aluminium to degrade is between 100 and 500 years, while it is 1 million years for plastic.

Electrical appliances and gazettes are the next category. In developing countries, due to the widespread availability of electrical and electronic goods, there has been a tremendous increase in amount of e-waste which has become a serious environmental concern (Pandey and Govind 2014). These electrical goods range from toys, personal care items (such as hair dryer, electrical razor), entertainment and/educational products (television, video, and CD players, iPads, laptops, computers, and mobile phones), and appliances that are used for household chores and activities, for example, washing machines, microwave machines, toaster, mixer-grinder, and so on. All the households surveyed for the study reported of having these products, though the quantity and brand varied. One of the respondents replied, 'these days we have become so used to these appliances, like washing machine and microwave that it is impossible to think of a life without these'. Another respondent stated that 'at times I wonder earlier how we managed our lives without cell phones (laughs). I mean now it is so much easier to stay connected with your friends all the time'.

When we asked the respondents whether they were aware that such items generate huge amount of e-waste and the adverse effect they have on the environment, their responses were interesting. About 43% said that they were aware about e-waste but not specifically about environmental hazards caused by them; 26% reported they thought only computers and laptops produce e-waste; 19% stated they were not sure about how everyday use of electrical appliances can produce e-waste and the environmental effects were limited only to those who deal with these wastes; and only 12% expressed concern about reducing e-waste production. Respondents were given the option that if they were willing to use less of these products to minimise e-waste production, their responses were almost anonymous as they stated that one has to lose something for enjoying comforts in life. From in-depth interviews it was evident that the purposes of these goods are as means of communication to express identity and mark status (Stillman 2003). Lodziak (2002) suggests that nowadays sources of identity dwell in the world of images, symbols and signs. Giddens (1991) thus observes that a new kind of consumer had emerged for whom consumption itself plays a central role in constructing new senses of identity based on and around the possession and ownership of status-conferring goods.

Not far behind we have the category that covers *personal care products and sanitary items*. A large proportion of the MSW consists of personal care items such as cosmetics, deodorants, diapers, and so on. There has been an increase in consumption of these items whose values and comforts are being reinforced through daily advertisements. In every household these items are very common. In fact, from the survey it was evident that the levels of consumption of these products are almost at par with the household's consumption of grocery items. For example, about 87% of the respondents reported that they buy such products of personal care more than twice every month. This suggests the frequent use of these items. Bourdieu (2003) argues that consumption is the articulation of a sense of identity. According to him, our identity is made up by our consumption of goods, which displays our expression of taste. Many people's sense of identities then, are affirmed and contested through specific acts of consumption (Jackson and Thrift 1995). People define themselves by what they buy and by the meaning that they give to the goods and services that they acquire. Lodziak (2002: 51) argues that – for those with the financial means – there exists a 'self-identity industry' that includes health clubs, fitness gyms, therapy centres, beauty salons, cosmetic surgeries, and the use of specific products. The same is true for the respondents of this study. They all agreed that their consumption of particular personal care items were influenced more by advertisements to forge a distinct personal identity which is characterised by living a comfortable lifestyle. To illustrate this with an example from another context, and as reported by Colon et al. (2013), all households that had children below three years of age uses diapers for them, but unfortunately these diapers are not disposed of in a sanitarily hygienic manner, causing adverse environmental effects. The situation is similar even in Patna.

Real estate is another significant category in Patna these days. As mentioned earlier, a large amount of MSW in Patna is also produced through construction and demolition. A tour of Patna illustrates that new buildings and shopping complexes, including malls, are being constructed in various places. With a rise in disposable income among the middle class as well as easy availability of various home loan schemes provided by the banks, Patna has witnessed a steady rise in the real estate market. Another factor that adds to this real estate boom can be contributed to the opening of different offices and state headquarters of various non-governmental organisations (NGOs). There is also an increasing influx of students from parts of Bihar to Patna in search of better educational and livelihood opportunities. Almost 35% of the household surveyed lived in house and/or apartment which they owned, while the remaining 65% lived in rental accommodations. Of those who lived in rental accommodations, approximately 85% mentioned that they have a pre-booked apartment in Patna which was under construction. Seventy-two percent of those who lived in their own house reported they plan to have some construction in their premises for commercial uses. This could be either to rent it as office space or else open student accommodation. Interestingly, all the respondents were aware that such activities would generate a lot of solid waste, but to them the attraction of income superseded their concern for environment. All these imply that apart from consumption of products to reinstate their social status, people in Patna also indulged in consumption of space (Jackson and Thrift 1995), which is also responsible for generating solid waste in the city.

Transport vehicles can be an environmental problem and an arena in which consumers are both the senders and receivers of symbolic meaning. By choosing to cycle or by selecting one rather than another type of car, individuals convey information about themselves. This is just as they interpret the social meaning of other' transport practices. Transport vehicles are important in connecting people between different spatial locations. Population growth in Patna is accompanied by growth of transport vehicles as well. Among these, the number of personal transport vehicles is ever increasing. Easy loans from different banks serve as a lubricant. However, it is the family's competition to have better car than the neighbour that sets the process. Having an expensive car is a conventional symbol of high social status all over the world. The roads here are unable to support the increasing number of vehicles, resulting in traffic congestion. Also, while new cars have taken to the road, the old means of transport are still there. Animal-driven carts, human-driven rickshaws, or slow-moving tractors adds to the slow traffic situation and ever-increasing sound and air pollution. What concerns us here in this chapter is solid waste. We have found a correlation between standstill traffic and disposal of waste in the city by people using transport vehicles to connect between two spatial locations. Participant observation at three select traffic points show that throwing of wrappers and other leftovers from a car increases with increasing traffic congestion. Participant observation also guides us to comprehend the consumption pattern in Patna, and thereby waste production reflects a complex admixture of tradition and modernity. We will discuss these and other significant points after we have delineated the consumption pattern and waste production.

The glocal paradox

It is cultural practice, then, and the knowledge production mechanism that are at the root of the problem. Rapid material and technological growth gave rise to a cultural modernisation with materialism and consumerism at the core. A common theme which emerges from all these cases is the changing definition of what it is to be modern. Throughout, the pattern is one in which the life which people aspire to or expect relies on an increasing number of appliances and environmentally problematic services relating to mobility, hygiene, and increasing standards of indoor comfort. The availability of these services and the technologies which make them possible symbolise modernity. This modernity is the yardstick for normality. Any deviance, either through inability of economic or cultural capital, desires enforcement for achieving normality. Consumers have their own yardsticks with which they measure levels and patterns of sufficient consumption. The moving mark of what is enough and pleasurable is negotiated in moral terms. Consumers legitimise their own high levels or aspirations of personal consumption with reference to a repertoire of justifications and excuses. Justifications include pleasure, connoisseurship, instrumentalism, or altruism, while excuses tend to focus on external forces, including arguments about the way of the modern world, or the need to make up for past deprivation, or to reward success. Paradoxically, the prevalence of these defensive vocabularies highlights the extent to which the ethos of consumption is legitimised.

The process of knowledge production and appropriation is led by the presiding deities of European enlightenment. Dualism leads the way. Either you are good or you are bad. Your modernity may be de-contextual, but you must aspire to be one. Formalistic knowledge production trajectories give emphasis to the Newtonian, Baconian, and Cartesian rationality. It is rooted in everything we produce and consume. This monocultural rationality negates local context as well as environmental concerns. Also, environmentalism in India has only been mild and controlled by the modernised elite, several budding environmentalists have been integrated into environmental departments in universities and in government agencies and municipalities. Such institutionalisation and professionalisation fostered a consensus-oriented form of environmentalism within the wider society. This background helps explain the proliferation of government initiated programs for citizen participation in local environmental improvements, new non-radical, professional environmental organisations and a growth in environmental journalism in the mass media.

In the preceding section, we tried to connect the missing lines between consumption pattern and waste production. This could be pertinent to comprehend the nature and type of waste produced, especially municipal solid waste. We have seen that it is the misplaced and raging consumption pattern that goes for increasing waste production. The 'positivistic' knowledge machine only justifies the conspicuous consumption and has become part of way of life of people in places like Patna. Next we would like to examine what re-enforces these patterns especially in our research site.

Drawing from our earlier discussion on globalisation we contend that in this specific context globalisation takes local root and re-emphasises the theories of glocalisation, especially in the manner it implicates the class structure. We believe that the growth of middle class in Patna is based on a pattern where lumpenism as a cultural practice has been the harbinger of social change. Through history the notion of the middle class has remained highly contentious in the social sciences. The liberal pluralists tend to regard the middle class as primarily a cultural entity defined by values of individualism and rationality, as well as by indicators of status, occupation and income. Accordingly, the middle class cannot be distinguished from the bourgeoisie and there is no means of distinguishing between the type of social power that they derive from property on the one hand, and salaries and qualifications on the other. However, while scholars continue to struggle to provide a comprehensive definition of the middle class, there has emerged in the literature a sub-group within this class, namely the *new middle class*. This conceptual framework originates in opposition to the official Marxist theories of the late 19th century. Betz (1992) relates the growth of the new middle class with changing production systems in a society and analyses it against a postmodern background. Betz (ibid.: 100) points out that

> the theoretical approaches to describe the new middle class in post-industrial, consumer and information society generally characterise the new middle class as a rather homogenous class (the service class of employers, managers and professionals) united in its members' shared pursuit of social status.

He argues that based on this theorisation, the new middle class emerges at a particular stage in a country's economic development where its precise function is to promote consumption ethics. In the present context we contend that globalisation has generated substantial employment in a number of developing countries like India. This in turn has given birth to a new urban middle class in these countries. An important majority of the members of this emerging class are employed in the service sector and constitute a growing and increasingly large proportion of these countries populations (Shurmer-Smith 2000).

Betz (1992: 99) concludes that the new middle class is intricately connected to the growth of the '*societe de consommation*'. Featherstone (1987) states that consumption and tastes become vital channels in the struggle between various classes and a particular class, the new middle class, is formed leading to a growing aestheticisation of everyday life via signs, symbols, and images of pleasure for consumption. Hence, the very nature of the new middle class puts heavy emphasis on consumption. In such a situation the new middle class are the 'new heroes of consumer culture'. In developing Asian countries, with economies predominantly based on extensive agriculture, the new middle class did not gain prominence either in number or in interest among researchers, media or politicians due to their insignificant numbers until the 1970s. From that decade onwards globalisation trends triggered a range of liberalisation policies across Asia (albeit to very different degrees and not in Burma) causing a shift in many occupational structures and the rapid growth of export-focused industries leading to an employment boom.

In Asia the term 'new rich' is used interchangeably with 'new middle class'. This term is used to describe in broad terms the new wealthy social groups that have emerged from industrial changes in Asia, with their social power based either on capital and expertise or rent and/or position in the extensive state apparatus (Gerke 2000). The new rich are thus the professional middle class. Nonetheless, this term is a starting point for examination rather than an analytical tool. This needs to be clarified because the new rich is neither a cohesive category nor does it have common historical roots, and its impacts vary from one country to another depending on the pattern of economic transition in the country. Therefore, there are likely to be several patterns in the emergence of the new rich and its influence on the cultural, social, economic and political life of the country under study (Robinson and Goodman 1996). This group is commonly characterised by a newly emerging lifestyle – a metropolitan, or *nouveau rich* lifestyle – in which the consumption of items such as brand-name clothes, personal adornments, and expensive pleasurable pursuits has become central (Bocock 1993). In this article we suggest that changing consumption patterns is directly linked to their change in lifestyle which has impacted upon the production of waste in these cities.

The new rich in Patna are a product of lumpenism. The lumpen way of life was epitomised during the last few decades when the agrarian and rural classes became the dominant caste. The unequal utilisation of resources by the previous regimes, mainly led by upper caste, was rightly resented and giving back was purposely engulfed in behaviour patterns not appreciated by the upper echelon. Investment in infra-structure was stopped as the institutions were so designed, by the ear-lier political administration, that the benefits would be utilised only by the established classes. Patna, pathetically, became a victim of its own people who in trying to get back to each other took resort in unruly behaviour that can at best be classified as lumpenism. Ascertain of this behaviour patterns was visible in every walk of life. Cattle on the road became an important signifier of getting back at the urban elite who had neglected rural Bihar. The political class enjoyed the benefits while the rot only stemmed further. The bureaucracy resented but was only concerned with their immediate neighbourhood. The bureaucracy encompassed more funds through increasing corrupt practices. The flow of funds in the market for unparalleled consumerism has direct co-relation with corruption in most branches of the bureaucracy here. The boom in real estate is also helped with incomparable extortion of funds by the lumpen political class and the corrupt bureaucracy. These two are joined by the expatriates of Bihar, especially those who have made a mark for themselves in other local in India. There are noteworthy instances of contribution of the expatriate Bihari in social work – mostly around education and identity branding. However, the spurt in consumerist behaviour is a gift from them as well.

The use of lumpenism to comprehend the social formation and cul-tural patterns in Patna may draw from but is not directly related to the concept of lumpen bourgeoisie espoused by A. G. Frank (1972). How-ever, like the class discussed by Frank, even the culture of the class in Patna is insensitive to the local need. Whether it is the condition of pollution in the river Ganga or the streets, people are only bothered about themselves and their loved ones. They are insensitive to the com-munity and their environment. They learn from practices of the other culture(s) and try their best to catch up to it. But, when it comes to the practices which sustained their own environment, people feel that by continuing those practices they may not be considered modern. The local word here for adopting the so-called modern practice is *vikashit*, which in English would mean developed. But, as one elderly respond-ent concluded, this attitude shows *vikrit* (meaning, that which has lost its mainstay) mentality. Overt rowdiness has been curbed during the current political regime, but insensitivity and an attitude of communal ownership is missing. While living rooms should be clean, there is no concern for the streets and the way inappropriate disposal of waste can create different kinds of health hazard, for instance.

In retrospect

There are occasions when city like Patna rises and cleans up its act, including the waste from its environment. It further needs an integrated approach when different stakeholders can join hand and do not allow the situation to deteriorate further. One needs informed public policy from the municipal and provincial government as well as a strict adherence to the process which will streamline such acts to help the city of Patna to rejuvenate. The recent *Swach Bharat* ranking puts Patna way down and puts a question mark on practices of governance to minimise the negative influence of global practices like consumption and their like. Nevertheless, there are examples of citizen groups when city like Patna is clean – *Chat puja*. This does provide a silver lining for a better Patna. We believe that change in attitude will change behaviour pattern of people here in Patna as well as any other place struggling to properly dispose of their wastes. One can have awareness programs that can be supported by the community and the local governance. The awareness programs must put emphasis on connecting people with their local community as well as with the larger environmental hazards. Increasing interest and motivation has no effect if it is not followed up by resources, support and structural improvements which make it possible, sensible, and normal for consumers to change their routines, habits and daily consumption practices. Only then can the locals resist and channelise any adverse impact of globalisation and its like.

References

Appadurai, Arjun. 1999. 'Globalisation and the Research Imagination', *International Social Science Journal*, 160: 229–238.

Appadurai, Arjun. 2003. *Modernity at Large*. Minneapolis: University of Minnesota Press.

Baudrillard, Jean. 1998. *The Consumer Society*. London: Sage.

Betz, Hans-Georg. 1992. 'Postmodernism and the New Middle Class', *Theory, Culture and Society*, 9: 93–114.

Bocock, Robert. 1993. *Consumption*. London: Routledge.

Bourdieu, Pierre. 2003. 'Classes and Classifications', in D. B. Clarke, M. A. Doel and K.M.L. Housiax (eds.), *The Consumption Reader* (246–250). London: Routledge.

'Census of India 2011, Government of India', www.censusindia.gov.in, accessed on 4/2015.

Clarke, David B. 2003. *The Consumer Society and the Postmodern City*. London: Routledge

Colón, Joan, Mestre-Montserrat, M., Puig-Ventosa, Ignasi and Sánchez, Antoni. 2013. 'Performance of Compostable Baby Used Diapers in the Composting Process with the Organic Fraction of Municipal Solid Waste', *Waste Management*, 33: 1097–1103.

Cox, Kevin R. 1997. *Spaces of Globalisation: Reasserting the Power of the Local*. New York: Guilford Press.

Das, Arvind N. 1992. *The Republic of Bihar*. New Delhi: Penguin Books.

Dicken, Peter. 1994. 'Global-Local Tensions: Firms and States in the Global Space Economy', *Economic Geography*, 70(2): 101–128.

Dicken, Peter. 1998. *Global Shift Transforming the World Economy*. London: P.C.P.

Fagan, G. Honor. 2003. 'Sociological Reflections on Governing Waste', *Irish Journal of Sociology*, 12(1): 67–84.

Featherstone, Mike. 1987. 'Global and Local Cultures', in J. Bird, B. Curtis, T. Putnam, G. Robertson and L. Tickner (eds.), *Mapping the Futures: Local Cultures Global Change* (169–178). London: Routledge.

Frank, Andre G. 1972. 'Lumpenbourgeoisie – Lumpendevelopment Monthly Review', *An Independent Socialist Magazine*. New York.

Ger, Gilliz and Belk, Russell W. 1996. 'I'd Like to Buy the World a Coke: Consumptionscapes of the 'Less Affluent World'', *Journal of Consumer Policy*, 19(3): 271–304.

Ger, Guliz. 1999. 'Experiential Meanings of Consumption and Sustainability in Turkey', E.J. Arnould and L.M. Scott (ed.), *Advances in Consumer Research*, 26: 276–280.

Gerke, Solvay. 2000. 'Global Lifestyles Under Local Conditions: The New Indonesian Middle Class', in C Beng-Huat (ed.), *Consumption in Asia: Lifestyles and Identities* (135–158). New York: Routledge.

Giddens, Anthony. 1990. *The Consequences of Modernity*. Cambridge: Polity Press.

Giddens, Anthony. 1991. *Modernity and Self-Identity: Self and Society in the Late Modern Age*. Cambridge: Polity Press.

Grant, Richard and Rennie Short, John. 2002. 'Globalisation: An Introduction', in R. Grant and J.R. Short (eds.), *Globalisation and the Margins* (3–14). England: Palgrave Macmillan.

Hannerz, Ulf. 1996. *Trnasnational Connections*. London: Routledge.

Harvey, David. 1989. *The Condition of Postmodernity*. Oxford: Basil Blackwell.

Held, David. 2000. 'Regulating Globalization? The Reinvention of Politics', *International Sociology*, 15(2): 364–408.

Hirst, Paul and Thompson, Grahame. 1996. 'Introduction: Globalisation – A Necessary Myth', in Paul Hirst and Grahame Thompson (eds.), *Globalisation in Question* (1–17). Cambridge: Polity Press.

Hoogvelt, Ankie. 1997. 'Globalisation', in *Globalisation and the Postcolonial World* (114–131). London: Macmillan Press.

Hoornweg, Daniel and Bhada-Tata, Perinaz. 2012. *What a Waste: A Global Review of Solid Waste Management*. Washington, DC: The World Bank, http//cpcb.nic.in/divisonofheadoffice/pcp/management_solidwaste.pdf, accessed on 4/2015.

Huntley, S. 2010. *Recycling Household Wastes: Composition Collection, and public participation*, http://www.lineone.net/ngooovemit/extra/wmessay. htm, accessed on 7/2010.

Jackson, Peter and Thrift, N. 1995. 'Geographies of Consumption', in D. Miller (ed.), *Acknowledging Consumption* (204–237). London: Routledge.

Jha, Arvind Kumar, Singh, S. K., Singh, G. P. and Gupta, Prabhat Kumar. 2011. 'Sustainable Municipal Solid Waste Management in Low Income Group of Cities: A Review', *Tropical Ecology*, 52(1): 123–131.

Kellner, D. 2000. 'Globalisation and New Social Movements: Lessons for Critical Theory and Pedagogy', in N. C. Burbules and Carlos Alberto Torres (eds.), *Globalisation and Education: Critical Perspectives* (299–322). New York: Routledge.

Kelly, Philip. 1999. 'The Geographies and Politics of Globalization', *Progress in Human Geography*, 23(3): 379–400.

Kjeldgaard, Dannie. 2003. 'Youth Identities in the Global Cultural Economies', *European Journal of Cultural Studies*, 6(3): 285–304.

Lodziak, Cornad. 2002. *The Myth of Consumerism*. London: Pluto Press.

Luke, Timothy W. 1994. 'Placing Power/Sitting Space: The Politics of Global and Local in the New World Order', *Environment and Planning D: Society and Space*, 12: 613–628.

Mason, Roger S. 1981. *Conspicuous Consumption*. New York: St. Martin's Press.

Mason, Roger S. 1983. 'The Economic Theory of Conspicuous Consumption', *International Journal of Social Economics*, 10(3): 3–17.

McGrew, Anthony G. 1992. 'Conceptualising Global Politics', in Anthony G. McGrew and Paul G. Lewis (eds.), *Global Politics: Globalization and the Nation State* (1–28). Cambridge: Polity Press.

Mittelman, James H. 2001. 'Mapping Globalisation', *Singapore Journal of Tropical Geography*, 2(3): 212–218.

Newman, David. 2006. 'The Lines That Continue to Separate Us: Borders in Our 'Borderless' World', *Progress in Human Geography*, 30(2): 143–161.

Pandey, Pooja and Madhav, Govind. 2014. 'Social Repercussions of e-Waste Management in India: A Study of Three Informal Recycling Sites in Delhi', *International Journal of Environmental Studies*, 71(3): 241–260.

Peck, Jamie and Tickell, Adam. 1994. 'Jungle-Law Breaks Out: Neoliberalism and Local Disorder', *Area*, 26(4): 317–326.

Robertson, Roland. 1992. *Globalisation: Social Theory and Global Culture*. London: Sage.

Robertson, Roland. 1995. 'Glocalization: Time-Space and Homogeneity-Heterogeneity', in M. Featherstone, S. Lash and R. Robertson (eds.), *Global Modernities* (25–44). London: Sage.

Robinson, Richard and S. G. Goodman, David. (eds.) 1996. *The New Rich in Asia*. London: Routledge.

Shurmer-Smith, Pamela. 2000. *India – Globalization and Change*. London: Arnold.

Stillman, Todd. 2003. 'McDonald's in Question: The Limits of the Mass Market', *American Behavioral Scientist*, 47(2): 107–118.

Thapar, Romila. 1966. *The History of India*. 1. New Delhi: Penguin Books.

Valentine, Gill. 2001. *Social Geographies: Space and Society*. England: Prentice Hall.

Veblen, Thorstein. 1992. *The Theory of the Leisure Class*. New Brunswick: Transaction.

Yeung, Henry Wai-chung. 1998. 'Capital, State and Space: Contesting the Borderless World', *Transactions of the Institute of British Geographers*, 23(3): 291–309.

8 Neo-liberal development, environmental sustainability and social justice

Contextualising the Mahatma Gandhi National Rural Employment Guarantee Scheme

B. N. Prasad

In a narrow sense, 'environment' is understood as a biophysical world order and environmental problems are considered simply to be negative impacts on the natural world, such as degradation of air, water resources, and loss of biological diversity. But environmental problems cannot be analysed without its social context, because nature neither exists independently of human intervention nor its social activities. It is in this broader sense that our understanding and application of the concept 'environmental degradation' should be based on the interaction of society and nature. Ability of human beings to manipulate nearly every aspect of the natural world challenges the notion that nature is somehow separate or autonomous from human culture. Environmental problems reflect inter-relationships among resource change, human productive activities and accompanying transformations of people's lives. An environmental problem is therefore logically understood to be a situation in which human action affects natural resources in such a way as to place people's welfare, income and livelihood at risk. In this sense environmental problems are social problems. There is a binary relationship between environment and social structure. Different social structures impact environment differently and in turns get impacted by environment differently. Inequitable social structures, such as unequal control over resources on the basis of class or gender, have contributed differently to environmental deterioration. Social groups are affected differently: some may benefit from changes in price structures or social relations that result from scarcities caused by environmental stress. On the flipside, environmental distress limits productive opportunities of marginalised masses in rural areas and seriously threatens their livelihood conditions. United Nations Conference on Environment and Development (UNCED 1992) and United Nations Research Institute for Social Development (UNRISD 1994) reports suggest that more than 2 million deaths and billions of illnesses per year are attributed to water pollution; ozone depletion is responsible for 3 million additional cases of skin cancer and 1.7 million cases of cataracts per year globally. The worst sufferers are those at the bottom of the population.

Although environmental degradation has multidimensional effects, but there is a direct link between environmental disequilibrium and poverty. It is argued that environmental degradation causes poverty, and poverty is one of the principal reasons for environmental destruction. The 'poverty-environment' debate has become more sophisticated in recent times among environmentalist and social scientists. One set of arguments blames that environmental degradation is largely due to ignorance and wasteful use of forest resources by the poor; the other advocates that the poor are forced to overexploit environment by factors outside of their control. This set of arguments explains the linkage between poverty and environmental degradation in terms of two main processes. First, environmental degradation causes poverty because degradation involves erosion of the resource base upon which the poor often depend for their livelihood, while adverse impacts of environmental decline on people's health further limits their productive potential. Second, poverty causes environmental degradation because the poor largely depend on the forest resource base for their survival and expansion of their marginal agricultural lands. In addition, the poor do not have sufficient security to invest in maintenance of environmental health. It is rightly argued that environmental conservation is a luxury that the poor cannot afford because their livelihood and their immediate survival are at stake. These twin processes create a vicious circle. Therefore poverty and environmental degradation must be attacked simultaneously. This type of synthetic debate draws together two schools of thought: scholars whose primary concern is environment and those whose focus is on equitable development. It has been able to forge this coalition between the people-centred development lobby and environmentalists by asserting that trade-offs between environmental rehabilitation and poverty alleviation are minimal and there is no general conflict between environmental protection and economic development in developing countries, particularly not where the poorest people are concerned.

There are three primary policy approaches to address environmental degradation: environmentalism for *nature, people,* and *profits.* First is the environment-centred approach, which is based largely on the assumption that human activities are detrimental to nature, so these activities should be controlled. Second is a more people-centred approach, which has been advanced in recent years. This approach is called primary environmental care (PEC approach). This assumes that human activity is not necessarily or inherently detrimental to nature, and that, given the opportunity, people will manage their environment sustainably because it is in their best interests to do so. Third is a range of tax, pricing and accounting-based policies which has been proposed with intention of creating incentives for those behaviours which are positive or neutral for the environment, and creating disincentives for environmentally destructive behaviour. Such market-based policy proposals define their goals in terms of balancing trade-offs between human activity and environmental conditions to achieve maximum economic efficiency. The reductionist approach ignores livelihood concern of poor social groups to those of stronger ones. Several environmental groups that originally assumed a purely conservationists stance have come to realise that environmental protection must go hand-in-hand with development policies that provide alternative livelihood opportunities for the rural poor. This is the PEC approach, which rests on assumption that it is essential to focus on community level when making sustainable development operational. The PEC approach is not the cure of all illness, but it certainly addresses the root of the problem. The lesson derived from the above explanation is that it is essential to avoid fundamentalist policy approaches that isolate and emphasise a single dimension of social-environmental dynamics. Environmental problems must be understood as part of larger social framework and must be addressed from this perspective. Much can be done at local level to address the problems, but it would be ineffectual unless it is carried out within a context of supportive institutions at local, national and global levels. Treating various dimensions of environment-development relationship in isolation will obscure as much as it reveals. In the phase of neo-liberal development 'sustainable development' has emerged as a buzzword and Mahatma Gandhi National Rural Employment Guarantee Scheme (MNREGS) has potential for sustainable development in rural areas with community support at local level.

Some economists have dubbed MNREGS as the 'dole' of the UPA government. Criticism of this sort has seriously implications on concept, theory and practice of development, especially in developing country like India. During the last eight and a half decades, the practice of development has undergone an evolutionary process.

Evolution of development discourse

Till the 1930s development was synonymous with economic growth, thus perceived as quantitative concept. During the 1940s and 1950s; multiple socio-economic problems cropped up in third world countries due to economic backwardness and colonial exploitation. This forced academia to rethink the concept and formulate a new approach. As a result a 'multidimensional approach' has been adopted and non-growth parameters, like poverty, unemployment and inequality occupied centre stage. This evolutionary process continued in the 1970s and the issue of 'environmental sustainability' became an important attribute of it. During the mid-1990s, a neo-liberal development paradigm has significantly changed the discourse of development. Now, a 'human development approach' has become an integral part of it which includes parameters like health, education, gender, inequality, environment and cultural capital, along with economic issues (i.e. income, credit, labour and market). The approach has been impacted by Amartya Sen's (1989) concept of 'capability improvement' of the individual and community through state-market-civil society partnership. Today, economic development is identified with 'sustained development', which has three major components: social, economic and environmental. Thus during the last eight decades the concept of development has evolved from economic growth to sustainable development and approach has changed from income to capability. In this theoretical backdrop, let us analyse sustainability dimensions of Rural Employment Guarantee Scheme.

Sustainable development and mandatory provisions of MNREGA

In the 59th year of independence, the Indian Parliament passed the National Rural Employment Guarantee Act (NREGA) in September 2005. The Act ensures 'right to work' as legal right that is not dependent on the benevolence of the state but legally binding to provide employment for any rural family that demands. It is the largest developmental initiative by the state which is demand driven. The Act ensures 100 days of wage employment in a financial year to every rural household at prevailing minimum wages, for public asset creation in rural areas. The Act also ensures equal wage rate for both male and female – a significant step towards gender equality. A well-designed employment program has potential to increase volume of employment, promote pro-poor development and has multiplier effect to income generation. Thus ensures economic sustainability aspect. NREGA received the president's assent on 5 September 2005 and notified on 7 September the same year. The scheme was initially introduced in 200 of the most backward districts and later extended to another 130 districts. From 1 April 2008 it was launched in all districts. On 2 October 2009 scheme has been re-christened as Mahatma Gandhi National Rural Employment Guarantee Scheme. Of late scheme started convergence process with other flagship programs in order to increase its efficiency. Its mandatory provisions address three critical components of sustainable development – social, economic and environmental.

Major provisions of the Act are to convene a Gram Sabha meeting at least twice a year for site selection, choice of works, crèche facilities, drinking water and first aid at worksites, medical treatment in case of injury and ex-gratia payment due to death or disability during employment in the scheme, right to check muster rolls and right to unemployment allowance if employment is not provided within 15 days of submission of application, social audit, village vigilance committee, wage payment through bank and post office, at least one-third women beneficiaries. These provisions ensure participatory development, empowerment of weaker section in general and women in particular, good governance on the principles of transparency and grass-roots democracy (Government of India 2008: 194). These measures significantly ensure social sustainability aspect of sustainable development.

Along with socio-economic sustainability, the scheme has an environmental sustainability dimension as well. Major permissible works under the Act are micro irrigation projects, preservation and renovation of traditional water bodies, flood control, water harvesting and conservation, drought proofing through afforestation and tree plantation, development of drainage system in flood affected areas, improvement of rural connectivity by construction of all-weather roads, land development, soil fertility, reclamation of degraded lands, carbon sequestration, and horticulture (Government of India 2014: 6). The aim of permissible works is to enhance natural resource base, strengthen the rural economy and protect the environment. Thus promote environmental sustainability dimension.

Empirical dimensions of MNREGS and sustainable development

In order to achieve sustainable development through capability enhancement, the Indian state introduced numbers of developmental programs, and MNREGS is one of them. Empirically, let us examine developmental potential of the scheme under critical components of sustainable development – social, economic and environmental.

Economic sustainability: Rate of growth of employment in agriculture during 1993–94 to 2004–05 has been 0.40% compared to 3.52% in the non-agriculture sector during the same period (Planning Commission 2010). This shows limited employment potential of Indian agriculture. India is one of the most rural countries; more than two-thirds of its population is dependent on agriculture for their livelihood. The cherished goal of 4% growth rate of agriculture has never been achieved till now. Due to demographic pressure and continued division and sub-division of land; land-man ratio has deteriorated over the years. Lack of viable employment opportunities outside primary sector has made the situation even more pathetic. Table 8.1 illustrates an economic picture of the country.

Out of total main workers, 30% are agricultural labourers where the female percentage is much higher than their male counterparts. The percentage of marginal workers is significantly high. More than two-thirds of marginal workers get employment only for 3–6 months in a year, which is largely underpaid. The worst sufferers of precarious condition are in the marginalised population, including women. The picture that emerges out of the above indicates that employment elasticity of Indian agriculture is quite dismal. Therefore scheme like NREGS has great potential for employment generation and poverty reduction in rural economy. Rs. 2.39 lakh crore has been spent under the scheme from its inception till 2013–14. Annual rate of growth of budget allocation has been widely varying from as high as 60% in 2007–08 to as low as 21.2% in 2011–12. Expenditure in successive year has been impressive, ranging from 67% to 88%. As per provision ratio of wage and material should be 60:40. Wage ratio has been higher than the provision in each financial year (Table 8.2).

Scheduled Castes (SC), Scheduled Tribes (ST) and women have derived maximum benefit. An impact study conducted by Kareemulla et al. (2010) in four states – Andhra Pradesh, Karnataka, Rajasthan and Maharashtra – shows that major beneficiaries of the scheme were marginal and small farmers, followed by landless labourers. In India, 80% of farmers and 40% of land under agriculture belongs to small and marginal farmers (NCEUS 2008). They outnumbered landless labourers in terms of employment beneficiaries under the scheme. The scheme has been useful to resource poor small and marginal farmers who otherwise remain unemployed after their own small farm

Table 8.1 Distribution of total workers and marginal workers in India

| Persons | Total workers | Main workers (in %) | Percentage to total workers | | | | Marginal workers (in %) | Percentage to total marginal workers | |
			Cultivators	Agricultural labourers	Household industry workers	Other workers		Marginal workers (3–6 months)	Marginal workers (< 3 months)
Males	331,865,930	82.3	24.9	24.9	2.9	47.2	17.7	82.7	17.3
Females	149,877,381	59.6	24.0	41.1	5.7	29.2	40.4	80.0	20.0
Total	481,743,311	75.2	24.6	30.0	3.8	41.6	24.8	81.3	18.7

Source: Primary Census Abstract, Census of India 2011

Table 8.2 Status of budget, expenditure and works completion in India

Financial year	Budget outlay (in crore Rs.)	Annual growth rate in %	Expenditure in %	Expenditure on wages in %	Works completed in %
2006–07	11,300	5.8	73	66	46
2007–08	12,000	60.0	82	68	46
2008–09	30,000	23.3	73	67	44
2009–10	39,100	2.5	76	70	49
2010–11	40,100	−0.3	73	68	51
2011–12	40,000	−21.2	76	70	34
2012–13	33,000	0.0	88	72	24
2013–14, till December 2013	33,000		67	76	10

Source: MNREGA, (Report to People), Ministry of Rural Development, Govt. of India, February 2014, N. Delhi.

operations. The dominant source of income of beneficiary households was MNREGS wages only after agriculture wages, which accounts for 12%–18%. Ensuring food security has been major objective across all surveyed districts, followed by education of children and family health. The scheme played a crucial role to ensure food security and survival during lean periods when no other source of income was available locally. A study conducted by Jha et al. (2011) in three states (Andhra Pradesh, Rajasthan and Maharashtra) of 1,500 households found that share of income from MNREGS has been 17%, 10% and 7%, respectively. A study conducted by the author in Uttar Pradesh has also shown significant impact of MNREGS on income and livelihood conditions of marginalised population (Prasad 2008). Ravi and Engler (2013), Banerjee and Saha (2010), Hirway and others (2009) have demonstrated the multiplier impact of MNREGS on income and employment of the participatory poor. The above data and studies by development scholars show that the scheme ensures critical minimum economic security of the labouring poor by strengthening rural livelihood resource base and thus acts as a growth engine for sustainable development of a predominantly agrarian economy.

Social sustainability: Till the 1990s dominant paradigms of Indian rural development has been microcredit, Self Help Groups (SHGs), poverty reduction, social protection, gender equality and environmental sustainability. In the new millennium there is a paradigm shift, and now the focus is on sustainable development, social protection and gender justice. The development imperative of MNREGS is to provide an alternative source of livelihood to the labouring poor, reduction in distress migration, augment education and health spending, thereby strengthening participatory development and women empowerment in particular. Women empowerment refers to change in gender relation and reduction in gender inequalities. Asset ownership and economic participation are two components of economic empowerment of women that provides confidence and capacity to change power relations in their favour. Lack of ownership and control over productive assets and income impacts gender equality, development outcomes and inclusive economic growth (Kelkar 2011). Globalisation offers new opportunities to the excluded social groups (Dalits, minorities and women) and frees them from traditional occupational hierarchy, but poses a threat to traditional ways of livelihood. Use of opportunities of globalisation depends upon inclusion of excluded in new ways of earning and skills (Sen 2000: 8).

The scheme provided employment to 1,439.77 crore households at an average of 46.14 person-days from 2006–07 to 2012–13. Most vulnerable groups (SCs and STs) have derived maximum benefit; together accounted for 50.71% of total employment during the same period. Women beneficiaries have been almost equal to their male counterparts: 49% and 51%, respectively (Table 8.3).

One of the mandatory provisions of MNREGA is to provide at least one-third employment to women and also ensures gender parity of

Table 8.3 Status of employment under MNREGS in crore (% of total person-days)

Financial year	Total	SCs	STs	Women	Others	Average person-days per employed HHs
2006–07	90.5	25	36	40	38	43
2007–08	143.59	27	29	43	43	42
2008–09	216.32	29	25	48	45	48
2009–10	283.59	30	21	48	49	54
2010–11	257.15	31	21	48	48	47
2011–12	218.76	22	19	48	59	43
2012–13	229.86	22	18	51	60	46
Total	1,439.77	186	169	326	342	323
Average	205.68	26.57	24.14	46.57	48.86	46.14

Source: MNREGA, (Report to People), Ministry of Rural Development, Govt. of India, February 2014, N. Delhi: 9.

wages. The table shows that percentage is much higher than the provision. This is indicative to the fact that the scheme infused significant amount of social and gender equality in rural areas. Development practitioners have highlighted multiple social impacts of the scheme. A study in Jharkhand observes that due to the scheme there is a decline in labour exploitation on rural public works, rural wages and bargaining capacity of labourers have gone up, productivity norms are more reasonable, delay in wage payment is shorter and complaints at worksite harassment are rare. MNREGS is a valuable and valued opportunity for the rural poor, and particularly for women, to earn a living wage in a dignified manner (Dreze 2008). It is important to note that Jharkhand is not one of the best performing states. Pankaj and Tankha (2010) observed that women empowerment has emerged as an unintended consequence largely due to independent earning avenues. They have made a tangible contribution to household income and it has also impacted their socio-economic status. The scheme has facilitated women access to credit and financial institutions. Mandatory provision of wage payment through banks and post offices has brought greater number of women into institutional finance from which they had been largely excluded (Shah 2012). Study shows that women participation in scheme is much higher than all other forms of recorded rural works.

Women workers of MNREGS program opined that scheme has provided greater degree of economic independence and self-confidence and they feel empowered as they are also earning members of the family (Jandu 2008, as quoted in Kelkar 2011). Now they are able to use their income for food and consumption needs, health care and education of their children independently. A survey showed that 79% women employees collect their own wages and 68% keep their wages on their own (Frontline 2009: 13). Another study conducted by Institute for Human Development in Uttar Pradesh, Karnataka, Maharashtra and Andhra Pradesh recorded that 68.48% women workers have bank and post office accounts in their name and 13.70% have joint account with husband. Eighty-two percent of women reported that they operate the account on their own (IHD 2011).

The woman is not only a resource creator but also a homemaker. She spends significant time and unpaid labour power in home maintenance and caring. She spends 20%–25% of productive time on collection of basic livelihood goods like fuel wood, water, vegetables and so forth, as well as acquiring fodder for cattle (Hirway 2008). Effective measure has been taken by the government of Bihar to address the problem. The government has relaxed task norms for women. One day work for man is 80 cubic feet, whereas for women it is 68 cft, 15% lesser than their male counterparts (PRIYA 2008). Traditionally women have been denied productive assets other than their own labour power. Women's unmediated control rights to income and productive assets provides them and their households a livelihood with dignity. Study conducted by Panda (2015) in five districts of Assam shows that target group has definite edge over control group in terms of children education, better networking (formation of SHGs and other associations), distress migration, women empowerment and improvement in health status. In the study it has been recorded that 74% workers have attended a Gram Sabha meeting where agenda of the program was discussed, 95% of them admitted that social audit has been undertaken in all cases, 84% agreed for existence of transparency and accountability in the scheme. The picture that emerges out of the above discussions indicates that the scheme has increased people's participation, substantially reducing exclusion of women from social processes, enhancing productivity and reducing inequality, bring transparency to a great extent, thereby ensuring social sustainability aspects.

Environmental sustainability: There is a symbiotic relationship between environment and social structure. Environmental crisis limits productive resource base, productive activities, and impacts people's livelihoods. Soil erosion, deforestation, loss or depletion of animal and plant species limits productive opportunities of vast numbers of people in the countryside, specifically of the historically marginalised population. Therefore environmental sustainability is extremely important for toiling masses in general and labouring women in particular.

The scheme is the world's largest ecological security program which can strengthen foundation for sustainable agriculture (Swaminathan 2009). Sustainable agriculture integrates the goals of economic profitability, socio-economic equity and environmental sustainability. In the present century, food security has emerged as a major global concern and agriculture production directly affects food security. There is more to this direct link; a rise in agricultural production increases rural income, lowers food prices and makes food more accessible to poor (World Development Report 2008). However, expenditures under MNREGS would be non-inflationary because it will spur agricultural growth upon whose foundation a whole range of sustainable livelihoods will be built with private investments leading to secondary employment opportunities (Shah 2012). This aspect has been further strengthened by amendment and enlargement of scope of MNREGS works to small and marginal farmers. One of the major imperatives of MNREGS falls within the sustainable development paradigm by holding the philosophy of creation of environmentally sound productive assets that are created by the local community and also managed by them. Several studies highlighted that the scheme has enhanced environmental services, reduced vulnerability of agricultural production, through improved soil fertility and livelihoods (Tiwari et al. 2011). An impact study conducted by the Indian Institute of Science (2013) in selected districts of Andhra Pradesh, Karnataka, Rajasthan and Madhya Pradesh shows that the program has substantial environmental benefits in terms of improvement in water, land and forest resource base. Another study undertaken by Centre for Science and Environment (2008) has highlighted positive environmental impact of the scheme. A study by Panda (2015) in selected districts of Assam reveals that 75% of beneficiaries have reported that MNREGS has improved environmental base of their rural economy. Eighty-nine percent of third-party stakeholders stated that convergence has happened among schemes because of MNREGS which has positive impact on environment of their society. It is important to note that emphasis on creation of rural productive assets under the scheme, for example water conservation and harvesting, micro and minor irrigation canals, provision of irrigation facility to land owned by SCs, STs and beneficiaries of Indira Awas Yojna, flood control, drought proofing, renovation of traditional water bodies, rural connectivity and so forth has significant bearing on agricultural productivity, basic services to health, education and communication, thereby enhancing environmental sustainability and well-being of labouring masses of remote rural areas.

There are definite linkages between development and environmental protection more so natural resources is an integral part of developmental activities in general and agrarian activities in particular. The goal can be achieved through participatory resource management and decentralised decision making process. MNREGS has mandatory provision of social audits with potential to facilitate a bottom-up approach to decision making in this regard. Along with democratic decision-making at the grass-roots levels; involvement of civil society and other major groups can further strengthen the role and importance of the program. MNREGS along with convergence with other rural agricultural programs, like National Food Security Mission, Rajiv Gandhi Watershed Development Programme, Rashtriya Krishi Vikas Yojana, National Rural Livelihood Mission and so forth has a potential to impact both fund flow and regeneration of rural ecosystem. In practice, except few, many of these departments do not prefer to converge, because of fear that norms and processes of the scheme will be benchmarks of their projects and thereby pressure would be built to follow

MNREGS norms and processes in implementation of their projects as well (Panda 2015). According to one estimate, by 2020 half of the Indian population would be in the age group of 15–44 years, the bulk of which would be concentrated in rural areas. Percentage of male and female in the same age group would be 24.52% and 23.11%, respectively (Adlakha 1997). This shows approximately half of the nation's population would be in the active age group. In order to reap the demographic dividend and realise aspirations of new generations, development policy interventions like MNREGS would be extremely important.

On the basis of the preceding analysis one gets a rosy pictures of the scheme, but it is not free from bottlenecks and misuse of public finance. The program has been attacked by academia, non-governmental organisations (NGOs) and concerned citizens regarding corruption, executive apathy, quality of created assets, inclusivity, lack of awareness and so forth. These criticisms are valid to a great extent, but one should realise that MNREGS is the world's largest experiment in contemporary sustainable development. The program is at a defining moment with an immature age of eight years. It is the first right-based economic scheme in independent India which has tremendous potential to impact socio-economic status of labouring poor. Instead of counting failures of the scheme, development practitioners should focus on corrective measures to consolidate sustainable development through MNREGS; one of the important steps in the direction may be by strengthening grass-roots democratic institution, like Gram Sabha.

References

Adlakha, A. 1997. 'Population Trends: India International Policy Brief', http://census.gov, accessed on 15/1/2016.

Banerjee, K. and Saha, P. 2010. 'The NREGS, the Maoists and the Developmental Woes of the Indian State', *Economic and Political Weekly*, 55(28).

Centre for Science and Environment. 2008. 'An Assessment of the Performance of the National Rural Employment Guarantee Programme in Terms of its Potential for Creation of Natural Wealth in Indian's Villages', report submitted to Ministry of Rural Development, http://knowledge.NREGS.net, accessed on 25/1/2016.

Dreze, Jean. 2008, 'NREGA: Ship Without Rudder?' *The Hindu*, 19 July.

FRONTLINE. 2009, 26(1), January 3–16.

Government of India. 2008. *The National Rural Employment Guarantee Act 2005*, Operational Guidelines (3rd ed.). New Delhi: Ministry of Rural Development.

Government of India. 2014. *Mahatma Gandhi National Rural Employment Guarantee Act, 2005, Report to the People.* New Delhi: Ministry of Rural Development, 2 February.

Hirway, I. 2008. 'NREGA: A Component of Full Employment Strategy for India, An Assessment', http://nic.in/release, accessed on 28/1/2016.

Hirway, I., Saluja, M. R. and Yadav, B. 2009. 'Analysing Multiplier Impact of NREGS Works through Village SAM Modelling', in *National Rural Employment Guarantee Act: Design, Process and Impact.* New Delhi: Ministry of Rural Development.

Indian Institute of Science. 2013. 'Environmental Benefits and Vulnerability Reduction through Mahatma Gandhi National Rural Employment Guarantee Scheme', report submitted to Ministry of Rural Development, http://NREGS.nic.in, accessed on 1/2/2016.

Institute for Human Development. 2011. 'Engendering Development through MGNREGS: A Study of Women Workers in the State of Uttar Pradesh, Maharashtra, Karnataka and Andhra Pradesh', New Delhi: U N Women, South Asia Office.

Jha, R., Gaiha, R. and Pandey, M. K. 2011. 'Net Transfer Benefits Under India's Rural Employment Guarantee Scheme', *Journal of Policy Modeling,* 34(2).

Kareemulla, K., S. Kumar, Reddy, K. S., Rama Rao, C. A. and Venkateswarlu, B. 2010. 'Impact of NREGS on Rural Livelihoods and Agricultural Capital Formation', *Indian Journal of Agriculture Economics,* 65(3), July–September.

Kelkar, G. 2011. 'MGNREGS: Change and Continuity in Gender Relations', *Journal of Economic and Social Development,* VII(2).

NCEUS. 2008. 'The National Commission on Enterprises for Unorganised Sector (NCEUS): A Special Programme for Small and Marginal Farmers', http://nceus.gov.in, accessed on 14/1/2016.

Panda, B. 2015. 'National Rural Employment Guarantee Scheme: Development Practice at the Crossroads', *Economic and Political Weekly,* 50 (23).

Pankaj, A. and Tankha, R. 2010. 'Empowerment Effects of the NREGS on Women Workers: A Study in Four States', *Economic and Political Weekly,* 45(30).

Planning Commission. 2010. 'Data Tables-Statistics', www.planning commission.gov.in.

Prasad, B. N. 2009. 'Impact Assessment of National Rural Employment Guarantee Scheme in Sonbhadra and Hamirpur districts of Uttar Pradesh', Report submitted to Department of Rural Development, Government of Uttar Pradesh.

PRIYA. 2008, 'Role of Panchayati Raj Institutions in Implementation of NREGS', National Study: Phase III, New Delhi.

Ravi, S. and Engler, M. 2013. 'Workfare as an Effective Way to Fight Poverty: The Case of India's NREGS', http://ssrn.com/abstract, accessed on 27/1/2016.

Sen, Amartya. 1989. 'Development as Capability Expansion', *Journal of Development Planning*, 19(2).

Sen, Amartya. 2000. 'Cooperative Conflict', in Irene Tinker (ed.), *Persistent Inequalities: Women and World Development*. New York: Oxford University Press.

Shah, M. 2012. 'MGNREGA Sameeksha, an Anthology of Research Studies on the Mahatma Gandhi National Rural Employment Guarantee Act, 2005–06–2012', MORD, GoI.

Swaminathan, M. S. 2009. 'The Synergy Between NREGA and Food Security Act', *The Hindu*, June 1.

Tiwari, Rakesh et al. 2011. 'MGNREGA for Environmental Services Enhancement and Vulnerability Reduction: Rapid Appraisal in Chitradurga District, Karnataka', *Economic and Political Weekly*, 46(20), May 24.

United Nations Conference on Environment and Development. 1992, http://sustainabledevelopment.un.org, 3–14 June, accessed on 10/2/2016.

United Nations Research Institute for Social Development. 1994. 'Environmental Degradation and Social Integration', http://unrisd.org, November, accessed on 13/2/2016.

World Development Report. 2008. 'Agriculture for Development', World Bank Group.

Part II

Globalisation, marginalised sections and social justice

Problems and challenges

9 Institutional challenges of common pool resource management

Insights from Tawa Reservoir Fisheries Cooperative

Amlendu Jyotishi, R. Parthasarthy and Sajiv Madhavan

The limited availability of natural resources, coupled with multiple types of usages among different user groups, has made natural resource management an important subject in development discussions. Management system is dependent on the resource characteristics. It is often being concluded from various researches that a community-based decentralised system of management is one of the best forms of natural resources management. However, the management system and the rules and regulation that work best in a system might not work in other contexts. The scale, character of the resource and other socio-economic factors play important role in the effectiveness of any management system. There are subtle issues controlling the cooperation and decision-making process in a decentralised community management system where cooperative is one form of manifestation. If the decision-making process is not defined properly, then it is highly probable that pressure groups and interests of other members control the process and others are marginalised. In this chapter, we discuss the critical parameters of reservoir fisheries management system in the Tawa reservoir context. While doing so, we attempt to understand the property rights and resource characteristics. Tawa is an interesting case as it has witnessed various regimes of management of fisheries.

Characterising reservoir fisheries: a property rights perspective

In this section, our interest is to understand the reservoir fisheries in terms of property rights. *Property* is a benefit (or income) stream, and economics refers to it as a bundle of entitlements defining the owner's right, privileges and limitations for the use of the resource (Tietenberg and Lewis 2003).

Depending upon who possesses these rights, the property regimes can be defined into four types: private property regime, government property regime, common property regime and open access regime (Jyotishi et al. 2017). Of these, the common property regime is generally followed where the subdivision of the property is not possible and the community uses the resource in common. Generally forests, rivers and water bodies are these kinds of resources.

Different property regimes require different management system. The main types of management regimes are state management (government), collective management (people's cooperative), co-management, private management or systems without management. There are social, legal, environmental and political contexts that determine the management regime for the properties. Over a period of time, with change in the resource base and change in resource use, the management regimes also change.

Van de Laar (1990) defines the goods or resources in terms of their intrinsic characteristics of excludability and subtractablity. These intrinsic characteristic of the resource demands different property rights regime and institutions to manage the resource. Reservoir fisheries are kind of resources, while excludability is difficult, the resource use is substractible. Reservoir fisheries management involves varieties of stakeholders often with conflicting interest. At the same time, different management regime would have priorities associated with the regime. For example, a private management system may consider profit maximisation through resource extraction as a priority; a community or cooperative management system may have equitable distribution as priority; a state-managed system may identify maximum social welfare and sustainability as priority. This requires an analytical understanding of the reservoir fisheries management system.

Understanding of reservoir fisheries as a common pool resource

In a resource base like reservoirs, there is a clear requirement of stocking similar to culture fisheries. At the same time, especially large reservoirs are large enough to be managed at individual capacity, and hence, require collective engagement for resource extraction unlike aquaculture fisheries. Therefore, reservoir fisheries management challenges are peculiar and different from aquaculture as well as capture fisheries like marine and riverine fisheries. Historically, there are many interesting observations on condition of such common pool resources (CPR). Gordon (1954: 135) represents the most commonly held view of the commons.

There appears then, to be some truth in the conservative dictum that everybody's property is nobody's property. Wealth that is free for all is valued by no one because he who is fool hardy enough to wait for its proper time of use will only find that it has been taken by another.

In a situation where individuals have a shared responsibility and benefits, they have an incentive to defect from the rules, known as a moral hazard problem. By defecting, an individual can maximise his or her own benefit. The underlying assumption in this behaviour is that everyone else would perform his or her functions well and defection by the individual would have little impact on overall outcome. This inherent problem with the commons leads to what Hardin (1968: 1244) termed as 'tragedy of the commons'. In his famous example of herders sharing a common grazing ground, he writes,

Therein is a tragedy. Each man is locked into a system that compels him to increase his herd without limit – in a world that is limited. Ruin is the destination toward which all men rush, each pursuing his own best interest, in a society that believes in the freedom of the commons.

This theory concludes that no rational individual would find it beneficial to act in interest of the group, and everybody would try to maximise their individual benefits. These concepts conclude that it is impossible for a rational individual to cooperate. As Campbell (1985: 3) puts it,

Quite simply, these paradoxes cast in doubt our understanding of rationality and in the case of prisoner's dilemma suggest that it is impossible for rational creatures to co-operate. Thus they bear directly on fundamental issue in ethics and political philosophy and threaten the foundation of the social sciences. It is the scope of the consequences that explains why these paradoxes have drawn so much attention and why they command a central place in philosophical discussion.

However, Van de Laar (1990) argues that rationality and opportunism (self-interest seeking with guile) are the guiding principles behind any collective action. Rationality in this theory is not perfect but bounded by limited information processing capability and information cost. In case of prisoner's dilemma (Dawes 1973, 1975), two individuals do not have information about other person's strategy, and hence they would act in their individual self-interest. However, if this information gap is filled and if it is in the interest of the members to cooperate, this leads to Olson's (1965: 2) logic of collective action:

> If the members of some group have common interest or object and if they would all be better off if that objectives were achieved, it has been thought to follow logically that the individuals in that group would, if they were rational and self interested, act to achieve that objective.

Ostrom (1990: 17) argues in *Governing the Commons* that this logic extends to monitoring defection by others, because their self-interests would be compromised if others defect

> the herders, who use the same meadow year after year, have detailed and relatively accurate information about carrying capacity. They observe the behaviour of other herders and have an incentive to report contractual infractions.

But that cannot be applied in all the cases of the commons. Where the resource system and number of users are large, there is inherent problem in monitoring. Even in other situations, the problem of mutual monitoring is widespread. As Elster (1989: 40–41) puts it,

> Before a union can force or induce workers to join it must overcome a free-rider problem in the first place. To assume that the incentives are offered in a decentralised way, by mutual monitoring, gives rise to a second order free-rider problem. Why, for instance, should a rational, selfish worker ostracise or otherwise punish those who don't join the union? What's in it for him? True, it may be better for all members if all punish non-members than if none do, but for each member it may be even better to remain passive. Punishment almost invariably is costly to the punisher, while the benefits from the punishment are diffusely distributed over the members. It is, in fact, a public good. To provide it, one would need second-order selective incentive, which would, however run in to a third-order free-rider problem.

Runge's 'Assurance Problem' model, which sees individual behaviour as being motivated not only by self-interest but by the degree of assurance a person has that others will cooperate. This theory in a way takes us toward collective adherence or collective defection by the community. Our case study of Tawa poses similar problems as we will discuss later.

However, in case of reservoir fisheries, the theory provided by Ostrom (1990) seems to be more relevant. She argues that the fundamental choices facing appropriators are whether to defect from rules and whether to monitor defection by others. It cannot be reduced to a simple game structure. She clusters the problems facing CPR appropriators in to two broad classes: appropriation problems and provision problems (Gardner et al. 1990). Appropriation problems are concerned with the effects that various methods of allocating a fixed, or time-independent, quantity of resource units will have on the net return obtained by that appropriator. While the provision problems are concerned with effects of various ways of assigning responsibility for building, restoring, or maintaining the resource system over time as well as the well-being of the appropriators. Both kinds of problems are involved in every CPR to a greater or lesser extent, and thus, the solution to one problem must be congruent with the solution to the other. We would now turn to our case of Tawa reservoir in order to understand the inherent management challenges and problems.

Tawa reservoir: a case study

The Tawa reservoir is an interesting case to study different institutional arrangements for management of common pool resources. Tawa is a tributary of the Narmada River in the state of Madhya Pradesh in India. The dam on Tawa was constructed in 1974. It is one of the first dams to be built under the Narmada Valley Development Project (NVDP). It is situated in Hoshangabad district. The reservoir that emerged after the construction of the dam led to submergence of about 20,000 hectares of land and displacement of 44 villages.

Fishing in the reservoir started in the year 1975. It was under state government, which was transferred to the Madhya Pradesh State Fisheries Development Corporation (MPFDC), which was continued till 1994. In 1994 the reservoir was given to a private contractor for a year. Then for a year it was left as an open access resource. In year 1996, after a long struggle with government agencies, the displaced tribal groups got fishing rights in the reservoir as a livelihood option to compensate displacement related livelihood losses. A cooperative structure was formed to manage the reservoir, and it was responsible for stocking, fishing, marketing and distribution of benefits to the fisherfolk. This cooperative structure has 34 primary fishing cooperatives of the Scheduled Tribe communities and six affiliated societies (three traditional fisherfolk and three consisting Bengali fisherfolk). The reason for giving rights to the affiliated societies by the federation is not explicit. According to Sunil and Smita (1996), these Bengali and other traditional fishermen had started fishing in the reservoir before the formation of the cooperative, maybe because of their traditional dependence on fisheries and owing to their skills in the fisheries, keeping in mind that they can train the tribal population and help the federation to meet the standards set by MPFDC, they were affiliated with the cooperative. Besides, prior appropriation rights of these fisherfolk were also respected through this arrangement.

The Tawa Matsya Sangh (TMS) is often being cited as the best management practice for this reservoir by the media and newspapers in India.[1] Comparing this system with earlier management regimes also confirms that the condition of local fisherfolk has improved after the formation of the TMS. However, over the period of time, the functioning of this institution has undergone changes. There are external and internal factors contributing to this change.

Comparison of the management regimes in Tawa

Any analysis of management regimes where large user groups are involved must look into equity and efficiency aspects. Though resource sustainability earlier was an incidental point in management regime; this too has become an important aspect of management practice in recent years. In case of Tawa, a comparative analysis shows a considerable increase in fish production after 1996–97 (Figure 9.1).

The poor performance under MPFDC regime can be attributed to following reasons. First, because of inconsistent level of stocking, the maintenance of production level becomes difficult. Second, due to irregularity in marketing and lower wage, the fishermen were forced to sell their catch to illegal marketing networks (Sunil and Smita 1996). And finally, the average number of fishing days was much lower than what could otherwise be possible in a normal year[2] (Jyotishi and Parthasarathy 2005).

For a year, when the reservoir was under private contractors, as it can be seen in Figure 9.2, the stocking was reduced and fish extraction was high. As a result, the wages and employment increased (Figure 9.3).

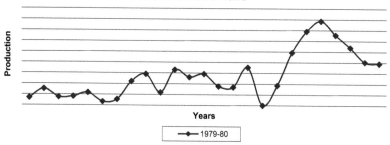

Fish Production of Tawa

Figure 9.1 Fish production in Tawa under different regimes

Note: Production in metric tonnes

Source: Jyotishi and Parthasarathy (2007), pp. 412–413

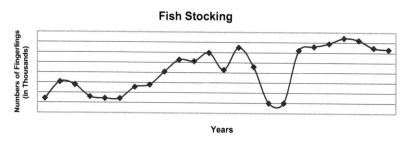

Fish Stocking

Figure 9.2 Stocking scenarios in Tawa from 1980–81 to 2003–04

Note: Stocking in thousands of fingerlings

Source: Jyotishi and Parthasarathy (2007), pp. 412–413

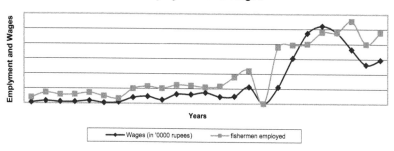

Employment and Wages

Figure 9.3 Wages and employment scenario in Tawa from 1979–80 to 2003–04

Source: Jyotishi and Parthasarathy (2007), pp. 412–413

However, during the private regime the employment was confined to the fisherfolk from outside whom the contractor had brought to increase production. In this case equity was out of question because the benefit was accrued to select few in terms of employment or even subsistence. With the over-fishing of the reservoir, the productivity for that particular year was improved, but the resource base was exploited to an extent that could have serious implication on the production in years to come. Such production regime without adequate regulatory mechanism puts a question mark on the resource sustainability.

In 1995, when the reservoir was left as an open access resource, no responsibility was assigned on stocking, although almost 300 fishermen were fishing and on an average five-quintals of fish was harvested in a year (Sunil and Smita 1996). But without stocking, the productivity would decline leading to what is known as 'tragedy of the commons'. Production system is not a sufficient condition without appropriate management and plan for marketing. Revenue stream would be adversely affected without market expansion and better price realisation.

In 1996, after the formation of the cooperative, the reservoir was leased to the cooperative. Since then, the cooperative is performing the task of stocking, catching, marketing and distribution of benefits to the fishers. The production has increased since the cooperative management. After four years, however, the fish production has started declining and it is a matter of concern. The causes for this decline in production are yet to be established. The possible causes given by TMS include:

1   Damaged nets are not replaced; stems in the riverbed cause damage to nets.
2   Stems also reduce the effective fish catch area. However, this problem was in existence during other management regimes too.
3   Floods causing damage to nets are also another regular feature; however damage to nets is a matter of concern when the investment required for replacement is not available.
4   Fish and fingerlings being washed away when dam gates are opened, as they do not have any protective device. This is again a regular feature; the gates of the dam always cause some loss of fish to the command area.
5   Pollution created by the ashes of the Sarni thermal power station is also a regular problem, however in the years when the water in the reservoir is lower, the pollution may create major problem because the intensity of the problem would be higher in those years.

6 Illegal fishing: this is a sign of crumbling of the 'social fencing' that was proclaimed as one of the major advantage of the cooperative, claiming that the fishermen living around the periphery would not allow outsiders to fish in the reservoir.

7 Lack of a hatchery (once again, this problem was there at the starting of the cooperative, it can at best militate an increase in efficiency, but cannot be given as a cause of decline).

8 Lack of sufficient area for rearing of seedlings: this is possible, if number of fishermen has increased, then there would be overcrowding and there may not be enough space for rearing of seedlings. However, the number of fishermen has declined because of non-replacement of nets. Therefore this does not seem to be the case.

That leads us to the observations that the major causes of decline in production are non-replacement of damaged fishing gear and illegal fishing. This is also reflected in the causes of increase in production given by the TMS. They proclaim that distribution of more nets to the fishermen and increase in number of fishermen are two important factors for increase in fish catch in the current year.[3] However, the cooperative needs to address the problems mentioned earlier to increase productivity to ensure growth of the cooperative.

Such situation is a case in point to analyse the internal dynamics of the TMS system, which has direct and indirect implication on fish production. This prompts us to understand the structural framework of the TMS, and hence the internal dynamics of the cooperative.

Structural framework of Tawa Cooperative Management System

The Tawa Matsya Sangh (TMS) is a two-tier federation. There are 34 primary fishing societies with six affiliated fishing societies. The fishers in different groups work in a fishing society. The affiliated fishing societies includes three Bengali fishing societies, which include Bangladeshi refugees who settled in India after the 1971 war. The other three societies include traditional fishers, mostly from Kahar community, who were fishing in the river before the construction of the dam; and other scheduled caste members, who came as labourers at the dam site and started fishing in the reservoir after the completion of the dam. Though they were not having tribal origin, but were settled in this area before the formation of the cooperative. They were therefore included in the cooperative group.

At the apex level, the cooperative works like an organisation to carry out fishing activity in the reservoir. It is at this level, the decisions about stocking are taken; working rules are formed; deferred wages are decided; negotiations with government department are undertaken. Marketing of fish, procurement of seedlings, rearing of fingerlings and monitoring are some of the responsibilities of TMS, at the apex level.

At the individual cooperative level, the organisational structure is homogenous, having all the members from the same community and village. They have their own norms and decision-making systems. Each primary society has its own committee. It has 13 members and a president among them. It is the responsibility of the president to keep record of the individual fishermen and give him his wages. A secretary may support the president in keeping the accounts. The president and the secretary are given commission on the fish caught by their members. Generally they get 60 paisa per kilogram of fish caught.[4]

The decisions about stocking as well as distribution of profits in the form of deferred wages (or 'bonus' as it is popularly known among the fishers) is taken at the time of annual general meeting of the federation. The president, secretary, accountant and other staffs are permanent employees of TMS. They have the responsibility of marketing of fish among other responsibilities. They receive allowance for travelling and boarding expenses at the time of marketing and other work-related trips. The federation does not have permanent staff to monitor the fishing activity. The person working at the federation office visits the reservoir and checks the identity of the fishers.

For the purpose of our study, we have categorised the villages as per their location along the reservoir. We distributed our samples on the basis of location of the village with reference to the reservoir (i.e. the head, middle and tail portion of the reservoir). Further, care has been taken to see to it that we get representative sample of both tribal and non-tribal villagers. The total numbers of sample observations in head/middle/tail of the reservoir are given in Table 9.1.

Table 9.1 Distribution of sample tribal, traditional and other fishermen in head, middle and tail end of the reservoir[5]

Caste/location	Head	Middle	Tail	Total
Scheduled tribes	36	30	36	102
Traditional fishermen	24	0	0	24
Others (Scheduled Caste, Harijans, Bengali)	12	11	0	23
Total	72	41	36	149

Source: Primary survey

With this basic understanding of the structural characteristics, it would be worthwhile noting the internal dynamics of the cooperative.

Internal dynamics of the cooperative

The TMS has been functional since 1996. The formation of the cooperative, after a long struggle with the government, was a positive development and the cooperation continued till the benefits are distributed more or less equally among the stakeholders. But the flexibility to change the institution to meet new demands of the circumstances usually determines the sustainability of the cooperative. In this section we look into some of the internal issues in the functioning of the cooperative.

The main issue within the cooperative is equity,[6] as this has implications on adherence or defection from the rules laid by the cooperative, which in turn would determine the production efficiency. The following are the salient challenges of TMS cooperative structure.

1   Heterogeneous composition of the group leading to fractionalisation of the cooperatives.
2   Uneven spatial and temporal distribution of water resource resulting in differential participation of members.
3   Conflicts over the land for drawdown cultivation causing local-level conflicts in the primary societies.
4   Uneven distribution of means of production (nets, labour, etc.) is increasing disparity.
5   Bureaucratisation of the cooperative decreasing its efficiency.
6   Administrative apathy over decreasing efforts of marginal tail end villagers.
7   Exclusion of potential beneficiaries from the project, giving rise to poaching.
8   Disguised defection from the cooperative to gain from difference between cooperative and market rates.

First, because of the inclusion of the traditional and Bengali fishermen, the composition of the federation is no longer homogenous. These two groups are more skilled than tribal fishermen. The fishing technique they use is also comparatively efficient. Actually, the deployment of Pesijaal[7] and Mahajaal[8] for increasing production to meet the target laid in the contract with the government has led to inequality among fisherfolk. Employing these techniques and methods, the fish catch has been increased up to more than 10 times of that with traditional methods. Apparently it would seem that the benefits from higher production would accrue to all the fisherfolk. However, deeper observations suggest that the real benefit to the fishermen might decline because the deferred payment of wages is based on their yearly production. Now with deployment of efficient fishing techniques, the fish catch gets accumulated with a small number of fishermen, thus increasing inequalities.

Second, the fishermen in the head, middle and tail end of the reservoir have differential access to the water resource. Because there are no specified areas allotted to fishermen, the access is based on prior appropriation. Obviously, those in the head can start fishing and laying their nets earlier than others who are staying away. Moreover, fishermen from faraway villages cannot keep a watch on their nets because that would require them to stay at the reservoir for the whole night.

However, with disparity in access to water resource, there is also additional access to the drawdown land to those in middle and tail portions, which they can use for cultivation. In areas, which do not get water in summer, the land of the reservoir is used to cultivate summer crops like green gram and watermelon. The access to this land for cultivation was not there before the formation of the cooperative. The distribution of land for cultivation is not looked into by the cooperative but it is based on principle of prior appropriation.[9] There are number of conflicts for this land because it goes underwater every monsoon and re-emerges after the water level goes down. The boundaries are shifting and the conflicts are unavoidable.

Further, extent of nets that one can employ for fishing is not restricted. The fishermen with more capital investment in nets would be on a comparative advantage over others. This inherent inequality would be determinant in the fishing effort. Fishers with more amounts of nets would be on a virtuous cycle and their capacity to fish would increase with time. While those with fewer nets would go through a vicious cycle. When the nets are damaged or stolen, they would have to rely on TMS to get nets on credit. Now, this amount they have to pay through their wages for the fish catch to be sold to TMS. People with limited access to water resource and limited labour would not opt for getting more nets. Worse, they would be discouraged by the fact that the fish catch is anyway declining because of the deployment of Pesijaal and Mahajaal.

In our primary survey, some fishermen told us that the authorities in TMS are acting like bureaucrats, and at times would threaten them not to indulge into defection. However, there is not a single case in those 10 years that shows that TMS has taken any action against the defectors. One respondent went on to tell that the workers at the weighing centre let go a whole boat full of the fish to big fishermen while when he tried to keep 2 kg of fish for entertaining guests, they caught him and threatened to seize his boat and nets. Another respondent, had similar complains about TMS officials when he somehow got hold of disco nets[10] somebody had disposed of in the reservoir. These allegations might be faulty, but that also shows the displeasure of the fisherfolk with the cooperative.

Small fishermen especially from the tail end villages have stopped fishing since last two years because their nets have been stolen from the reservoir. This is because of substantial distances they have to travel to get to the fishing area. They cannot keep a watch on their nets properly. This is similar to the assurance problem discussed earlier in this chapter.

There is a revealing example in the tail end villages about the community that has not been included in the cooperative. People of this community collect the small fish from the fishermen in the village and they go to sell it in local markets. This system gives incentive to the fishermen to defect and catch the small fish. Since this community is not part of the cooperative, nobody has direct control over them. They do not go to catch fish in the reservoir themselves; they only sell other people's catch in local markets. However, whether they were excluded by mistake or it was their own choice is to be found out. But the fact remains that they are facilitating defection from the cooperative. It has been seen that some of the fishermen in this village did have disco nets, which are being used to catch small fish.

While it is true that people pushed to the margin would do anything for survival, it is not necessary that those who are better off would not defect; given a chance everyone has a tendency to maximise his or her self-interest. However, if it were still profitable to them to stay as a part of the system, they would not accept the fact openly, but they may defect in disguise. In a revealing example, quite by chance we interviewed two different individuals (a couple) from the same household. When we asked the husband about selling outside the cooperative, he said they do not indulge in such activities and sell only to the cooperative. When the same question was put to his wife, she said – unknowing of the implication – that every fortnight in the peak season, they do sell outside the cooperative in local market. The reason for this is that the cooperative gives uniform yearly rate for fish. While

Table 9.2 Comparative prices of local and predator fish in closing and regular season at cooperative and local markets

Place	Season ——————— Type of fish	Closed Season (Monsoon)	Regular
Cooperative	Rohu/Katla/Mrigal	No transaction	16 Rs. per kilogram
	Palhin/Singad	No transaction	30 Rs. per kilogram
Local Market (Tawanagar/Itarsi/ Kesla/Sukhtawa/ Chandrakhar)	Rohu/Katla/Mrigal	10 to 15 Rs. per kilogram	20 to 40 Rs. per kilogram
	Palhin/Singad	40 to 45 Rs. per kilogram	60 to 70 Rs. per kilogram

Source: Primary survey and personal conversations with locals

in the local market, the same fish would fetch four times the value. Table 9.2 shows the comparative prices of fish at the cooperative and local market in monsoon as well as non-monsoon season. The information in the table 9.2 is obtained through personal conversation with fishers during primary survey.

The livelihood of fisherfolk in Tawa

Fishing and cultivation are two major sources of income for tribal population living around Tawa reservoir. However, because of irrigation and drying up of the reservoir, not all the fishermen can do fishing for the entire year. Apart from two months closing season, the fishermen in the middle and tail end villages of the reservoir have to stop fishing in summer because of receding water level. In general, the livelihood options for tribal population around Tawa can be summarised as shown in the table 9.3. The villages are grouped into head, middle and tail portion of the reservoir.

Now, for carrying out fishing activity, the means of production other than access to water are boat, nets and labour. The fishing technique used in these villages requires two persons on a boat – one to sail and the other to put the net. The mutual need for boat and labour is generally negotiated easily because one cannot go alone for fishing. The major controlling factor is fishing gear (nets). Because of the stems in the riverbed, the lifespan of the nets is very low. In general they need to invest in nets every year. For a consistent income they have to buy 5

Table 9.3 Livelihood activities by population dependent on the reservoir round the year

Portion of the reservoir	15 August to December	December to March	March to 15 June
Head	fishing	fishing	fishing + drawdown cultivation
Middle	fishing	fishing+ cultivation on their own land	drawdown cultivation
Tail	fishing + cultivation on their own land	drawdown cultivation	other labour jobs

Source: Primary survey and field observations

Table 9.4 Number of fishermen with varying amounts of nets in the head, middle and tail area of the reservoir

Location/ amount of nets	Less than 10 kg	11–15 kg	16–20 kg	More than 20 kg	Total
Head	34 (22.81%)	14 (9.39%)	9 (6.04%)	15 (10.06%)	72 (48.32%)
Middle	17 (11.40%)	4 (2.68%)	8 (5.36%)	12 (8.05%)	41 (27.51%)
Tail	8 (5.36%)	8 (5.36%)	14 (9.39%)	6 (4.02)	36 (24.16%)
Total	59 (39.59%)	26 (17.44%)	31 (20.80%)	33 (22.14%)	149 (100%)

Source: Primary survey

kg nets every year.[11] TMS does provide credit to buy nets, however it can be understood from the above matrix that some fishermen do not have access to water for entire year, and they would have difficulties to pay back the borrowed money with limited access to means of production. To compensate the deficiency in fishing period, they would need to ensure that they catch as many fish as possible in limited time. Thus they would require more amounts of nets. However, it is not necessary that increasing the amount of nets is the only solution. Those who can go for fishing to the head of the reservoir would be able to sustain. This is reflected in Table 9.4.

The minimum means of production for agriculture activities are land, water, labour, seeds, pesticides, fertilisers and a pair of bullock. Those who are cultivating in other than monsoon season need to invest in pump sets to draw water from the reservoir and need to pay water charges to the irrigation department. Seeds generally they keep aside each year from the production for cultivating next year. A pair of bullock is part of their livestock. The recurring investment here is fertilisers, pesticides and sometimes seeds and bullocks. Thus, here also the controlling factor is credit. People indulging in drawdown cultivation has problem in availing credit from bank because they do not have legal ownership of the land.

In absence of credit facility for cultivation, people borrow from informal sources like the moneylenders at an exorbitant interest rate of 10% per month (this means 120% annual interest rate). Needless to say that they would be barely able to return the money and might never be able to save money for future. A descend down in this vicious circle of debt can compel them to do anything for money. A small defection from the cooperative is not a sin.

The decision to adhere or defect from the rule or norm is a complex phenomenon. There are several internal and external factors affecting the decision. In cases like reservoir fisheries and that too amid forest, it is often the livelihood question that has maximum impact on decision making.

Institutional issues related to the cooperative management system: a discussion

In order to understand performance of the cooperative in the institutional economics realm, let us define the institution in the first place. According to North (1991, pp. 97),

> Institutions are the humanly devised constraints that structure human interaction. They are made up of formal constraints (rules, laws, constitutions), informal constraints (norms of behaviour, conventions, and self-imposed codes of conduct), and their enforcement characteristics. Together they define the incentive structure of societies and specifically economies.

Leach et al. (1999: 226) says that *Institution* includes all the structures and practices that influence the question of who has access to and control over what resource, and arbitrate contested resource claims. *Indigenous institutions* represents organisations, conventional knowledge, regularised practices, or customary rules and practices. Policymakers have heralded each of these as a valuable resource for the development process (Leach et al. 1999). Chambers (1983) sees them as risk minimising, sustainable and adopted to precarious microenvironments

(Chambers 1983, 1997; Richards 1985, 1997; Reij et al. 1996). Warren et al. (1995) says indigenous organisations are seen as a ready-made set of power structure that enable a group of people to organise themselves, to take decisions, to enforce regulations and to resolve conflicts.

The concept of *moral economy* states that within a small group the premises of rational choice do not apply as people are bound by close mutual relations of kinship and reciprocity (Douglas 1987). There are 40 primary fishing cooperatives in TMS federation, which are bound together by the movement for the fishing rights for the displaced tribal communities. These societies represent different groups based mainly on community and villages they belong to.

Ostrom (1986) defines institutions as the set of working rules that are used to determine who is eligible to make decisions in some area, what actions are allowed or constrained, what aggregation rules are used, what procedures must be followed, what information must or must not be provided, and what payoffs will be assigned to individuals dependent on their actions. In the TMS context, working rules are common knowledge[12] and are monitored and enforced. According to Ostrom (1990), three levels of rules cumulatively affect the actions taken and outcomes obtained. These levels are operational rules, collective choice rules and constitutional choice rules.[13] The operation level rules affect the operational choice of appropriation, provision, monitoring and enforcement. Operational rules are based on collective choice by the cooperative and it is manifested in terms of policy-making, management and adjudication. These collective choices are dependent on constitutional choices like formulation, governance, adjudication and modification at the highest level. Now with this background, let us see what the issues at Tawa are. The major issues in this context are royalty, the price structure of TMS, conflicts with the irrigation department, conflicts between fisheries, irrigation and forest department and the looming threat of displacement for wildlife conservation. We will discuss these issues in detail.

First, at the time of formulation, it was decided that Rs. 6 per kilogram royalty would be paid by TMS to MMS (Matsya Maha Sangh).[14] In fact, in other reservoirs in the state, MMS is getting more royalty. But, the TMS argues that MMS does not have any function in the reservoir unlike other reservoirs. As they do not provide any facility, this imposition of royalty is an unjust burden on TMS.

Second, the price of fish that the fishermen get is uniform throughout the year; this decision was a collective choice to provide consistent income to the fishermen. The deferred wages in the closing season is also a step towards that direction. But there is an inherent problem in the uniform pricing. At the operational level, with existence of local markets, fishermen would be attracted to sell outside the cooperative to get higher prices.

Further, in India, use of reservoir for irrigation and power generation are the top priorities, while fishing is the last priority. The ownership of the reservoir is also with the irrigation department. The fish production is greatly affected by the water level in the reservoir. Often, the fish would flow out of the dam because of release of water for irrigation or power generation. This affects the efficiency of stocking.

Apart from this, the fact that part of the reservoir is in the sanctuary area is also a matter of concern. The forest department in India is powerful, having both policing and judicial powers. They claim that sanctuary rules would apply to the part of reservoir falling inside the sanctuary area. Therefore, activities like fishing could not be allowed here. They often seize nets and boats from the fishermen who venture in to those areas.

On top of all these, there is a looming threat of displacement because of growing concerns of wildlife conservation. When we were conducting our survey, there was a protest going on in response to the proposal of moving 17 villages out of the Bori Sanctuary area. The media carried an article on formation of a wildlife corridor connecting two sanctuaries and a national park in the state. If that happens, then whole reservoir would become part of a biosphere reserve and all the forest residents would have to move out.[15] However, the website of Madhya Pradesh forest department carries a different proposal. The proposal envisages merging of three sanctuaries in the state to make a biosphere reserve (see Box 9.1). The resulting implications of the proposal are yet to be established because; the existing Wildlife (Protection) Act does not mention the concept of biosphere reserve at all.

As the reservoir belongs to the irrigation department and they are not bothered about anything other than water, the allocation of land for drawdown cultivation[18] is much disorganised. Neither the irrigation department nor the TMS is intervening for equitable share of land to farmers. The irrigation department charges money for use of water for cultivation based on the amount of land the farmer occupies. But the boundary disputes remain there because there is no legal document showing the location of the land. Prior appropriation is only way the land allocation is determined.

There is an interesting example in case of this drawdown land. The tribal have to pay tax for water use to the irrigation department. The TMS has a *usufruct right*[19] over the resource. This means that they do

---

Box 9.1 The conservation versus livelihood debate

The major portion of the Tawa reservoir falls into the Satpura National Park and Bori wildlife sanctuary. By definition, the only difference between the national park and wildlife sanctuary is that the claims of ownership in a sanctuary may be considered and allowed, while in case of national park, all the rights are forfeited. The section 24, subsection 2(C), which is the only additional clause in case of sanctuary states: 'Allow, in consultation with the chief wildlife warden, the continuance of any right of any person in, or over any land within the limits of the sanctuary'.[16]

Although the studied villages are outside the national park area, most of the portions of the reservoir are under Satpura National Park and Bori Wildlife Sanctuary. This makes the fishing operations in the reservoir a challenging proposition leading to conflict with the forest department.

The Government of India, in consultation with Environmental Planning and Co-ordination Organisation[17] has constituted Pachmarhi Biosphere Reserve which covers three civil districts of Hoshangabad, Betul and Chhindwara. The total area is 4,926 km^2 and it envelops three wildlife conservation units: Bori Sanctuary, Satpura National Park and Pachmarhi Sanctuary. Satpura National Park comprises the core zone (524 km^2) and the remaining area of 4,502 km^2. surrounding the core zone serves as a buffer zone. The resulting implications are yet to be established, but there are reasons for concern.

---

not have ownership over the land; but since they have been given the reservoir on lease, they can use the land for cultivation. The fishermen, in turn, have started cultivating on this land. Thus, they have de facto right over the land. The receipt of the irrigation department mentioning the area of land given to tribal is the only proof of the right. The physical boundary of the plot is not mentioned anywhere in the document. In one village, the revenue officer of the irrigation department had ordered that he would start charging for irrigation water if he would receive any complaint regarding conflict over this land. This has the effect that the conflicts are resolved within the village *panchayat*[20] itself and the revenue officer need not intervene in the matter. This shows how external pressure can reduce the conflicts at the community level and increase the cooperation.

These internal and external issues have a direct bearing on the livelihood of the people. The decisions about collective action, cooperation or defection from the prevailing rules and norms are determined by the livelihood condition of people.

Conclusion

Although cooperative is the best model available for management of natural resources, there are internal and external issues which needs to be understood to ensure equity, efficiency and sustainability of the cooperative. Equitable distribution of the means of production and the benefits from the resource is necessary to maintain cohesiveness among the members. Here, the inequitable opportunities have led to a decline in the trust with the cooperative, which has led to decline in the efficiency of the operation. To ensure efficiency, it is necessary to address appropriation and provision problems. Though, restrictions on smaller nets and voluntary closures during breeding season are important milestones reached by the cooperative, there are still appropriation problems to be addressed. Parity with the local markets in terms of the price structure can ensure that all the fishermen sell their catch only to the cooperative. In terms of provision problems, the need to establish their own hatchery tops the list. However, establishment of hatchery would only be feasible if the lease period granted to TMS is extended for a longer time, or some agreement with the fisheries department to ensure the reprieve in the revenue or payment of the money spent on the development of infrastructure is given to the cooperative.

Apart from these, the up-gradation in the technology is essential to increase the efficiency, but this growth need to be inclusive to ensure that equity is maintained. Alternatively, the reservoir could have been given to Pesijaal players to get optimum output, but this would make locals unemployed. The purpose of forming the cooperative for betterment of local communities would perish. It is therefore necessary to balance efficiency and equity.

Cooperative can work efficiently even when the composition of the group is heterogeneous, as we have seen in the initial years of operation of TMS. As it has been observed in tail end villages of Tawa reservoir, it is important in common pool resource management that everyone who can derive potential benefits from the resource system be made a part of the cooperative. Exclusion of potential stakeholders would result in defection.

As observed, livelihood of the people has a direct impact on sustainable exploitation of the resource base. To ensure livelihood of people, it is necessary to provide credit facility to satisfy recurrent need for investment in fishing gear as well as agricultural implements. Though agricultural implements might not feature within the purview of the fisheries cooperative, the fact that a good number of members in the middle and tail end reservoir engage in both fishing and agriculture needs to be taken into account. They would benefit if certain kind of credit cooperative, with additional responsibility of management of drawdown cultivation, would go a long way to enhance livelihood of the people.

Apart from the internal issues, the cooperative needs to address larger issues, which have direct bearing on the lives of forest dwellers. The long-standing conflict between the fishers and forest department needs to be resolved. The main strength of the cooperative lies in the unity among members. How efficiently TMS deals with these issues will determine the sustainability of the cooperative and livelihood of the fisherfolk.

As we observe the scenario after the year 2007, the external issues became the main cause of failing TMS as an institution. In the year 2006, the lease period of TMS ended and was not renewed by the Madhya Pradesh Matsya Mahasangh (MPMM), the nodal agency for fisheries in the state. This issue was contested in the court of law that remains subjudice. In addition to this, a large part of the reservoir falling under Satpura National Park makes the issue more complex. Fishing is not allowed inside the national park region. This has resulted in conflicts between the fishers and the forest authorities leading to confiscation of boats and nets of the fishers and subsequent protest by them.[21] These two external factors apart from internal issues discussed earlier in the chapter played the critical role in failing TMS as a sustainable cooperative institution.

Notes

1 *Nayi Duniya*, 6 July 2001; *The Hindu* Business line, 4 July 2000; *Express Magazine*, 25 February 2001; *Samaj Kalyan*, October 2000.
2 For a detail description of the problems of MPFDC regime, refer to Sunil and Smita (1996), pp. 455–457.
3 Both the causes for decline of production after four years and increase in production in the current year are based on the personal interview of the TMS office bearers.

4 The TMS pays Rs. 17 per kilogram and the fisherman gets Rs. 16 per kilogram. From the remaining Rs. 1, 20 paisa goes towards the share of the primary society with TMS and another 20 paisa is used to fund nets and boats. The remaining 60 paisa per kilogram goes towards the salary/commission of the president and secretary.

5 The Bengali fishermen, who reside at Hoshangabad and other locations, are not shown separately in this table. However, they do feature in other tables, as they are part of our sample. The numbers in the table shows the number of samples households considered for the study.

6 'Equity' here is different from 'equality'. Equity means a distribution of a whole into parts that is acceptable to all members of a community, which need not to be equal. So, in this reference, equitable distribution need not mean equal distribution. Here, since the entire tribal were part of the struggle, they have more or less equal stake in the reservoir. However, traditional fisherman and Bengalis were working before TMS also, so they are allowed to fish but if they prosper at the cost of tribal fishermen, then it would lead to disaster because of the growing impatience of tribal fishermen.

7 It is a technologically advanced system of fishing in which the fishermen cordon a big area in the middle of the reservoir with the help of a group of boats and then make noise to frighten the fish so that the fish would move frantically and would be caught in the net. This technique requires 10 to 12 fishermen with one expert diver, who can free the nets from the tree stems in the bottom of the reservoir.

8 This is also an advanced system of fishing. In this method a part of the riverbed is cleaned up of all the tree stems. A group of 10 to 12 fishermen drags a big net so as to form a 'C' shape boundary along one bank of the river. The entire riverbed is dredged with this net and all the fish are captured. These two techniques have helped in dramatically increasing the fish production. But there are concerns from the small fishermen that this has adversely affected their individual harvesting.

9 A concept in economics that suggests that the first person to arrive on land has the superior claim on the resource it has to offer. This is the most common way in which traditional societies define rights.

10 This is a type of net with small mesh size and nylon material. It is used to catch small fish. After the formation of TMS, it has been banned. Anybody found using these nets could be punished.

11 This is a rule of thumb the experienced fishermen said they are following.

12 'Common knowledge' is an important assumption frequently used in game theory and essential for most analysis of equilibrium. It implies that all participants know X, that the participants know that each of the other knows X, and that each of the others knows that each of the others knows X (Aumann 1976)

13 For understanding of all these three rules, refer to Ostrom (1990), p. 52.

14 Matsya Maha Sangh (earlier MPFDC – Madhya Pradesh Fisheries Development Corporation) is the state level federation managing all the reservoirs having area greater than 2,000 hectares. While they have greater say in the functioning of all the co-operatives of the state, Tawa Matsya Sangh is given greater autonomy. TMS has been given the reservoir on lease and

in return they have to pay royalty. The marketing of fish is also done by TMS, while in other cases it is performed by MMS.

15 For details of the project and its impact, see K. S. Shaini, 'The Cost of Tigers', p. 66, *Outlook* magazine, 13 June 2005.

16 Chapter IV, Section 35, subsection 3 of The Indian Wildlife (Protection) Act, 1972.

17 An autonomous body under the department of Housing and Environment, Government of Madhya Pradesh.

18 It is a spin-off of the dam project. The tribal people use the land that emerges out of water by receding of water in summer for cultivation. It was not practiced until the formation of TMS. Now that the fishing rights are with these people, they can indulge in this activity. It's an important means of livelihood for people in middle and tail portions of the reservoir, because they do not get water near their villagers and the long distance to the actual water level prevents them to go for fishing.

19 This is a concept in economics in which the subjects have right to use the resource but it is not the ownership right.

20 Village *panchayat* is the grass-roots level institution in India. It signifies the 'decentralisation of power' or *Panchayaatiraaj* as it is often referred to in policy documents of government of India.

21 For details, see www.downtoearth.org.in/news/tawa-matsya-sangh-fishing-cooperative-in-madhya-pradesh-loses-licence-5650.

References

Aumann, R. J. 1976. 'Agreeing to Disagree', *The Annal of Statistics*, 4(6).

Campbell, Richmond. 1985. *Background for the Uninitiated*. Vancouver: University of British Columbia Press.

Chambers, Robert. 1983. *Rural Development: Putting the Last First*. Harlow: Longman.

Chambers, Robert. 1997. *Whose Reality Counts? Putting the First Last*. London: IT.

Dawes, Robyn M. 1973. 'The Commons Dilemma Game: An N-Person Mixed-Motive Game with a Dominating Strategy for Defection', *Ori Research Bulletin*, 13(2): 1–12.

Dawes, Robyn M. 1975. 'Formal Models of Dilemmas in Social Decision Making', in M. F. Kaplan and S. Schwartz (eds.), *Human Judgment and Decision Processes: Formal and Mathematical Approaches* (87–106). New York: Academic Press.

Douglas, Mary. 1987. *How Institutions Think*. London: Routledge & Kegan Paul.

Elster, Jon. 1989. *The Cement of Society: A Study of Social Order*. Cambridge: Cambridge University Press.

Gardner, Roy, Ostrom, Elinor and Walker, James M. 1990. 'The Nature of Common-Pool Resource Problems', *Rationality and Society*, 2(3): 335–358.

Gordon, Scott H. 1954. 'The Economic Theory of a Common-Property Resource: The Fishery', *Journal of Political Economy*, 62(2): 124–142.

Hardin, Garret. 1968. 'The Tragedy of the Commons', *Science*, 162(3859): 1243–1248.

Jyotishi, Amalendu and Parthasarathy, R. 2007. 'Reservoir Fisheries Management: Experiences of Tawa in Madhya Pradesh', *Economic and Political Weekly*, 42(5), 409–415, February 3–9.

Jyotishi, Amalendu and Parthasarathy, R. 2005. 'The Tawa Reservoir Fisheries Management: Experiences and Options', Working Paper No. 28, CEPT, Ahmedabad.

Jyotishi, Amalendu, Sivramkrishna, Sashi and Lahiri-Dutt, Kuntala. 2017. 'Gold Mining Institutions in Nilgiri – Wayanad: A Historical – Institutional Perspective', *Economic and Political Weekly*, 52(28), 57–63, July 15.

Leach, Mellisa, Mearns, Robin and Scoones, Ian. 1999. 'Environmental Entitlements: Dynamics and Institutions in Community-Based Natural Resource Management', *World Development*, 27(2): 225–247.

North, Douglass C. 1990. *Institutions, Institutional Change and Economic Performance*. Cambridge: Cambridge University Press.

North, Douglass C. 1990. 'Institutions', *Journal of Economic Perspectives*, 5(1): 97–112.

Olson, Mancur. 1965. *The Logic of Collective Action*. Cambridge, MA: Harvard University Press.

Ostrom, Elinor. 1986. 'An Agenda for the Study of Institutions', *Public Choice*, 48(1): 3–25.

Ostrom, Elinor. 1990. *Governing the Commons: The Evolution of Institutions for Collective Action*. Cambridge: Cambridge University Press.

Reij, Chris, Scoones, Ian and Toulmin, Calmilla. 1996. *Sustaining the Soil: Indigenous Soil and Water Conservation in Africa*. London: Earthscan.

Richards, Michael. 1997. 'Common Property Resource Institutions and Forest Management in Latin America', *Development and Change*, 28(1): 95–117.

Richards, Paul. 1985. *Indigenous Agricultural Revolution: Ecology and Food Production in West Africa*. London: Unwin Hyman.

Sunil and Smita. 1996. *Alternative Forms of Management in Reservoir Fisheries: Comparative Case Studies from Madhya Pradesh*. Anand: Institute of Rural Management.

Tietenberg, Tom and Lewis, Lynne. 2003. *Environmental and Natural Resource Economics*. New Delhi: Pearson Education.

Van De Laar, Aart. 1990. *Framework for the Analysis of Common Pool Natural Resources*. The Hague and The Netherlands: Institute of Social Studies.

Warren, Dennis M., Slikkerveer, Jan L. and Brokensha, David. 1995. *The Cultural Dimension of Development: Indigenous Knowledge Systems*. London: IT.

10 Social justice for women and girls: global pacts, unmet goals, environmental issues

Jan Marie Fritz

This chapter examines the difficult situation for women and girls in a world that is increasingly connected[1] but also has become more unequal[2] and has profound sustainability issues. And while many are discussing and/or intervening to address the world's daunting problems, there are increasing calls for these interventions to be based on social justice (inclusion and fairness) principles.

The first section of the chapter discusses the global situation of women and girls to learn to what extent their world is inclusive and fair. The second section focuses on the goals outlined in three very important international documents about human rights for women – the UN Convention on the Elimination of All Forms of Discrimination Against Women (1979), the Beijing Declaration and Platform for Action (1995), and UN Security Council Resolution 1325: Women, Peace and Security (2000). The analysis is done particularly with an interest in environmental issues (e.g. climate change, land use, pollution). The third section looks at some interesting initiatives to move us toward meeting the goals noted in the human rights documents regarding women and the environment. The chapter's concluding section discusses the role of human rights documents in meeting goals and indicates what needs to be done to improve the situation of women and girls.

The status of women and girls

The difficult situation facing women and girls has been repeatedly discussed in international forums and there have been serious efforts on different levels[3] to see that women and girls are centrally included and safe. What have been the outcomes of these efforts?

According to the 2012 World Bank Report on Gender Equality and Development (The World Bank 2011), gains have been made for females, since the mid-1980s, in educational enrolment, life expectancy, and labour force participation. The report also indicated 'change has come slowly or not at all for many women and girls in many . . . dimensions of gender equality'. Persistent gender gaps were noted in four particular areas: *excess deaths* (in comparison to males) of girls and women; *disparities in girls' schooling* (particularly in Sub-Saharan countries and some parts of South Asia); *unequal access to economic opportunities* (e.g. 'women everywhere tend to earn less than men'); and *less say in making decisions and control of resources in households and society*.

A 2014 report from the UN Secretary-General indicated 'Overall progress . . . has been unacceptably slow, with stagnation and even regression in some contexts'. Change has not been 'deep enough, nor has it been irreversible'. Among the points that were stressed:

> Overall progress . . . has been slow for women and girls who experience multiple and intersecting forms of discrimination. Stark gaps exist for poor women and girls living in rural areas and in poor urban settlements on several indicators, including enrolment in education, maternal mortality and access to such services as water and sanitation. . . . Violence against women and girls persists at alarmingly high levels, in many forms, in public and private spaces.

And the 2015–16 report by UN Women (2015a) on the progress of the world's women discusses some gains, but also underlines that 'changes have not yet resulted in equal outcomes for women and men'. The 2015 study for the European Parliament (Debusscher 2015: 9) noted some global progress for women and girls (e.g. there are laws promoting gender equality, important gains in the enrolment of girls in primary and secondary education, and women's labour market participation has increased). The overall assessment, however, is similar to the other analyses – 'global progress has been "slow, uneven and limited"' (Debusscher 2015: 10). Of particular concern:

- Women and girls who experience multiple and intersecting forms of discrimination
- Low levels of participation and leadership of women in decision-making
- Persistence of violent conflict
- Chronic underinvestment in gender equality globally
- Absence of strong accountability mechanisms.

Human rights for women and girls

Just as organisational, local and national efforts to agree on social justice principles are important, so are international efforts. There are three very important international human rights documents specifically concerned with human rights for women and girls. They will be discussed and examined in the order each was put in place, with special attention given to any mention of women's rights in relation to the physical environment (e.g. climate change, pollution, and land use).

UN Convention on the Elimination of All Forms of Discrimination against Women (1979)

The UN General Assembly adopted the Convention on the Elimination of All Forms of Discrimination Against Women (CEDAW) on 18 December 1979. The treaty (United Nations General Assembly 1979; UN Women 2015b) has 30 articles and covers topics such as educational opportunities, sex trafficking, women's rights in political and public life, access to health care, rural women, women's economic and social rights, and equality in marriage and family life. In Article 14 (about rural women), CEDAW indicates that women should have 'equal treatment in land and agrarian reform as well as in land resettlement schemes' as well as 'adequate living conditions, particularly in relation to . . . sanitation . . . (and) water supply'. The expectation is that the specifics in all the CEDAW articles should be incorporated into national law in order to fully realise women's rights.

The treaty, often called an 'International Bill of Rights for Women', was adopted 130 to 0, with 10 abstentions. It should be noted, however, that more than 50 of the countries that ratified the treaty have done so specifying certain reservations and objections and that a handful of member states (Iran, Somalia, Sudan, Tonga, Palau and the United States) have not ratified the treaty.

CEDAW does expect member states that have ratified the treaty to provide reports (about their goals and progress regarding the central inclusion of women and girls in their societies) to the CEDAW Committee at least every four years[4] (e.g. Hungary 2006; Hungary 2013; India 2012). In addition, supplementary/alternative/shadow reports can be submitted that support and/or challenge the government reports (e.g. Hungarian Women's Lobby and the European Roma Rights Centre 2013). The CEDAW Committee then responds to a government (e.g. CEDAW Committee on the Elimination of Discrimination against Women 2013) about its written and oral presentations taking into account any supplementary statements. Sometimes the CEDAW Committee takes particular note of a situation and asks for a special report. For instance, the Committee asked India to submit a special report on violence against women and girls (CEDAW 2014).

In addition to CEDAW's formal process, there are other CEDAW-related activities. In the United States, for instance, there is a movement to have cities declare themselves as CEDAW cities. This initiative has the support of the US Conference of Mayors (2014). This kind of effort raises awareness about CEDAW, provides a framework for local/community action[5] and calls attention to the fact that the United States is one of a very small number of nations that has not ratified the treaty.

The Beijing Declaration and Platform for Action (1995)

In September 1995, an 'unprecedented 17,000 participants and 30,000 activists' (UN Women 2015c) from around the world came to Beijing for the Fourth World Conference on Women. Representatives from 189 countries agreed to the Beijing Declaration and Platform for Action, 'the most comprehensive global policy framework for gender equality, the empowerment of women and the realization of the human rights of women and girls' (UN Secretary-General 2014: 3). According to Debusscher (2015: 8), the 123-page Platform for Action has been, for the last 20 years, 'the world's most powerful framework for international and national gender equality policies and practices'.

The Platform for Action has 12 critical areas of concern: (1) women and poverty, (2) education and training of women, (3) women and health, (4) violence against women, (5) women and armed conflict, (6) women and the economy, (7) women in power and decision-making, (8) institutional mechanisms for the advancement of women, (9) human rights of women, (10) women and the media, (11) women and the environment and (12) the girl child. In addition to the areas of concern, strategic objectives are identified and actions are listed for the international community, governments and civil society.

The section in the platform on women and the environment has three strategic objectives:

1   Involve women actively in environmental decision-making at all levels.
2   Integrate gender concerns and perspectives in policies and programs for sustainable development.
3   Strengthen or establish mechanisms at the national, regional and international levels to assess the impact of development and environmental policies on women.

There are over 30 specified actions and these include increasing women's access to relevant education, integrating women – including indigenous women – and their views and knowledge in decision-making, and sponsoring research on the role of women, particularly rural and indigenous women, in food gathering/production as well as many other areas. In the platform's first section on women's poverty, it is noted that the poverty is directly related to a number of factors including the lack of land ownership.

UN Security Council Resolution 1325: Women and Peace and Security (2000)

United Nations Security Council Resolution (UNSCR) 1325 was adopted unanimously by the Security Council on 31 October 2000. This acceptance was due, in part, to the work of dozens of women's organisations; the efforts of UNIFEM (now UN Women); the work of the NGO Working Group on Women, Peace, and Security; the initiative of Netumbo Nandi-Ndaitwah, then Minister of Women's Affairs in Namibia; and the continuing support of Ambassador Anwarul Chowdhury. The resolution (United Nations Security Council 2000), a three-and-a-half-page document with 18 points, highlights the terrible consequences of violent conflict on women and girls as well as the important role of women in the peace building processes. It is one of the most important UN resolutions within the field of peace and security policy (Fritz et al. 2011: 1–2).

A number of important international and regional documents have a bearing on the full participation and advancement of women. UN Security Council Resolution 1325 is particularly significant because it mandates (requires)[6] all UN member states to centrally involve women in the political life of their countries and take additional actions to address the situation of women and girls (Fritz et al. Gumru 2011; Fritz 2014a, 2014b). While UNSCSR 1325 does not discuss women in relation to environment, land use, pollution or water, one of the follow-up Security Council resolutions to 1325 – UNSCR 1889 (United Nations Security Council 2009) – mentions the 'particular needs of women and girls in post-conflict situations in regard to . . . land and property rights'.

There has been a pressing need for the Security Council resolutions (e.g. 1820, 1888, 1889, 1960, 2106, 2122) about women, peace and security. In contemporary conflicts, soldiers are not the highest number of casualties; instead, according to the UN secretary-general (2008: 2), 'millions of women and children continue to account for the majority of casualties in hostilities, often in flagrant violation of human rights and humanitarian laws'. Mass displacement, use of children in combat, and violence against ethnic and religious groups, as well as gender-based and sexual violence, are common in certain places of the world. The secretary-general's 2009 report noted that 'sexual and gender-based violence remained one of the most pernicious consequences of armed conflict as a weapon of war' (UN Secretary-General 2009: 2–3).

When UNSCR 1325 was adopted in 2000, it did not mention the need for national action plans (NAPs) to address the situation facing women and girls. In 2002 and 2004, the UN Security Council president and then the UN secretary-general noted the lack of progress and invited UN member states to prepare NAPs in order to take strong steps toward implementing UNSCR 1325. In 2009, UNSCR 1889 welcomed 'the efforts of Member States in implementing . . . resolution 1325 (2000) at the national level, including the development of national action plans'.

Some of the national action plans do refer to land, climate change and/or the environment. Liberia (2009), in its plan for 2009–13, noted as indicators of change: 'Quality and frequency of education courses on land and property rights offered to women and level of increased understanding of women'. Finland's 2012–16 national action plan (Ministry of Foreign Affairs for Finland 2012) includes the following:

> The destruction of the environment, issues related to land ownership and disputes regarding the use of natural resources may give rise to violent conflicts. Correspondingly, transparent and equitable management of natural resources increases political stability and plays an important role in conflict prevention and resolution.

One of Finland's objectives is 'to promote women's participation in environment and security related issues and in the mitigation of climate change and adaptation to its consequences' (Jukarainen and Puumala 2014: 21).

Miller et al. (2014: 11) reviewed the 1325 national action plans and identified examples of 'institutional progress' they think are plausibly connected, either directly or indirectly, to UNSCR 1325 and the subsequent related resolutions. One of these outcomes concerned the environment:

> Many governmental and non-governmental organizations have appointed, and are appointing, Gender Advisors to promote policy and implementation in WPS (Women, Peace and Security) as

well as in areas such as climate change and conservation, agriculture, and more.

There are now over 45 nations and regional action plans,[7] but having plans and making substantial progress are not the same. As indicated in the remarks at the beginning of this chapter, there still is a remarkably long way to go for countries to achieve substantial progress. In fact, McMinn (2015: 7), writing on behalf of Cordaid, a Netherlands-based civil society organisation that fights poverty and exclusion, as well as its partners, says:

> Despite the high expectations for UNSCR 1325 to build transformative change and strengthen women's participation, the Women, Peace and Security (WPS) agenda has failed to deliver on both counts. In the current context, confidence that the WPS agenda will enable women's participation and leadership is diminishing at global, national and local levels . . . The focus in WPS global policy has been on rhetoric and advocacy rather than action, and on the bureaucratic rather than the transformative approach to gendering peace and security.

Women, environmental concerns and actions

This is a time of very serious environmental challenges. In addition to treaties and agreements about principles, we must specify desired outcomes, collaborate on developing creative actions, set timelines and monitor implementation strategies and outcomes. Ken Conca (2015: 2) identifies some of the reasons why this must be done:

> The World Health Organization estimates that more than three million people annually die prematurely due to air pollution. More than two billion people lack a sanitation system of the sort that was introduced at the height of the Roman Empire, two thousand years ago. As much as one-third of the world's population extracts its living and its food supply from degraded land that has suffered a long-term loss of ecosystem functions and services.

Climate change refers to differences in the distribution of regional or global weather patterns for extended periods of time (i.e. decades to millions of years).[8] Climate change affects the whole world and will affect all its people, particularly the 'poorest people, in the poorest regions who have contributed least to the causes. The majority of these deeply affected are women' (Halonen 2015). In different socie-ties, however:

> women and men will feel the impacts in differentiated ways, with a disproportionate burden on women very likely in some contexts due to structures that marginalize them socially, politically and economically. In parallel, these same structures prevent women from being active participants in addressing climate change.

The UN Secretary in his 2014 report noted a number of problems regarding women and the environment:

> there is evidence that women farmers control less land than do men and that they have limited access to inputs, seeds, credits and extension services . . . Critically, data disaggregated by sex do not exist for tracking and assessing women's access to and use of water and energy services. Indoor air pollution, primarily pro-duced by inefficient and dirty cook stoves and fuels, causes some 4.3 million premature deaths worldwide, above all among women and children . . . Women and girls are also the most exposed to waterborne diseases . . . Women and children bear the main nega-tive impacts of collecting and transporting fuel and water.

In beginning to address these problems, there are a number of inter-esting initiatives regarding gender and the environment. In 2008, for instance, the Global Gender and Climate Alliance (GGCA) – 'a first-of-its-kind multi stakeholder network to advance gender-responsive climate change policies, plans, and actions' (Aguilar et al. 2015: 10) – with the International Union for Conservation of Nature (IUCN) and key partners, such as the UN Development Programme (UNDP) and Government of Finland, created the *Training Manual on Gen-der and Climate Change* (https://cmsdata.iucn.org/downloads/eng_version_ web_final_1.pdf). This training material was the first com-prehensive document on gender and climate. It has been translated into all the UN languages and used in trainings around the world. The 2008 publication has just been fully updated and the 467-page publi-cation is now available (Aguilar et al. 2015) as *Roots for the Future: The Landscape and Way Forward on Gender and Climate Change*.

Another important initiative – an index – was developed by IUCN's Global Gender Office (GGO) in collaboration with UN Women (http://genderand environment.org; Granat 2015). The GGO operates with a basic principle: that female empowerment and gender equality are required for sustainable development. In November of 2013, the GGO of IUCN (2013) launched the Environment and Gender Index (EGI; environmentgenderindex.org). The EGI was developed because no quantitative tool was available to monitor, assess and compare the 'implementation of mandates that mainstream gender equality issues in the environmental sector'.

The pilot phase of the EGI used environmental and gender variables in a composite index to rank 73 countries based on six categories: ecosystem, governance, gender-based rights and participation, livelihood, country-reported activities and gender-based education and assets. Countries for which data were available were put in three performance categories: strongest, moderate and weakest. The strongest performers were found to be Iceland, Netherlands, Norway and Sweden. The weakest were Democratic Republic of Congo, Yemen, Mauritania, Syria and Burundi.

One of the newer datasets is Women in Environmental Decision Making (Granat 2015). In collaboration with UN Women, the EGI team in IUCN's Global Gender Office provided the dataset to better understand a finding of the 2013 pilot study – that women, at all levels, have less access to environmental decision-making spheres. Indicators are compiled for women's participation in environmental delegations, leadership of large environmental institutions, green parties and national environmental ministries. The UN Secretary-General (2014: 83), in his 2014 report, discussed EGI's information about female representation in government delegations for selected meetings of each of the Rio Conventions and noted 'Despite improvements in some cases, gender parity is far from being achieved in . . . government delegations'.

While women – and particularly poor women – bear a heavier burden because of climate change, many of these women also are leaders (e.g. decision-makers, experts, stakeholders, organisers and/or educators) in the struggle to deal with the effects of climate change. The work of these women and their organisations has been profiled in many publications (e.g. Fritz 2006, 2008, 2014a, 2014b, 2014d; Porio 2014) also is now highlighted in a much broader way by the Secretariat of the United Nations Framework Convention on Climate Change (UNFCCC).[9]

The UNFCCC Secretariat showcases the important roles women play in responding to climate change through its Momentum for Change initiative. The initiative (Figueres 2015: 7):

> highlights women-led activities that are making a real difference in the fight against climate change – activities that can be replicated and scaled up at the local, national and international levels. (It)

tell(s) the stories of women making transformational change, such as the Thai industry leader who has turned her solar company into a billion-dollar business, or the Australian trailblazer who is creating a movement to get 1 million women across the country to act on climate change, or the Ghanaian entrepreneur who is bringing bamboo bicycles to the global market.

This Momentum for Change initiative began in 2012 with support from the Rockefeller Foundation. It showcases 'particularly innovative – but also scalable and replicable – projects that help to create a highly resilient, low-carbon future'. The initiative identifies 'innovative and transformative solutions that address both climate change and wider economic, social and environmental challenges' (Aguilar et al. 2015: 73).

There has been some movement to address the many issues faced by women in dealing with environmental issues. The UN Secretary-General (2014: 85) identified five trends:

1   Increasing women's access to land and other resources
2   Supporting women in responding to environmental degradation
3   Supporting women's participation and collective action
4   Mainstreaming gender perspectives in sustainable development policies
5   Increasing attention to changing patterns of consumption and production.

While there is movement, much more needs to be done to improve the lives of women. Implementation strategies, for instance, need to include financial support for individual women and organisations to be part of the solutions to environmental problems. Gender-specific effects of pollution and environmental health risks need to be documented. Representatives of civil society and government need to work together to identify problems and put action plans in place.

Interventions need to be monitored, reviewed and revised, as needed. Serious problems (as well as small ones) require the recognised leadership of men as well as women.

Conclusion

A number of national leaders have noted the problems faced by women and girls in their societies and called for and initiated change. Among them was Dr. Bhimrao (known as Babasaheb) Ambedkar

(1891–1956; Gauher 2015). Ambedkar, an economist and social reformer, was independent India's first law minister and the principal designer of India's Constitution. He worked tirelessly to end discrimination against Untouchables (Dalits) and women (Chandra and Mittra 2003: 154–157; Sharma 2003: 158–163). Ambedkar knew the importance of declaring and emphasising human rights principles in a country's basic documents (such as a constitution) as a strong platform for change (Khan 2001: 174).

It is very important to emphasise human rights in basic documents (such as national constitutions, international treaties and UN Security Council resolutions). Human rights documents with a review component, such as CEDAW's committee review of country reports and the submission of additional documents by civil society organisations to assess those reports, are particularly helpful. Human rights documents can be enduring and set the stage for a broad range of possible actions. Without the acceptance of these documents, some actions may not be considered or taken and it may be difficult to put comprehensive approaches in place. Basic human rights documents need to be at all levels including the global. As Conca (2015: 2) has concluded:

> It is difficult to imagine a world of peace and prosperity unless the problems of climate change, water shortages, the loss of forests, and the destruction of critical ecosystems are addressed. It is also hard to imagine effective responses to these problems without a strong role for the UN.[10]

In addition to accepting basic human rights documents at all levels (e.g. organisation, community, global), effective actions are necessary to achieve progress in the central inclusion of women and girls. To make progress in this area, the advice is much the same if one looks at the situation in a general way or in terms of a specific sector (e.g. work force, decision-making, laws or environment).

Political will, in which leaders prioritise central inclusion, is of the utmost importance in change initiatives (Fritz et al. 2011; McMinn 2015). In addition, there has to be the central and effective participation of women in all stages of informal and formal decision making (e.g. United Nations Environmental Programme et al. 2013: 7), adequate financial support for change efforts (e.g. The Global Network of Women Peace builders and Cordaid 2014), data collection that takes gender into account, and adequate protection of women and girls from harassment and physical violence (e.g. United Nations Environmental Programme et al. 2013: 8). Also of importance: the identification of obstacles that prevent effective gender mainstreaming in planning and implementing change efforts and actions to deal with these obstacles (e.g. Aguilar et al. 2015: 332); recognised leadership of women (e.g. UN Women 2015c); dissemination of information about innovative programs and solutions[11] and accountability (e.g. McMinn 2015). Our developing global partnership for sustainability will only work if it is based on human rights principles of inclusion, access to knowledge for all and full (respectful/effective) participation in decision-making.

Notes

1 As Kenneth Gould (2014: 251) has noted, 'The people and societies across the globe have never been more closely interconnected, interdependent, and in close contact than they are now. The world has never been smaller in terms of the insignificance of great distance and the ability to instantaneously communicate across space'.

2 According to the 2015–16 report by UN Women on the progress of the world's women, 'The world is both wealthier and more unequal today than at any point since the Second World War. The richest 1 per cent of the world's population now owns 40 per cent of the world's assets, while the bottom half owns no more than 1 per cent'.

3 Information about the different levels of intervention (e.g. individual, small group, community, national, global) is available in *Community Intervention* (Fritz 2014c: 15–16).

4 Countries that don't meet a deadline (e.g. Hungary 2013) may file combined periodic reports.

5 Some actions are taken within city administration (e.g. Garcetti 2015) and others are in the broader community.

6 Under the UN Charter, the UN Security Council 'alone has the power to take decisions which member states are obliged to carry out' (Fritz 2009).

7 It is difficult to have an accurate count of the national action plans. Some, for instance, are out of date (e.g. ended in 2014) and may or may not be included in a list of the total number of plans. While it is not a requirement to have a national action plan, it should be noted that only about one-fourth of the 193 UN member states have developed plans.

8 According to UN Secretary-General Ban Ki-moon's address at the opening of the UN Climate Summit in 2014, 'Climate change is the defining issue of our age. It is defining our present. Our response will define our future. To ride this storm we need all hands on deck' (Aguilar et al. 2015: 17)

9 UNFCCC is an international environmental treaty. It was negotiated at the Earth Summit in Rio de Janeiro (3–14 June 1992) and entered into force on 21 March 1994.

10 Conca (2015: 193) suggests 'Embrace a human right to the environment and acknowledge an environmental responsibility to protect'.

11 Aguilar et al. (2015: 382–466) provide '35 examples from around the world of innovative mitigation and adaptation programmes and projects that have successfully integrated gender equality concerns'.

References

Aguilar, Lorena, Granat, Margaux and Owren, Cate. 2015. *Roots for the Future: The Landscape and Way Forward on Gender and Climate Change.* Washington, DC: International Union for Conservation of Nature and Global Gender and Climate Alliance.

CEDAW Committee on the Elimination of Discrimination against Women. 2013. 'Concluding Observations on the Combined Seventh and Eighth Periodic Reports of Hungary adopted by the Committee at Its Fifty Fourth Session', 11 February–1 March. CEDAW/C/HUN/CO/7–8, www.refworld.org/publisher, CEDAW, HUN, 514b022c2,0.html.

CEDAW Committee on the Elimination of Discrimination against Women. 2014. 'Concluding Observations on the Combined Fourth and Fifth Periodic Reports of India', Adopted by the Committee at its 1219th and 1220th meetings on 2 July, www.ohchr.org/EN/Countries/AsiaRegion/Pages/INIndex.aspx.

Chandra, Ramesh and Mittra, Sangh. 2003. *The Ambedkar Era.* New Delhi: Commonwealth.

Conca, Ken. 2015. *An Unfinished Foundation: The United Nations and Global Environmental Governance.* Oxford: Oxford University Press.

Debusscher, Petra. 2015. 'Evaluation of the Beijing Platform for Action +20 and the Opportunities for Achieving Gender Equality and the Empowerment of Women in the Post-2015 Development Agenda', Brussels: European Union, www.europarl.europa.eu/studies.

Figueres, Christiana. 2015. 'Prologue' by UNFCCC Executive Secretary, in Aguilar, Lorena, Granat, Margaux and Owren, Cate. 2015. *Roots for the Future: The Landscape and Way Forward on Gender and Climate Change,* 7. Washington, DC: International Union for Conservation of Nature and Global Gender and Climate Alliance.

Fritz, Jan Marie. 2006. 'Confrontando o Racismo Ambiental: Boas Idéias, Vozes Femininas, Perspectivas Globais', in Selene Herculano and Tania Pacheco (eds.), *RacismoAmbiental* (148–163). Brazil: FASE.

Fritz, Jan Marie. 2008. 'Environmental Justice', in Amy Lind and Stephanie Brzuzy (eds.), *Battleground: Women, Gender and Sexuality* (143–150). Westport and London: Greenwood Press.

Fritz, Jan Marie. 2009. 'Women, Peace and Security: National Plans, International Interests, Sociological Possibilities', *Bulletin of the Kharkiv National University (Ukraine),* (881): 25–31.

Fritz, Jan Marie. 2014a. 'Women, Girls and Transitions from Autocracy', in Sari Hanafi, Marlene Nasr and Diab Chebib (eds.), *Arab Uprisings: Sociological Perspectives and Geographical Comparisons* (102–135). Beirut and Lebanon: Farabi.

Fritz, Jan Marie. 2014b. 'UN Security Council Resolution 1325, Inclusive Peace building and Countries in Transition', in Jan Marie Fritz (ed.), *Moving Towards Just Peace: The Mediation Continuum* (245–272). Dordrecht, Heidelberg, New York and London: Springer.

Fritz, Jan Marie. 2014c. 'Essentials of Community Intervention', in Jan Marie Fritz and Jacques Rhéaume (eds.), *Community Intervention: Clinical Sociology Perspectives* (15–30). Dordrecht, Heidelberg, New York and London: Springer.

Fritz, Jan Marie. 2014d. *Moving Toward a Just Peace: The Mediation Continuum*. Dordrecht, Heidelberg, New York and London: Springer.

Fritz, Jan Marie, Doering, Sharon and Gumru, F. Belgin. 2011. 'Women, Peace, Security and the National Action Plans', *Journal of Applied Social Science*, 5 (1): 1–23.

Garcetti, Eric. 2015. 'Gender Equity in City Operations: Mayor's Executive Directive Number 11', City of Los Angeles, 26 August, https://d3n8a8 pro7vhmx.cloudfront.net/mayorofla/pages/17070/attachments/original/ 1440645063/ED_11.pdf?1440645063.

Gauher, Rajesh Kumar. 2015. 'Dr. Ambedkar on Women's Progress', *International Journal of Applied Research*, 1 (9): 697–700. www.allresearchjournal. com/archives/2015/vol1issue9/PartK/1-9-196.pdf.

The Global Network of Women Peacebuilders and Cordaid. 2014. 'Financing for the Implementation of National Action Plans on UN Security Council Resolution 1325: Critical for Advancing Women's Human Rights, Peace and Security', October, www.cordaid.org/media/medialibrary/2014/10/ FinancingUNSCR1325_2014_27oct.pdf.

Gould, Kenneth. 2014. 'Global Dynamics', in Kenneth Gould and Tammy L. Lewis (eds.), *Ten Lessons in Introductory Sociology* (251–276). New York: Oxford University Press.

Granat, Margaux. 2015. 'Telephone Interview with a Program Officer in the Global Gender Office', International Union for Conservation of Nature, Washington, DC, December 2.

Halonen, Tarja. 2015. 'Foreword' by the President of the Republic of Finland (2000–2012)', in Lorena Aguilar, Margaux Granat and Cate Owren (eds.), *Roots for the Future: The Landscape and Way Forward on Gender and Climate Change*. Washington, DC: International Union for Conservation of Nature and Global Gender and Climate Alliance.

Hungarian Women's Lobby and the European Roma Rights Centre. 2013. 'Alternative Report Submitted to the UN CEDAW Committee for Consideration in Relation to the Examination of the Combined Seventh and Eighth Periodic Reports of Hungary', January, http://daccess-dds-ny.un.org/doc/ UNDOC/GEN/N06/402/22/PDF/N0640222.pdf?

Hungary. 2006. 'CEDAW Report: Sixth Periodic Report', http://daccess-dds-ny.un.org/doc/UNDOC/GEN/N06/402/22/PDF/N0640222.pdf?Open Element.

Hungary. 2013. 'CEDAW Report: Seventh and Eighth Periodic Reports', www.refworld.org/publisher, CEDAW, HUN,514b022c2,0.html.

International Union for Conservation of Nature. 2013. 'The Environment and Gender Index (EGI) 2013 Pilot', Washington, DC: IUCN, environmentgen derindex.org.

Jukarainen, Pirjo and Puumala, Eeva. 2014. 'The Nordic Implementation of UNSCR 1325: A Comparative Evaluation', Finland: The 1325 Network Finland and Acaide Oy. www.1325fi/tiedostot/Nordic_Implementation_1325_report_2014_final.pdf.

Khan, Nazeer H. 2001. 'Ambedkar on Gender Equality: Myth and Reality', in Nazeer H. Khan (ed.), *Ambedkar on Federalism, Ethnicity and Gender Justice* (173–190). New Delhi: Deep and Deep.

McMinn, Karen. 2015. 'Candid Voices from the Field: Obstacles to a Transformative Women, Peace and Security Agenda and to Women's Meaningful Participation in Building Peace and Security', The Netherlands: Cordaid, The Global Partnership for the Prevention of Armed Conflict and Women Peacemakers Program.

Miller, Barbara, Pournik, Milad and Swaine, Aisling. 2014. 'Women in Peace and Security through United Nations Security Resolution 1325: Literature Review, Content Analysis of National Action Plans, and Implementation', IGIS WP 13/GGP WP 09. May. Washington, DC: Institute for Global and International Studies, www.peacewomen.org/assets/file/NationalAcitionPlans/miladpournikanalysisdocs/igis_womeninpeaceandsecruitythroughunsr1325_millerpournikswaine_2014.pdf.

Ministry of Foreign Affairs for Finland. 2012. *Finland's National Action Plan 2012–2016*. Jyväskylä, Finland: Ministry of Foreign Affairs for Finland.

Open Element India. 2012. 'CEDAW Report', Combined fourth and fifth periodic reports. http://daccess-dds-ny.un.org/doc/UNDOC/GEN/G12/470/51/PDF/G1247051.pdf?OpenElement

Porio, Emma. 2014. 'Climate Change Adaptation in Metro Manila: Community Risk Assessment and Power in Community Intervention', in Jan Marie Fritz and Jacques Rhéaume (eds.), *Community Intervention: Clinical Sociology Perspectives* (149–166). Dordrecht, Heidelberg, New York and London: Springer.

Republic of Liberia. 2009. *The Liberia National Action Plan for the Implementation of United Nations Resolution 1325*. Liberia: Republic of Liberia.

Sharma, Sanjay Praksah. (ed.). 2003. *Dr. B.R. Ambedkar: A Crusader of Social Justice*. Vol. I. Jaipur: RBSA.

Sharma, Sanjay Prakash. 2003. *Dr. B.R. Ambedkar: A Crusader of Social Justice*. Jaipur: RBSA.

UN Women. 2015a. 'Progress of the World's Women 2015–2016: Transforming Economies, Realizing Rights', http://progress.unwomen.org.

UN Women. 2015b. 'The Beijing Platform for Action: Inspiration Then and Now', http://beijing20.unwomen.org/en/about, accessed 8/12/2015.

UN Women. 2015c. 'Gender Equality and Women's Empowerment in a Changing Climate: UN Women Key Messages for the Climate Conference – COP 21', November 17, http://webcache.googleusercontent.com/search?q=cache:PMW0GSCbuP0J:www2.unwomen.org/~/media/headquarters/attachments/sections/how%2520we%2520work/intergovsupport/un%252

0women%2520key%2520asks%252010_28.docx%3Fv%3D1%26d%3D
20151124T040426+&cd=2&hl=en&ct=clnk&gl=us
United Nations Environment Programme, United Nations Entity for Gender
Equality and the Empowerment of Women, United Nations Peace build-
ing Support Office and United Nations Development Programme. 2013.
Women and Natural Resources: Unlocking the Peace Building Potential.
Nairobi: UNEP.
United Nations General Assembly. 1979. 'Convention on the Elimination of
All Forms of Discrimination Against Women', www.un.org/womenwatch/
daw/cedaw/cedaw.htm.
United Nations Secretary-General. 2008. 'Report of the Secretary-General on
Women, Peace and Security', www.un.org/Docs/sc/.
United Nations Secretary-General. 2009. 'Report of the Secretary-General on
Women, Peace and Security', www.un.org/Docs/sc/.
United Nations Secretary-General. 2014. 'Review and Appraisal of the
Implementation of the Beijing Declaration and Platform for Action and
the Outcomes of the Twenty-third Special Session of the General Assem-
bly', December 15, www.un.org/ga/search/view_doc.asp?symbol=E/CN.6/
2015/3&Lang=E.
United Nations Security Council. 2000. 'Resolution 1325 on Women and
Peace and Security', www.un.org/Docs/sc/unsc_resolutions.html.
United Nations Security Council. 2009. 'Resolution 1889 on Women and
Peace and Security', www.un.org/Docs/sc/unsc_resolutions.html.
United States Conference of Mayors. 2014. 'Resolution in Support of Cities
for CEDAW Initiative and Encouraging Cities to Implement the Principles
of the UN Convention on the Elimination of all Forms of Discrimination
Against Women', www.usmayors.org/resolutions/82nd_Conference/csj18.
asp.
The World Bank. 2011. *Gender Equality and Development: World Development Report 2012.* Washington, DC: The International Bank for Reconstruction and Development and The World Bank.

11 Globalisation, environmental degradation and tribal identity

With particular reference to Central India

S. N. Chaudhary

Broadly there are two faces of globalisation both as an ideology as well as a process. It is fruitful for some but it has created anxieties among many others. Sociologically it is both functional and dysfunctional. It is functional for those groups, individuals and regions who have required pre-condition of globalisation in their possession which enable them to avail its benefits. Many of them avail benefits due to their high bargaining power. In contrary to them, those individuals and groups among whom pre-conditions of globalisation is insignificant are forced to suffer. And their number is much bigger. Along with this in many cases development of former small segment of population and region is dependent on under-development and marginalisation of the latter. The best example is of tribes of Central India and regions inhabited by them. Majority of them are poor, engaged in primary sector, illiterate, low level of social capital and live in resource-rich rural areas.

The chapter is an attempt to examine how globalisation has contributed to environmental degradation in tribal regions of Central India, namely, in the states of Orissa, Jharkhand, Chhattisgarh and Madhya Pradesh, which in turn has affected tribal identity in a negative manner.

Globalisation and Scheduled Tribes

In the strict formal sense of the term globalisation was introduced in India in July 1991. But the history of certain elements of globalisation in this part of Asia is very old. If we restrict only to the features and indices of the ongoing globalisation, it stands for breaking down of boundaries and barriers. It stands for universalisation and oneness. It believes in the formula of survival of the fittest at the cost of the culture of 'live and let live'. It believes in maximum exploitation of natural resources to meet not basic need rather unending greed of population across the globe whose number is increasing day by day. Globalisation stands for regulation by market forces, IMF and World Bank. Contemporary social scientists discuss globalisation as a process by which the world is becoming increasingly interconnected and unified, subject to homogenous and uniform process of cultural, technological and economic unification. Hence, globalisation is an economic plus process. It has two sides. If the one side is shining, the other side is full of discord, differences, demarcation, discrimination and dissonance. It is full of threats and exclusion particularly in the third world. To Dasgupta (2005), globalisation has created a three-tiered structure across national boundaries. The globalists represents the core of circle; at the second level are those who are in the secured form of employment and cut throat competition in the global market; at the third level is the excluded population. McLuhan (1964) gave the concept of a 'global village'. In the realm of globalisation of the total 100 villagers, for example, 70 are illiterate, 50 are suffering from malnutrition and 80 are living in the substandard house. Huizer (2003) said that if the world is like a village with 100 population, only six are Americans but they have control over 50% of the resources and remaining 94 residents have control over remaining 50% resources only. If resources are distributed in this manner we can easily guess about the term 'global village'. Of course globalisation creates opportunities even in the third world countries, but here also it is controlled and possessed by only few. Most of the others who are the victim of marginalisation, are forced to remain at the bottom by globalisation. And suffering of these dispossessed are further bound to increase manifold due to number of interconnected factors including ever increasing environmental degradation. There are different indicators of environmental degradation. Important among these are climate change, biodiversity loss, unregulated population growth, water pollution, contamination, air pollution, greenhouse effect, deforestation, land degradation and desertification. The existing technology is incapable to rectify environmental and ecological loss. Of course, ecological degradation has negative impact at the local and at the macro level but the immediate victims of this process are the poor. Due to limited needs and resources neither they are serious polluters nor are they able enough to overcome impact of ecological and environmental loss. Studies on environmental and cultural dimensions of globalisation clearly reflect, particularly with reference to tribals that they are experiencing irreparable loss. They are forced to enter into insecurity zone since long. But globalisation is also contributing to this process in a massive manner. Neither, the state civil society organisations or local culture nor the corporate houses are eager enough to address these issues in a successful manner. Tribes have been largely left at the mercy of their own and heritage nurtured by them have been significantly either grabbed or destroyed by others.

Impact of globalisation on environment

As discussed above, there are different components of environment. Over time and particularly since the introduction of globalisation, there is intense degradation in the health status of these components. All such changes are taking place particularly in tribal areas partly because of unregulated industrialisation in the area. There are examples and studies to prove that a number of mines,[1] power plants and other growth centres have been established in these resource-rich areas without respecting local ecology, local culture and other concerns of tribes. Thousands of hectares of land have been encroached either by the state or investors or both without respectful and effective rehabilitation package for displaced tribals. The following example support the argument and show the intensity of displacement and establishment of mega-development projects for the economic development of the country at the cost of tribal people, tribal areas and tribal concerns. Padel (2013) called this process as 'investment induced displacement'. States who are rich from natural resources point of view have carelessly signed countless memorandums of understanding (MOU) with investors and industrial houses.

According to Dungdung (2013) in Odisha state alone, for example, more than 90 MOUs has been signed with corporate houses. These initiatives are likely to industrialise and strengthen the state but, on the other hand, locals are also likely to suffer and become deprived. They are bound to suffer health, economic, social and culture related problems. The chairperson of National Human Rights Commission K. G. Balakrishnan apprehended: 'As Odisha is emerging as an industrialized state, we apprehend more cases of human rights violation' (as quoted by Dungdung 2013: 162).

According to Iyer (2013), in a span of less than a decade, the Government of Jharkhand for example, has signed well over 100 MoUs. Notable among these are Arcellor-Mittal, Jindal, Essar, Tata, Hindalco, Abhijit Group and so on. According to a human rights report published by Jharkhand Human Rights Movement (JHRM), the state government of Jharkhand has so far signed 102 MoUs that go against the 5th schedule of the Constitution that guarantees to tribals their right over the land they live in. The Jharkhand Industrial Policy 2001 and the Jharkhand Vision Document 2010 strongly wish to exploit its natural resources by making it investor-friendly by providing various concessions and government help to industrial houses by acquiring land for private industrial estates and making it available at acquisition cost.

The same process of industrialisation and signing of MOUs with investors and subsequently displacement is going on in the neighbouring states of Chhattisgarh,[2] Odisha, Madhya Pradesh, Andhra Pradesh and Maharashtra. According to the Annual Report 2007–08 of the Ministry of Rural Development, a total of 105,491 cases alleging alienation of 104,742 acres of land have been filed in the court in Orissa. An estimated 104,644 cases were disposed of by the court. Out of these 61,431 cases were disposed of in favour of tribals and 56,854 acres of land was restored to tribals. What will happen to the human rights of the locals, mostly tribals, in these states? Who will ensure the future of forests, water, land, climate, biodiversity and so on which are immediately and directly responsible for the survival of tribal masses? How to insure survival of tribal masses, their culture and tradition and their geographical space under the given economic and political scenario? Padhi and Panigrahi (2011) documented consequences of deforestation and displacement in Orissa. More or less similar is the situation in other parts of Central India. They said:

> The impact of massive deforestation has been observed in the lifeway processes of tribal people and can be categorized as environmental effects, social effects and economic effects. The social effects of deforestation restrict tribal people's access to the forest and affect their religious activities, life-cycle rituals, customs, practices and habits. Similarly, the economic effects of deforestation have drastically influenced the traditional livelihood resource of tribal people, which were providing them with food and economic security.
>
> (Padhi and Panigrahi 2011: 16)

Of course there are some areas where the amount of forests as well as Non-Timber Forest Produces (NTFPs) are found in plenty but poor tribals are far away from these resources. It seems that during globalisation period maximum parts of these resources are grabbed by the agents and representatives of market forces. Tribals have now no access to these resources. It is claimed that rehabilitation policy was adopted for the welfare of the displaced. But it appears that functioning of rehabilitation measures is not up to the mark (Chaudhary et al. 2013). There is wide gap between what is promised and what is performed. It appears that the implementing agencies are not serious on these issues. But the theoretical question is, even if implemented honestly, can any scheme rehabilitate, social, psychological and cultural displacement? Can it address health-related problems? In many cases tribals are either forced to displace themselves or they are terrorised to out-migrate so that land encroachment drive is not opposed strongly (Dungdung 2013).

It seems that injustice of all types generated by globalisation and environmental degradation have individually and collectively frustrated tribal masses. Institutional initiatives taken during last decades are by and large failed to arrest the amount of frustration of tribes particularly tribal youths. There is no ray of hope from any corner to restore their environment and human rights. Sometimes it appears that either tribals or their non-tribal advocates fight a lost battle. The amount of frustration is high in those areas where so-called alternatives of traditional livelihood are totally missing and coping mechanism to adjust with the adverse situation is either ineffective or beyond the reach of tribal masses.

Change in environment and tribal identity

Identity of any community, region or society is a construct of historical forces. But these historical forces are not uniform in constructing identity, rather it is the worldview of community which help to construct the identity. But worldview is not at all detached from ecology, local culture and ongoing socio-economic and political environment. All these domains of life are organically linked to each other. As a result of such organic linkages between these components of space, ways of life is constructed which subsequently become culture as the degree of interaction and sharing among its practitioners increases. And in the due course of time some elements of culture become crucial among a section of population. Such elements are termed as identity of the practicing group. Hence, identity is a product of physical and social environment. And change in the environment, which is inevitable, either notionally or structurally, either due to internal forces or outside, there is change in or loss of identity or some of its spirits. Hence, identity is not at all a complete historical reality rather its root lays in both contemporary context and history. Without comprehension of these two contexts,[3] therefore, it is difficult to underline heritage and subsequently identity of any group or sub-group. The foundation of identity of a community is affected by external forces over the time. And, a foundation of identity relevant at one point of time becomes irrelevant at another point of time. According to Miri (1993) identity is an emotive concept. Hence, all such phrases like 'identity crisis', 'threat to one's identity', 'search for identity' and so forth are most often used in an emotive manner. Since these concepts are emotionally used, therefore, it may not tag with cognitive and objective comprehension. And emotive use of such phrases not only prohibits objective understanding but also it may have disastrous practical consequences.

If there is entry of an alien identity either voluntarily or involuntarily, there is every possibility of conflict between the constituents of once own identity and identity imposed by external forces. In this situation either the entire community or a section of them are confused either to adopt or retain the newly imposed or traditionally practiced identity or some of its elements. This state of affairs leads to identity crisis and also identity conflict and the practitioners are confused to adopt either any of these two identities or both the identities. For example, a person from Gond tribe historically practicing the Gondi language is confused when he is directed to read and write in the classroom in Hindi or any other non-tribal language. At this level, of course, he is confused between old and the new and both these identities have its own support base and sources of legitimisation, but the ego is confused to adopt the new identities at the cost of the old identity for various practical objectives. In course of accepting otherwise alien identity, of course supportive environment may be there but its encouragement and legitimisation from the century old traditional identity is most often not there. As a result, when in the remote villages of Bastar district of Chhattisgarh, a Hill Maria student of the 1st or 2nd standard is asked to read and write in Hindi by the class teacher, the student does not get any encouragement and legitimacy from the traditional Gondi language, which they have practiced since long. This example clearly refers to the conflicting situation between the old and established and the new, emerging and an alien identity. The net result of this conflicting situation is loss of traditional identity for newly constructed identity. But examples may be cited to prove coexistence of both traditional and the modern identity. For example, the Gonds of Betul village in Madhya Pradesh worship their own gods and goddess as well as the gods and goddesses of their Hindu neighbours. They also practice their own festivals as well as festivals of Hindus (Chaudhary 2012). Identity also shapes and reshapes our choices. It provides freedom. It also works as problem solving institution and it has long history of doing such service to its practitioners. It provides them sense of belongingness and oneness. But if such identity with long history are either slowly or abruptly suppressed and the new identity is imposed, members of a community at large are for long period incapable to adopt the new identity by heart which they have been doing since long with the ongoing traditional identity. Hence, identity is a backbone of groups and communities, no matter at what level of development they are placed in the society. There are also a large number of examples to show that how newly imposed identity, initially with small support base gradually, becomes dominant identity over the time and in this way it becomes part and parcel of the said community. For example, once upon a time the English language was not at all a symbol of identity in India, but over time the support base of English language increased in India, and today the number of persons speaking and practicing English is much higher here than the original followers of this language in England. Today for many, the English language is their identity symbol in India. But shift from one identity to another identity is neither smooth nor an overnight phenomena. The practitioners have to face the pain and trauma of transition, no matter whether they are the recipient of fruits of new identity or not. In course of expansion of new identity, which have support from the macro level social processes, theoretically the social groups are likely to go through number of conflicting social processes.

As discussed above, identity is the backbone of any community or social group. And in the situation of identity crisis which is perceived as transitional phase in the life of an individual, social groups and the community, actors are confused. They are confused to adjust with the emerging identity at the cost of the existing identity. They are also confused to synthesise certain elements from the existing and the emerging identity which are suitable for them. But ultimately, in the due course of time, they have to move ahead to achieve a point which is acceptable to both traditional and the modern identities and its practitioners. So far as tribes are concerned, of course historically they have lived in the compartment of both homogeneity and heterogeneity, but because of these two realities all the tribes either commonly or separately have developed their own identity or indicators/marker of identification. And these identities have subsequently become core features of tribes practicing it. One can take example of Baiga and Agaria tribes of Mandla district of Madhya Pradesh. Historically, adolescent girls have availed the freedom to select their life partner as per their own choice and Baiga and Agaria people have always encouraged them. According to Guha (1994), Elwin praised the exalted place of women and children in aboriginal life, its non-repressive attitude to sex and marriage, its finely developed aesthetic sensibilities, and its collective and cooperative spirit. Miri (1993) highlighting importance of identity in the life of tribes over the time said:

> That tribal identity, in this sense, can become a powerful reality we all know. It is something for the sake of which one may be prepared to give one's life, and also frequently, as we know too well, to take another's life. What greater proof, one might ask, can there be of the reality and power of tribal identity?
>
> (Miri 1993: 172)

Pandey (2007) identified seven common indicators of identity found with most of the tribes of the country. These are:

1   Inter-dependent and friendly relationship between natural resources and tribal culture.
2   Collection-based and not destruction-based living habit.
3   Egalitarian and social justice–based social institution, economic life and cultural practices.
4   Collective and need-based economic system.
5   Tolerance-based animistic religious heritage.
6   Folk-centric art, culture and folk tradition equally respecting nature and culture.
7   Governance system totally informal, transparent, honesty based, participatory, local and based on common consensus.

Munda perceived eight indicators of tribal identity. These are (1) casteless, classless and egalitarian society; (2) community-based economic system; (3) symbiotic with nature; (4) democratic policy based on consensus; (5) fight for dignity and self-respect; (6) change according to the demands of the times; (7) accommodative history; and (8) people-oriented art and literature. Munda strongly disagreed with the indicators of tribal identity provided by non-tribals (see Louis 2000) particularly indicators provided by the Scheduled Castes (SC) and Scheduled Tribes (ST) Commission. Many more scholars have narrated identity of individual tribes from across the country.

But these indices of tribal identity which historically served number of social functions are at crossroads and the history of disintegration of their identity is not new. In many cases its history began as their interaction with and exposure to the outside world increased. And the history of such interaction is very old. By taking examples from

Madhya Pradesh state, we can say that even during pre-British days there were Hindu kings, Muslim rulers and tribal kings like Gond-Raja and the Bhil Raja, who promoted interaction of tribals with other cultures and regions. There are several examples to prove that long back tribals were engaged in trade and commerce with foreign countries. But gradually as acculturation increased, diverse interest groups interacted with tribes and their culture. For example, when Maratha rule was established in certain parts of Madhya Pradesh, they not only invited Jats and Patidars from Gujarat but also encouraged massive logging or deforestation which negatively affected tribal identity. The Bhils of Western Madhya Pradesh opposed massive logging during British and pre-British period, but a large number of them were killed and their revolt could not succeed. There are many more examples from across the country to support the view that Britishers were necessarily against land and water based natural resources which were mostly available in plenty in the tribal dominated areas. Since these natural resources were the foundations which led to emergence and continuation of tribal identity as mentioned above, with the deterioration in the status of natural resources, the condition of tribal identity also deteriorated in the due course of time. According to Guha (1983: 1883):

> The forest dwellers, of course, depended on their natural habitat in a multitude of ways. An adequate forest cover was ecologically necessary to sustain cultivation on hilly terrain, whether it was *jhum* (shifting cultivation) or cultivation of the terraced variety. In addition, the forests themselves provided a reserve of food that could be consumed throughout the year. The Indian Famine Commission of 1881 has detailed 31 species of trees whose produce was consumed as food by the tribes of the Satpura Hills, in different seasons – including fruits, flowers, buds, young shoots, seeds etc. both in raw and cooked form (in fact peasants and tribals in forest areas normally know of over a hundred natural products, besides the staples, that can be gathered without cultivation). And where animal husbandry was a valuable appendage to cultivation (as in the Himalayan foot hills), the forests were a prime source of fodder, in the form of grass and leaves.

He further said that organic linkage between tribals and forests were institutionalised through number of socio-cultural mechanisms. According to a Government of India Report (1967),'It is striking to see how in many of the myths and legends the deep sense of identity with the forest is emphasized'. According to Brandis (1897) the first inspector general of forests, a large number of sacred groves were found in the Indian forests. These groves have been analysed as an ancient strategy for sustainable use of the forest. These groves are part of the belief systems among many tribal groups which have been used as a conservation mechanism. According to Sen and Lalhrietpui (2006: 4205–4210),'in pre-colonial days, there was greater diversity of landscapes, and sacred groves and shifting cultivation contributed to this diversity'. Similarly according to Kothari (1996), totemic social organisations have contributed to protection of plants and animals. Also, as late as in 1953 an eminent botanist Bor (1963:18) reported that 'the largest *deodar* (Himalayan cedar) are those which are planted near temples and which are venerated and protected from injury'. According to Guha (1994), for forest-dependent communities like charcoal iron makers and shifting cultivators, control over the forest was vital to their economic and cultural life. Rituals, myths and sense of self of Baiga and Agaria tribes were all deeply interwoven with their forest world. Consequently, the takeover of forests by the state and their subsequently working on commercial lines, when coupled with the alienation of tribal agricultural land to outsiders destroyed their livelihood and culture. This process had resulted in a deep sense of helplessness or what Elwin (1939) termed a 'loss of nerve'.

Hence, the role of British administration, Christian missionaries,[4] industrialisation and urbanisation, gradual spread of Hindu rituals and ways of life in the tribal areas and forces of globalisation since 1991 are by and large responsible for degeneration of tribal identity and imposition of alien identity directly or indirectly, in the historical perspective. It is needless to mention that in order to increase their social status some of the tribal kings in present Jharkhand state invited *Pandits* to perform rituals from plain areas. These *Pandits* subsequently settled there and managed situation also in their own favour which had its impact on tribal identity. According to MacDougall (2008: 5),

Among the Mundas and Oraons, as among the Santals, there were headmen who possessed authority over whole groups of villages. Many centuries before the British assumed control over Ranchi district one of these superior headmen emerged as the chief of such headmen. This headmen, who came to be known as the Maharaja (or chief) of Chotanagpur, was paid nominal rents by *Adivasi* villagers, and seems to have occasionally provided them with military protection. However, the *Maharaja's* position changed markedly in the seventeenth century, after one *Maharaja* came into closer contact with the Moghul empire. Maharajas began to aspire to high caste – Hindu status, and to bring non-*Adivasis* from the Gangetic plains to serve as priests, artisans and soldiers. These newcomers were supported economically by the *Adivasis*, through higher rents, forced labour and the expropriation of *adivasi* lands by the newcomers.

Similarly Christian missionaries addressed basic health and basic education related issues in many tribal areas. It had positive and negative consequences. It significantly destroyed tribal identity. It brought the feeling of 'in-group' and 'out-group' between converted and non-converted tribals. But for those who embraced Christianity, many of them received benefits. According to Sinha (1993: 153) for example:

> The Baptist Mission in Nagaland played a salutary role among the Aos. Indirectly it made a common cause with the British rulers to end the practices of head chopping and slavery. It introduced a strict moral code of conduct, marital fidelity and prohibition against drinking of intoxicant beverages among the believers. A number of fruits, vegetables, edibles, dresses were made in vogue. Construction of living houses, segregation of animals from the living quarters, personal hygiene and physical cleanliness, disposal of dead through burial in a community cemetery were some of social practices, which were initiated by the church. Mission literacy programme resulted in a number of positive reactions such as spread of education, women employment through the church and production of literature in Ao language. Again it was the Baptist church, which made certain occupation such as teaching, nursing, evangelical etc. as honourable ones. The Baptist always emphasized the socio-economic upliftment of the new converts leading to the emergence of a new urge among the Aos for economic prosperity.

These are the development issues. A section of converted tribals has gained in development terms but gradually they have also lost at least some elements of their traditional identity. A number of industries have been established in the tribal belt which have affected tribal life particularly tribal identity negatively. It has displaced hundreds and thousands of tribal families without rehabilitating them properly. Even construction of a big dam has proved to be dysfunctional for tribes. Baviskar (2005), with reference to Sardar Sarovar Dam in western Madhya Pradesh and Gujarat said, Dam supporters received a jolt when the Morse Commission conducted an independent review of the Sardar Sarovar Dam and advised the World Bank to withdraw its funding from the project on the grounds that it harmed tribal cultures (Baviskar 2005: 109). The report held the bank accountable to its own guidelines and to international conventions on the rights of indigenous people. Interestingly on the basis of this recommendation the World Bank loan was cancelled. Industries have also contributed to social disorganisation among them without any meaningful gain even in the material sense (Sachchidananda and Mandal 1985). Of course a number of tribal revolts took place in tribal areas which were addressed to their basic concerns relating to land, forest and culture, but these movements[5] could not arrest the ongoing process of disintegration of tribal support base, tribal heritage and finally tribal identity. In short, throughout the British period the process of disintegration of tribal identity remain active.

After independence capitalistic model of development was followed with reference to tribes also like other communities. It was said that neither isolation of Elwin who gave the concept of 'national park' nor assimilation but only integration approach will solve tribal problems. Keeping this model from time to time a number of institutional and voluntary interventions has been made. From time to time a number of constitutional provisions were made to protect and promote tribal concerns in the light of the integrative approach. All the major Articles can be classified into four broad categories. These are protective provisions (Articles 15, 16, 19, 23, 29, 46, 164, 330, 332, 335, 338, 339, 342 and 371), development-related provisions (Articles 15, 16, 19, 46, 275 and 399), administrative provisions in the Sixth Scheduled (North-East states) areas (Articles 344, 338 and 339) and reservation facility (Articles 330, 332, 334, 335 and 340). In order to actualise the spirit of these provisions, from time to time hundreds of development schemes have been formulated and implemented. However, in the recent past few very important provisions/schemes have been formulated and launched to improve physical and social quality of life of tribals in particular and other marginalised groups in general. These schemes are:

1   The Provisions of the Panchayats (Extensions to the Scheduled Areas) Act, 1996 (PESA).
2   The Scheduled Tribes and other Traditional Forest Dwellers (Recognition of Forest Rights) Act, 2006 (Commonly known as the Forest Rights Act).

Besides these specific provisions and many more development schemes, at the Government of India level tribal policy is also in the pipeline. There are 15 specific points in the proposed policy document. If the draft policy is passed and implemented, it would be a milestone on the part of the state to address socio-economic problems of tribal masses. It is needless to mention that Pt. Nehru by strongly advocating the importance of tribal heritage opposed homogenisation process and said that they should be developed without compromising with their identity. In other words, he was in favour of giving them the largest measure of autonomy. His five-point program that he mentioned in his foreword to V. Elwin's book *A Philosophy for NEFA* (1955) says:

1 People should develop along the lines of their own genius and we should avoid imposing anything on them.
2 Tribal rights in land and forests should be respected.
3 We should try to train and build up a team of their own people to do the work of administration and development.
4 We should not over administer these areas or overwhelm them with a multiplicity of schemes.
5 We should judge results not by statistics or the amount of money spent, but by the quality of human character that is evolved.

But this is one side of the coin. Panchsheel is pleasant to the ear, but in practice the situation is totally different. Making comments on the second point of Panchsheel, Burman (1996) said, 'Tribal rights in land and forests should be respected', said Nehru in the second point of his Panchsheel. Apart from the Sixth Scheduled area, this has not been implemented elsewhere. Protection of their ownership of land is the most important for them. They and their ownership of land is the most important for them. They and their forefathers have lived on the same land for a long time. Land and its resources are their livelihood. Their religion is based on forests and trees. Their Gods and Goddesses live there. They are born and would die there. It is this basic pillar of their life that is being not adequately taken care of by the government in some places for economic development of the people in general. Simultaneously, land grabbers, liquor vendors and moneylenders have cheated them of their land' (Burman 1996: 74). The nature and direction of changes taking place among tribals during last several decades after independence clearly reflect the failure of the Panchsheel agenda and expansion of homogenisation process in the tribal world in favour of non-tribal tradition and culture. Many tribes are assimilated with the Hindu culture in such a way that sociologically it is difficult to say whether they are tribe or they are heading towards Hindu religion. Many of them are practicing food habits, dress pattern, means of entertainment, language, religious practices and so forth, which are theoretically not their own and these changes have taken place because of culture contract and external intervention. Miri (1993: 173) rightly said:

> The March of modernity has all but crushed tribal identity, and for the tribesman to gain an authentic, detailed insight into it has become a near impossibility. The search for tribal identity seems thus an endeavour that is doomed to fail. And the desperation accompanying this realization is immense.

Further, during last 20 years one can see expansion of globalisation, alien culture and market forces along with some new institutional initiatives like new panchayati-raj system. The Provisions of the Panchayat (Extension to the Scheduled Areas) Act, 1996 (PESA), The Scheduled Tribes and Other Traditional Forest Dwellers (Recognition of Forest Rights) Act 2006 (FRA) Mahatma Gandhi National Rural Employment Scheme (MNREGS), Self Help Groups (SHGs) and so on. The numbers of mobile phones and televisions, two-wheelers and so forth have also significantly increased in the tribal areas. Most of the tribal areas are connected with the main road through the village all weather *pucca* roads constructed under the Prime Minister Rural Roads scheme. Because of all these interventions there is significant change in their material and non-material culture. The ever-decreasing traditional local resources, particularly forest is not capable enough to meet their ever increasing requirements. Also, neither the wage work nor the farm work is attractive enough to draw the attention of tribal youth. Neither tribal youths nor their parents are interested to keep them with their traditional sources of livelihood. Establishment of modern schools in tribal villages has shown them a ray of hope in favour of modern occupations. But most of these occupations which are secondary and tertiary in nature have its own requirements and pre-conditions. The pre-conditions are largely absent among tribals. Even at the primary level of education, of course, there is high enrolment rate but the quality of teaching and learning is very poor. Also, as we move from primary to secondary to higher education there is very high rate of dropout and non-enrolment among them. A very small number of tribal youths, particularly those who have adopted Christianity, are graduates and post-graduates. Most of the non-converted tribal boys and girls who have passed high school examination are unable to see the gate of higher education. Besides lack of education, neither majority of tribals have money nor other resources to enter into new occupations which are created either by the state or by the globalisation forces. Other development initiatives, mentioned above, are largely away from them. Hence, tribals at large are neither satisfied with their traditional sources of livelihood which is either disappearing day by day or it is passing out of their hands, particularly to the globalisation forces nor they are capable enough to avail benefits of new sources and new opportunities created by both the state and the globalisation forces. But one can easily see negative consequences of globalisation on their environment, culture and sources of livelihood. If we examine impact of all these external forces on their identity, it is not friendly. Relationship between their ever-changing culture and ever decreasing status of local natural resources are incapable to ensure their development as well as to retain their identity. Many of the mobile tribals are rather what Fernandes (1996) called 'destructively dependent' on forest resource. There is class and elite formation among them and over the time attitude of tribal elites towards their identity such as collective economic structure, tolerance, animistic nature of their religion and other social and cultural practices based on local ecology, tribal art and culture, folk tales and folk lore, status of folk tradition, informal community panchayat, shifting cultivation, communitarian ways of life, community panchayat, importance of institutions like totem, youth organisation, freedom availed by girls and women and so forth have significantly disappeared from their life and for this change factors and conditions, mentioned above, are largely responsible. Hence, the pertinent question at this juncture is who will address their plight and problems which are of recent origin for which they are not at all responsible? In the situation of identity loss who will mitigate their plight and problems which were earlier solved by their culture and tradition? Who will solve, for example, their health and disease-related problems which were earlier solved by their medicine men who have lost their importance and the new formal health management institutions are either poorly equipped and managed or are beyond their reach?

In short, for the degeneration of tribal identity both globalisation and schemes initiated by the state for the cause of national development along with rays coming out of modernisation in different walks of life are responsible. One can say with confidence that the famous integrative approach is miserably failed to address plights of tribal masses. But the crucial question at this juncture is that in the near future in the absence of tribal identity who will perform those functions which were performed in the past by their environment and ecology centric cultural heritage? Under the given scenario who will ensure the tribal friendly functions of both state and globalisation forces? What will happen to the tribals who are politically and socially dispersed? To what extent the type of identity formation which is taking place under an umbrella of integrative approach of the state will be fruitful and functional in the psychological and instrumental sense? What is the nature of relationship between nature and tribal culture? What is the state of collectivism and tolerance among them? What is the state of their material and non-material culture? These are some of the basic issues which needs to be probed. Insights emerging out of such problem and its analysis will not only help to understand the state and importance of tribal identity academically but also it will help to harmonise and humanise the face of both state and globalisation in the wider interest of tribes. To Miri (1993) since identity is an emotive concept, it is necessarily subject to change. Over the time either some of the elements of identity or the entire identity complex may be replaced by another set of identity. In the case of tribals, even today, there is no total loss of identity. But to him the pertinent question is how and to what extent basic problems of tribes are successfully addressed by the new and emerging identity of tribes? If the emerging identity is capable enough to address some of the pertinent problems encountered by tribes then only such identity will command respect and continue for longer time. To him

> Things that could happen which will help create a situation that is better than the one prevailing are: (i) an open-eyed awareness, on the part of the tribesman, of his *real* predicament; (ii) an attempt, bold as it will have to be, to articulate a conception of intelligibility, coherence and knowledge, which is embedded in the idea of a tribal tradition (this will have to be done in opposition to the powerful, coercive, uniformity-imposing conception of intelligibility, coherence and knowledge implicit in the notion of modern science and modernity generally); and (iii) relatedly, the development of an intellectual, moral-spiritual, self-confidence, on the part of the tribesman, which will enable him to face the world outside without being overwhelmed by it, and yet with a natural sympathy free from self-deluding exclusivist fears and arrogances. Needless to say, this is a tall order, but certainly not impossible to achieve, at least in moderate degree.
>
> (Miri 1993: 174).

Conclusion

All the components of environment are historically related to tribes in a symbiotic manner. Culture was constructed in the light of these components which in turn protected local environment in favour of tribes. Tribes developed their languages, religion, food habit, dress pattern, customary laws and rituals relating to vital demographic events and so forth in the light of their environmental setting. These elements of environment became the foundation stone for the formation and sustenance of tribal identity. This state of affairs, with certain changes, continued for generations without harming core identity issues. Low population pressure, insignificant and adhoc interaction with outside world and limited requirements retained and strengthened symbiotic relations.

But over time, because of various reasons there was appropriation of environment primarily by external forces in an unregulated and speedy manner which in turn affected both local environment and tribal identity in a negative manner. Gradually with the increasing amount of relatively one sided interaction with non-tribal forces, the process of environmental degradation became fast. No successful effort was made by all the concerned to regulate interaction in favour of local environment and tribal concerns. Rather the process of environmental degradation became fast after 1991 when globalisation was formally introduced. In practice globalisation is opposed to environmental stability, especially in third world countries and particularly when there is clash of interest among stakeholders including tribal vested interest on the issue of land, forest and water. Environmental degradation has caused serious harm to majority of tribes, their material and non-material culture, livelihood and other issues directly responsible for the formation of tribal identity. For want of required resources, they are failed to associate themselves with the so-called mainstream process of development and form new identity. Many of them are failed to retain their traditional identity due to rapid environmental degradation. Hence, environmental degradation in general and globalisation led speedy process of environmental degradation in particular have made tribals nearly rootless in social, psychological and cultural term. It has contributed to what Cernea (1988) called landlessness, joblessness, homelessness, marginalisation, food insecurity, high morbidity, loss of access to community property resources and community desertification in the tribal regions of Central India. And coping mechanisms of all varieties are largely failed to restore human rights of tribal masses.

258 S. N. Chaudhary

Notes

1 According to a Report of an Expert Group of Planning Commission (2008), mining dust causes pneumoconiosis (a group of lung diseases), eye infection, conjunctivitis, corneal ulcers, glaucoma and squint trachoma. Silicosis is caused by dust from coal, mica, silver, lead, zinc and manganese mines, pottery and ceramic units, sand blasting, metal grinding, building and construction work, rock mining, iron and steel plants, slate pencil factories and so forth.

2 In Chhattisgarh since the beginning of globalisation, 121 MOUs have been signed. The total proposed budget of all these MOUs was Rs. 192,126 crore. About half of them have already started functioning. In Madhya Pradesh, 324 MOUs were signed of which 12 MOUs have been implemented and 18 are in process. The areas where MOUs have been signed are agriculture and food processing, forest and herbal, industries, infrastructure, minerals, power, textiles and tourism. In Odisha, 235 MOUs were signed during the above period. These were in the following sectors: air products (04), alumina and aluminium (12), aviation (01), cement (P. 26), ferro products (09), food processing (08), mining (03), others (13), paper (05), pelletisation (14), petroleum (05), power (63) and steel (72) (Source: Different web site sources of the concerned state governments dated 24 June 2014).

3 Dealing with the socio-political context which led to formation of identity among tribes of Jharkhand Louis (2000) underlined four factors, namely (1) the feeling of being a tribal who have suffered marginalisation united all the various tribal groups in favour for separate state of tribes; (2) sense of being the original settlers of the Jharkhand region which united them; (3) Christianity provided them a sense of history myth about the golden age sense of separateness by providing them modern education and the ethnic sense of 'We' tribals and they *dikus* or outsiders united them for struggle.

4 The spread of Christian missions in the tribal world was both dysfunctional and functional from the point of view of their identity as well as improvement in their quality of life. Mills (1973), Elwin (1955), Haimendorf (1980) and host of other scholars, for example, apprehended that Christianity poses a threat to the tribal identity. But according to Sinha (1993) in the light of the views of the tribal Christian intellectuals and elite of the region the above apprehensions appear to be notional. Can one ignore the emergence of ethnicity and ethnic movements prevalent among the highly Christianised tribes of the region? If Christianity is not synonymous to the Western culture, how can it be equivalent to a distinct ethnic identity, especially when the ethnic elite are conscious to maintain their identity? (p. 155).

5 For instance Kol revolt (1821), Bhumij revolt (1832), Santal revolt (1763), Birsa Munda Movement (1890), Tana Bhagat Movement (1915) and Jharkhand Movement (1950) in present Jharkhand state, Juang Movement (1837–1856) and Kaujhar Movement (1891–93) in Orissa state and Gond revolt against British Raj (1911) and Movement for Separate Gond State (1940) in Madhya Pradesh may be taken as an example.

References

Baviskar, A. 2005. 'Adivasi Encounters with Hindu nationalism in MP', *Economic and Political Weekly*, November 26.

Bor, N. L. 1963. *Manual of Indian Forest Botany*. New Delhi: Oxford University Press, 18.

Brandis, D. 1897. 'Indian Forestry', *Working*, 12.

Cernea, M. M. (ed.). 1988. *Putting People First: Sociological Variables in Rural Development*. London: Oxford University Press.

Chaudhary, S.N. et al. 2013. *Adivasi Gramo me Tikau Vikas Ka Yathartha*. New Delhi: Concept.

Chaudhary, S. N. 2012. *In search of Sustainable Development: Scenario in a Tribal Village of Madhya Pradesh*. New Delhi: Serials.

Dasgupta, Samir. 2005. 'Introduction', in S. Dasgupta (ed.), *The Changing Face of Globalization*. New Delhi: Sage.

Dungdung, G. 2013. *'Whose Country Is It Anyway?': Untold Stories of the Indigenous Peoples of India*. Kolkata: Adivaani.

Elwin, V. 1939. *The Baiga*. London: John Murray.

Elwin, V. 1955. *A Philosophy for NEFA*. London: Oxford University Press.

Fernandes, Walter. 1996. 'Tribals, Forests, Displacement and Sustainable Development', in K. G. Iyer (ed.), *Sustainable Development: Ecological and Socio-Cultural Dimensions*. New Delhi: Vikas Publishing House.

GOI. 1967. 'Report of the Scheduled Areas and Scheduled Tribes Commission', Vol. I, 1960–61, New Delhi: Government of India.

Guha, R. 1983. 'Forestry in British and Post British India: A Historical Analysis', *EPW*, October 29.

Guha, R. 1994. *Sociology and the Dilemmas of Development*. New Delhi: ICSSR.

Haimendorf, Christoph Von Furer. 1980. 'Recent Developments in the position of Indian Tribal Population', in S. G. Deogaonkar (ed.), *Problems of Development in Tribal Areas*. New Delhi: Leeladevi.

Huizer, Gerrit. 2003. *Globalization from Above and from Below: A Dialectical Process*. Inhoud.

Iyer, K. G. 2013. 'Globalization, Jharkhandi Identity and Rural Transformation', in S. N. Chaudhary (ed.), *Globalization, National Development and Tribal Identity*. Jaipur: Rawat.

Kothari, A. 1996. 'Is Joint Management of Protected Areas Desirable and Possible?' in Ashish Kothari, N. Singh and S. Suri (eds.), *People and Protected Areas: Towards Participatory Conservation in India*. New Delhi: Sage.

Louis, P. 2000. 'Jharkhand: Marginalization of Tribals', *EPW*, XXXX (47): 4087–4090.

MacDougall, J. 2008. *Tribal Resistances*. New Delhi: Critical Quest.

McLuhan, Marshall. 1964. *Understanding Media*. London: Routledge.

Mills, J. P. 1973. *The Ao Nagas*. Bombay: Oxford University Press.

Miri, Mrinal. 1993. 'Identity and the Tribesman', in M. Miri (ed.), *Continuity and Change in Tribal Society*. Shimla: Indian Institute of Advanced Study.

Munda, R. D. (2001). 'Adivasi Identity: Crisis and Way Out', in *Rising Fascism* (53). New Delhi: Update Collective.

Padel, Flex. 2013. 'Tribal Identity and Real Development in a rapidly Globalizing World', in S. N. Chaudhary (ed.), *Globalization, National Development and Tribal Identity*. Jaipur: Rawat.

Padhi, S. and Panigrahi, Nilkantha. 2011. 'Tribal Movements and Livelihoods: Recent Developments in Orissa', CPRC-IIPA working paper, No. 51, New Delhi: Chronic Poverty Research Centre, Indian Institute of Public Administration.

Pandey, Gaya. 2007. *Indian Tribal Culture*. New Delhi: Concept, 421–443.

Planning Commission. 2008. 'Development Challenges in Extremist Affected Areas', Report of An Expert Group to Planning Commission, New Delhi: Government of India, 18.

Roy Burman, B. K. 1996. *Tribal Situation and Approach to Tribal Problems in India*. New Delhi: Rajiv Gandhi Institute for Contemporary Studies.

Sachchidananda and B. B. Mandal (1985) *Industrialization and Social Disorganization: A Study of Tribes in Bihar*, Delhi: Concept.

Sen, Arnab and Esther Laihrietpui (2006): Scheduled Tribes (Recognition of Forest Rights) Bill: A View from Anthropology and Call for Dialogue, *Economic and Political Weekly*, September 30, pp. 4205–4210.

Sinha, A. C. 1993. 'Christianity and Ethnic Identity Among the Nagas', in Mrinal Miri (ed.), *Continuity and Change in Tribal Society*. Shimla: Indian Institute of Advanced Study.

12 Sacred landscape, modes of subsistence and Adivasi rights in the globalised world

Gomati Bodra Hembrom

Highest God in heaven,
Mother Earth down below
Rising like milk, setting like curd
You are the beginning, you are the earliest
All four corners, ten directions
East west north south
It is your creation, it is your making
Forests, hills, rivers, plains
Animals and birds, creatures of all kind
They are protected by you, they exists through you.
The hill spirits of the hills
The water spirits of the deeps
The forest goddess of the grove
The village spirit of the village
chandi, goddess of the boundaries
Our forefathers, our ancestors
We call upon you, we invite you all of you
We pray to all of you, we beseech all of you
        –A Munda prayer of Jharkhand region (Munda, Ramdayal 2000)

Every living being requires certain basic necessities that nature provides, such as land, water, atmosphere, light, forest, and biodiversity. Ecology plays an important role in human adaptation and maintenance of the culture and the life style of a community. The geographical location of a place is mainly responsible for its people's social system, customs, behaviour, religious beliefs and tradition and shaping their livelihood. Different ecological settings and practices are linked to the use of available natural resources.

Human beings have made unprecedented changes to ecosystems in recent decades to meet growing needs for food, fresh water, fibre and energy. These changes have improved the lives of billions but at the same time weakened nature's ability to deliver other key services such as purification of air and water, protection from disasters and the provision of medicines. The ecosystems contribute in provisioning, regulating and cultural services to enhance human well-being.

The role of environment in securing subsistence and in sustainable development is crucial. The more fragile an environment is, the more are the subsistence conflicts and challenges to sustainable development. An environment or ecosystem and thereby culture becomes fragile on account of various factors ranging from climatic change, over-population induced by population, changes in land use or livelihood practices, technological changes, over exploitations, depletions and destructions of resources and so forth. According to anthropologist Marvin Harris, even hunting-gathering and agricultural societies lapsed into endemic warfare and gender violence when their recourses bases were depleted and over stretched. An ecological system under stress renders people vulnerable. Already vulnerable groups like indigenous people, women, children and old and disabled especially are the worst sufferers of such environmental stress (Menon 2012).

Sacred landscape, ecology and commons

As the most impressive features of the landscape, mountains, dense forests, life-giving water bodies like lake, river, ponds, waterfalls, trees and so forth imbue people with an aura of mystery and sanctity. It has an unusual power to awaken a sense of the sacred. In that aura, indigenous people, experience a deeper reality that gives meaning and vitality to their lives. Efforts to conserve the environmental integrity and cultural diversity associated with sacred landscape need to involve the whole community and many diverse traditions that revere and care for them. The indigenous/tribal[1] population the world over has shared a symbiotic relationship with their environment and natural resources. They have developed cultural traditions, economy, social-control mechanism, religious institutions and production techniques to retain these relationships. Their cultural system ensured that there should be sustainable use of resources, and it continued to be their livelihood for their several generations. They did this by using them judiciously to live on, while at the same time ensuring their renewability. It is a fact that, indigenous and tribal communities inhabited in different regions of the globe have been playing a vital role in preservation and management of natural resources within the frame of their indigenous knowledge. It is not a surprise to find that about 80% of the world's cultural and biological diversity has been reported in their inhabited regions. Their identity as a community is closely linked to the natural resources such as a mountains, forest, land, water bodies and so forth. Ramdayal Munda (2000) in his detailed descriptions on Adi-dharam, which is based on the forms of beliefs scattered among the Adivasis in India and also known as sarana, sari, sansari, jehar, bongaism and so forth, clearly points out that one of the most distinctive characteristics of it is that the various forms of nature like hills, trees, forests, water bodies (rivers, lakes, ponds, etc.) and others are accepted as the best dwellings of God. The survival of the Adi-dharam is, therefore, crucial for the survival of all, the toiling and peace loving people of the world, both indigenous and non-indigenous. But one should not forget that like any other faith the Adi-dharam is premised on a certain mode of production. If agriculture is the provider of life, the forest and land, provide the economic and cultural base of the Adivasis' faith (Mullick 2014).

The forest environment satisfies the deep-rooted tribal traditions and sentiments throughout their life until death. Even after death, the deceased tribal is laid to rest in a grave close to a forested region by most of the hunting and gathering tribes of India. Thus, even after death, the tribals are close to the forest. Forests have played a vital role in the socioeconomic and cultural life of the tribal people of India. It is well-known that majority of the tribal population lived in isolation in the forested regions of India with harmony, security and trust for many centuries and developed a symbiotic relationship with the forest.

In the Adivasis' society, traditional ecological knowledge is closely linked with the nature especially the landscape. The importance of forests, particularly in the form of sacred groves, water in the form of springs and rivers, mountains and forested hills (Bir-Buru) in Adivasis' social, cultural and spiritual life. Many rituals are still used to show respect to hills, forest and water. One must be reverent to the spirit of the sacred groves, water bodies, hills and forest. Not only are these considered to be sacred, but also, because these landscapes are considered a living being. Mountains have both social and spiritual significance for tribal people. These mountains are considered to be a biodiversity hotspot because of their relatively high proportion of organic species and also source of life as streams and rivers flow from it. Sukan Buru (where an annual fair is held every year) in Khunti district, Sursi Buru in Sraikela-Kharsawan district of Jharkhand, the Ajodiya hills in Purulia district of west Bengal and the Niyamgiri hills in Odisha are few examples. The annual hunt or *Disumsendra* is of great important among many tribes like Santhal, Mundas and Ho in this region. So before hunting, the forest spirit was worshiped. In the traditional set-up Adivasis have a strong rule against taking more than is needed (herbs, firewood, fish, fruits, etc.).

Deep inside the forests of south-western Odisha, in the Niyamgiri hills, people of small tribal, unlettered forest dwellers – Dongria Kondh and Kutia Kondh tribals, and Gouda and Harijan non-tribals – spoke of a religion embedded in the hill's pristine ecology. The people stressed that the Niyamgiri hills, spanning 250 km^2, is abode of their supreme deity and ancestral kin Niyamraja, who is the protector and preserver of Niyamgiri, the mountain of law. 'Your temples are made of bricks and cement; ours are these hills, forests, leaves and streams. If you dig these, we will die with our gods', says Bejuni, village priestess of a Dongria Kondh tribal hamlet in Kesarpadi (Bera 2013). Living trees were treated as living forest capital and were not cut unless absolutely necessary, and only when they could be taken without damaging wildlife or other aspects of the natural ecosystem. Tribes in the northwest accord a special status to the mahua tree, whose flower, fruits, seed and wood can be used for food, oil and mineral feed. Many places sacred to indigenous peoples are sources of both material and spiritual sustenance. Harvesting certain crops, catching a particular fish, or hunting certain animals reflects both economic needs and sacred customs.

Apart from sacredness, another component related to nature is that of the commons. The forests, hills, grazing field water bodies in the whole habitat, where the tribals live, were designated as common property resources or commons, which, were traditionally conserved by the tribal (or local) communities, with the most effective mechanism, not only for monitoring the environmental conditions, but also for negotiating with outsiders. A common property resource is a natural resource with social, cultural, economic and political importance subject to collective ownership as well as communal use. Common property resource utilisation applies mainly in communally owned land where traditional regulations are applied to manage resources. The characteristics of common resources are that they provide subsistence needs for local cultures in terms of food, shelter, income, health care delivery and promote cultural orientation. The management of common resources is enforced by traditional beliefs which nevertheless are seriously eroded, has been kept alive by local culture. Historically, the maintenance of these resources reflected people's concern for their collective sustenance and for protection of fragile natural resources. Still today the tribals with limited alternatives increasingly depend on low pay-off options offered by such resources. Sursi Buru situated in

Kuchai block of Kharswan Saraikela district is considered a sacred mountain. This forested hill which is under the state government and become highly degraded, but tribal people in the neighbouring villages still look at not only as a sacred site but also as an important source of livelihood, food, water, biomass and so forth almost in all seasons. The elderly people in this area vividly remember how it was a dense forest full of sal trees, as thick enough which could not be hugged even by two people. And later on all these were cut down as timber contractors from the cities would come and bribe the forest guards and middle of night these trees were gradually cut down and taken away, in trucks as it was managed by the state forest department, under the broad principle of joint forest management. The local village council like the *paraha-panchyat* has become very weak in this region. The Sanutola which is situated in the bank of Sona river still remember a huge banyan tree which was the biggest tree in the river bank and that part of the forest was so dense that even in the daytime wild bear used to reside in that tree and nobody would dare to venture into that part of the forest. Elderly people clearly remember that in their childhood days they would hear the roaring of tigers in the forest and in the morning when they graze their cattle in the forest, it was a common sight to find tiger and bear litter all over the place.

Later the change in the whole socio-cultural perspective towards ecology can be understood as the influence of major religions in the whole of the South Asian region. A study by Madhav Gadgil and Ramachandra Guha (1992) is important in this aspect. In their work *This Fissured Land: An Ecological History of India*, they discuss various historical, distinct modes of resource use, where they focus on the aspects of technology, economy, social organisations and ideology. They point out that the belief system of the food gatherers, with its conservation orientation, saw spirits that were respected in the trees, groves, ponds, rivers and mountain peaks. In contrast, in the belief system of the food producers, namely agricultural and pastoral communities, conquering new territories, worship focused on elemental forces such as fire, water and the great God of war, Indra, with the pattern of resource use becoming grounded in a continual march of agricultural and pastoralism over territories held by food gatherers, who had a great stake in the conservation of the resource base of their territories. Since the forests with its wild animal population served as a resource base for the enemy, its destruction rather than its conservation would now assume priority. Supernatural power would now no longer reside in specific trees, groves or ponds, but would be the more abstract forces of nature: fire, earth, wind, water and sky, whose assistance could be evoked in the task of subordinating the hunter-gatherers and colonising their resources base. Fire to clear the forest and water to nourish crops in the fields, would be the most valuable of these forests; therefore Agni and Varuna were the major deities. The main rituals were fire worship, ritual in which huge quantities of wood and animal fat were consumed. The burning of Kandava forest, as depicted in the *Mahabharata*, beautifully illustrates the operation of this belief system. The burning of the forest and killing of the wild animals and the tribal food gatherers is couched in the terminology of a great ritual sacrifice to please Agni. Later, as the frontier receded and there were no longer large fertile tracts to move forward, there emerged the belief systems of Buddhism and Jainism, which rejected the supernatural and advocated a rational arrangement of human affairs. Their belief system included an important sense of conservation; they advocated that resources should not be used wastefully.

Interplay between nature, totemism and cultural beliefs

Durkheim (1912) attempts to locate the source of the sacred and what religion is all about. He considers totemism (of Australian aborigines) as the most basic type of religion. In totemism, tribes are divided into clans whose solidarity derives not from kinship, but from a religious relationship between its members. As Durkheim understands it, this relationship is based on a sacred association between the clan, its members and a totemic entity, usually a local animal or plant species. In Durkheim's view, the idea was that the totemic emblem, a design representing the clan's totemic entity, was sacred. Its sacredness lay in the fact that it conferred sacredness on whatever was marked with it. Totemism assures the continuing fertility of the totemic animal or plant etc. Where the totemic entity was an animal or a plant, its sacredness was a matter of it being prohibited as ordinary food to clan members, though it might be obligatory to consume it in ritual situations.

The concepts of totemism, animism, ritualism and shamanism should all be considered to gain a full love for forest and nature is natural for the tribes of Jharkhand state of India from the ancient times. The idea and concept behind totemism is that people have a spiritual connection or kinship with creatures or objects in nature, making the practice very similar to animism. Animism is a belief based on the spiritual idea that the universe, and all natural objects within the universe, has souls or spirits. It is believed that souls or spirits exist not only in humans but also in animals, plants, trees, rocks and all natural forces understanding of the religious beliefs of the tribes of Jharkhand that included animal totems. There are ideological, mystical, emotional, reverential, and genealogical relationships of social groups or specific persons with animals or natural objects, the so-called totems. Most of the indigenous tribal cultures in eastern India, in the states of Jharkhand, Orissa, West Bengal and Chhattisgarh, derive their family clan or kinship identification from particular plants, habitat, fish and food groups.

Native beliefs further explain that a totem animal is one that is with you for life both in the physical and spiritual world. Though people may identify with different animal guides throughout their lifetimes, it is this one totem animal that acts as the main guardian spirit. The totem animal, when it dies is ceremonially mourned and buried as a member of the clan concerned In other words totem is a belief in a spiritual association between a clan/lineage/moiety and a bird, animal or a natural phenomenon.

The anthropologists of modern time look at totemism as a recurring way of conceptualising relationships between kinship groups and of the natural world. A number of tribal groups believe that they are related to some plants and animals that are sacred to them. The Ho of Jharkhand state has clans (*killis*), and each killi bears a totemic object that is sacred to them. The Gond, the Munda and the Oraon also have totemic clans. The Mundas have got the totem Soi (sol fish), Nag (serpent) and Hassa (goose); similarly the Santhals have the totem Murmu (a forest based wild cow), Chande (a lizard), Boyar (a fish); similarly the Ho have Hansda (a wild goose), Bage (tiger), Jamuda (spring) and Tiyu (fox). Every climatic region has its own trees, animals and rocks peculiar to its own. The animal totems in Chhotanagpur region of Jharkhand state consists of those animals which can be found in the plateau and from which various endogamous totemistic groups have originated. The totemistic names are from those animals generally found in the tract, such as Karkha (the cow), Tirki (a young mouse), Lakra (the tiger), Kindu (the saur fish), Toppo (a small bird), Kerketta (the quail), Khalko (a fish), Ekka (the tortoise) and so forth. All clans within a tribe have different versions of their origins and the origin of their totems. Special interests attaches to the fact that the Kharwars of South Lohardaga regard the Khar grass as the totem of their tribe, and will not cut or injure it while it is growing. In Kharia community the totem objects are not injured or eaten. According to different experts, the Santhals have more than 100 totemistic clans. Hos have more than 50, Mundas 64 and Bhils 24, many castes in Orissa, the Kurmi, the Kumhar, the Bhumia, who have advanced in culture in recent years are named after the serpent, pumpkin, jackal, and other totems. The Birhor, a people that were traditionally residents of the jungle of Chhotanagpur Plateau in Jharkhand state (India), are organised into patrilineal, exogamous totem groups. According to one imperfect list of 37 clans, are based on animals, plants, localities, and the rest on objects. The totems are passed on within the group, and tales about the tribe's origins suggest that each totem had a fortuitous connection with the birth of the ancestor of the clan. The Birhor think that there is a temperamental or physical similarity between the members of the clan and their totems. Prohibitions or taboos are sometimes cultivated to an extreme degree. In regard to eating, killing, or destroying them, the clan totems are regarded as if they were human members of the group. Moreover, it is believed that an offense against the totems through a breach of taboo will produce a corresponding decrease in the size of the clan. If a person comes upon a dead totem animal, he must smear his forehead with oil or a red dye, but he must not actually mourn over the animal; he also does not bury it (Priyadarshini 2013).

As with the names of the animals, so with the names of trees; some trees are considered sacred and are worshipped in two forms, namely the worship of the tree itself in its natural form and the worship of the tree spirit. The names of trees, which are quite natural, are only those that grow in this plateau, namely the Sal which is associated with the great festival, the Sarhul, Udbaru (the kusum tree), jojo (the tamarind), Bara (the ficus *Judica*), and the Kujur which are minor jungle trees and creepers not to be found elsewhere.

Those observances of sacredness of their totems are unique only with the indigenous people of Jharkhand. Thereby they not only protect the equilibrium of the biodiversity, but also continue the wisdom and collective excellence related to forest and their protection of biodiversity (Priyadarshini 2013).

Forests, local ecological knowledge and Adivasi cosmology

The significance of forests to the maintenance and use of biodiversity is limitless. As a resource and environmental stabiliser, a tropical moist forest is the most important ecosystem. It provides timber, non-timber products, tourism income, and plant genetic material, raw materials for biotechnology, medicines, pharmaceuticals, food and shelter for its people. It prevents erosion, maintains soil fertility, regulates water runoff, moderates climate, reduces stream and river sedimentation which kills fish, stops nutrient washout which pollutes waterways, and fixes carbon dioxide.

Forests have a considerable importance in the life of the tribes. In India forests and tribes are inseparable to historically, the forest provided plentiful food to its people. Particularly during times of severe droughts, the forest acted as a saviour and adivasi people were known to spurn relief works and return to the forest for their food. Valentine Ball noted in the 1880s that he had frequently seen large numbers of men, women and children grouping in half-dried-up tanks for Singhara (water chestnut), fresh water snails and small sluggish fish. Adivasis are less affected by famine for the jungles produce their ordinary food whether there is drought or an abundant rain. In Palamau of Chhotanagpur region, most of the people obtained a good supply of flowers, fruits, barks, roots and tubers which formed important articles of food almost throughout the year and as district officers noted to this chiefly is due the immunity of the district from famine (Deb et al. 2014). The tribal culture developed, and in spite of large scale depredations of the forests, still today thrives in the lap of nature.

Since time immemorial, one finds that tribal hunters and food gathers, Swidden cultivators and pastoralist have been using the forest, as a major source of livelihood. There are some tribal groups like Shara or Sa-ara in the vicinity of temple towns in ancient towns, who had the main source of livelihood in cutting fuel wood in the jungle and selling it to the town dwellers and villagers. There are other tribal groups who made charcoal in the forest and sold it to blacksmiths and others as a major means of livelihood. All tribal people residing near the forest or inside the forest use wood and bamboo and reeds (chhana) as a building material. Their cattle and other domestic animals regularly graze in the forest. Even when tribal group is not a hunter and food gatherer who has to depends on forest as a sole source of livelihood, other tribal groups including who live in the vicinity of the forest but practice settled agriculture like Santhal, Munda and so forth also depend on forest for various food and non-food products including herbal medicines. Medicine, as a matter of their cultural tradition, has an age-old linkage to forests. There are tribal people like the Karia in the Simlipal forest who collect and sell honey, arrowroots, sal rasin and other minor forest products including mynah birds. In a nutshell, the tribal people and the forest as the source of their livelihood and as the place where they mostly reside and prefer to live are inseparable. But since the colonial period their utilisation of minor forest produce has been a vital link with the outside world economy as also a very important source of cash income as a part of their life support system (Mahapatra and Mohapatra 1997).

Sanjay Kumar (2004), in his case study of indigenous people's management of community forest in Jharkhand show the extent of indigenous people's knowledge of the local environmental services provided by the forest and manner in which there management takes account of these environmental service functions. He points out that the indigenous communities in the eastern Indian Chhotanagpur plateau region are the bearers of extensive local ecological knowledge that revolves around the forests of that area. This knowledge could be an extremely useful tool to involve the tribals in the forest management and development programs and also to ensure the long-term sustainability of management in that area. He clearly points out that the Adivasis have deep understanding of how the forest influences on the air and water quality, drinking water sources, aquatic food, other uncultivated food items, relationship between forests and farmlands, farm soil erosion, the hydrological cycle of forests and so forth. He also describes the strong cultural beliefs about forest. Forests are integral to the cosmos vision of indigenous communities in the whole Chhotanagpur region which manifest in direct relationship between cultural events and beliefs with the tree and forests. For example, Sarhul is one of the important festival of the forest population across the eastern India plateau is observed to mark the flowering of the Sal tree in April–May. No person can bring any flower for consumption or otherwise before Sarhul as it is believed that it will invite deadly snake bite. The custom coconsciously keeps the flower unharmed until pollination and seed setting is over in most tree species of the area. Other festivals of importance are Karma in which the Karam tree (*Adina cordifolia*) is worshiped. There is forest prayer (Birbonga) in the month of May, to propitiate the wild animal god. Rog-her diseases eradication prayer observed during summer month performed at a particular place having a specific type of vegetation. In some villages for example, Rog-her place is called Loa-Ikir which is encircled with the Loa tree (figtree). Another one is Sarjom Ikir which is encircled by Sal trees. Bishu Shikar, the community wild animal hunt in which the game, however small has to be shared equally between all households of the participating villages. Most people believed that tree should be protected because it propitiates the rain god and bring rain fall by stopping clouds as mountain do when causing orographic rainfall. Elderly people also believed that the bog tree should be conserved because of the cuckoo bird sings for rain and likes to rest on these big trees. Ancestors' spirits also come and rest on these trees particularly in those sacred groves

(Sarna). The fear of retribution that they will be punished by the god (bonga) if they cut or harm the Sarna trees is common among all age groups and classes. The local knowledge and management of forest tree resources for cultural and religious purposes set within the complex social framework of the area. Conservation of tree resources can best be understood in the context of control by the rural elite, namely the *pahan* (priest) who was the most venerated person of Munda society in pre-British days. The pahan high position in the society even today strengthen by the ecological argument for these religious and cultural rituals and same time these rituals serves as potent tool that keeps outsider/immigrants from ever using the villagers natural resources as it is argued that it will displease the bonga.

Significance of sacred groves and conservation of environment

James Frazer in his famous ethnographic study of religion and ritual, *The Golden Bough* (1922), mentions the supreme importance of worshiping the holy trees and the sacred groves, as the most powerful force in making of primitive religion. He also explains the significance of a priest who bore the title of King of the Wood, and one of whose titles to office was the plucking of a bough – the Golden Bough – from a tree in the sacred grove.

There are multiple layers of meaning in understanding human ecological relationships. Anthropologist have highlighted that interventions and intrusion into indigenous population's habitats and their lives have contributed to ecological stress as indigenous population did not over exploit their habitat and had harmonious adaptations to environment changes. Conservation of natural resources has been an integral aspect of many indigenous communities all over the world. The traditional ethics of many tribal people directly or indirectly protect forest patches by dedicating them to local deities. Such forest patches are referred to by these people as 'Sacred groves' – a place of religious importance as well as a socio-cultural ground for observing various ceremonies. In *The Elementary Forms of Religious Life* (1912), Durkheim view the sacred is far from being synonymous with the divine. Not only may gods and spirits be sacred, but also things like rocks, trees, pieces of wood, in fact anything. For what makes something sacred is not that it is somehow connected to the divine but that it is the subject of a prohibition that sets it radically apart from something else, by which it is thereby made profane. Durkheim describes religion in terms of beliefs and rites. For him, the details of these in particular religions are particular ways of dealing in thought and action with the fundamental dichotomy of sacred and profane. Durkheim addresses next the question of how people come to see the world the way he claims: as two separate worlds, in fact. He starts by dismissing theories of the origins of religions based on animism and what he calls naturism.

The sacred grove for tribal is an adobe of deities who remain inside the grove and care for the villagers, animals and plants. It is a holy religious place which consists of a cluster of that exists in a circular shape and varies according to its nature and type. Generally there are number of groves around the village named after different deities. Tribal consider their grove as mirroring their culture and have a family type of ties with the gods and goddesses who believe to reside in the sacred grove. They believe that trees provide them with all types of amenities like food, shelter, clothing, medicines and animal feed, and bring happiness and well-being to them. The tribal have a profound knowledge of their own environment, especially of their forest-based ecosystem. The sacred grove is one of a kind where trees of different nature are preserved. The indigenous knowledge about the utility of these has been passed on from generation to generation, mostly orally through stories and cultural practices. The knowledge may be a simple life lesson, a tale with a moral ending or practical knowledge on cultivating crops, health care and observations of ceremonies relating to their well-being; it is a tradition they are expected to maintain. The plant resources in the sacred grove have socio-cultural importance for the tribe and the indigenous knowledge and ethno-medicinal information are usually preserved in the sacred groves and also in their forest environment by an action-oriented nature, like cultivation and propagation of important medicinal plants, generating awareness among the people about the importance of different plants by extending sacred grove complex through afforestation and to get the indigenous knowledge relating to medicinal plants of the area. The sacred groves irrespective of their nature and size, would find scope to blend an ecological function and cultural justification of biodiversity on the one hand and indigenous system on the other. There is an urgent need not only to protect the grove but also to revive and reinvent such traditional practices of natural conservation, and encourage people to protect, preserve and regenerate sacred groves in tribal areas to maintain biodiversity and ecosystem. It is imperative that sacred groves be explored in terms of ecological and cultural perspectives in order to develop a strategy for revival of the tradition in conservation (Sahoo and Nanda 2012).

Every village has a small patch of forests called 'Jahera' or 'Sarna' in the Jharkhand region, which is place of worship for them. It is quite right for them to worship forests, because their entire living depends on forests. If forests are destroyed they will lose their source of food, medicines, fruits and fodder for their animals, and they will lose their source of cooking and warming themselves.

Sacred groves figure prominently in efforts to create community-based conservation in tribal region. The intersections of ecological and social dynamics in sacred groves, offers a framework for understanding them as resource management systems with the potential to conserve biodiversity and mitigate deforestation. Sacred groves are the repositories of rare and endemic species and can be regarded as the remnant of the primary forest left untouched by the local inhabitants and protected by them due to the belief that the deities reside in these forests. In India, as elsewhere in many parts of the world, a number of tribal communities practice different forms of nature worship. One such significant tradition of nature worship is that providing protection to patches of forests dedicated to deities or ancestral spirits. An empirical study of sacred grove in the Purulia district of West Bengal is called Sarana or Jahersthan, by the tribal people while the Bengali people call it by the name of 'Pabitra Kunjaban'. In Purulia district, each sacred groves owned and managed by the members of the associated (tribal) village community. In India, tribal people also have unprecedented proneness or propensity toward religion. In addition, they also worship earth or nature as Mother Goddess. Religious beliefs, practices, sentiments, emotions and sustainability are all interwoven. For maintaining social sustainability or stability, religious sanctions are also assumed to produce more social welfare compared to social sanctions. Prior to the inception of global unsustainability, a consistency between the religious sacredness and sustainability was persisting in tribal society. There are some sacred groves from which biomass can be collected. But in most cases, these are treated as 'no-entry zone' due to social or cultural taboos or sanctions. Some act as the means of indicating the cultural or ethnic identity. The ecological functions performed by these are as follows: The sacred groves act as the pool of biological diversity owing to the rigid restrictions imposed by the communal taboos or sanctions against free entry and exit of the people. Due to sustained destruction and degradation of preexisting forests, these have become the last refuge for many threatened and endangered plant and animal species. The sacred groves also act as the repository of many medicinal plants. Water resources, particularly in the form of ponds, springs, lakes, streams or rivers, are seen in most of it. The water resources act as the last resort for the age of inchoate sustainability revolution. Sacred groves exist throughout the tribal region which consists of dense patches of forest in agrarian landscapes. The term sacred does not imply, however, that these sites are purely religious institutions, separate from politics, social organisation, and land tenure, but it shows how community-based conservation often leads to institutional coherence and effective management (Konar 2010).

A 2005 symposium on the management of sacred sites called for administrators, scholars, and activists to work toward 'safeguarding the cultural and biological diversity embodied in sacred natural sites and cultural landscapes' (UNESCO 2005), efforts that surely would contribute much to the diversification of conservation policy. The implication for conservation policy is that sacred groves are not simply local forms of conservation; groves should be oriented not simply toward empowering locals to protect and maintain these sites, but rather toward adaptive co-management by various institutions at local, national, and global levels (Sheridan 2009).

Today the current crisis and pressures related to sacred groves as contested sites are very apparent. The sacred groves are also going through the phase of unsustainability syndrome due to the following factors such as, commercialisation of forestry, execution of development projects, diminishing trend in the sacredness (loss of faith in the deities), conversion of people into other religions, voluntary or involuntary Hinduisation of tribal people, aversion of current generation toward traditional culture or custom, marketisation, monetisation and commoditisation of diverse facets of human social life, lack of mass awareness and so forth. The Ajodhya Hills in Purulia district West Bengal covered with forest layer have become the important tourist spots, which are being socialised or humanised by the inflow and outflow of people coming from various communities and lands. Earlier the Ajodhya Hills were inhabited by only tribal people. But now these hills and their forest cover are being colonised by non-tribal people of close and distant origin in the sense that almost all types of economic activity (e.g. road construction and repairing, reforestation or replanting, hotel and motel businesses, primary health services, primary and secondary educations, running of different administrative departments or units, etc.) are undertaken by the non-tribal colonists to satisfy their own interests (Konar 2010).

Indigenous system of ecological management and culture of the conservation

Most of the indigenous communities the world over are mainly concerned to regulate their own use of natural resources, including collection of firewood and thatch, and grazing by livestock. The original common property resource management system operated under an indigenous institution, which was enforced through sanctions and punishments imposed by the community.

Thus the management of the common property resources was part and parcel of the wider tenure and administrative system of any tribal community. Outsiders, and even rightful owners not abiding by the rules and regulations governing the mode of resource appropriation, were excluded or subject to severe punishment. The common property resources became a kind of sacred entity, with the prestige, power, and authority of important local level institution. The old system was based on kinship and tribal religion both of which are tremendously important to communal belief and unity. And this sacred area was not supposed to be brought under crop cultivation or extensive tree plantation, despite the general craving for land, hence there is no permanent human settlement in this area. However, the area plays an important role in the economics and survival strategies of adjacent tribal communities.

The traditional land use institutions are based on mythological and cultural beliefs. These lead to common interests, open access and free user rights on natural resources. Because the attributes of common property resource utilisation are influenced by traditional rules and aspirations, their management had in the past been in harmony with the environment. The forest communities or indigenous people have always viewed forests as a multiple-use resource and they were, actively engaged in preserving its multiple-use character, likewise the forest has flourished. Sustainability of the forest depends on collective-action rights being vested in a forest community committed to preserving its multiple-use character. Wildlife was managed through traditional regulations to meet subsistence requirements for food, income, recreation and health care. The tribal economy is highly dependent on forest products like leaves, fruits, fuel wood, timber, mushrooms and others to generate income and to provide food and medical care. Animal wildlife and surface water are conserved through taboos and other communal regulations aimed at protecting the resources (Geores 1998).

Since independence in India large scale deforestation had occurred either for locating major industries, water management schemes, mining etc. or for commercial purposes. Both these requires clear feeling. But in swidden cultivation clear feeling is not resorted to. The tree stumps remain and help regenerate the trees from new suits. Many kinds of tree are spared from burning by swidden cultivators in their self-interests. Trees, yielding edible and non-edible oil, many variety of food, trees on which silk or Taser worms grow by feeding on the leaves or the tree on which stock lac organism grow, tree with edible leaves, flowers, one left standing in the swidden. The tribal people pursuing food gathering and hunting do destroy neither the animals nor birds nor plant resources wantonly. As matter of fact, tribal hunters do not kill wild animals during the periods the animals are pregnant. Hence, they conserve nature in their own interest. Similarly the food gatherers leave a portion of tubers, yam or roots in the grounds, the tribals dig up for food. Therefore, the tribals on no account destroy the forest resources, but on the contrary they conserve the forest resources. Only when in a traumatic situation for example, under threat of displacement do the tribal people develop a thoroughly destructive attitude towards the forest.[2]

Forest resources mean the difference between life and death to rural economies. For example, forest products are used for traditional health care delivery, recreation, and food and income generation. Around homes, forests are protected for various uses: to bury the young (bad bush), to design and fabricate masquerades, to prepare rituals for the installation of traditional rulers and for religious worships. Plants are managed in line with land tenure systems at communal level. In sacred or forbidden forests, free access and open access user rights are held by few individuals: priests, village heads and elders of a community. The forests are usually protected for gods or goddesses for the performance of rituals and for worship. The communal rules and regulations prevent all members from exploiting forest resources from sacred forests except for rituals or to worship deities. Notable fruit bearing indigenous species are protected by the community. The user rights to these plants are absolute but the plants cannot be killed physically by an individual but their fruits are usually harvested when matured to avoid wastage.

In the past, the regulations controlling common resource utilisation were based on traditional beliefs and administration when the structure of the economy was homogeneously agrarian and the forests supplied all requirements for food, cash and shelter. The stability of the ecosystems was maintained because of low human population relative to the demand for forest resources. The regulations were forced on individuals from birth and defaulters were either disbanded from taking part in communal functions or sent on exile by the community or forced to perform some rituals. Taboos are compelling on individuals, families or the entire community. Taboos arose from religious differences, experience of founders of settlements and from traditional curative medicine or from traditional medicine used to acquire mystical power. Taboo was a significant management tool applied to wildlife in the past and had substantive positive impact on conserving the resources so concerned. Unfortunately, the traditional arrangement for the management of common property resources are breaking down due to a combination of factors: forest depletion, trade in wild animals and changes in the beliefs of the people with regards to religion.

Land use changes and common resource utilization

Common property resource utilisation is successful under four conditions: communally owned land, unindustrialised agricultural production, and low population density and subsistence economy. Today with structural changes such as the transformation of land ownership into state or public land tenure meant that the common property regime that had formerly guaranteed the sustainable availability of resources on which all rightful owners collectively depended was no longer fully functional (Geores 1998).

In the traditional set-up of the Adivasis village, the watchman would make regular announcement (at night), regarding 'rules of conservation'. For example during the summer when it is the season of mango, jackfruit, jamun and so forth, a meeting would be held by the village council to fix various rules to procure these fruits from the forests which acted as common property resources, for the whole community. The rules clearly states that the fruits should be only picked from the ground and no one is allowed to climb or shook the trees, in order to get more than their needs. Some fruits like tamarind are being plucked from the trees situated in and around the village; everybody participates, than it is being equally distributed among all the households. In the tribal region of eastern states in India, strict rules are still applicable and are operationalised, specifically, related to, sacred groves. In Sanutola of kuchai block in Jharkhand, outsiders are forbidden to enter the sacred grove (Sarna) or to take photographs, even members of the village staying in cities are being told to, seek permission from the 'Sarnabonga' the ancestral holy spirit, residing in the trees, show respect and then enter. The land of the 'sarna' should not be encroached upon by any cost.

Adivasis culture's inherent respect to ecology specially forests, trees, rivers etc. becomes clear with the historical fact that during the colonial, period, when they left their home and hearth for distant places (like tea plantations in Assam) under the indentured system, to work as laborers. In the tribal region of Jharkhand, people still tell stories about the pain people felt during the time of leaving, the Adivasis would cry aloud looking at their field and forests, when they were compelled to migrate. Even though well versed with the skill of clearing the forests and making agricultural fields, they could have easily cleared the remaining forests and transform them into farmlands, but still they didn't do that. Even in such situation of crises they safeguard the forests. The indigenous ecological knowledge categorically strengthen the cultural norm of environmental and biodiversity conservation rather than destroying it for individual needs, which gets reflected in their cultural beliefs which define landscape as sacred, rituals and festivals.

Modes of subsistence, livelihood patterns and environmental sustainability

The livelihoods among tribal communities in India is complex, dynamic and multidimensional phenomenon, the perception of which varies with geographic location, type of community, age, gender, education, fluctuations in resources, services and infrastructures and social, economic, cultural, ecological and political determinants (Ajazul-Islam et al. 2013)

Rita Brara (2011) discuss about various combinational modes of subsistence such as hunting, pastoral-nomadism and settled agriculture and its impact on environment. As a combinational practice small scale animal husbandry dovetails well with one-crop agriculture. Most rural inhabitants keep livestock that are fed on the vegetative resources of uncultivated lands. Livestock such as cows, buffaloes, hens, pigs, goats, yaks, horses, are commonly reared by sedentary agriculturalist for various uses: meat, milk, wool, hides, draught power and so forth. From the environmental angle it is vital to note that the stall feeding of livestock is conceived largely as a supplement to the pasturage that is found in commons. The streams, rivers, and ponds that dot the countryside furnish additional water bodies for cultivating and harvesting aquatic species. This water bodies are mostly commons. The legal system in India distinguishes the villager's right in arable fields from the rights of villages over common tracts. The combinations of swidden cultivation and hunting or animal husbandry and dry land agriculture required more extensive tracts for their viability but this aspect was overlooked in the legislation concerning land rights. The changing environment conditions influences the life, culture, interrelation and interdependency between man and its environment. Overall the local technology, management strategies and local culture are interrelated with environmental condition of a particular region which helps adapt to natural phenomena.

Even today, Adivasis in central and eastern India are heavily dependent on land and forest for their livelihood. The principles of equity, group rights, egalitarian norms, woman's status, health, well-being and ecological balance are the basic components of their socio-cultural and religious life. Indigenous spiritual and cultural practices depend upon access to their traditional lands, including historically and spiritually significant sites. Besides, there are other healthy dimensions of their lifestyle and habitation (e.g. less crowding, greater intimacy with natural environment). Even recent researches on some major tribes in Jharkhand show that their traditional food habits and diets (including usage of roots, tubers, vegetables, fruits, etc.) have sufficient nutritive value. The global literature on health and survival of traditional (mostly tribal) societies is broadly suggestive of their greater adaptability to such aspects of nature and environment, but they generally lose this type of adaptation (hence their health and survival advantage) in course of acculturation.

Tribals need continued non-market access to critical livelihood resources, land and forest. A case study of Bundu block in Jharkhand clearly shows that, there is a strong inter-sectionality between livelihood pattern, mode of subsistence and environmental sustainability. Forests of Bundu block in Ranchi district of Jharkhand state are the common thread in all aspects of life, whether it is birth, marriage, livelihood or death among the tribal communities. The forests include a considerable wealth of land, soil, water, fuel, minerals, natural vegetation, wild life including the aquatic fauna having multifarious uses constitute an important source of livelihood among tribal people in the block. Forests are the source of revenue, employment, shelter, housing materials, cloth, ornament, fuel, fodder/grazing, timber, food, vegetables, medicines, fertiliser, fibre, floss, oilseed, cottage industries and handicrafts and other non-timber forest products (NTFPs) besides playing a vital role in the environmental amelioration in the block. About 70% of the population mainly depends on rain fed agriculture characterised by low productivity, un-predictive weather and calamities, degraded soil with low fertility, un-protective irrigation and degraded environment. These factors aggravated the problems of poverty, migration, unemployment, under-employment, food insecurity and malnutrition. The capability of agriculture and livestock production is unable to form sustainable livelihoods of tribal poor. Consequently, the tribal people are constrained to earn their livelihoods from forest resources. Forest is the second largest land use in India after agriculture covering

21.05% of the total geographical area of the country. Forests provide a wide spectrum of livelihoods for tribal communities in the form of direct employment, self-employment and secondary employment. The results of the study revealed that the forest resources are the important contributor to the total livelihoods among the tribal communities in the block. The forest resources are viewed as a viable source for both subsistence and cash income among the surveyed households as the alternative options are scarce or even absent, land for agriculture is in short supply and the returns to agriculture is low in the study area. The poorer households use greater amounts of forest resources for earning income than wealthier households. Although the cash earned from forest resources is small, participation in the trade is an important source of self-esteem, pride and independence, especially for women. The study leads to conclude that the livelihoods of tribal communities in the area have traditionally been dominated by subsistence agriculture. However, the forest resources play a vital role in the livelihoods of tribal people through direct paid employment and NTFPs based self-employment. (Ajaz-ul-Islam et al. 2013)

A recent study of uncultivated foods from forests and food and nutrition security of Adivasis in Odisha clearly points out that Adivasi communities' dependence on uncultivated foods from the forest still persists. Apart from this, there is an enormous wealth of biological knowledge associated with these foods with members of the community, including children. Whether it is about where a particular species grows seasonality characteristics, identification and appearance, or its nutritive and medicinal properties, properties related to processing or storing, cooking methods and quality, veterinary and livestock uses are all valuable knowledge that community members possess. Several of these foods is especially tubers, greens and various fruits etc. hold great cultural significance for the communities dependent on them. Technical and nutritious analysis of these foods shows that most such foods are highly nutritious, safe, diverse and nutritious food that is in several ways superior to the food (Deb et al. 2014).

There is close relation between environment and livelihood among tribals. But at the same time, deprivation is the norm mainly because project planning ignores the role of the environment in the lives of the poor, particularly the dependents on natural resources or commons. They suffer more than the *patta* owners do since often they are not even considered displaced. Besides, development literature never mentions the 'indirect displaced' who move out 'voluntarily' because of environmental degradation, for example when fly ash from cement or thermal plants destroys their land or explosions, noise and air pollution from mines affect their houses. Their number is substantial but no estimates exist. That is where the meaning one gives to the environment becomes relevant to the poor. According to the Brazilian President Fernando Henrique Cardoso (1998), the first danger the global environment faces is biodiversity loss and linked to it, the value system of the communities depending on it (Fernandes et al. 1988).

State intervention, forests and exclusion of Adivasis

The forests support unique cultural systems, societies of hunter-gatherers, which are not only an integral part of the forests, in balance with (and vital for) the stability of the ecosystem, but also its most intelligent guardians, capable of being the most important asset for future sustainable and profitable use of forests (Swingland 1993). The tribal communities in India largely occupy forested regions where for long period in their history they have lived in isolation but in harmony with nature. They draw their sustenance largely from the forest. They have had symbiotic relationship with the forests which continues undisturbed in the interior areas even now (Burman 1982).

In the succeeding section, I shall denote with reference to the forest legislation in India that state intervention in natural resources, has been generally based on the principle of 'exclusion' than 'inclusion' and 'equity' in the management of these resources. The history of formation of forest lands in India can be traced to the Indian Forest Act of 1865, replaced in a span of 13 years by the core comprehensive Forest Act of 1878. Baden Powell traces the sources of forest lands to the large areas of wastelands (mostly common and community-owned lands) adjoining zamindari estates and other village communities. The Indian Forest Act aimed at commuting or eliminating the rights of the people existent prior to the declaration of these lands as reserved or protected forests, particularly those rights which were deemed to clash with the interests of the state. But while in the case of protected forests, only the 'harmful rights' of the people such as shifting cultivation were eliminated, for the reserved forests, a variety of other rights were also eliminated, since the resources of reserved forests were considered for 'first degree protection' by the state. Philosophically the creation of forest lands in India represented the symbolic assertion of the difference between the rights of the state and that of the people, through a mutual separation of rights which was achieved in space by a two-faceted principle: (1) segregation of discrete resources (e.g. reserved trees) occurring in the land declared as forests; and (2) through a discrete segregation of resources by enforcing exclusion of people in spatial terms (by keeping them out of 'core' resource areas as a whole). It is not difficult to conceive that a common land constituted into a forest land underwent a change in its 'open-access' trait. Thus the former users of the common lands would have been excluded from using certain resources over which the state had established property rights, or it may have been that the users would have been excluded from a part of their former common lands through a total spatial exclusion. In the case of forest lands in respect of which all user rights were exterminated this not only meant an end to the 'open mode of access but also to 'open-access'. Thus no attempt was made to ensure that the community of users (Adivasis), denied physical access to the forest lands got an equitable access to the common resources growing in these lands. Even worse was the situation with regard to those forest lands where the state imposed selective control through segregation of resources. Here while physical access to the reserved resources was totally denied, for the non-reserved resources the state permitted 'individual' user rights rather than 'community' user rights. Only those 'individuals' whose rights have been taken cognisance of by the state were to have access to non-controlled forest resources, as compared to their fellow community members. This meant an 'unequal' access to forest lands and its non-reserved resources for some individuals as compared to the former common property situation wherein they could have only shared equal rights with their fellow users (Chopra 1995).

Forest has always played pivotal role in the economy of the tribal people even before historical times. In the colonial period, there was commercialisation of forest produce for the first time in vast scale. Even in the interior region of Orissa, commercial exploitation of the forest goes back at least to 1920, when companies from outside brought in sawyers into the forest and slippers for railways were made and exported. Blocks of mahua forest were auctioned for commercial purpose. Although forest produce was collected and sold in the weekly market or otherwise buy the forest dwelling tribes, the commercialisation of minor forest produce is a colonial phenomenon with the rise of Biri factory and with large scale distillation of mahua spirits by the wine makers. Some forest produce assumed disproportionate importance in the economy of the forest dweller during the colonial period. Use of tobacco and maize among other things, may have taken roots after the European intrusion, but today everywhere in tribal India one finds tobacco made in use. Similarly, when the tribal people are used for decades to depending on collection and sale of minor forest produce, these have entered into tier economy as an irreversible component (Mahapatra and Mohapatra 1997).

Colonial rule in India led to the imposition of laws and practices which gave the rulers a greater control over forest resources, the colonial laws disrupted people's livelihoods. Some of the significant laws such as the Indian Forest Act were passed in 1865, 1878 and once again in 1927. Post-independence, the National Forest Policy 1952 and laws such as the Wild Life Protection Act of 1972 and the Forest Conservation Act of 1980 continued to curtail the local use of forest, further alienating village communities from their resources. The Odisha Forest Produce (Control and Trade) Act 1981 continued to give monopoly control over forest produce to the state. In all these years, there was little attention paid to food gathered and consumed from the forest. Several thousand villages across Odisha have been conserving their forests for generations on their own initiative, much before an official recognition dawned on the importance of involving local communities in forest protection and conservation. The adivasi community and others living close to the forest started the community forest management programs to conserve forests to ensure access to fuelwood and fodder and protect the forests for ecological gains. This was a purely community initiative supported by civil society. The Joint Forest Management (JFM) program was aimed at the forest department working in partnership with communities for mutual gain. The JFM was meant to ensure livelihood improvement of the forest dependent people by involving the local communities through re-generation of forests and their rehabilitation. In 1993, the emerging JFM program visualised a three-way partnership between forest department, community and non-governmental organisation (Deb et al. 2014).

The forest policy of the state both colonial and post-colonial clearly indicated a historical injustice to the tribal people in India (Chaithanaya 2012; Kakada 2012; Fernandes et al. 1988). The extended process of state intrusion into forest areas that characterised the colonial and post-colonial period brought about a far reaching change in the ownership and management of forests. In India the tribal people had rights to collection and use granted by the state but not having ownership or even recognised tenure. They become at best interlopers on their own lands or worse law breakers because of their daily action, whether of gathering conversion to agriculture or other uses, becomes criminal acts on state's property (Dev Nathan et al. 2004). In Jharkhand, the history of 'crime against ecology' can be studied in three phases. The first phase began with the British occupation of forests of as eminent domain and clearing of flora and cleansing of fauna for the production of agricultural surplus. The second phase started with British conservationist policy was challenged by zamindar during Second World War and by the forest department after independence till the central government tried to revive the policy of conservation in the 1980s by the enactment of 1980 Act. And the third phase begin after that with a series of laws, resolutions and directives aimed at completing the unfinished jobs of the colonial masters of legally serving all relationship between forests and forest dependent people, the Adivasis (Paty 2007).

Globalisation, indigenous economy and environment

Economic globalisation proposed by the World Trade Organization is patently unsustainable and based on environment degradation. Industrial development and the lifestyles of the 'advanced' countries have become universal with the advent of economic globalisation policies. By universalising this form of production and consumption, environmental degradation is also being globalised, with most countries of the world following a common pattern of economic development that is uniformly unsustainable and environmentally destructive. On the other hand, environmental globalisation stress upon the need for environmental protection and the need to move towards an alternative form of development based on eco-friendly methods of production and consumption. While economic globalisation wants free markets, environmental globalisation pleads for stricter government intervention and control over the market. So there is a conflict in the tenets, practices and policies between the two forms of globalisation (Panth 2007).

This whole process of modernisation and development got accelerated due to globalisation, which resulted in impoverishing those who lost access to the natural resources and at the same time it enriched those who have took possession of it. Dev Nathan, Govind Kelkar and Pierre Walter (2004) in their work *Globalisation and Indigenous People in Asia* mention that the economically indigenous have been outside systems of accumulation, carrying on combination of swidden and terraced agriculture along with gathering of forest products. Environmental services like, controlled hydrological flows or carbon sequestration and the preservation of biodiversity taken from them without any compensation. The current process of globalisation in the context of weak property rights of the indigenous people enhances the risk of further marginalisation. Indigenous people are marginal to the growing national and global networks of capital in a number of ways. First they are national minorities enhance politically marginal. Second economically they have small role to play in labour market (as workers) capital market (as investors). Commodities markets (as consumers) or even debt markets (as taxpayers). They are marginal as per as their worldviews and cultures are concerned, usually being dismissed as primitives. Policies, for the indigenous people, so far being framed mainly, with view to the benefits that can be extracted for the outside economies. What the state covet from the hill forest area are the resources like timber and minerals which they extract from local economy. When deemed necessary for the national interest be it for the irrigation or for power supply, the indigenous people have been displaced to make way for dams, with most of them are losing their livelihood. In most cases the indigenous people do not own the forest and mineral resources of their economy. Consequently revenue from mines and forest accrue to the economies of the lowlands. At best the indigenous people get low wages at the bottom of the working class. In cases where the indigenous people do have some forms of ownership rights over the forest and mineral resources, they have been often forced in the name of national interest to submit to policies that are not in their interest. Indigenous people are being increasingly displaced from land ownership namely the hill forest region which have been opened up essentially to extract timber, minerals, NTFPs and other natural resources, but these investment have enabled the advance of non-tribal population into the area and tribals are losing their best lands.

With accelerating frequency, state and private actors enter indigenous territories to extract resources, develop energy, promote recreational and tourism activities, and expand industries. These activities often take place without consulting or benefitting indigenous communities. Indigenous children get less schooling, go hungry more often, and have less access to health care. Rather than improve these conditions, commercial activities often expose indigenous communities to hazards, risks, and wastes that contaminate their lands and interfere with their access to the cultural and life-sustaining resources found in their traditional territories (Willis and Seward 2006).

In today's scenario, the ecosystem are suffering due to the negative impacts of the every stage of ecological degradation and its life cycle – from exploration, production, refining and distribution, to consumption and disposal of waste. If deforestation and other ecological devastation continue at current rates, it is certain that climate change will result in increased temperatures; sea level rise; changes in agricultural patterns; increased frequency and magnitude of 'natural' disasters such as floods, droughts and intense storms; epidemics; and loss of biodiversity. The world over, ecosystems are in crisis. We are experiencing an accelerating spiral of climate change and global warming. Caused by the excessive build-up of heat-trapping greenhouse gases in the Earth's atmosphere – in particular carbon dioxide emissions from the burning of oil, gas and coal – climate change threatens virtually every segment of the biosphere and human society. Yet climate change doesn't affect everyone equally. Indigenous peoples, who rely on the land and water for food and culture, are most threatened by these.

In the eyes of many indigenous spiritual leaders, the source of these pressures can be traced to the long historical processes by which humans have become increasingly alienated from the Mother Earth. This results in an alienation from self, community and nature. The alienation has roots in imperialism and colonialism, and is currently being exacerbated by economic globalisation initiatives of free trade, privatisation and development policies that have no tie to nature. These trends propel an unsustainable concept of the natural world as 'property', and therefore a commodity to be exploited freely, and bought and sold at will. This paradigm has resulted in disharmony between human beings and the natural world, as well as the current environmental crisis threatening all life. It is totally incompatible with a traditional Indigenous worldview (Goldtooth 2004).

Mainstream society's lack of environmental concern disrupts the ability of Indigenous peoples to protect their traditional territories. Indigenous communities are finding it difficult to maintain sustainable economic systems, to practice their traditional ceremonies, and to preserve their hunting, gathering and fishing cultures. Indigenous spiritual and cultural practices depend upon access to their traditional lands, including historically and spiritually significant sites. Yet mineral and mining extractions, flooding of lands from mega-hydro dams, and toxic chemical contamination of traditional food systems seriously affect their deeply ingrained spiritual and cultural relationship with the ecosystem.

Indigenous peoples throughout the world are expressing their concern about the agenda of economic globalisation and imperialism. Indigenous tribes' inherent rights to sovereignty and self-determination are undermined by the World Trade Organization (WTO) and by most free trade agreements. Whether through environmental degradation; bio piracy and the patenting of Indigenous medicinal plant and seed knowledge; or the militarisation and violence that often accompanies development projects, the impact of these agreements is disproportionate and devastating these communities. The Indigenous Environmental Network and other US-based indigenous non-governmental organisations are challenging the WTO by applying indigenous rights and human rights based approaches that redefine principles and practices in regards to trade and development. They envision a 'sustainable communities' paradigm, a transparent and democratic process, as well as alternative worldviews and models of development. The Kimberly Declaration and the Indigenous Plan of Implementation developed at the Indigenous Peoples' International Summit and the World Summit on Sustainable Development affirmed the vital role Indigenous people play in defining this new paradigm. Indigenous peoples of the United States and the world – especially those that still maintain and practice their land-based cultures – are a threatened people (Goldtooth 2004).

Adivasis in a globalised world

> Imperialism and colonialism are not something that happened decades ago or generations ago, but they are still happening now with the exploitation of people. . . . The kind of thing that took place long ago in which people were dispossessed from their land and forced out of subsistence economies and into market economies – those processes are still happening today.
>
> (John Mohawk, Seneca 1992, cited in Goldtooth 2004)

Since independence the tribals are gradually denied access to the support system of their livelihood and human rights violation in the name of development. Most of the 'Tribal Development Programme' of the government has become too elusive and ineffective to reiterate, owing to lack of political will, inefficiency and corruption of the government officials. Displacement is treated as inevitable for development, while rehabilitation and resettlement are demoted or disregarded. Today Adivasis are suffering the five 'Ds': dispossession, displacement, dislocation, disempowerment and disentitlement (Konar 2010).

The construction of big dams, new mining, forest and land acquisition policies displaced millions of Adivasis from their home and habitats. Jharkhand being the largest producers of 'ecological refugees' as tribal people were displaced under the development projects (Paty 2007).

In spite of the enormous natural wealth of the region, a majority of the Adivasis people face widespread poverty and underdevelopment, which characterise a marginal economy, are historical. Whatever development was brought about by the colonial and post-colonial state, did not reach the Adivasis. On the contrary it, brought in capitalism, which eroded the traditional economy and redirected production toward the capitalist market. The formerly stable and viable economy was completely drained out and destroyed, as it has to deal with capitalist market. The large enterprises owned by multinational corporations and powerful local businessmen, industries and infrastructure projects continue to extract the wealth of the land, leaving the communities with land depleted of mineral resources, denuded forests, and pollution. It became difficult for Adivasis to survive only on marginal subsistence agriculture, and also displace the people from their land and livelihoods.

Since 1991, the process of neo-liberalism has been greatly accelerated by the new economic policies, which have been brought in by the Indian government under the grab of 'structural adjustments' ostensibly to rescue itself from financial disaster. These policies have been blueprinted by the World Bank and the International Monetary Fund (IMF) in response to the government's request for badly needed foreign exchange loans. So the earlier project-based role of the World Bank in India has moved to a much more powerful policy-based role. Invariably, the worst sufferers of this degradation are the most vulnerable sections of the society-forest dwellers, Adivasis, labourers, Dalits, farmers, women and children, rural and urban poor.

In 1991, India's liberalisation policy boosted the mining sector. Exploitation by coal, iron and related industries has adverse environmental impacts. But the Indian state appropriates land for industry without contextualised negotiation, undermining adivasi cultures based in land-related livelihood patterns. Displacement of Adivasis, often violent, accompanies this. Land encroachment has historically placed Adivasis at a structural disadvantage, with their migration induced by loss of access to subsistence resources. Traditional commons, or shared natural resources like forests, are being converted to private property by invoking a nature versus culture relationship that restricts access and control, with local communities paying the price for private gain from such commodification. This creates land alienation for Adivasis, including loss of rural natural commons. Such loss causes breakdown of inclusionary structures for joint resource use, deepening poverty and forcing migration.

Today, the contemporary forms of oppression of Adivasis are assimilation, development schemes, privatisation of land and water, and now economic globalisation. The nation state, ruling economic elites and multinational corporations have replaced the earlier colonisers as the beneficiaries of stolen and forcefully acquired indigenous lands, knowledge and resources. Ironically, territories where indigenous peoples live are resource-rich and serve as the base from which governments and corporations extract wealth, yet they are also areas where the most severe form of poverty exists. Abundant natural resources were found to exist upon these tribal lands, like timber, minerals, coal and water and so forth. Hence, the state wanted to gain direct access and control over the remaining indigenous natural resources, so environmental and economic exploitation gained currency shortly after independence in the name of national development. But these developments have not directly benefitted indigenous peoples, in fact, modern Western forms of production and business development have forced Indigenous peoples to depend on the cash economy and markets, while their traditional economies collapsed.

Most of the region's indigenous people combine agriculture, hunting, fishing, and forest collection for subsistence and seasonal migration to cities. Many tribes are still adjusting to changes in livelihoods, trade, and migration initiated by the modern forces.

According to Jose Kalapura (2010), the ill effect of globalisation especially in the area of industrialisation and modernisation of tribal lands have been devastating. Some of these are increasing materialism, consumerism, greed for power and money, use of violence, lack of concern for others and trampling ruthlessly upon the rights of poor, the weak, women and children. These are directly opposed to the tribal value of honesty, simplicity, hard work, community living, solidarity, equality and hospitality. All these are signs of socio-cultural degradation of tribal communities under the impact of globalisation. Constitution of India assures these tribal protection through many committee and commissions under the central and state government for their development and upliftment but still the tribal's rate very low on the most important indicators of human development: health, education and income. Today because of globalisation, they face the challenges of becoming extinct. A case of Adivasis in Jharkhand state clearly shows this. The state of Jharkhand is spread over an area of 79.71 km^2 and has a population of 26.91 million. This land of tribal is rich in mineral resources. The economy of tribals depends on land, forest and various minerals. In the name of development of tribal areas, many development projects have been launched by MNCs (Multinational corporations), TNCs (Transnational corporations), the World Bank and IMF (International Monetary funds) that have been approved by central and state government for the improvement of the economy. However the economic development of the tribals has been destroyed over the recent years. The major ecological problem which has emerged due to the greed of globalisation is that of deforestation. At the time of independence, in 1947 the total forest land in Chhotanagpur and Santhal Pargana amounted to 54 lakh hectares. Contractors, in collusion with, the police and forest officers rapidly carried out the ruthless cutting down of forest. As a result, the traditional rights of the villages over forest were blatantly flouted as the governments become the owner. The tribals of this region have thus lost their secondary source of income. Now a days, there is a massive deforestation to exploit the natural resources and established new development projects. The reforestation program of the government is not popular among the tribals due to fear resulting from their past experience. Besides the trees planted are commercially oriented and not bolstering the economic condition of the tribals.

The main reason for the degradation of environment which is happening in a very fast pace are the development model, market forces and the social, political and legal system in India. Open cast mining in the whole of Chhotanagpur plateau region have caused environmental damage for example in the Gandamandan Mountain in Orissa, BALCO has been doing bauxite mining. Natural resources have been exploited in an unorganised and unplanned manner due to which the whole region is experiencing different types of environmental crises like draught, climate change, change in rain fall cycle, soil degradation, pollution and so forth due to which the local indigenous people have been suffering both physically and psychologically.

Policy framework, social justice and strategic measures for conservation

Tribal economy are characterised by 'ecosystemic multifunctionality' and natural resources as commons, have the scope for providing income diversification opportunities to the weaker sections of the adivasi communities through a restructured program of development of these resources. In most regions incentives from the state to manage the resource for sustained use are missing, for the local communities and likewise there is both under provision of services for maintenance and over extraction from the resource, leading to environmental degradation and depletion. Poor people are being systematically excluded from customary access to natural resources such as forests.

The globalisation processes of privatisation of property and marketisation of common goods for the profit of a few were at play here, and the upshot is a relative decline in tribal poor people's livelihoods. It is a well-known fact that, modern national development and the process of globalisation have impacted the adivasi forest dwellers and made them vulnerable to food and nutrition, security, comprehensive health and well-being. Adivasis communities are getting more and more impoverished in India.

What is unfortunate is that most of these issues have not entered the discourse of even the civil society groups which have worked for Adivasi rights, sustainable forestry models or ones who have sought to address food rights. Needless to say, if they have not entered the discourse, they have not entered into the action plans. Forest area being replaced by plantations of various kinds, some are by the forest department of monocultures. At the same time, forests have rarely been looked at as food producing habitats in our policy discourse or implementation of any development efforts related to food security. Forest department has always focused on plantation revenues, ignoring the real and imputed value of NTFPs and unmarketed forest foods have to be challenged. The forest department has always chosen the more lucrative as well as easy way out in its functioning, and ignored the more challenging conservation function, along with communities. The government-supported JFM was appreciated not only for providing access to the forest for better governance but for seeking favours to implement infrastructural development activities such as roads, drinking water, renovation of tanks, schools, health centres in lieu of protection to nearby emerging forests. Across the tribes, perception of JFM varied, but an overwhelming majority of the respondents feel that it was not people friendly but bureaucratic (Deb et al. 2014).

The whole idea of life, well-being and culture are intimately woven into their traditional pattern of subsistence revolving around forest. But at the same time, tribals are deprived from their natural habitat. Earlier the forest policies were against their interest which led to many protests and movements. Project planners, government officials and aid donors thus need to pay more careful attention to the rural and forest economy and what poor people do within it. They need to consider poor people as actors rather than passive beneficiaries of outsiders' largesse, and to examine how to build on poor people's capabilities such as their ability to utilise the natural resource base. At the very least, they should work towards the creation of an enabling policy environment that does not increase the exclusion of poor women and men from customary resources. Finally, we have the wider lessons of history which tell us that 'modernised', capitalist societies may be no kinder to the poor than 'traditional' ones. In the recent times two

Acts in India can be considered of great importance. These are the PESA Act and the FRA Act.

The Panchayats (Extension to the Scheduled Areas) Act of 1996 is described as: it will strengthen the tribal people's struggles on issues of natural resources, mega projects, displacement and self-governance. The Act can also pave the way for other communities outside the scheduled areas who are aspiring for some rights, some regulations to manage their own natural resources and protect their lives and livelihood in a sustainable manner. The Act and its implementation open up new areas of struggle for self-governance in any community, in this era of globalisation and hegemony of market forces (Mukul 1997).

The Scheduled Tribes and Other Traditional Forest Dwellers' (Recognition of Forest Rights) Act 2006 recognises and vests the forests rights and occupation in the forest land to the forests dwelling scheduled tribes and other traditional forest dwellers who has been residing in the forests for generations, but whose rights could not be recorded. This recognised rights include the responsibility and authority for sustainable use, conservation of biodiversity and maintenance of ecological balance and thereby strengthening the conservation regime of the forests while ensuring livelihood and food security of the forest dwellers. This Act categorically state that the forest rights on ancestral lands and their habitat were not adequately recognised in the consolidation of state forests during colonial period as well as in independent India resulting in historical injustices to scheduled tribes and other forests dwellers who are integral to the very survival and sustainability of the forest ecosystem. It was only in 1996 that PESA (Panchayats Extension to the Scheduled Areas) Act came into force. The Act provided for the Gram Sabha to manage community resources. It gave powers to manage minor water bodies and also powers to control local plans for development. While the intent was excellent, control over resources remained a distant dream.

In 2006, the Government of India passed the Scheduled Tribes and Other Traditional Forest Dwellers (Recognition of Forest Rights) Act, which acknowledges, for the first time in India's legislative history, that the traditional forest dwellers are integral to the very survival and sustainability of the forest ecosystem. By recognising the customary rights of 'forest dwellers', this Act seeks to ensure livelihoods and food security of the forest villagers, while empowering the people to sustainability use and manage forest biodiversity.

The fact is that, the socio-cultural linkages with forests, including in terms of food, have a great potential to create a more symbiotic relationship once again for forest communities and their forests. Civil society has a critical and important role to play here, in striking dialogues with communities on this front. PESA and FRA are constitutional and legal spaces that are already available, whose full potential has to be actualised. FRA implementation in terms of community claims is still awaited. The shift to a new approach in policy discourse towards forests as food producing habitats should be balanced to ensure that it happens in a non-exploitative and sustainable fashion. (Deb et al. 2014). The recent PESA Act, Forest Rights Act and Rehabilitation and Resettlement Act received great applause from the civil society and advocacy groups.

Conclusion

Interestingly today, destruction of natural resources is escalating and so are the efforts at conservations and regeneration of nature. It is clear that unless the bio-physical constraints in the various ecological areas are substantially reduced, the environmental stresses would increase in a faster pace

Most of tribal population, in eastern Indian states population, are worst hit by the unprecedented poverty, hunger, malnutrition, illiteracy, poor housing facilities, starvation, lack of employment, assets and also face extreme forms of exploitation, marginalisation exploitation and violence. Under the existing socio-economic system, a majority of the adivasi population is unable to meet its food, shelter, livelihood, total biomass and energy requirements comfortably (affordable in terms of cost, technology, suitability and other inconveniences) both through the market mechanism and administered price mechanism. The general economic activity does not generate sufficient employment and income for the tribal people even in normal times. The only viable option left for them is to depend on the existing natural resources and commons such as forests regardless of their productivity and sustainability to meet their biomass requirements and for a supplementary source of income and employment. Thus the pressure on the existing ecological resources has increases, which would result in their overexploitation and degradation. Initially, the demographic factors, technological factors, structural factors, market factors and public policy pursued by various governments are held responsible for the depletion and degradation of environment. And hence it falls into the vicious circle of depletion, overexploitation, degradation and negligence.

The point which I want to argue is that this ecological crisis cannot be resolved only by seeking practical solutions, such as securing sustainability of the natural resources, like land and forests, but also by implementing religious practices intended to cosmologically restore and safeguard the environment. By using a model of Adivasis ideology, we propose that a strong religious complex involving nature worship, and the cosmological control of natural phenomena, particularly certain groves, hills, mountains, water bodies like lakes, rivers, waterfalls and forests can coexist with modern methods and practices of conservation.

A sacred landscape is thus seen as complementary to the established political landscape and providing a supernatural justification. Ideology defines and explains religious, political, social, and economic aspects of a society. Religious ideology is perhaps the strongest and most enduring, in traditional and preliterate society where religious beliefs and their material associations are both conservative and pervasive. Religious ideology is also where we find symbolic meaning to be most consciously and precisely expressed. In interpreting religious ideology through analogy, the probability of total disjunction of form and meaning over time can be significantly lessened by addressing a complex formal configuration that is unlikely to be duplicated without conveying similar meaning. Beliefs and practices of a religious ideology should be recognised by their unique symbolic representational elements and configurations and, consequently, in all situations, human activity is being directed toward making the spatial and temporal needs more compatible. This is the objective of all environmental management (Glowacki and Malpass 2003). If one looks at the ecological status of these natural landscape or sites, which is linked to the indigenous worldview and have socio-cultural, religious and spiritual importance. It becomes easy to understand that how a sacred grove or landscape provides different layers of meaning in the form of their values, specifically related to the indigenous system of ecological conservation. All these layers of meaning contribute to preserve nature and natural resources, which have a tangible effect on the ecological dynamics of these culturally significant landscapes.

More recently, scientists from fields as diverse as biology, ecology, geography, and anthropology (to name just a few) are altering the ways in which they view, study, and portray humans in relation to global environmental change generally, and climate change in particular. Changes in the conceptual models and practices of scientific inquiry are coinciding with the emergence of new forms of visual and political representation. Research into the effects of climate change on human-environment systems increasingly emphasises the importance of human agency, human-environment interactions, social, cultural and economic factors, and local knowledge as essential for understanding the implications of global environmental phenomena (Martello 2008). Many nation states might even consider indigenous ecological knowledge and socio-cultural beliefs and practices as backward and non-modern economy that requires modernisation. But there is very little evidence that processes of modernisation are kind to poor households, or that customary access is being replaced by other equally valuable sources.

In various global forums, indigenous peoples are becoming recognised as holders of specialised knowledge, which is crucial for identifying and understanding local manifestations of global environmental change and attendant nature-society interactions. They appear as embodiments and harbingers of what climate change has in store for the rest of the world. Standing for and speaking on behalf of at-risk cultures and livelihoods, indigenous groups are now spokespersons. Their voices are buttressed by the authority of a science that recognises and validates their history, experience and knowledge, in part through visual imagery (Martello 2008). Drawing on the wisdom passed to indigenous communities from one generation to another and a lifetime's experience can actually change and enrich the way people think and experience nature, describing them deep-seated, sustainable reasons for conserving the environment.

As economic globalisation introduces commerce to new regions and private actors seek to exploit new resources, indigenous peoples' cultural identity and very survival may hinge upon their ability to design new tools and breathe fresh life into existing mechanisms to change the thinking of governments, businesses, and the public at large. By guiding the public to a new understanding of the environment and the continuing relationship of the indigenous people to the land, indigenous communities have shown that it is possible to change the way people think. Notwithstanding international norms and national laws to protect indigenous peoples' customary use and tenure of their lands, persuading non-indigenous authorities and businesses to respect natural resources of cultural importance of the indigenous people, they demands innovative strategies that blend a variety of approaches and tools (Willis and Seward 2006).

The Washoe Tribe of Nevada and California has successfully expanded its authority and responsibility with respect to its place of origin, Lake Tahoe, and indigenous Buryats from the Russian state Buryatia in southern Siberia show how to protect Lake Baikal and the lands are classic examples.[3]

Closer home it has been found by the partially excluded areas committee for Orrisa (so-called Thakkarbapa committee) that the forests in Koraput district managed by the tribal people is in much better conditions of growth than the forests managed by the forest department under the British government (Mahapatra and Mohapatra 1997). After independence the same situation was found, Roy Burman (1982) who was the chairman of the committee on forests and tribal in India, reports that some of the *khutkhatti* communal land were better managed that the reserved under direct management of forest department. Sanjay Kumar (2004) in his study clearly points out that that the forests under Mundari-khutkhatti[4] land tenure, which are owned and managed by the local Munda tribe in Jharkhand is better managed and ensures ecological stability. In these villages the *Munda* (headman) and the *pahan* (priest) were also able to maintain their leadership positions because forests in these villages are communal property and their management required regular village meetings under the chairmanship of the *Munda*. This process allows the traditional resource management systems to be strictly adhering to. On the other in the forests under the control of state forest department, there is a complete breakdown of the local ecological link between forests and its surrounding habitat, the village aspects of traditional society have broken down, the central role of traditional leaders like *Munda* and *pahan* has become weak and subsequently traditional natural resource management systems in such villages too have become dysfunctional. Hence the degradation of forests controlled and managed by state forest department continued at a faster pace. He also points to the importance of tenure in the manner in which environmental services functions are integrated into local management decisions in community owned forests of Mundari khutkhatti system, the Munda understanding of the water and nutrient cycling functions of forests is integrated into forest management decisions. Forests are protected from logging so as to allow for the satisfactory provisions of these services. On the other hand, where the forest is state owned and the local community has no control over logging and other forests use decision, the villagers try to increase their area of agricultural land. Today, both forest and land are under gravest threat. Thus, the struggle to protect the land, forest and water (*jal, jangal, jamin*) is the precondition of the survival of the Adi-dharam (Mullick 2014).

The policy of state to takeover of natural resources and commons has not ensured equitable and sustainable management of common lands for community purposes. For 'equity' and 'sustainable' management of common lands to be a reality, their management by the community of users is necessary and desirable. There is a need to evolve and set up appropriate management structures of the communities concerned. While constitution of such management structures may not automatically ensure participation of the user community in the sustainable management of natural resources, it will at least create necessary pre-conditions for realising the potential of common natural resources. At the same time, there is the urgent need to sustain or promote local-level management bodies of the user communities. The basic pre-condition for local management of ecology would be to confer, the property rights of these lands or its resources on the community. All users should have access to these resources in their capacity as members of the community and no individual user enjoys any preferential access to these lands by virtue of any social and economic advantages vis-à-vis other fellow users. While the debates and efforts for access and control of adivasi communities over forest rights continue, their access to resources from the forest have been severely restricted so for the purpose of conservation and local management of natural resources, it has to be devoted with proper participation of tribals in their habitat.

But Indigenous peoples are fighting for all life put in jeopardy by corporate globalisation and its agenda for world domination and control. Indigenous peoples from the United States and global community believe that they can offer viable alternatives to the dominant export-oriented economic growth and development model. Indigenous peoples sustainable lifestyles and cultures, traditional knowledge, cosmologies, spirituality, values of collectivity, reciprocity, respect and reverence for Mother Earth are all crucial in the search for a transformed society where justice, equity and sustainability will prevail (Goldtooth 2004). The active participation of indigenous people reflected their traditional willingness to take action against political decisions that negatively impacted the environmental, cultural, and religious values of their homeland that such a shift requires investments in processes of dialogues and knowledge-sharing within the community wherever needed.

Notes

1 In this chapter, I have used the terms 'adivasis', 'tribal' and 'indigenous' interchangeably.
2 The Jharkhand andolan (agitation) for separate statehood started as the self-assertion of indigenous in the 1970s. State-owned forests, mainly reserved forests, became the target of the opposition during the period of agitation, which resulted in politically motivated felling of trees (Kumar 2004).
3 For details of the cases regarding Washoe Tribe of Nevada and California and Buryat indigenous people in the region of southern Siberia, refer

to 'Protecting and Preserving Indigenous Communities in the Americas' by F. Michael Willis and Timothy Seward Source in *Human Rights*, 33(2) (Spring 2006), pp. 18–21.

4 Mundari-khutkhatti is a unique type of land tenure guaranteed by the Chhotanagpur Tenancy Act 1908. It allows the Munda (headman of a village, who is the direct lineage of the original founders of the village) to own and maintain village wasteland (including forests) for the exclusive use of the village community. Under this Act the adivasis' Munda community enjoys a special status and they collectively own and manage the forests within the boundary of the village (Kumar 2004; Paty 2007).

References

Ajaz-ul-Islam, Mohammad, Sulaiman Quli, S. M., Rai, R. and Sofi, P. A. 2013. 'Livelihood Contributors of Forest Resources to the Tribal Communities of Jharkhand', *Indian journal of Fundamental and Applied Life Sciences*, 3(2):131–144, April–June, www.cibtech.org/jls.htm.

Bera, Sayantan. 2013. 'Niyamgiri Answers', *Down to Earth*, August 31, wwwdowntoearth.org.in/coverage.

Brara, Rita. 2011. 'Ecology and Environment', in Veena Das (ed.), *Oxford Handbook of Indian Sociology* (88–120). New Delhi: Oxford University Press.

Chaithanaya, E. P. 2012. 'Historical Injustice Towards Tribals: A Reflection on Forest Policies of India', *International Journal of Social Science & Interdisciplinary Research*, 1 (11), November.

Chopra, Kanchan. 1995. 'Forest and Other Sectors: Critical Role of Govt. Policy', *Economic and Political Weekly*, 30(25), June.

Deb, Debal, Kuruganti, Kavitha, Rao, Rukmini and Yesudas, Salome. 2014. 'Forests as Food Producing Habitats: An Exploratory Study of Uncultivated Foods and & Nutrition Security of Adivasis in Odisha', *Living farms*, Odisha, July 14.

Durkheim, Emile. 1912. 'The Elementary Forms of Religious Life', in W.S.F. Pickering (ed.), *Durkheim's Sociology of Religion: Themes and Theories*. London: Routledge & Kegan Paul.

Fernandes, Walter, Menon, Geeta and Viegas, Philip. 1988. *Forest Environment and Tribal Economy*. New Delhi: Indian Social Institute.

Frazer, James. 1922. *The Golden Bough*. New York: Macmillan and Bartleby. com2000, www.bartleby.com/196/17html.

Gadgil, Madhav and Guha, Ramachandra. 1992. *This Fissured Land: An Ecological History of India*. New Delhi: Oxford University Press.

Geores, Martha E. 1998. 'The Historic Role of Forest Communities in Sustaining the Black Hills National Forest as a Complex Common Property Multiple Use Resources', *Mountain Research Development*, 18(1), February.

Glowacki, Mary and Malpass, Michael. 2003. 'Water, Huacas, and Ancestor Worship: Traces of a Sacred Wari Landscape', *Latin American Antiquity, Published by: Society for American Archaeology*, 14(4), 431–448, December.

Goldtooth, Tom B. K. 2004. 'Stolen Resources: Continuing Threats to Indigenous People's Sovereignty and Survival', *Race, Poverty & the Environment, Reclaiming our Resources: Imperialism & Environmental Justice*, 11(1), 9–12, Summer.

Kakada, Jayprakash. 2012. 'Short Essay on Forest and Tribal', *Preserve Articles*, January, www.preservarticle.com.

Kalapura, Jose. 2010. 'Globalisation and Livelihood: Increasing Marginalization of Dalits and Tribals in India', in Debal K. Singharoy (ed.), *Surviving Against Odds: The Marginalized in a Globalized World*. New Delhi: Manohar.

Konar, Arup Kanti. 2010. 'Tribal Communities and Their Age-Old Sacred Groves: A Fair Fieldwork in the Purulia District of West Bengal, India', *Kamla-Raj 2010 Stud Tribes Tribals*, 8 (1): 1–12, www.krepublishers. com/02 Journals.

Kumar, Sanjay. 2004. 'Indigenous Communities Knowledge of Local Ecological Services', in Dev Nathan et al. (eds.), *Globalisation and Indigenous People in Asia: Changing the Local-Global Interface*. New Delhi and London: Sage.

Mahapatra, P. M and Mohapatra, P. C. (eds.) 1997. *Forest Management in Tribal Areas: Forest Policy and Peoples Participation*. New Delhi: Concept.

Martello, Marybeth Long. 2008. 'Arctic Indigenous Peoples as Representations and Representatives of Climate Change', *Social Studies of Science*, 38 (3), 351–376, June.

Menon, Vineetha (ed.). 2012. *Environment and Tribes in India: Resource Conflicts and Adaptations*. New Delhi: Concept.

Mukul. 1997. 'Tribal Areas: Transition to Self-Governance', *Economic and Political Weekly*, 32 (18), 928–929, May 3–9.

Mullick, Samar Bosu. 2014. *Preface in Ramdayal Munda – Adi-dharam – Religious beliefs of the Adivasis of India*. Kolkata: Adivaani.

Munda, Ramdayal. 2000. *Adi-Dharam-Religious Beliefs of the Adivasis of India*. Bubaneshwar: Sarini and BIRSA.

Nathan, Dev, Kelkar, Govind and Walter, Pierre. (eds.) 2004. *Globalisation and Indigenous People in Asia: Changing the Local-Global Interface*. New Delhi and London: Sage.

Panth, Prabha. 2007. 'Globalisation and Sustainable Development: Economic and Environmental Conflicts', in Pushpam Kumar and B. Sudhakara Reddy (eds.), *Ecology and Well-Being*. London and New Delhi: Sage.

Paty, Chittranjan Kumar (ed.). 2007. *Forest, Government and Tribe*. New Delhi: Concept.

Priyadarshini, Nitish. 2013. 'Sacredness of the Totems Is Unique Only with the Indigenous People of Jharkhand: Totem Also Protects the Equilibrium of the Biodiversity', May 11, 13, wwwnitishpriyadarshini.blogspot.in/2013/05.

Roy Burman, B. K.1982. *Report of Committee on Forests and Tribals in India, Tribal Development Division*. New Delhi: Ministry of Home Affairs.

Sahoo, P. R. and Nanda, P. M. 2012. 'Sacred Groves-Diversity in Forest Eco-System', in Vineetha Menon (ed.), *Environment and Tribes in India: Resource Conflicts and Adaptations*. New Delhi: Concept.

Sheridan, Michael J. 2009. 'The Environmental and Social History of African Sacred Groves: A Tanzanian Case Study', *African Studies Review*, 52 (1), 73–98, April.

Swingland, Ian R. 1993. 'The Ecology of Stability in Southeast Asia's Forests: Biodiversity and Common Resource Property', *Global Ecology and Biogeography Letters, The Political Ecology of Southeast Asian Forests: Trans disciplinary Discourses*, 3(4/6), July–September–November.

United Nations Educational, Cultural, and Social Organization (UNESCO). 2005. *Conserving Cultural and Biological Diversity: The Role of Sacred Natural Sites and Cultural Landscapes*. Geneva: UNESCO.

Willis, F. Michael and Seward, Timothy. 2006. 'Protecting and Preserving Indigenous Communities in the Americas', *Human Rights*, 33(2),18–21, Spring.

13 Re(caste-ing) justice

Globalisation and Dalits in India

Antara Ray and Ramanuj Ganguly

The post-independence India has seen a sudden upsurge in the construction of the discourse of subalterns. Here the term 'subaltern' purely indicates the downtrodden of a society and does not signify any theoretical connotation. India has been given a special place in the world for its uniqueness of social structure that is based on the so-called caste system. Though it cannot be denied that hereditary occupation and rituals and privileges based on one's ascribed status is not a unique phenomenon of India rather is seen throughout the world in all kinds of society at some epoch of history. But nonetheless India characterises this generality in its truest form which makes it unique. Nothing so far was able to break the centrality that caste has in Indian social structure. In 1940s and 1950s, it has been communicated by the intellectuals, scholars and nationalists that caste is going to wither away in the independent India which has now established itself on the ethos of democracy, equality and fraternity. But none except few people like Srinivas, Rajni Kothari who argued otherwise and renewed the debate on caste by putting forward the relevance of caste in the contemporary, modern, democratic India. They have been criticised extensively for that. Caste has not lost its relevance and importance in any form in the modern-day Indian society. The more we talk about it, the more it confirms and affirms its existence. It has in no way lost its being in the everyday discourse. But the important aspect to acknowledge is the fact that caste has changed its structure. No social phenomenon withers away just like that. It is a major faux pas if someone thinks that an institution will suddenly wither away. Here we are not talking about Marxian theory of revolution which changes the base of a society all of a sudden. The reality is far more complex and very difficult to foresee. A society does not change in a day or night. Just by invoking certain ethos from above, it is not going to change the base whose roots are much stronger than we tend to understand.

Caste is present in the conscious, sub-conscious and unconscious of the people of India that is hard to eradicate. Some acknowledge its presence some do not. But our reality, being and situations are many a times structured by caste.

If we talk about caste in the contemporary society, it draws our attention to the construction of the discourse of Dalits. Though untouchability or low caste movement are not something new and can be traced from Bhakti movements but the issue of untouchability and discrimination as well as exploitation of low caste has been granted a public discourse in the everyday world by the emergence and creation of the identity Dalits which got legitimised specifically in the post-independence India. Without going too far in the history of Indian society, if we examine the early 20th century, we will find at that point of time Gandhi was major force in the society and he introduced the discourse of 'Harijan' in the social context. At the same time Ambedkar was also rising with his glory and charisma among the low-caste people of India and especially Maharashtra. Both the figures were prominent in their fields but were contradictory in their arguments and mobilisation. Where Gandhi propounded Harijan discourse, Ambedkar most of the time refrained from creating any kind of jargons. He synonymously used the term Depressed classes, scheduled castes and rarely Dalits to denote the marginalised people with respect to caste. Later after independence, Harijan as a marker of identity lost its gained visibility and Dalit as a term took prominence. It got further re-instilled with the Dalit Panthers movement of 1970s in Maharashtra. It tried to revive or re-create Dalit's lack of history and acknowledgement in literature and academia.

Dalit conceptualisation

The question we confront as to who are the Dalits? Can we have a uniform definition of Dalits? Dalit scholars and thinkers have tried to do so. S.M. Michael argues in his book,

> the term Dalit is not merely a rejection of the very idea of pollution or impurity or 'Untouchability', it reveals a sense of a unified class, of a movement toward equality . . . the word 'Dalit' particularly emphasizes the dehumanizing 'caste oppression' that makes them outcastes and untouchables (a degradation not shared by the tribals or soshits), within the context of the Hindu caste system with its religio-social organizing principle of 'purity and pollution'.
>
> (Michael 2007: 33, 108–109)

In another place, Hardtmann in her book conceptualises Dalit as follows:

> Scholars and activists use the term 'Dalit' in more ways than one: according to the criteria of either social status or economic position. A common usage among scholars, activists as well as the public is to mean the so-called untouchables, or those who are officially defined in 1935 when backward groups were listed on a schedule to get access to reserved seats. The most common usage among today's scholars and activists seems to be to include all caste groups that were traditionally regarded as 'untouchables', although not all of them are now among the official list of 'SCs'. Sometimes 'Scheduled Tribes' (STs) and even 'Other Backward Classes' (OBCs) are included. The other definition in which an economic criterion is used includes the economically disadvantaged, regardless of caste category. This has been among common usage among Marxists scholars. More recently Dalit activists have come to include other categories outside of India in their definition, like Burakumin in Japan, to mention just one. In this study 'Dalit' will be used as an emic concept, referring to people who use it self-ascribingly.
>
> (Hardtmann 2011: ix)

If we notice carefully then dalit has a very wider context which we always try to ignore. At one point of time Dalits were regarded to all those people who are and were outcastes but now it has a much wider scope. It includes all the people who are discriminated, exploited and marginalised with respect to their caste position.

It is inevitable that when we deal with Dalits, the issue of social justice becomes crucial. How is the concept of social justice related to Dalits? Before we move on to this relationship we must first understand the concept of social justice.

Concept of justice, being a continually evolving concept constricted by time and space, has to be understood by its variable – synonymously expressed as unbiased, impartial, objective, neutral and unprejudiced principles – formulated in contrast to bias, partial, subjective, prejudice and predisposed conditions prevailing in sphere of life. To understand the various forms of injustice and discrimination in society, one has to take into account the socio-historically constructed forms of disempowerment prevalent in society that impedes achievement of natural justice even if its norms are committed to in the political system of the society. In India, despite its constitutional safeguards and principled recognition of equal opportunity in social, economic and political affairs, distributive justice towards achieving egalitarian access to assets, position, rights and privileges has continue to elude the communities in line of caste identity.

It has been debated over and over again regarding the principle of caste-based affirmative action (Yadav and Deshpande 2006) where it has been argued that such program over the last seven decades has given a new salience to caste in society for which it has not been possible for Indians to transcend their caste-identity. Tarunabh Khaitan (2015) is of the view that 'affirmative action is necessary . . . but caste-based reservations are unimaginative, crude and costly for the intended beneficiaries'. Such arguments have drawn credence from the fact that in Indian democratic set up, reservation policy has been seen as an everlasting electoral milch cow, which instead of correcting the evil of caste based disability, by creating a provision to address this social and economic gap between caste groups, has yielded political dividends for political parties that have been suffering from poverty of ideology since countries independence. However, by being blind to the historical burden of caste based discrimination, alternative discourses, often forwarded by the civil society groups with a majoritarian bent, are mostly utilitarian in nature that neglects the social-cultural-political bases of vulnerability of caste groups. Contrary antithesis also have emerged in last three decades in India, which argue strictly on caste-identity lines, neglecting the multifaceted nature of disadvantage. Thus, numeric strength in elections and the economic gains by being in power have been a heady mixture, diminishing the advantages of so-called Dalits combine to become their own destiny maker, because on gaining power either they have followed the corrupt practices of higher caste or have given shape to their hidden agenda of individual success to devise exit strategies from their community existence.

One has to concur with the consultation paper of the National Commission to Review the Working of the Constitution entitled 'Pace of Socio-economic Change Under the Constitution', 2001, where it refuses to consider development merely in terms of increasing per capita income and economic growth. Inspired by the ideas of the Nobel Prize–winning Indian economist Amartya Sen, the paper notes that the level of human development achieved should be the criterion for evaluating progress. Human development means expanding the freedoms of and assuring human rights to all people so that they have the capability to lead the kind of life they value. Human development therefore means attaining freedom from fear, repression, discrimination and exploitation, freedom to lead a life of dignity, freedom from hunger and ignorance and freedom to participate in decision-making in an informed and intelligent manner. It finds that Scheduled Castes (SCs) and Scheduled Tribes (STs) who are nearly a quarter of the Indian population have not attained this level of human development during the last five decades.

The *Dalit Manifesto* (Krishnan 1996: 1–23) appropriately states that

> almost all of them dwell below the 'Line of Economic Freedom' and the 'Line of Self-Respect'. An important instrument of progress emphasised by Dr. Babasahab Ambedkar, viz; education, has not been made available to them either in full quantity or in quality. There is no educational equality for them with the dominant elite minority. In fact, the qualitative gap between the educational availability to this majority and the dominant elite minority has been alarmingly widening in the last one or two decades. Thus, there is no true equality of opportunity for them. Indian governance at the Central as well as State level, has not till now addressed itself totally, comprehensively and consistently to measures which would bring economic freedom, educational equality and true equality of opportunities to SCs, STs and BCs in an integrated and comprehensive manner. Developmental assistance has been and is usually sporadic, patchy, truncated and inadequate.

Dalit and heterogeneity

Can we have a uniform construction of Dalits despite of having a uniform idea of the concept? Now generalisation is useful when we talk about censuses or to find a definite pattern. But when it is about social justice, generalisation is not going to take us anywhere. The question thereby arises what is the problem with generalisation? Why do we have to look into particular issues and situations in order to have an inclusive and effective social justice? Earlier in this chapter attention has been drawn towards the effort of creation of a uniform idea about 'Dalits' but when one is dealing with social justice and its effective applicability, just by having a uniform theoretical idea of Dalits creates a lopsided view of social justice. The reason lies with the fact that creation of Dalits as a category for both theoretical and action purpose, does not make it devoid of its multifaceted characteristics. Even at the level of theory, social justice must encapsulate the overarching features of the category Dalit in order to do justice at the level of action when enacted. Typifications and categorisations are methods of simplification both at the level of theory and practice. In case of everyday life typification helps us to relieve the burden of complication and also helps the society to run its course in day to day world (Schutz 1967). It's the basic human nature to categorise and typify everything around them in order to have a smooth way of life. So we, for the sake of ourselves, categorise even people into various groups and assign that group with specificities and characteristics in order to fulfil the aim and aim is 'interpretation and understanding of behavior and action'. Something similar happens with the category of Dalits. Dalit as a category put forwards few characteristics that include extreme form of exploitation, marginalisation and discrimination on the basis of caste position by the dominant and upper castes of Indian society and specifically Hindu society. This category also forms the idea that people belonging to this group are also sometimes poor and impoverished. But if we need a proper social justice then can we have a uniform construction of Dalits? It is really not that simple as there exist multiple realities of Dalits and not one. Dalit is not a homogenous category and it's influenced by class, gender, region, religion, language, aim, status, occupation and so on. Let's take each category one by one.

Variations on the basis of gender

Among Dalits, Dalit women remain triply exploited in terms of caste, class and gender. Dalit women, till in the recent past, has remained outside the fold of Dalit movement and women's movements. Dalit feminism came into existence only after late 1980s and it has taken a structured form and trying to make them visible in the recent scenario by participating in national and international conferences and also by bringing out testimonies of Dalit women. Despite the numerous posts held by Dalits at various public offices, we cannot escape the question that why Indian women in general despite being made highly visible advances and promotion, and empowerment-oriented work – are still not developing as they should? Moreover, in case of Dalit women, they continue to remain overshadowed and veiled, known yet ignored. There is little understanding of the economic, religious, political and ideological isolation of Dalit women. There are innumerable cases of rape of dalit women but only a fraction of the victims lodge reports, an even smaller fraction is filed by the police, while actual conviction is negligible. According to SC/ST commission report between 1981 and 1986 about 4,000 dalit women became victim of rape. In 1993–94 these figures rose to 798 and 992, respectively. This means annually about 700 dalit women fall prey to sexual assault by high-caste people (Pal and Bhargav 1999). The atrocities against dalit women include gang-rape, murder, parading them naked, making dalit women eat human excreta and so forth (Human Rights and Dignity of Dalit Women 2006). Not only that, Dalit woman also suffer in terms of access to health care, education and subsistence wages as compared to women of higher castes. This severe gender and caste discriminations faced by dalit women in the contemporary world is due to the outcome of imbalanced social, political and economic power relations. In 2001, about 57% of SC and 37% of ST women respectively were agricultural wage labour in rural areas, as compared with 29% for non-SC/STs. In urban areas, 16% SC and 14% ST women were daily wage labourers as compared with only 6% from non-SC/STs. Only 21% of SC women were cultivators compared with 51% for STs and 45% for non-SC/STs. SC/ST women also faced differential treatment in wage-earning, particularly in urban areas. In 2000, SC and ST women casual labourers received daily wages of Rs. 37 and Rs. 34 respectively, compared with Rs. 56 for non-SC/ST women; the national average was Rs. 42. Besides this, a large number of SC women are engaged in so-called unclean occupations, like scavenging. Because of their association with these occupations, Dalit women face discrimination in the social and economic spheres (Thorat 2008).

Class, status and occupation as a basis of variation

Max Weber (1924) articulated three major dimensions of stratification in his discussion of class, power, and status. This multifaceted framework provides the background concepts for discussing status inconsistency as can be seen also among the Dalits with differential life course. For Dalits, it seems correct, as predicted by status inconsistency theories that people whose status is inconsistent, or higher on one dimension than one another, will be more frustrated and dissatisfied than people with consistent statuses. With regard to Dalits, we find that Gerhard Lenski's (Boundless 2015) original prediction that people suffering from status inconsistency would favour political actions and parties directed against higher status groups have come to be true. Here we will do well to remember, as observed correctly by Erik Olin Wright (2003: 1–16) when he says,

> for Pierre Bourdieu . . . he differs from Weber and other Weber-inspired class analysts . . . expanding the idea of life-chances to include a variety of non-economic aspects of opportunity (e.g. cultural opportunities of various sorts) and expanding the kinds of

resources relevant to explaining those life-chances from narrowly economic resources to a range of cultural and social resources (called 'cultural capital' and 'social capital'). 'Class' for Bourdieu, therefore, is a much more expansive concept, covering all inequalities in opportunities (life chances) that can be attributed to socially-determined inequalities of resources of whatever sort.

As it has already been mentioned that Dalit is not a homogenous category and furthermore the homogeneity has been lost due to education, occupational variation and globalisation. Specifically due to the catalysts of globalisation, we find a rise of Dalit middle class and elite-Dalits within the broad category of Dalits. The result of protective discrimination and globalisation has given rise to a new class of Dalits which has managed to utilise the benefits of reservation effectively. The neo-dalit class has been the most ardent supporter of caste based reservation (Prakash 2014). The process of sanskritisation of Dalits and co-option has given rise to a new bourgeoisie class among the Dalits in the form of elite-Dalits (ibid.). As the elite-Dalits join the life styles of the privileged class of the country, their life style changes not only in material terms but also in terms of values. Not only that, a vast majority of dalit middle class has also emerged within the minority Dalit. This leads to the differences in statuses due to differential access and adaptation of lifestyles. In explaining the above phenomenon, we will follow the explanation given by Cecilia L. Ridgeway (2014: 1–16) where she explains that

> to understand the mechanisms behind social inequality, this address argues that we need to more thoroughly incorporate the effects of status – inequality based on differences in esteem and respect – alongside those based on resources and power. As a micro motive for behavior, status is as significant as money and power. At a macro level, status stabilizes resource and power inequality by transforming it into cultural status beliefs about group differences regarding who is 'better' (esteemed and competent). But cultural status beliefs about which groups are 'better' constitute group differences as *independent* dimensions of inequality that generate material advantages due to group membership itself. Acting through micro level social relations in workplaces, schools, and elsewhere, status beliefs bias evaluations of competence and suitability for authority, bias associational preferences, and evoke resistance to status challenges from low-status group members. These effects accumulate to direct members of higher status

groups toward positions of resources and power while holding back lower status group members. Through these processes, status writes group differences such as gender, race, and class-based life style into organizational structures of resources and power, creating durable inequality. Status is thus a central mechanism behind durable patterns of inequality based on social differences.

Now these differences in statuses, lifestyle and creation of various classes of dalit have emerged also due to differential ways of adaptation of occupation. Thanks to reservation, a part of dalit has progressively motivated itself to move forward. But even this reservation has created various strata within the category of Dalits. It will not be wise to claim that all Dalits enjoy the protective discrimination equally as we will see that there are many Dalit groups who are yet to come forward to utilise the pathways given by globalisation. It has been seen that basically reservation is enjoyed by only few sub-castes of Dalits and not all in most of the states of India (Teltumbde 2009). Reservation is one crucial method of social justice in India to create an equal society. But this method of reservation has not helped all. In the era of globalisation only the progressive Dalit sub-castes have enjoyed the benefit of reservation. The motive behind the reservation has not served completely. Much debate is going on whether reservation should be there or not. Without going into that debate, the reality is where some Dalits have achieved high social mobility whereas there are numerous cases where majority of dalit sub-castes were not benefitted by reservation due to their acute state of conditions (ibid.). Teltumbde draws attention to the fact that it has been assumed while formulating reservation that the entire mass of SCs are cohesive and reservation will benefit all and slowly the society will absorb all the SCs. He says that in contrary to this view castes are difficult to unite rather easier to divide. The reservation helped the caste consciousness to remain alive also within the SCs. In the post-independent period, the unity of twice born castes were achieved and mainly due to the steps taken by few forward castes. The same was expected out of the SCs but Teltumbde further argues,

> Among the SCs, the castes which were in the forefront in the Ambedkarite dalit movement were expected to perform this task. To name, in Maharashtra it would have been the Mahars as it would be the Malas in Andhra Pradesh, the Jatavs in Uttar Pradesh, the Palars in Tamil Nadu, the Holeyas in Karnataka, and so on. But they proved themselves utterly incapable of fulfilling

this historical task. On the contrary, they imbibed the caste consciousness of superiority over the other castes as is reflected in the argument of the Malas in countering the Madiga Reservation Porata Samiti's (mrps) demand for their share of reservations in Andhra Pradesh. The Malas argued that the Madigas should not grudge their progress because they had worked hard for it while the Madigas just ate, drank and loafed. The same could be said of any of the above castes. It is essentially the prowess of the caste system that even its victim easily forgets his/her own victimhood and assumes the high-caste oppressor's posture vis-a-vis others when the opportunity arises. It is even forgotten that it is basically the anti-reservationist argument that they are repeating. The upper castes have always justified their privileges on the basis of their 'merit', earned in the previous birth until yesterday, as a result of hard work, efficiency, potential, and so on. It is never realised that in India it is the accident of birth in the social structure of differential privileges that is more important than individual 'merit'. And this view is not confined to only the upper castes; it very well applies to even the SCs'. The son of a Mahar Indian Administrative Service officer in Mumbai is certainly privileged, while the son of a Mahar landless labourer in a remote village of Gadchiroli district is equally handicapped, in both cases, because of the accidents of their births.

(Teltumbde 2009: 16–18)

Variations as per region

Furthermore Dalit communities differ from one region to another. It will be controversial and incorrect to argue that Dalit community faces problems which are universal. The situations and way of life differ from region to region. At some places one may find that caste disabilities, exploitation and violence are much more acute. Like for example it is observed that caste violence against Dalit communities is much higher in regions like Haryana, Rajasthan, Uttar Pradesh, Andhra Pradesh compared to rest of the places. We see the existence of Khap panchayat especially in the North Indian states which proves the incidences of caste violence. Also in these states, Dalit communities play a major role in the state politics. Where Dalits are given importance in politics, they are mostly ignored in state like West Bengal where the visibility of Dalits in the public discourse is very limited though significant numbers of Dalits are present here. Dalits of West Bengal are not progressively motivated and conscious of their acute state of misery. Except the Namashudra community, most of the Dalit groups in West Bengal are significantly and conspicuously absent from the mainstream public discourse. This situation of West Bengal shows a stark contrast to that of states like Maharashtra, Andhra Pradesh and Uttar Pradesh where Dalits have a significant visibility in the public discourse.

Language as the basis of diversions

The heterogeneity within the category Dalit can also be identified in terms of variations of language and dialects. Exclusion and discrimination in terms of language is not something alien for us to know. Simply put, discrimination based on Language happens when prejudicial action experienced by an individual style of speech, pronunciation, choice of words, and composition. It need not be forgotten that due to poverty of ideology and bigotry of political parties, most of Indian states have endorsed their own languages as the medium of instruction in state aided schools. With reservation in such educational institutions, clientele of these schools are mostly from poor and downtrodden section of society. This has resulted in communicative disability among youth even though they have all requisite degree and percentage of marks.

Religion as the basis of diversions

Dalits differ not only on the basis of occupation, status, class, incidences of violence, but also in terms of religion. The common myth is that Dalit is a category exclusive to Hindu religion. But the reality is much different. Though Dalit category can be theorised in terms of Hindu religion but in reality this category has an overwhelming presence among the Christians, Muslims and Buddhists in the Indian peninsula. It is because of the fact that at various epochs of history, the outcastes and low castes of Hindus have adopted religions like Christianity, Islam and Buddhism in order to extract themselves out of their miserable conditions due to their caste category. It has already been argued that Dalits are those people who were considered to be outcastes of caste Hindus. So these outcastes can be any and every community which does not belong to the caste system and are considered to be untouchables. So, it is peculiar to Indian subcontinent that all the major religion here consists of Dalit as a category which is ignored not only by state but also by human rights and social justice mechanisms. The Constitution originally recognised all the tribes and castes listed in the official Schedules that were part of the Government of India Act of 1935. In these schedules, persons belonging to only Hindu religion could be enumerated as SCs. In 1956, a presidential order was passed to include within the purview of the schedules those ex-untouchables belonging to the Sikh faith. In 1990, a similar presidential order served to include ex-untouchables of the Buddhist faith.

Caste equally plays an important role among the Christians in Indian society. The relations between Dalit and non-Dalit Christians of Kerala are depicted by Alexander in his article where he shows that there exist lack of integration between Syrian Christians and those who have converted into Christianity from ex-untouchable castes, at all levels. The converted Christians from lower castes are known as *Putu Christians* (Neo-Christians), *Chermar Christians*, *Pulaya Christians* and so on, while the old Christians are known as Syrian Christians. Furthermore, it was found that only the Syrian Christians are referred to as Christians and others like Pulaya Christians are referred to as *Pulayas* not only by others, but also among themselves. The Syrian Christians are addressed by the Pulaya Christians with honorific titles like *Panikke* (Master), *Tampuran* (Lord). The division is so much so that the low-caste converts have to remove their head-dress in the presence of rich Syrian Christians. Moreover while speaking to Syrian Christians, they have to cover their mouth with one hand. Syrian Christians accept food from these low-caste converts only outside the house in some broken dish which they later wash. The priests of Syrian Christians do not perform rituals for Pulayan Christians not even in the church of Pulaya Christians. Pulaya Christians have separate persons to perform their rituals. It has been also found that Pulayas are not given proper representation within the church. Despite the fact that Mar Thoma Church and Church of South India officially do not approve these segregation, such distinction and divisions still persist (Alexander 1977: 54–55).

In Table 13.1 it can be seen the population of Dalits within the various religious communities of India. The NSSO data clearly shows the presence of Dalit community in other religions in rural and urban India.

From Table 13.1 it is evident that Dalit is not an exclusively category of Hindus but they are also present within other religions in the Indian sub-continent. The Dalit people within the other religions are also the converts from Hinduism. Their statuses are much grimmer than that of the Dalits within the folds of Hinduism.

Table 13.1 Estimated population of Dalits in major religions (NSSO estimate of caste shares applied to Census religion totals)

Major religious communities	RURAL INDIA			URBAN INDIA			ALL INDIA
	Census 2001 count of population (Lakhs)	NSSO 2004–05 estimate of Dalit popn. Share (%)	Estimated Dalit population (Lakhs)	Census 2001 count of population (Lakhs)	NSSO 2004–05 estimate of Dalit popn. Share (%)	Estimated Dalit population (Lakhs)	Estimated Dalit population (Lakhs)
Hindus	61,12.6	23.35	14,27.3	21,63.2	18.20	3,93.7	18,21.0
Muslims	8,87.9	0.55	4.9	4,93.9	0.63	3.1	8.0
Christians	1,58.9	9.40	14.9	81.9	10.51	8.6	23.5
Sikhs	1,41.1	34.76	49.0	51.1	15.17	7.8	56.8
Buddhists	48.9	84.97	41.6	30.6	97.01	29.7	71.3

Population estimates column = (Census count × NSSO share) = 100 and rounded to nearest 10,000.

Source: Deshpande and Bapna (2008: 25)

Conclusion

To draw a conclusion, as noted earlier, term 'dalit' has a very wider context, about which we often blind. Though at some point Dalits were regarded to all those people who are and were outcastes but now it has a much wider scope. It includes all the people who are discriminated, exploited and marginalised with respect to their caste position. For instituting social justice vis-à-vis the dalit discourse in India, in the context of globalisation calls for us to look into the inclusion-exclusion practices in contemporary times. Naila Kabeer's (2000: 91–93) exposition seems pertinent in explaining the above, where she identifies three types of attitudes and social practices which result in exclusion. These can be conscious or unconscious, intended or unintended, explicit or informal. They are:

- *Mobilisation of institutional bias*: This refers to the existence of 'a predominant set of values, beliefs, rituals and institutional procedures that operate systematically and consistently to the benefit of certain persons and groups at the expense of others'. This mechanism operates without conscious decisions by those who represent the status quo.
- *Social closure*: This is the way in which 'social collectivities seek to maximize rewards by restricting access to resources and opportunities to a limited circle of eligibles'. This involves the monopolisation of certain opportunities based on group attributes, such as race, language, social origin and religion. State institutions cause exclusion when they deliberately discriminate in their laws, policies or programs. In some cases, there are social systems that decide people's position in society on the basis of heredity.
- *Unruly practices*: This refers to the gaps between rules and their implementation. Institutions unofficially perpetuate exclusion when public sector workers reflect the prejudices of their society through their position; in this way institutionalising some kind of discrimination.

In view of the above, if we have to reconcile the ambiguity that manifests in the term 'dalit' so that the understanding of caste based discrimination and inequality are not waylaid, we need to delve into the politics and economy of caste's contributory processes over the ages in independent India. Here we may remember to note the concepts 'othering' and 'bordering' that seems to have afflicted the Dalits.

'Othering' is the process through which a dominant group defines into existence a subordinate group. This is done through the invention of categories and labels, and ideas about what characterises people belonging to these categories. The literature defines 'othering' as what happens when a person, group or category is treated as an 'object' by another group. This 'objectification' allows actors to break the moral rules of social relationships. 'Bordering' often accompanies 'othering' and involves maintaining spatial and symbolic borders or boundaries to keep people excluded. These boundaries prevent people from equitable access to jobs, services and political spaces.

(Eyben 2004: 32–39)

Dalit discourse though attempted to break such labelling processes that determine the distribution of social, political and economic powers, however, became victim of their own attempt of securing hegemonic meanings and values through framing. Thus, unless there is a shift from motivated program to developmental politics, and from interventionist patronisation to long-term developmental strategies, challenges of globalisation will further weaken social justice.

References

Alexander, K. C. 1977. 'The Problem of Caste in the Christian Churches of Kerala', in Harjinder Singh (ed.), *Caste Among Non-Hindus in India* (54–55). New Delhi: National Publishing House.

Boundless, 2015. 'Status Inconsistency', *Boundless Sociology*, 21 July, from www.boundless.com/sociology/textbooks/boundless-sociology-textbook/ stratification-inequality-and-social-class-in-the-u-s-9/social-class-73/status-inconsistency-436–1358/, accessed on 30/11/2015.

Deshpande, Satish and Bapna, Geetika. 2008. 'Dalits in the Muslim and Christian Communities: A Status Report on Current Social Scientific Knowledge, prepared for the National Commission for Minorities Government of India with the assistance of Department of Sociology University of Delhi', 25, http://ncm.nic.in/pdf/report%20dalit%20%20reservation.pdf, accessed on 12/12/2015.

Eyben, R. 2004. 'Inequality as Process and Experience', in R. Eyben and J. Lovett (eds.), *Political and Social Inequality: A Review*, IDS Development Bibliography 20, Brighton: Institute of Development Studies, pp. 32–39

'Human Rights and Dignity of Dalit Women', *Report of the Conference in The Hague*, 2006, http://www.indianet.nl/pdf/humanrightsdalitwomen.pdf, accessed on 16.6.2016.

Hardtmann, Eva-Maria. 2011. *The Dalit Movement in India: Local Practices, Global Connections*. New Delhi: Oxford University Press.

Kabeer, N. 2000. 'Social Exclusion, Poverty and Discrimination: Towards an Analytical Framework', *IDS Bulletin (Institute of Development Studies)*, 31(4): 83–97.

316   *Antara Ray and Ramanuj Ganguly*

Khaitan, Tarunabh. 2015. 'A Better Design for Social Justice', *The India Express*, September 8, http://indianexpress.com/article/opinion/columns/a-better-design-for-social-justice/, accessed on 30/11/2015.

Krishnan, P. S. 1996. *Dalit Manifesto*. New Delhi: National Action Forum for Social Justice.

Michael, S. M. 2007. *Dalits in Modern India*. New Delhi: Sage.

Pal, R. and Bhargav, G. 1999. *Human Rights of Dalits: Societal Violation*. New Delhi: Gyan.

Prakash, Ojha Jai. 2014. *DNA of Dalit Movement*. Patridge India.

Ridgeway, Cecilia L. 2014. 'Why Status Matters for Inequality', *American Sociological Review*, 79(1): 1–16.

Schutz, Alfred. 1967. *Phenomenology of the Social World*. Evanston, IL: Northwestern University Press.

Teltumbde, Anand. 2009. 'Reservations Within Reservations: A Solution', *Economic and Political Weekly*, 44(41/42): 16–18.

Thorat, Sukhadeo. 2008. *Dalit Exclusion: The Empirical Evidence*. Info Change News & Features, October.

Weber, Max. 1924/1978. *Economy and Society*, (eds.). Guenther Roth and Claus Wittich. Berkeley: University of California Press.

Wright, Erik Olin. 2003. 'Social Class', www.ssc.wisc.edu/~wright/Social%20 Class%20 – %20Sage.pdf, accessed on 30/11/2015.

Yadav, Yogendra and Deshpande, Satish. 2006. 'Redesigning Affirmative Action', *Economic and Political Weekly*, 41(24), 17 June.

Part III

Globalisation and questions of equity and social justice

Issues from various sectors

14 Service-level benchmarking

Some emerging global lessons for Indian water governance

Ravi S. Singh and Dipankar Roy

Water governance primarily has three basic forms across the globe. The first includes the state-owned utilities (agencies) which take care of both the infrastructure development and their operation and management (O&M) tasks (Chakraborty 2008). Water is generally considered as a free social good and supplied at subsidised rates to the population. Here, a strong political compulsion acts as a safeguard for the lower income households for their daily water requirements. However, the observed O&M standards of the water utilities remain very poor (ibid.). It results in recurring monetary losses for the government and unchecked wastages of the resource. To minimise these losses, the governments have to seek partnerships from the free market economy. Consequently, various types of public-private partnership (PPP) models are put into practice which characterises the second form of water governance (Tiwari & Nair 2011). At this stage, water is treated as an economic good, and full cost recovery and wastage reduction become the bywords for market-led reforms. The government still remains a major stakeholder in the institutional framework and generally exerts its influence through regulating the tariff rates of bulk water supply. Water rate subsidies are partially or completely removed, but the private players are not allowed to injudiciously maximise their profits from bulk water supply. The utilities are subjected to the corporate work ethics and thus pass through a phase of structural transformation (ibid.). Finally, the third form of water governance is emancipated with growing decentralisation of the resource management sector and a minimum direct involvement of the government in 'water business' (Armitage 2012). The water utilities work according to the motive for a maximum profit at this stage. Tariff rates of water are decided solely by the free market interactions and domestic prices of supplied water become exorbitantly high (Alam 2004).

These said three forms of water governance models are practically interlinked and dependent upon both internal and external factors (Shah et al. 2015). Here, population growth, water demand-availability gap, farm land expansion and cropping pattern changes, political nature of the state etc. are the major internal factors (ibid.). At the same time, globalisation has been the strongest external factor that is bringing unprecedented changes in the form of water governance especially in the developing nations (ibid.). In case of the developed nations like the United States or Australia, the emergence of integrated water market has been a product of internally based social, economic, and political factors (Griffin 1999; Hoffmann 2006). Here, the elements of decentralisation, democratisation and private sector participation have successfully been bought together under the common shade of integrated water resource management. Similarly, the supporting governance functionaries are placed at relatively a favourable equation with the larger society, and events of marginalisation or exclusion is the minimum (ibid.). Conversely, in most of the developing nations like India or China, such efforts have basically been esteemed by the external globalisation process (Shah et al. 2015). The big international financial institutions (IFIs) like the World Bank or Asian Development Bank (ADB) are seeking business opportunities in the increasing population of these countries and their growing water demands. Creation of the Global Water Partnership in 1996 is the landmark display of the process of globalisation in the water economies of developing nations (Rogers and Hall 2003).

As a process while the GWP is trying its best to integrate and organise the supply side of the resource, its involvement in organising the demand side (i.e. the population) is virtually nil (Rogers and Hall 2003). This may be a problematic issue as the population in most of these developing nations is already suffering from some serious problems like deficient water quality and quantity, incomplete coverage, growing water disputes and so forth (World Health Organization and UNICEF 2006). Additionally, in India the problem of social exclusion is perhaps the strongest in case of water accessibility and equity. This exclusion is equally evident in the form of social (caste) and economic (class) marginalisation of the poor and weaker sections of the population (Prakash 2006). Even after following a socialist model of water governance for more than six decades, these problems of exclusion or marginalisation could not be eradicated. So, the institutional model of water governance is visibly very weak and seriously in need of reforms from inside. However, the current state affairs are showing a great faith on GWP which is thrust from above as an external solution of the internally created problems of mismanagement and ineffective policy doctrine. Currently, the urban water supply sector is the hotbed of such experiments. The service-level benchmarking (SLBM) initiative introduced in 2008–09 by the Ministry of Urban Development has included four basic urban services, namely, water supply, sewage, storm water drainage and solid waste management (Government of India 2009). Clearly, it is a drive for measuring the present level of efficiency of urban water supply management so as to reduce the wastages and leakages of the resource. This measurement of efficiency is based only on monetary principles like minimising the cost of supply and recovering the full cost from the end users. The actual problems of access inequality and inequity have no references in the bench marks (ibid.). Thus how much positive change such measures can brought is very uncertain.

Service-level benchmarking initiatives in India

Service-level benchmarks are a set of technical, financial and social/ environmental indicators which can describe the performance of a service (Perez-Corral 2007). This performance includes a variety of aspects like the service level, service quality, operational efficiency, financial management etc. (ibid.). These benchmarks aids the management and decision making tasks. The earliest effort towards service-level benchmarking in Indian water resource management sector was made by the Central Water Commission (CWC) in 2002 for the irrigation sector (Government of India 2005). This policy initiative was a result of a need of a comparative performance assessment of the state irrigation infrastructure. The CWC had been conducting performance evaluation studies since 1992, and there was a need for standardising their performance indicators. So here, the internal factors strongly influenced policymaker's decision. However, in case of the drinking water service-level benchmarks' introduction, the external factors had a more powerful role than the internals. The first consolidate compilation of SLBMs for 20 selected urban centres was published in 2007 by the Ministry of Urban Development with the financial assistance from the Asian Development Bank (ADB 2006). Crucially, this report came into light after the 4th World Water Forum (Mexico) in 2006 when ADB announced its new water financing program for 2006–10 (ADB 2006). This program sought to double the ADB's water investment during the following four years, and create a Water Financing Partnership Facility with $100 million in grant in aid for those governments willing to reforms their water resource management sectors.

This new investment plan has three major foci, namely, rural water services, urban water services and integrated river basin water management with an effective collaboration between the private sectors and civil society. Understandably, the SLBM handbook of the Ministry of Urban Development reflects the banking ethics of the ADB as it underlined the importance of full metering of connections, rational tariff structure, partnership based access designs etc.

The ADB's benchmark database (2007) is based on 13 selected indicators which is generally treated as the prescribed standard for measuring the service performance in India (see Table 14.1). Current

Table 14.1 List of performance indicators in SLBM

Indicators	Methods of assessment
Water coverage	[(population served by HC[1]) + (population served by PT[2])] × 100 / [total population in the area of responsibility]
Water availability (in hours)	—
Consumption/capita (in lpcd)[3]	[total annual domestic consumption (m³) × 1,000/365]/[number of people served]
Production/population (m³/day/c)	[annual production volume (m³) /365]/[number of people served]
Unaccounted for water (in %)	[total annual production (m³) – total annual consumption (m³)] × 100 / [total annual production (m³)]
Connection metered (%)	—
Operating ratio	[annual O&M cost (Rs.)]/[annual revenue (Rs.)]
Accounts receivable	[accounts receivable at end of the fiscal year]/[total annual billings/12]
Revenue collection efficiency (%)	[total annual collections (Rs.)/total annual billings (Rs.)] × 100
Average tariff (Rs./m³)	[total annual billing (Rs.)]/[total annual consumption (m³)]
New connection fee (Rs.)	—
Capital expenditure/connection (Rs.)	—
Staff/1000 connections	[number of utility staff]/[number of utility connections/1,000]

Notes:
1 HC= house connection
2 PT= public tap
3 lpcd= litre per capita/day

Source: ADB (2007)

household coverage indicators of the benchmarks are not disaggregated according to household income levels. So no authentic record is available about the poor household's water accessibility. Existing benchmark database clearly lacks a pro-public/community character as it does not include the aspects like public consultation mechanisms of the utilities or publicly available annual reports or budget statements and so forth. Also, the workforce management and skill assessment parameters are having a very narrow definition. Staff strength of the utilities are measured only in terms of number of staff heads per thousand of population, and the multi-skilled assessment of the workforce has not been generally given any weightage in the benchmarks. Healthy labour relation and collaborative decision making parameters like labour union activities has not find any reference which are otherwise instrumental in enhancing productivity of the workforce. This has been a major cause of the observed poor relationship between labour and management in case of a number of PPPs and management contracts endorsed by the international financial institutions like the World Bank (WB) or ADB (Koonan 2012). In some countries like Philippines, benchmark surveys have already revealed the importance of flexible connection charges (paying in instalment facilities) especially for the poor households (Perez-Corral 2007). But the ADB's promoted benchmarks yardstick has not facilitate these factors. So the actual effectiveness of these 13 indicators in service performance assessment is debatable. It appears as very flat and shallow estimation of the business scope of the Indian urban water supply sector which can do little more than supporting the regular water business plan of the ADB.

There has been much enthusiasm about a possible performance enhancement of the water utilities with a wider role of private sector funding in that sector (Tiwari & Nair 2011). However, there is no actual ground evidence for this assumption. On the contrary, there are incidents where public water utilities have performed better than their private counterparts. Water utilities in two Asian cities, namely, Manila and Jakarta have been under private hands in between 1997 and 2002. Here, the non-revenue water (NRW) contributes 62% and 51% of the total water supply in 2002, respectively (see Table 14.2), whereas in case of the city of Dhaka the NRW rate is 40% in 2002 whose water supply is taken care of by the public utilities. Again, the water supply system in London till 2002 has been managed by the private agencies for previous 15 years. Still, in 2002, London had the same NRW rate as Dhaka (i.e. 40%; Perez-Corral 2007). Even the ADB itself has acknowledged that in between 1997–2002, there was only very marginal improvement in a few performance indicators of

Table 14.2 Key performance indicators of private run utilities, 2001–02

City	Performance indicators					
	Coverage (%)	24 hours availability (%)	NRW (%)	Staff/1000 connections	Revenue collection efficiency (%)	Capital expenditure/ connection (US$)
Jakarta	51	95	51	5.3	98	47
Manila	58	88	62	4.4	97.3	18

Source: Perez-Corral, 2007

the utilities in Manila and Jakarta (ADB 2004). These indicators were customer's satisfaction level, human resources management, service coverage and so forth. On the other hand, the financial management quality has been below average. The coverage facilities in these two cities rank behind 11 other Asian cities with public run water supply systems. Still, the higher revenue collection efficiencies (97.30% in Manila and 98% in Jakarta) have couples with an impressive record in providing a 24-hour water supply (88% in Manila and 95% in Jakarta). It implies that in between 1997–2002, there has been very little efforts for supply coverage expansion, whereas, a maximum focus has been given for providing 24 × 7 water supply to comparatively higher income customers. So, benchmarks are actually serving to isolate the lower income households, as it has been already experienced in case of Philippines that a higher charge for new connection acts as a barrier for the poor households to apply for fresh connections.

International finance services and their benchmark propaganda

Between 1998 and 2012, the World Bank released a number of official assessment reports on the status and sectorial requirements of Indian water resource management practices (Sohoni 2012). These reports prepared the groundwork for the transition and transformation of national water resource management policies and institutions in India from an earlier people centred to a new customer based service delivery model. All these reports were financed by the Non-lending Technical Assistance Programme of the WB, and technically non-binding for the Indian states (ibid.). Still, a number of these states have been regular customers of WB's financial services and thus, these reports were indirectly perceived as an important conditionality for availing the investments from WB. In its report of 2012 on the state of Maharashtra, the bank shortlisted a number of benchmarks for an efficient urban water utility. These benchmarks were to promote the separation of these utilities from the urban local bodies (ULBs) and bring them under independent regulatory authority. Thus, the decision making power in case of water supply management was to be taken away from local level to higher order governing bodies. Such a move would be a clear violation of the spirits of the 74th Constitutional Amendment Act (CAA) which sought to empower local self-governance in the urban areas. These benchmarks show a stated commitment for private sector investments, but, also provide unparalleled concession to these investors from carrying out the risk (ibid.). This risk is to be solely borne by the ULBs who themselves would lose the decision-making power after the formation of the said independent regulatory authority. So thus, the ULBs will be left to deal only with the risks without any actual executive power, and the private investors are to enjoy the profits from 'water business' along with a maximum say in decision making on account of their funding conditionality.

As like the WB, the ADB's business plan on water also includes country specific strategies like technical assistance or project loans (Withanage et al. 2007). These measures ensure a slow but steady policy change for water resource management in these member countries without much public attention or participations. In neighbouring Sri Lanka for example, the bank has effectively financed a national water policy and legislation change in 1997 (ibid.). The ADBs first involvement in the Indian urban water supply sector was in 1995 in Bangalore city under the Karnataka Urban Infrastructure Development project (Budhya 2007). This project came under severe criticisms on account of the poor quality of physical developments and a gross exclusion of public opinion and consequent non-transparent nature of project management and planning. Similarly in Nepal, the controversial ADB-funded Melamchi project, the bank moved ahead for the physical works without clarifying some core question about future water accessibility to the government (Withanage et al. 2007). The project was also environmentally unsustainable as a large-scale withdrawal of water from Melamchi River left the livelihood options of the riparian communities under threat. The 'Running Dry' report in 2005 by the NGO Forum on ADB has vociferously discussed about the pressure building tactics of the ADB in forcing the governments to resign from providing basic services like water supply or sanitation. The SLBM initiatives in India by the ADB have a motivational overtone by its stated affiliation with the Millennium Development Goals

(MDGs). Interestingly, the MDGs even include an investment scale up to $75 billion annually to achieve the target of safe drinking water provisions to all (Withanage et al. 2007). Such projections have been supported by the Camdessus Report (2003) and the Gurria Task Force on Water Financing (Winpenny 2003, Hofwegen 2006). Such huge financial requirement has coupled with a strong market propaganda for top-down planning tools like SLBM. It leaves very little scope for alternative management strategies or community initiatives.

In the 4th World Water Forum in Mexico (2006), Kofi Annan's Advisory Board on Water and Sanitation presented its report (Withanage et al. 2007). The report officially launched the concept of Water Operators Partnership (WOP) or Public-Private-Partnership (PPP), and stressed the importance of a 'not-for-profit' work ethic of such partnerships. Thus, the report actually sought to revitalise the role of public water utilities with fresh policy initiatives. Still, due a very strong lobby inside the advisory board, the PPP mechanism could not exclude the private sector, and eventually, UN-Habitat delegated the multilateral development banks like the WB or ADB as the funding sources for PPP projects (ibid.). This leaves these IFIs with scope to twist the mechanism of PPP according to their own vested interests. The 'Winning through Twinning: SAWUN's Vision' report (2007) by the Global Water Intelligence has observed this behaviour by these IFIs (GWI 2007). In most of the cases the PPP mechanism has been used to open the business scope of domestic water markets of the developing nations to multinational finance houses. The IFIs do not follow any clear criteria for selection of private water companies for doing business in the developing nations (Sohoni 2012). In most of the cases, this selection is based on profit generation scope, and do not follow the not-for-profit objective as stated in the UN-Habitat's recommended mechanism (ibid.). One observed trend of these private supply vendors is their ambition for a complete monopoly of the water market that leaves their domestic partners (public utilities) excluded from actual decision making process. The Delhi Jal Boards experience with Pricewaterhouse Coopers (PWC) in was such an incident (ibid.). The company was recommended by the World Bank and their business plan was full of errors and irregularities. If a next step of SLBM is a possible entry of foreign direct investment (FDI) in domestic water supply, then, such experiences need to be rigorously evaluated at the outset.

Benchmarking serves for what and to whom

The ADB's water policy claimed to have a pro-poor approach and aims to reduce poverty. On the contrary its practices and strategies act only to marginalise the poor (Withanage et al. 2007). The ADB's Water Policy 2001 has faced severe objections from across Asia (ibid.). The ADB's sponsored projects have been found to be under achieving which have also caused large scale ecological harms and displacements of local populations. Likewise, ADB's promoted bench marks are more geared towards assessing the user's willingness to pay for their water requirements, rather than ensuring a scale of affordability for various income groups (ADB 2006). One observed obstacle for such affordable water rates would be the banks inclinations for expensive technologies and consultancy services (Withanage et al. 2007). The bank usually takes a negative approach towards locally available resources and solutions. In the selected benchmarks, a greater stress has been given on water rates and prices as a possible solution for allocation problem (ibid.). There is no clarification on how the apparently divergent policy aims of full cost recovery and poverty reduction would work together in Indian context. During the Karnataka Urban Development project in 1995, the ADB has attempted to depoliticise the nature of water supply services in the name of curbing corruptions (Ghosh 2005). On the flip side, these political elements within the decision-making circle are the voice for the poor people who otherwise, would not be having any representation at all. This political pressure has so far forced the public water utilities to maintain a basic standard of supply in the poor urban residential areas like the slums. The benchmarking drive by the ADB in India has also tried to bypass these political factors, and thus, failed to ensure equity for the urban poor in their promoted model of water governance. At the same time, the regular subsidy features of the bank cannot provide any effective relief to these poor populations as this subsidy is given on a case-to-case basis.

Of the urban population in India, 13.7% are still below the poverty line (GoI 2014). The National Family Health Survey (NFHS) data for the year 1998–99 shows that a 33.60% of the urban population is dependent on community drinking water sources, namely, public tanks, hand pumps and public wells (see Table 14.3). These people are either the slum dwellers who cannot afford a private connection of water supply or outside the supply coverage. If this NFHS data is used as an indicator for poverty measurement, then the actual estimate of poverty may increase well above 13.7%. A very important character of their water usage pattern is that they receives very little water and waste almost none. A survey in 1995 in Delhi by Zerah (2000) found that households with personal water supply connection actually contribute to this wastage. Further, there is a considerable percentage (%) of non-revenue water due to either leakages or illegal connections.

Table 14.3 Types of major drinking water sources in urban areas

Source(s)*	Dependent population (%)
Transported/diverted	51.9
Personal	13.9
Community	33.6
Natural	0.6

Note: (*)
Transported/diverted = piped into residence/yard/plot + tanker truck
Personal = hand pump in residence/yard/plot + private wells
Community = public tap + public hand pump + public wells
Natural = spring + river/stream + pond/lake + dam + rain water

Source: Computed on the basis of the National Family Health Survey 1998–99

A rampant corruption within the public water utilities has supported these illegal practices. The SLBM regime is projecting its water pricing measures as a regulating mechanism for such wasted and unaccounted water. Although, in reality, this pricing measure can only ensure a high value use of supplied water which may not necessarily be eco-friendly at the same time like water amusement parks, golf courses etc. At house hold level also the emerging urban middle class may willingly accept such water pricing, as they are already spending additional money to widen their water access. The 1995 survey by Zerah has effectively assessed this behaviour of the urban middle class. The SLBM regime is completely silent on the scope of redistributing this wasted and unaccounted water to the poor population at a reasonable price. Its ultimate target is only centred on achieving a 24 × 7 supply facility and not a judicious mechanism of supply that may also concerns for the weaker section.

The effect of private sector investment in water supply can be understood from the example of neighbouring China. Since 1988's Water Law, China has followed the 'reform path' and private players have received warm entry inside water governance affairs (Loong-Yu 2007). Average water rates in 35 cities had have an eight-fold increase in between 1988 to 2003 of which Beijing has the most dramatic record with a 23-fold hike. Generally, water expenses should not exceed the 2.5% critical limit of household income; otherwise, water becomes completely unaffordable for the poor. However, water bills at some instances, already account for at least 4.2% of the monthly income even of the poorest households in China. Despite this unprecedented price rise, two-third of the Chinese cities did not have adequate supply of fresh water, and supply conditions in 110 cities were critical. Even there has not been any considerable improvement in the quality of the supplied water. Privatisation has only worked towards inflating the profit for the private players, as the Chinese water market has been generating annual revenue of nearly US$8 billion since 2005, and 53% of the water enterprises are considered as profitable. Till 1997, the Chinese government even ensured a guaranteed profit between 12% and 18% for opening and operating water treatment plants, and it turned the business into one of the most profitable for foreign investors. Till 2005, the foreign firms accounted for 8.5% of the Chinese water market. Currently, in India, the SLBM program has set a priority lists for the selected 20 cities without any assessment of the persisting socio-economic character of the population or their purchasing power (ADB 2006). A total 60 priorities have been fixed, but the poor city dwelling population did not found any reference in anywhere. So already during the policymaking stage, the ADB have a clear demonstration of its future 'business plan'.

Democratisation versus privatisation

Many Western nations do not follow a full cost recovery based model of water supply, and rather, follow a 'social tariff' scheme (DEFRA 2012). Under this scheme, every household is entitled to a fixed volume of water free of cost on a monthly basis. Water charges are applied only beyond that particular volume. In this scheme, the high-usage households compensate for the low-usage ones which mostly belong to the low income and elderly people. Interestingly, the private water companies from the United States or Europe follow a completely different approach in case of the developing nations. IFIs like the ADB or WB has a core business idea of integrating the entire water supply network of a country or province under a single authority; so as to facilitate a larger market for their finance (World Bank 2012). So far, such move has only compounded the problem of inefficiencies and corruption inside the utilities (Davis 2004). Alternatively, the public water utilities perform much better with greater autonomy and decision making power. It provides them more options with respect to finance sources and management designs to meet the local needs. There has also been a biased tendency in viewing privatisation as an end in itself. Even market economies like Hong Kong or Japan have also avoided privatisation of their water supply sector in consideration of larger public interests. Like these developed nations, India too may need to keep pumping in capital investments in its water supply management sector as a part of these broader social commitments. Currently, the SLBM approach is closely associated with national level urban development programs like the Jawaharlal Nehru National Urban Renewal Mission (JNNURM). This is an indication of the deeply penetrating roots of the approach which may be regarded as a foundation stone towards private sector participation on a nationwide scale.

Despite these discussed evils of privatisation, there are also some bright aspects of the process. Public water utilities from across the world have successfully tied-up with the domestic and international capital markets to drive their own agenda of structural reforms and efficiency building. Table 14.4 shows two such exemplary PPP projects. Here, a strong equitable relationship between the public utilities and private financers has been supported by the national policy and legislation towards water resource management. The measurable positive outcome are better water access, judicious pricing and minimum wastages. At the same time, factors like transparency, political accountability, social responsibility and so forth have also made these public water utilities profitable and efficient. The utilities do not follow any externally imposed SLBM, but, still manage to bolster an outstanding performance in every parameter of an advanced water supply system. The service standards are designed completely according to locally available resources and solutions and outside interference is negligible owing to strong public opinion. The PBA water concession area of Malaysia is indeed one of front-run water supply system in the world which provides water at very low prices to its population. In a survey in 1999 across 38 countries in Asia, Europe, Africa and the United States, the PBA had the cheapest water rates. Even in 2001, the utility has revised its water rates downward for the consumers which

Table 14.4 Performance of some leading PPP ventures

Country	Water utility	Major private Partner	NRW (%)	Water rates	Revenue collection efficiency (%)	Metering (%)
Cambodia	PPWSA	ADB	<10	US$ 0.91/ month/7 m^3	99	100
Malaysia	PBA Water Concession	The Yayasan Bumiputera Pulau Pinang Berhad	18	ECU 10.13/ 200 m^3/year	99	99

Sources: Santiago (2007)

are completely a unique feature of water business. Noticeably, the PBA has maintained its position as the most profitable water company in Malaysia without even imposing a full cost recovery principle. So, the SLBM's propaganda about a direct positive relation between full cost recovery and efficient service is not justifiable. It also proves that the best nature of a PPP venture may be a combination between an easy private finance availability and public control over decision making with a maximum autonomy.

Example of decentralisation with more democratisation and less privatisation is not rare in India either. The southern state of Kerala has a long tradition of a decentralised water supply regime with 93 urban local bodies (Census 2011). Since 1996, these ULBs have been entrusted with an illustrative range of functional power as part of a statewide democratic drive called the People's Plan Campaign and managing water supply has been under their own jurisdictions as well (World Bank 2009). A number of international donor agencies including the World Bank have been supporting these local water utilities. Still, owing much to the pressure of the World Bank in 1980's, the Government of Kerala was forced to merge these different water utilities into a single state-run agency called Kerala Water Authority (ibid.). However, the targeted goal of this merger program could never be achieved due to the difficulties faced in maintaining such a large infrastructure network. The quality of services gradually declined and corruption multiplied. This series of event compelled the World Bank to revise its policy in 2001, and push back to the regime of local self-governance managed water supply (ibid.). In the new policy, a maximum stress was given on supporting the administration to improve community participation and civil society organisation's (CSOs) involvement. The O&M capacities were created and maintained at the local self-governance level to improve the technical standard of the services. Such interactions between private finance and democratic management always come with a number of innovative solutions for observed water problems. These solutions are like reducing unnecessary consumption to ensure sustainability of the source, scaling down leakages and theft by active community vigilance, minimising administrative costs with simple delivery models etc. This was an example that no single scheme of efficiency measurement can work under each and every environment which the ADB has also acknowledged (Withanage et al. 2007). So, a single SLBM scheme cannot bring all these essential factors of sustainability to bear in management planning. At best, it can only serve as a model indicative framework.

Role of a national water law

It has been already mentioned that private sector participation ventures have yielded positive outcomes only under a comprehensive legislative framework and policy environment (UN-Habitat 2011). Here, both the public-administration and private financers possess a clear knowledge of their responsibilities and limitations, and the term of reference (ToR) of their engagements is also equitably stated (ibid.). This aspect of water resource management is particularly of a very weak nature in India (Sohoni 2012). The urban drinking water sector is under the jurisdiction of the Ministry of Urban Development, while the Ministry of Water Resources is held responsible for guiding the national policies on water resources. This in fact has resulted in a condition of policy vacuum within urban water supply regimes. The situation may be better understood from the example that during post-independent period, the Ministry of Urban Development has been able to introduce only two major programs in the water supply sector, namely, Accelerated Urban Water Supply Program for small towns (1993–94) and Mega City Scheme (1994–95) for five metro cities (Jha 2010). Their timing has indeed coincided with the 74th CAA which was a major key factor for initiation of the said two programs. Still, the urban water supply sector had remained primarily in a bad shape even after more than 14 years since the programs' formation, and problems has aggravated in its all components like coverage, sustainability and technical capabilities (McKenzie and Ray 2009). India does not have an umbrella water legislation at the national level which can guide the local urban utilities in their management operation (Cullet 2007). The private finance market seeks to transform government's role from service provider into service facilitator, but, ironically, in India, the government does not have a clear service providing role; apart from provisioning the finance (ibid.). Even if the SLBM approach is finally incorporated into regular management framework, some serious questions on the legal authority of such a practice will always remain there.

Terms of reference of the private finance-market supported programs are currently outside the diameter of legal purview (Sohoni 2012). This has provided the IFIs with opportunity to skip the necessary clarifications over their terms and conditions (ibid.). Here, the major problem is that India does not have a constitutional definition of water right (Cullet 2007). Although, in the back drop of a number of the Supreme Court's hearings, it has been implied that access to clean water exists in the form of the Fundamental Right to clean environment under the Article 21: Right to Life (ibid.). Still, the implications of these court hearings for policymaking are negligible. The national water policy was formalised in 1987 and amended in 2002 and 2012, but, still, could not stabilise the impacts of the apparently strong external factors like globalisation or Global Water Partnership in urban drinking water supply management. In comparison to the drinking water, the irrigation laws are better developed in India owing mainly to the colonial interests on irrigation expansion and regulations (ibid.). This has been a major reason why formalisation process of irrigation economy is more successfully running in states like Maharashtra and Haryana with active financial supports from the World Bank (Bansil 2004). The urban drinking water PPP projects, however, are facing stiff public confrontations due to an existing mistrust between the community and private finance market (Koonan and Sampat 2012). Additionally, informal ad hoc rules and regulations have forged with formal management principles at local levels and produced unnecessary complications (Cullet 2007). One of such informal rule is the one that acts along the lines of castes (social) and class (economic). A direct product of this particular rule is the social and economic exclusions of different groups from water accessibility (ibid.). These principles are visibly very difficult to isolate from the regular management practices. If the privatisation process ever gain speed in drinking water supply, then, these informalities would produce a persisting challenge for them.

One major challenge before framing of a comprehensive national water law in India is an absence of a model international water legislation manual (Cullet 2007). Even circumstantially, the state water laws appear as more detailed and better developed than the international laws, like those under the various UN Convention on developments related issues including water resources (ibid.). Still, there exist some broader international avenues for partnerships before India becomes a serious player of the GWP business. The European Union's (EU) Water Framework Directive, for example, is a very up to date and well-perceived water management framework for ensuring the provision of safe and potable water to the population of the member nations of EU. It has effectively dictated the government's role and responsibilities towards the domestic water needs of their people. Although, the framework is reserved only for the nations within the EU, but, given the growing recognition of India as an important business partner of the EU, the framework may provide a scope of partnership engagement. Such a partnership may be helpful to form a safeguard when India would seek to articulate a national water framework law. Further, it would be helpful for the local water utilities in phrasing the negotiation terms with the international finance market without compromising with the local and national interests.

Conclusion

Possibilities for private sector participation or financing are quite bright in Indian urban water supply management sector. Given the high future growth potentials of urban economy, the public sector alone would not be able to provision the domestic water needs of the urban population. Here, market forces can effectively plugin the institutional and financial deficiencies of public-run water utilities, and service-level benchmarking should be regarded as a positive step towards this direction. Its implications are important for re-energising the age-old delivery models of urban water supply systems and upholding the standards of efficiency in management practices. However, current methods of benchmarking have an observed problem of overstated efficiency and under-represented water-access equity. This weakness has discredited the positive sides of benchmarking approach. So, the major objections raised against benchmarking initiative are primarily about its policy context and not about technical applicability. When benchmarking is imposed as a part of funding conditions, it undermines a range of essential socio-political aspirations of the ground level. Currently, the need is to device the nation's own standards of benchmarking, and not blindly trust the foreign donor-agencies' imposed schemes. At the same time, the inherent principles of democratic decision making should not be violated for a mad rush of modernisation.

References

ADB. 2006. 'Serving the Rural Poor: A Review of Civil Society-Led Initiatives in Rural Water and Sanitation', Asian Development Bank, Quezon City, Philippineshttp://hdl.handle.net/11540/2448.

ADB. 2007. '2007 Benchmarking and Data Book of Water Utilities in India', *Asian Development Bank*, Quezon City, Philippines, https://www.adb.org/sites/default/files/publication/27970/2007-indian-water-utilities-data-book.pdf

Alam, J. 2004. 'Water, Not for Private Ownership', *Economic and Political Weekly*, 39(30): 3351–3352.

Armitage, S. 2012. 'Demand for Dividends: The Case of UK Water Companies', *Journal of Business Finance & Accounting*, 39(3–4): 464–499. doi:10.1111/j.1468-5957.2011.02277.x

Bansil, P. C. 2004. *Water Management in India*. New Delhi: Concept.

Budhya, G. 2007. 'Struggles Against Failing Privatization, for People-Centered Model – Case of Bangalore, Karnataka', in M. A. Manahan, N. Yamamoto and O. Hoedeman (eds.), *Water Democracy: Reclaiming Public Water in Asia* (21–24), www.tni.org/books/publicwater.htm.

Chakraborty, L. 2008. 'Deficient Public Infrastructure and Private Costs: Evidence for the Water Sector', *Economic and Political Weekly*, 43(31): 65–69.

Cullet, P. 2007. 'Water Law in India: Overview of Existing Framework and Proposed Reforms', Working Paper. Geneva: International Environmental Law Research Centre, www.ielrc.org/content/w0701.pdf.

Davis, J. 2004. 'Corruption in Public Service Delivery: Experience from South Asia's Water and Sanitation Sector', *World Development*, 32(1): 53–71. doi:10.1016/j.worlddev.2003.07.003

DEFRA. 2012. 'Company Social Tariffs: Guidance to Water and Sewerage Undertaker and the Water Services Regulation Authority under Section 44 of the Flood and Water Management Act 2010', Department of Environment Food and Rural Affairs (DEFRA), Government of the United Kingdom, www.defra.gov.uk/publications/2012/06/22/social-tariffs-guidance.

Ghosh, A. 2005. 'Public – Private or a Private Public?' *Economic and Political Weekly*, 40(47): 4914–4922.

GoI. 2005. 'General Guidelines for Water Audit & Water Conservation, Central Water Commission, Government of India (GoI)', New Delhi, www.cwc.gov.in/main/downloads/Water%20Audit%20&%20Water%20Conservation%20Final.pdf.

GoI. 2009. 'Handbook of Service Delivery Benchmarking', Ministry of Urban Development, Government of India (GoI), New Delhi, http://moud.gov.in/pdf/57f1ef81d6caeHandbook06.pdf.

GoI, 2014. 'Report of the Expert Group to Review the Methodology for Measurement of Poverty', Planning Commission, Government of India, New Delhi, http://planningcommission.nic.in/reports/genrep/pov_rep0707.pdf.

Griffin, C. B. 1999. 'Watershed Councils: An Emerging Form of Public Participation in Natural Resource Management', *Journal of the American Water Resources Association*, 35(3): 505–516. doi:10.1111/j.1752-1688.1999.tb03607.x

GWI. 2007. 'Winning Through Twinning: SAWUN's vision', *Global Water Intelligence*, 8 (5), www.globalwaterintel.com/global-water-intelligence-magazine/8/5/general/winning-through-twinning-sawuns-vision.

Hoffmann, M., Worthington, A. and Higgs, H. 2006. 'Urban Water Demand with Fixed Volumetric Charging in a Large Municipality: The Case of Brisbane, Australia', *The Australian Journal of Agriculture and Resource Economics*, 50(3): 347–359. doi:10.1111/j.1467-8489.2006.00339.x

Hofwegen, P. V. 2006. 'Enhancing Access to Finance for Local Governments: Financing Water for Agriculture', Report 1 of the Task Force on Financing Water for All Chaired by Angel Gurria, World Water Council, www.worldwatercouncil.org/fileadmin/world_water_council/documents/publications/Financing_FinalText_Cover.pdf.

Jha, N. 2010. 'Access of the Poor to Water Supply and Sanitation in India: Salient Concepts, Issues and Cases', Working Paper No. 62 (Brasilia: International Policy Centre for Inclusive Growth), www.ipc-undp.org/pub/IPCWorkingPaper62.pdf.

Koonan, S. and Sampat, P. 2012. 'Delhi Water Supply Reforms: Public – Private Partnerships or Privatisation?' *Economic and Political Weekly*, 47(17): 32–39.

McKenzie, D and Ray, I. 'Urban Water Supply in India: Status, Reform Options and Possible Lessons'. *Water Policy*, 11 (4): 442–460. doi: https://doi.org/10.2166/wp.2009.056

NGO Forum on ADB. 2005. "Running Dry': Does the ADB Stand for 'Water for All'? Synthesis Report of the Civil Society Organizations to the Implementation Review of the Asian Development Bank Water Policy', www.yumpu.com/en/document/view/20952442/running-dry-ngo-forum-on-adb.

Perez-Corral, V. 2007. 'Labour-Management Cooperation: A PUP in Benchmarking Water Utilities in Asia', in M. A. Manahan, N. Yamamoto and O. Hoedeman (eds.), *Water Democracy: Reclaiming Public Water in Asia* (9–11), www.tni.org/books/publicwater.htm.

Prakash, A. and Sama, R. K. 2006. 'Contending Water Uses: Social Undercurrents in a Water-Scarce Village', *Economic and Political Weekly*, 41(7): 577–579.

Rogers, P. and Hall, A. L. 2003. 'Effective Water Governance, Global Water Partnership Technical Committee', Background Paper NO. 7, www.orangesenqurak.org/UserFiles/File/GWP/GWP%20TEC%20Paper%207_English.pdf.

Santiago, C. 2007. 'Privatisation vs. Public-Public Partnership in Malaysia', in M. A. Manahan, N. Yamamoto and O. Hoedeman (eds.), Water Democracy: Reclaiming Public Water in Asia (16–18), www.tni.org/books/publicwater.htm

Shah, T., Sadoff, C., McCornick, P., Molle, F., Samad, M., Suhardiman, D. and Koppen, B. V. 2015. 'Water Governance: Context is Crucial', Brief for Global Sustainable Development Report 2015, https://sustainabledevelopment.un.org/content/documents/630978-Shah-Water%20governance-context%20is%20crucial.pdf.

Sohoni, M. 2012. 'World Bank's Urban Water Report on India: Thinking Backwards', *Economic and Political Weekly*, 47(47–48): 22–26.

Tiwari, P. and Nair, R. 2011. 'Transforming Water Utilities Policy Imperatives for India', *India Infrastructure Report*, pp. 240–259, www.idfc.com/pdf/report/2011/Chp-16-Transforming-water-utilities-Policy-Imperatives.pdf.

UN-Habitat. 2011. 'Public – Private Partnerships in Housing and Urban Development', The Global Urban Economic Dialogue Series, United Nations Human Settlements Programme 2011, Nairobi, https://unhabitat.org/books/public-private-partnership-in-housing-and-urban-development/.

WB. 2009. 'Implementation Completion and Results Report on Kerala Rural Water Supply and Environmental Sanitation Project, No: ICR0000482', World Bank, Washington, DC, http://documents.worldbank.org/curated/en/969711468269099081/text/ICR4820P05545410Disclosed0041221091.txt.

WB. 2012. 'India: Improving Urban Water Supply and Sanitation Service Provision: Lessons from Business Plans for Maharashtra, Rajasthan, Haryana and International Good Practices', Vol 1, World Bank, Washington, DC, http://documents.worldbank.org/curated/en/599581468043490323/ Lessons-from-business-plans-for-Maharashtra-Rajasthan-Haryana-and-international-good-practices.

Winpenny, J. 2003. 'Financing Water for All, Report of the World Panel on Financing Water Infrastructure Chaired by Michel Camdessus', World Water Council, 3rd World Water Forum, Global Water Partnership, www.worldwatercouncil.org/fileadmin/world_water_council/documents_old/Library/Publications_and_reports/CamdessusReport.pdf.

Withanage, H. Manahan, M.A. and Hoedeman, O. 2007. 'The Asian Development Bank Water Policy: Privileging Private Sector Investment over Pro-Poor Access', in M.A. Manahan, N. Yamamoto and O. Hoedeman (eds.), *Water Democracy: Reclaiming Public Water in Asia* (3–8), www.tni.org/books/publicwater.htm.

World Health Organization and UNICEF. 2006. 'Meeting the MDG Drinking Water and Sanitation Target: The Urban and Rural Challenges of the Decade, WHO Library Cataloguing-in-Publication Data', www.who.int/water_sanitation_health/monitoring/jmp2006/en/.

Yu, A.L. 2007. 'China's Road to the Commodification of Water', in M.A. Manahan, N. Yamamoto and O. Hoedeman (eds.), *Water Democracy: Reclaiming Public Water in Asia* (16–18), www.tni.org/books/publicwater.htm

Zerah, M.H. 2000. *Water: Unreliable Supply in Delhi*. New Delhi: Manohar.

15 Shifting food production and consumption patterns in globalised India

Issues of sustainability, security and justice

Purba Chattopadhyay

Clinically speaking, food can be defined as a substance (of either plant or animal origin) which has one or more of the nutritional components such as carbohydrates, protein, fats, vitamins and minerals whose consumption provides nutritional support to the human body.[1] Food is ingested and assimilated by our cells to provide energy, maintain life and stimulates growth. The sum total of food that one consumes makes the diet of that person. Naturally, it depends upon several components as dietary habits, availability of food, and capability of purchasing the desired food by the individual. Dietary habits are the habitual decisions a person makes when choosing what foods to eat. Many cultures hold some food preferences and some food taboos. Dietary choices can also define cultures and play a role in religion. In addition, the dietary choices of different countries or regions have different characteristics influenced by the geographical location of the place, age-old tradition and so forth. This is highly related to a culture's cuisine.[2] Dietary habits thus have a significant influence on the food intake and the demand for a particular food by an individual. In totality these dietary patterns along with the purchasing power determines the actual food intake of any individual which becomes detrimental in the health and mortality of people. Imbalances between the consumed food and expended energy results in either starvation or excessive reserves of body fat.[3] Poor intake of various vitamins and minerals can lead to diseases that can have far-reaching effects on health. Whereas excessive intake of junk food[4] can result in lifestyle diseases and high mortality while less than or severely less than basic minimum food leads to malnourishment, morbidity and death.

Food consumption, food production and food choices are socio-economically and culturally determined continuously changing interactive processes which reflects upon a complex dynamic process of development, distribution and social justice in any economy at a given point in time. Globalisation has its distinct impact on all these three aspects of food. Economic growth is typically accompanied by improvements in a country's food supply, both quantitative and qualitative, and a gradual reduction in nutritional deficiencies. It also brings about changes in the production, processing, distribution and marketing of food. Diets evolve over time and are influenced by factors such as income, prices, individual preferences and beliefs, cultural traditions, as well as geographical, environmental, social and economic factors.

The aim of this chapter is on one hand to look into this dynamic process of food production and supply while on the other hand it would look into demand and distribution of food and how globalisation has a profound impact of all these aspects of food. The first section of this chapter discusses the food productivity and imports, that is the supply side of food in the Indian context. This portion deals with the basic question of what to produce and analyses how it is affected by the multi-national companies (MNCs) and the realities of globalisation and its consequent repercussions.

Next, the chapter looks into the demand aspect of food and the impact of globalisation on it. It analyses the determinants, economic costs and consequences of increased demand of these unhealthy food. As a direct consequence of such consumption there is a steep rise in non-communicable diseases like diabetes, obesity and cardiovascular diseases. Thus, India showcases worst of both worlds severely undernourished as well as over fed masses. Next the chapter tries to locate the gaps in this demand and supply interactions which are being reflected by the severe health consequences. The chapter in analysing the demand supply interaction looks into the cultural transition of India as reflected by food choices. Lastly as an interaction of the above, it analyses the direct as well as indirect impact of globalisation on the social justice.

Food: the supply side

To look into the supply side of food, it would be better if we start with the food production first, as, it is total productivity that determines the base of food availability for a given population. India's population is likely to reach 1.5 billion by 2030. The challenge facing the country is to produce more and more from diminishing per capita arable land and water resources and dwindling abiotic and biotic resources. Indian agriculture is broadly a story of success (Swaminathan and

Sinha 1986). It has done remarkably well in terms of output growth, despite weather and price shocks in the past few years. Food grains production reached a record level of 259.32 million tons in 2012–13. The growth target for agriculture in the 12th Five Year Plan remains at 4%, as in the 11th Five Year Plan. However, the average annual growth rate of 3.6% was actually achieved during the 11th Five Year Plan for the agriculture and allied sector. India currently produces about 235 million tons of cereals to meet the needs of a population of 1.15 billion. The current situation in India is that cereal production has to be doubled by 2050 in order to meet the needs of the expected population of 1.8 billion, in addition to meeting the needs of live-stock and poultry (Swaminathan 2009). The National Commission on Farmers (NCF) in late 2006[5] had warned that to double annual food grain production from the present 210 million tons to 420 million tons within the next 10 years, (by 2015), will call for producing at least 160 million tons of rice from 40 million ha, and 100 million tons of wheat from 25 million ha. Pulses, oil seeds, maize and millets will have to contribute another 160 million tons. In addition, the national goal is to raise the production of vegetables and fruits to over 300 million tons by 2017. This means that more productivity has to be achieved by smaller and smaller arable lands and shrinking water resources. What makes the situation critical is that the farm products have to face global competition from abroad both quality-wise and price-wise. On the positive side, taking into account the global scenario, India is the third largest producer of cereals, with only China and the United States ahead of it. India occupies the first position in milk production and is the third largest producer of fish and second largest producer of inland fisheries in the world. India ranks first in respect of cattle and buffalos and second in goats, third in sheep and seventh in poultry population in the world (Shetty 2002; Subramanian et al. 2009; Subramanian & Smith 2006).[6]

Looking at the growth rate of productivity, it can be noted that between 1950–51 and 2006–07, production of food grains (comprising production of rice, wheat, coarse cereals and pulses) in the country increased at an average annual rate of 2.5% compared to the growth of population, which averaged 2.1% during this period.[7] The rate of growth of food grains production however decelerated to 1.2% (lower than the annual rate of growth of population at 1.9%) during the post reform period 1990–2007. The per capita availability of cereals and pulses consequently witnessed a decline. Food grain availability declined by 4.5% between the two periods 1991–2000 and 2001–05, after having a lower rate of increase in the period 1991–2000 as compared to that in the period 1981–90. It was a point from where we have had to resort to import of food grains from the position of self-sufficiency that the green revolution helped us attain. Per capita availability of milk increased from 124 g/day in 1950–51 to 176 g/day in 1990–91 to 290 g/day in 2011–12, a figure comparable with the global trend.[8] Per capita availability of eggs increased from five eggs per head per annum at one time to 55 eggs per head per annum in 2011–12. Meat production from the recognised sector increased from 1.9 million tons in 1998–99 to 4.9 million tons in 2010–11. At the same time, the output of the export crops rose up to 10 times faster than food grains, owing to the diversion of land and resources to export crops. The growth of cereal output was insufficient to meet the rising domestic needs and to provide an adequate surplus for meeting the increasing deficit of the country (Patnaik 2009).

In the case of coarse cereals like *jowar, bajra, ragi*, maize, small millets and barley, the growth rate was negative in all the entire period from 1980–81 to 2011–12. With regard to pulses, while during the 1980s there was negative growth in total area under pulses and growth in production and yield was 1.52% and 1.61%, respectively, during 2000–01 to 2011–12 whereas area and production grew by 1.6% and 3.69%, respectively, growth in yield at 2.06% was almost stagnant. There has been progressive decline in per capita availability of pulses; it fell from 69 grams in 1961 to 32 grams in 2015. As compared to last year's production of 265.57 million tons, current year's production of food grains is lower by 8.5 million tons. This decline has occurred on account of lower production of rice, coarse, cereals and pulses due to erratic rainfall conditions during the monsoon season of 2014.

Availability of food also depends upon the volume of imports interestingly the expanding middle income groups of consumers in India and their spending patterns on consumption related items have resulted faster rising imports demands of the country. Major imports of India include cereals and edible oils. Recent Government of India (GOI) data[9] shows that over $1billion of imports of food products are sugars and sugar confectionery. It is followed by dried vegetables. In 2014, India imported dried vegetables worth over $850 million. This is in contrast to the fact that India is one of the biggest fruit and vegetable producer in the world. Fruits, especially nuts, apples and dates worth almost $700 million were imported from the United States, Côte d'Ivoire, Benin and Afghanistan. Coffee, tea and spices are procured mostly from Sri Lanka, Indonesia, Nepal and China. India imported cereals worth over $90 million in 2014. A substantial portion of our requirement of edible oil is met through import of palm oil from Indonesia and Malaysia. Any disruption in the supply of palm oil from these countries will put the country in a difficult situation, especially since a large quantity of the global production of vegetable oils is being utilised for production of biodiesel in Europe and North America. Such non-food use of edible oils ultimately reduces their availability and pushes up their prices.[10]

Food: choice and demand side

According to a study by National Council of Applied Agricultural Research (NACR)[11] consistent with the overall economic growth, the share of consumer spending on food has declined. According to some studies, the proportion of expenditure on food items over all income groups has declined by about 10 percentage points in the rural areas and by about 16 percentage points in the urban areas between 1987–88 and 2009–10.[12]

Let us first look into the consumption patterns of the inferior goods in the traditional Indian consumption basket. We begin with rice: it can be seen that the capita rice consumption in rural households declined from about 83 kg in 1987–88 to 80 kg in 1999–2000 and more rapidly to 73 kg in 2009–10. A similar trend was noticed in the urban households where per capita rice consumption declined from 64 kg in 1987–88 to 62 kg in 1999–2000 and to 55 kg in 2009–10. The trend in wheat consumption reveals a similar pattern as that of rice but at a less spectacular rate. Per capita consumption in rural households after remaining more or less unchanged at around 54 kg/year during 1988–98 to 1999–00 declined to slightly below 52 kg in 2009–10. In urban households the decline was more significant, from around 54 kg to around 50 kg. The reason could be attributed to direct consumption of wheat substituting rice and indirect consumption of wheat such as bread, biscuits, and noodles and so forth which are not included in the National Sample Survey Office (NSSO) wheat consumption data which may be substituting rice. For which fall in rice consumption is more spectacular. Moving on to coarse grains we can see that decline per capita consumption declined from around 38 kg in 1987–88 to 13 kg in 2009–10 in rural households and from 19 kg to 9 kg in urban households. This enormous fall in consumption was more than the fall in consumption of both rice and wheat. This divulges the natural economic consequence of the consumers replacing coarse grains for costlier grains as rice and wheat. Considering pulses we see that per capita pulse consumption after showing an upward trend during 1987–88 through 1999–2000 has shown a generally declining trend. Per capita consumption in urban households declined from 12 kg in 1999–00 to 9.6 kg in 2009–10 and from 10 kg to 8 kg in rural households. The steadily rising prices of pulses had actually more than offset the increase in demand the negative price effect more than offsetting the positive income effect.

Let us now consider the superior consumption goods as oils, milk and milk products, meat, poultry eggs etc. As far as edible oil are concerned, we can see that consumption has shown a steady upward trend both in rural and urban households with per capita consumption increasing from 4 kg/year to 7.7 kg/year in rural areas and from 6.6 kg to 10 kg in urban households during 1987–88 to 2009–10. Over the past two decades palm oil and soybean oil emerging as the major oils consumed after rapeseed and mustard oil (which are the traditionally consumed edible oils) this could be attributed mainly due to larger imports and lower international prices. As regards to milk; we can see that a significant increase in per capita milk consumption has taken place during the same period, both in rural and urban areas. This showcase positive income effects that is with rise in per capita income. The per capita milk consumption in rural households increased from 39 kl/year in 1987–88 to 52.5 kl in 2012–13, an increase of about 30%, whereas in urban households per capita (Government of India (GoI) 2012). Although consumption of mutton (goat and sheep meat) registered a declining trend during 1987–88 to 2009–10, more drastically in urban households than in rural households, the decline was more than offset by the increase in poultry meat consumption. Poultry meat consumption registered an exponential growth during this period, increasing from 240 grams to 1.5 kg in rural households and 240 grams to 2.2 kg in urban areas. The higher poultry meat consumption is attributed to larger supplies and its relatively lower prices vis-à-vis mutton. Per capita consumption of eggs also registered a significant growth over the past decades increasing from about six eggs per year in 1987–88 to 21 eggs in 2009–10 in rural households and from 17 eggs to 32 eggs during the corresponding period in urban households. Fish consumption has also registered a steady increase during the period. Per capita, per month milk consumption (in litres) almost doubled from 2.15 (1983) to 3.94 (1993–94) but has increased only marginally to 4.08 (2009–10) in rural areas. In urban areas, the corresponding quantities are 2.82 (1983), 4.89 (1993–94) and 5.39 (2009–10). Egg consumption (in numbers) increased from 0.42 (1983) to 1.09 (1999–2000) but declined to 0.95 (2009–10) in rural areas. In urban areas, it increased from 1.09 (1983) to 2.06 (1999–2000) but declined to 1.60 (2009–10). Fish consumption (in kg) increased from

0.17 (1983) to 0.21 (1999–2000) but declined to 0.18 (2009–10) in rural areas. In urban areas, this was 0.17 (1983), 0.22 (1999–2000) and 0.18 (2009–10). The only item of consumption which increased was chicken (in kg) which grew from 0.02 (1983) to 0.08 (2009–10) in rural areas and 0.01 (1983) to 0.12 (2009–10) in urban areas.

The consumption of most common items of fruits and vegetables also shows a decline after 1999–2000 compared with an increase before that. Potatoes, bananas, mangoes, apples and other vegetables and fruits show similar trends. The data below shows the falling consumption of inferior goods as cereals and pulses and rising consumption of superior goods as sugar and edible oils. Thus a comparison of the data from the pre- and post-reform period shows that the dietary patters have undergone distinct changes in the last few years. Initially with the low per capita income coarse grains, rice wheat and pulses occupied significant portion of the consumption basket. However, with rise in income over time and increased availability and choices of food due to globalisation consumption basket of Indian consumers have witnessed significant changes with the consumers substituting the inferior goods with superior goods like milk, meat, eggs, sugar and oils. This diet diversification is income-induced and globalisation driven. Studies have supported this nutritional transition occurring by the fact that the income elasticity for cereals in India is negative and the income elasticity for high quality food is positive. The noticeable fact is the change is occurring both among rural and urban households. Other factors contributing to the change in the consumption pattern is the increasing urbanisation. During the most recent decade globalisation has also played an important role in the transformation of food consumption patterns of Indian households. As discussed in the previous section there has been a significant increase in imports of fresh fruits such as apple dry fruits such as almonds, raisins and processed food products following removal of trade restrictions. Indian diet is diversifying with fruit/vegetable and animal-based food share increasing and cereal and pulses declining.

Table 15.1 shows the per capita availability of cereals and pulses on one hand and oils and sugar on the other hand. It could be seen that wherein the availability of cereals and pulses have stagnated or declined the availability of sugar and oils have increased significantly.

Figure 15.1 further elaborates the consumption trends of cereals and pulses as well as sugar and oils.

Coming back to the basic concept of food, we see that it is not only about availability or affordability but also about the contents of the commodity basket which is detrimental to the nutritional intake of a

Table 15.1 Per capita availability of select food items

Year	Cereals	Pulses	Oils	Sugar
1971	417.6	51.2	3.5	7.4
1976	373.8	50.2	3.2	6
1981	417.3	37.5	3.8	7.3
1986	434.2	38.3	5	11.4
1991	468.5	41.1	5.5	12.7
1996	442.5	32.7	8	14.6
2001	386.5	30	8.8	16.3
2006	412.8	31.5	11.1	19.7
2011	413.5	32	13.8	21.4

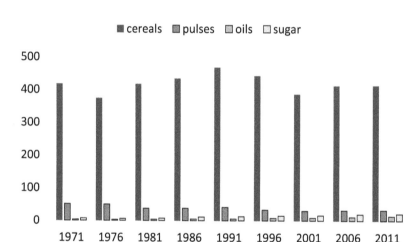

Figure 15.1 Consumption trends: cereals, pulses, oils and sugar

Source: Economic Survey 2012–13, Government of India[13]

person. With the rising level of income, per capita fat consumption is growing rapidly and the share of vegetable oil and sugar in the overall calorie intake is increasing necessitating large imports. Unless domestic production increases the import requirement will continue to grow with rising per capita income. India's per capita calorie, protein, and fat consumption still remains significantly below that of more developed countries which means that in near future with rising per capita income and rapid urbanisation, India's demand for various superior food products will continue to increase necessitating a possible change in the food production system and agricultural trade. In the next section we will look into the consequences of such supply and demand patterns and look into the process of globalisation and its significance.

The problem

India today is witnessing a perplexing food production versus consumption trend. On one hand food grain output is expected to touch a record 252 million tons. The NSSO consumption expenditure surveys also show that not only has poverty declined during 2004–05 and 2009–10, its pace has also been faster than recorded before. Yet, India's per capita food grain availability and intake is declining. Further the decline in food grain availability is confirmed by the food grain intake data from consumption surveys of NSSO, which show that per capita, per month consumption of cereals in rural areas declined from 13.4 kg per month in 1993–94 to 11.35 kg per month in 2009–10 and from 10.6 kg per month in 1993–94 to 9.37 kg per month in 2009–10 in urban areas. Pulses consumption declined from 0.84 kg per month in 1999–2000 to 0.65 kg per month in 2009–10 in rural areas and from 1 kg per month in 1999–2000 to 0.79 kg per month in 2009–10 in urban areas. Calorie intake figures from the same consumption surveys validate these findings and point to the uniform decline over the years. It would be interesting to see how the change in the nature of food consumption pattern has affected the nutrient intake in the Indian diet as the process of diet transformation has far-reaching consequences for public health. While an increase in the consumption of milk, animal protein and fruits and vegetables could result in reduced incidence of malnutrition, an increased consumption of high-calorie, fatty foods could lead to increased incidence of obesity and of diet-related diseases, like diabetes, coronary heart disease.

A study on the trends in macro nutrient (calorie, protein, and fat) intake in India shows the annual trend in all the three nutrients from which it appears that while calories and protein intake remained static or registered a modest growth, increase in fats consumption was more significant. Despite the changing diet pattern in India over the years, the overall calorie intake has registered only a modest increase from an average 2,250 kilocalories (kcal) during 1987–93 to 2,310 kcal during 2005–10. A decline in calorie intake from vegetable-based food, more importantly from cereal-based food, was more than offset by increased calorie intake from animal based food products.

Calorie intake by type of food shows that the contribution of cereals and pulses combined has declined from 1,580 kcal during 1987–93 to 1,460 kcal during 2005–10, a decline of around 8%. During the corresponding period calorie availability from fruits and vegetables increased by 43% to 156 kcal; from vegetable oils by 39% to 204 kcal; from milk by 6% to 105 kcal; from meat, egg and fish by 25% to 35 kcal; and from sugar by 9% to 200 kcal. A recent study shows that despite rapid economic growth during the past decades, India's average per capita calorie and protein intake has grown only modestly, although the per capita fat consumption has registered a higher growth. According to the study, what comes out from the recent data is the extent of decline in calorie intake during 2005–10, the highest in any five-year period. Per capita calorie intake in rural areas was 2,266 in 1972–73, 2,149 in 1999–2000, 2,047 in 2004–05 and 1,929 in 2009–10 on comparable basis. Calorie intake in urban areas was 2,107 in 1972–73, 2,156 in 1999–2000, 2,020 in 2004–05 and 1,908 in 2009–10. That is, while calorie intake declined by 117 calories per capita between 1972–73 and 1999–2000 in rural areas, it fell by 220 calories per capita in the last 10 years. In urban areas calorie intake rose by 49 calories in the first 27 years, it fell by 248 calories in the last 10 years. The trend in protein intake was similar with protein intake in rural areas declining from 60.2 Gross Domestic Product (GDP) in 1993–94 to 55.0 GPD in 2009–10 and declining in urban areas from 57.2 GPD in 1993–94 to 53.5 GPD in 2009–10. The fact that these trends have heightened in the last 10 years is now evident. In all the states the lowest 10% consumed less cereal than the average for the state itself. This is an alarming trend, since it means no growth in calorie intake. The average calorie intake for the lowest 10% in the urban areas for the country as a whole has remained stagnant. At least for the poor, cereal consumption and calorie intake go together, since cereals provide the major part of the calories consumed (M S Swaminathan Research Foundation (MSSRF) 2008).

These details have been noticeable during recent consumption surveys, but these figures are red renunciation instead of raising questions about the origin of these trends. What's alarming is this decline in cereal and pulses consumption together constitutes 60% to 70% of energy intake. However, the data from the last two rounds of NSSO data suggests that per capita consumption on the protein-rich items has either declined in the last 10 years or has seen marginal increase compared with previous decades. The bitter truth that comes to the fore is that despite improved incomes and increased production, not only per capita availability but also intake of most food items declined during the last decade. Moreover, this decline is not only restricted to cereals and pulses but has shown in fruits and vegetables also. This data has devastating consequences if we concentrate on the bottom

20% of the population where this decline manifests in its worst form and the direct consequence is malnourishment and morbidity.

On the other hand, driven by a robust economic growth a flourishing middle class estimated as 50 to 250 million people, with improved income has emerged. Propelled by the strong income effect of these rising middle class the dietary patterns are continuously evolving over time and are influenced by factors such as prices, individual preferences and beliefs, cultural traditions, as well as geographical, environmental, social and economic factors apart from income. The food consumption patterns of this class showcases income induced diet diversification, globalisation, increasing urbanisation and changing lifestyle of people. Globalisation is integrating not just trade, investment and financial markets; it is also integrating consumer markets around the world and opening opportunities. This has two effects: economic and social. Economic integration has accelerated the opening of consumer markets with a constant flow of new products. There is fierce competition to sell to consumers worldwide, with increasingly aggressive advertising. On the social side local and national boundaries are breaking down in the setting of social standards and aspirations in consumption. The augmented income is most likely to be used for not consuming more of the items which are already in their commodity basket instead they may increase their choices of goods with sensory appeal such as sweets, tobacco, drugs and intoxicants and also those goods and services associated with prestige and status. Food intake patterns reveal conspicuous consumption where consumption of traditional food is largely associated with poverty. People thus, change their dietary patterns to a typical westernised diet with a high fat content and low carbohydrate intake (Bourne et al. 2002).

Like India, many countries in the global south are facing a similar predicament. As their middle classes grow and rural to urban migration accelerates, more people are moving away from diets high in unprocessed starch, high-fibre vegetables, and plant proteins. Instead they are moving toward a Western-style way of eating, replete with animal protein and fat, refined carbohydrates, and sugar. This phenomenon has come to be known as the nutrition transition and it occurs in many developing countries. With more money and easier access to urban centres that provide cheap, tasty, filling food, people are lured to eat like the developed world. But for India and other transitioning countries, the situation is tricky as it's not just that the standard westernised diet leads to weight gain and chronic disease. It does, but for those who were not accustomed to such diets from early childhood, switching to a diet high in fat, sugar, and salt carries higher risk for developing chronic disease compared to their counterparts who have been affluent for generations.[14] Another study (Krishnaswamy 1999) reveals that obesity prevails mostly among the middle class and in the age group of 40 and above. The proportion of obese people to the total population for the western country stands at 50% and India, although it is at a lower level is catching up fast.

The impact of globalisation

Globalisation in the present world is entirely different from the age-old process of globally integrated world economy. In today's world globalisation integrates markets and cultures at a tremendous speed. It has multifarious players involved in it and thus has its influence both direct and indirect, at varying degrees on various sections and workings of the society. In this section we would look into the possible role of globalisation on the nutritional trends as discussed in the previous sections.

Now, as we focus on the supply side, we observe globalisation has expanded the markets however, to reap the benefits of globalisation the agricultural produce have to be marketed in appropriate way. The challenge is that there are limited access to the market information, and low literacy level among the farmers complicated by multiple channels of distribution that eats away the pockets of both farmers and consumers. The government funding of farmers is still at nascent stage and most of the small farmers still depend on the local moneylenders who are charge high rate of interest. There are too many middlemen that eat away the benefits that the farmers are supposed to get. Although technology have improved but it has not gone to the rural levels as it is confined to urban areas and some wealthy rural belts only. There are several loopholes in the present legislation and there is no organised and regulated marketing system for marketing the agricultural produce. The farmers have to face so many hardships and have to overcome several hurdles to get fair and just price for their hard work.

The small-scale farmers are still isolated from the benefits of agricultural produce as they are not yet integrated and informed with the market knowledge like fluctuations, demand and supply concepts which are the core of the globalised economy. Public sector investment particularly in research and technology transfer along with institutional reforms to make it more accountable towards delivery, conservation of land, water and biological resources, development of rain fed agriculture, development of minor irrigation and water use efficiency, timely and adequate increasing flow of credit particularly to the small and marginal farmers is still at low levels. The other components in the value-chain such as infrastructure supporting agricultural upstream and downstream activities, including transport, storage, processing and marketing facilities for agricultural products are also under-developed. This prevents the small farmers to reap the benefits of globalisation. Further with opening up of opportunities relatively better off farmers are diversifying their agro products in view of the exporting their produce. All these have its impact on the supply of cereals and pulses which are dwindling over time. This is detrimental to the bottom 20% of the population who are malnourished and due to falling supplies and increasing prices are further getting impoverished.

On the demand side the impact is more severe with far reaching consequences. Globalisation has increased the *choices* for the rising middle income groups (Pramanick et al. 2010: 95–113; Sethia 2013). The advent of mall and big brands are giving the concept of food new dimensions. The boundaries between the necessities and luxuries are getting blurred (Chattopadhyay 2013). The new age consumers are spoilt for choices. India is witnessing a tremendous growth in its fast food and restaurant industries (Pingali et al. 2004). It now accounts for roughly half of all restaurant revenues in the developed countries and continues to expand.

Second, globalisation has led to increased *monetisation* of the economy. Income being an important means of widening the range of consumption options, especially as economies around the world becomes increasingly monetised. Income gives people the ability to buy diverse, nutritious foods instead of eating only their own crops, to pay for motorised transport instead of walking, to pay for health care and education for their families, to pay for water from a tap instead of walking for many hours to collect it from a well. The increasing dependence of much consumption on private income means that changes in income have a dominant influence on changes· in consumption. When incomes rise steadily consumption rises for most of the population. But for the same reason, when incomes decline, consumption also falls sharply, with devastating consequences for human well-being.

Aggressive *advertising* is another key factor which is one of the manifestation of globalisation. According to Peter Drucker (1954), 'There is one valid definition of business purpose: to create a customer'. Customers created from the womb will be global players with their advertisement creating demand and soaring consumption. Information which is the key to raising awareness of the range of consumption options available and enabling the consumers to decide which choices are best. Without information there is no way of knowing what goods and services are available in the market and what services are being provided by the state and are by right, available to all. Advertising and public information campaigns play an important role in this respect. Here one has to factor in the role of media in contemporary society. The mass media carry with them prescribed attitudes and habits, certain intellectual and emotional reactions which bind the consumer and reduce them to a mindless mass (Herbert 1991).

> The fact is that the media have the power through selection and reinforcement to give us very influential portrayals of a whole range of groups, situations and ideas. We make sense of these representations in different ways according to the values and assumptions we carry around in our own heads. So representation is not just the way the world is presented to us but also about how we engage with media texts . . . representation is, therefore, just as much about audience interpretation as it is about portrayals that are offered to us by the media.
>
> (Connor 2001)

The problem is aggravated by the fact that media representation is assumed to be correct by masses, thus not realising that every time we encounter a media text, we are not seeing reality, but someone's version of it. Stuart Hall (1997) correctly points out that if something is 'represented' through the media there must exist the thing that is being portrayed – 'out there', is a reality – a 'set of unchanging meanings' – to be represented. Thus, for media to produce representations of reality there must, ultimately, be something that is 'really real' – otherwise it couldn't have a representation; there would, by definition, be nothing to represent. Anthony Giddens (1991) correctly observes that identity constructions; focuses on how we construct our identity, which is no longer given to us through socialisation and inheritance. We constantly work on our 'self' and seek to express who we are through the adoption of lifestyles often represented in the media. These representations play an important part in helping us structure and review our identity and help us to make personal decisions about ourselves, our relationships and the world around us. Unfortunately, it is often assumed that through social media, civil society can and shall stall many unsavoury attempts of the business houses to propagate practices that are harmful and unsustainable, both socio-culturally and economically.

> An informed citizenry depends on people's exposure to information on important political issues and on their willingness to discuss these issues with those around them. The rise of social media,

such as Facebook and Twitter, has introduced new spaces where political discussion and debate can take place . . . (however) that those who think they hold minority opinions often self-censor, failing to speak out for fear of ostracism or ridicule. It is called the 'spiral of silence'.

(Hampton et al. 2014)

Availability is another facet of food or so-called luxury items of consumptions.

Compared to standard goods, luxury goods are relatively expensive and scarce; regularly possess superior design, quality, and performance; offer their users a subjective value in use that cannot be easily quantified; and provide their users with social and economic status as ascribed by others. Subjective value and social and economic status derive from social relationships present in hierarchically arranged social groups. Luxury goods range from exotic, rare, and unique products affordable only to the elite to premium yet common products affordable to the many. Luxury goods are found throughout history and around the world, with identities and characteristics determined by cultures, sub-cultures, and reference groups.

(Moya 2012)

Going by the above definition, one may observe that choice and availability of food items are no more inward looking culturally, rather are progressively being imposed upon by the market and its projections. Giving the malls a run for their money; online mega stores like Amazon.com and Flipkart.com are giving availability and convenience a whole new definition by making products available at your doorstep. It has been found that traditionally, the Indian consumers have been eating at roadside eateries and stalls which still occupy a major share of the unorganised sector, where fast food has been eaten traditionally. However, with the changes in the economy of the country and injection of modern employment from the West, the non-home food market has now changed (Deivanai 2013; Malhotra 2010). The market is dominated by global players, especially in the organised fast food segment. Growing trend of consumption of multi cuisines and increasing brand awareness has led to the increase of global players. Organised modern formats like malls and supermarkets have also become a favourite destination for the outlets. Larger companies are teaming up with small franchisors and mall owners to promote their brand.

The growing segment comprises of formats like fast food chains, cafes and fine dining restaurants. The pizzas and burgers have now developed into part of the nation's eating habits. Their share is continuously growing with the key global brands such as Domino's, McDonald's and KFC making their marks quickly. The chains have had no problems accommodating different menus targeting specifically the Indian consumer.

The trend is radically changing the way people eat in India. For a nation that is particular about its food and significantly fond of home cooked and fresh food, this trend is showing the globalisation of India and increase of new markets not witnessed in India before. With increasing number of people eating out the industry offers major opportunities to the players to capture a larger consumer base. As a result of the trend, all the international food players are investing huge amount of money to grab a share of this highly lucrative market.

Increased w*omen workforce participation* has the dual impact of increasing income which can be splurged on consumption on the other hand due to the lack of time and leisure becoming a more valued good, convenience food and shopping are gaining importance. The 'Ready to Eat' (RTE) market in India for food is expanding at an enormous pace. RTE can be defined as food products that constitute complete meals; require minimal processing, if any, typically requiring re-heating to desired temperature or addition of water. They are often termed as 'convenience food' since they are positioned as 'value for money' products that solve the issue of time-constrains faced by consumers due to the pressures of urban life. Initially when RTE foods were familiarised first in India the concept failed however with time it gained importance. Changing consumer habits, preferences and perceptions has driven the market. A strong correlation exists between the growth of RTE foods and organised retail formats such as supermarkets, malls and hypermarkets.

Shrinking household sizes and *weakening of family ties* are making them more vulnerable to the manipulation of the market forces. Trends show that the modernisation of India is well on its way. These changes in the eating habits Indians are more than likely referring to middle class and upward earning society of India. The prospect of seeing fast food such as burgers and pizzas being the staple diet for middle income group is now a reality.

The basic question of an economy of what to produce and for whom to produce are thus being influenced by the process of globalisation as it has its impact on both the supply as well as the demand side of food.

Consequences

Thus from the above discussion it can be seen that globalisation has a profound impact on both the demand as well as the supply of food. It also becomes evident that consumption of so-called inferior goods like jowar, bajra, rice, wheat and so forth are on a decline while superior food consumption is on the rise. From an economist view point at first this substitution of inferior foods for the superior ones seems normal with increasing incomes as it is supported by the fact that as income rises people tend to eat well and their commodity baskets undergo quantitative as well as qualitative changes. However, when we closely scrutinise the data at a disaggregated level it reveals that the bottom 20% of the Indian population have not experienced any rise in income. So whatever they were eating is either same or have in fact deteriorated significantly both in term of quality as well as quantitatively. The situation became worse with the exponential rise in the price of pulses which used to provide the essential sources of protein for these bottom 20% populations.

On the other hand, those who have in fact experienced a rise in income are actually eating well. But a close scrutiny reveals that people are substituting traditional home cooked nutritious food with the fast food or RTE meals which are tastier as well as provide the pseudo satisfaction of eating well. Indians form the major markets for ice cream, pizzas and burgers. We are a part of the global culture for which potential consumers get confused between eating well and eating healthy. But this kind of consumption entails enormous health risks. Heart disease is responsible for the majority of deaths in India, and more than 60 million Indians have been diagnosed with diabetes. That's nearly 5% of India's people, and this number is expected to rise – and quickly. By 2050, India will have the dubious distinction of being home to the most diabetics of any country in the world (leaping over China). The traditional communicable diseases are being replaced by the non-communicable modern lifestyle diseases which are turning into an epidemic.

Studies have found that because of these biological mechanisms, people in developing countries are particularly at risk for type 2 diabetes and obesity (European Journal of Clinical Nutrition 2012). India thus has to bear the double burden of malnutrition, where the overfed masses suffer from obesity and other lifestyle diseases while the underfed mass die out of starvation. The sheer economic cost of this health imbalance will be an interesting case study which is beyond the purview of this chapter. Lastly from the socio-economic and moral stand point we can see that in the entire process the rich-poor divide as manifested itself clearly on this contentious issue of food. The inequality which already existed got accentuated largely due to the factors of globalisation and social justice had to be compromised with.

Conclusions

The Indian diet is diversifying with the share of edible oils, sugar and animal-based food increasing and cereal and pulses declining. The nutrition transition as is observed an inevitable process leading to a dual economy comprising undernourished impoverished masses and over fed masses posing a severe health risk. Problem is to provide the former with cheap affordable protein alternative while have to discourage the later from indulging in the high calorie fatty and sugary food appealing to the taste buds. What is clear is that both malnourishment deaths and accelerating rates of non-communicable diseases and the associated mortalities has to be curbed immediately.

The need of the hour is to reformulate the National Food Security Act which is cereal-based as it will have only a limited impact in achieving the goal of providing nutritional security to the vulnerable section of the population. There is need to include higher protein food such as pulses or protein-enriched cereals, micro nutrient supplements such as fruits in the program. Unfortunately, at present India is exporting a major share of soybeans which is a rich source of protein while the country is facing a protein-deficiency.

Policy analyst must concentrate on the fact file of the food consumption patterns of the entire economy at a disaggregated level to look into the cultural, social, economic factors influencing the dietary patterns and have to take immediate action to ensure social justice for all the sections.

Notes

1 Encyclopedia Britannica (https://www.britannica.com/). Accessed on 15.11.15.
2 A characteristic manner or style of preparing or cooking food.
3 Adipose tissue; a type of connective tissue that contains stored cellular fat.
4 A high-calorie food that is low in nutritional value.
5 National Commission on Farmers (NCF). October 2006. *Serving Farmers Saving Farming: Towards Faster and More Inclusive Growth of Farmers' Welfare*, Vol. I, 5th and Final Report. New Delhi: Ministry of Agriculture, Government of India; pp. 187–92.

6 National Commission on Farmers (NCF). April 2006. *Serving farmers and saving farming: Jai Kisan – A draft National Policy for Farmers*, 4th Report. New Delhi: Ministry of Agriculture, Government of India.

7 M. S. Swaminathan Research Foundation (MSSRF). 12. *Report on the state of food insecurity in rural India*. Chennai: M.S. Swaminathan Research Foundation; December 2008.

8 Government of India (GoI). 15. *Annual Report 2011–12*. New Delhi: Department of Animal Husbandry, Dairying and Fisheries, Ministry of Agriculture; 2012.

9 www.tradingeconomics.com/india/imports, accessed on 23.12.2015.

10 Department of Agriculture and Cooperation (DAC).18. *Guidelines for special programme on oil palm area expansion*. New Delhi: Ministry of Agriculture, Government of India; March 2014.

11 An Analysis of Changing Food Consumption Pattern in India, NACR 1956–2014.

12 Sharma (2012).

13 Economic Survey 2012-13, *Statistical appendix*, Pages, A21–A23, https://www.indiabudget.gov.in/es2012-13/estat1.pdf, accessed on 23.12.15.

14 Poor early-childhood nutrition leads to a host of metabolic and hormonal changes that actually help survival in nutrient-poor environments, according to Barry Popkin, Distinguished Professor of Global Nutrition at the University of North Carolina Gillings School of Public Health. However, when confronted with a calorie-packed environment in later years, these adaptive mechanisms may actually lead to obesity. An important 1976 study published in the *New England Journal of Medicine* found that mothers exposed to the 1944–45 Dutch famine during their pregnancies resulted in higher obesity rates among their children.

References

Bourne, L. T., Lambert, E. V. and Steyn, K. 2002. 'Where Does the Black Population of South Africa Stand on the Nutrition Transition?' *Public Health & Nutrition*, 5(1A): 157–162, http://mospi.nic.in/Mospi_New/site/inner.aspx?status=3&menu_id=31, accessed on 23.12.15.

Central Statistical Organisation, http://mospi.nic.in.

Chattopadhyay, Purba. 2012. 'Attaining Food Security. A Cautious Approach for India', in Biswajit Chatterjee and Asim K. Karmakar (eds.), *Food Security in India* (160–174). New Delhi: Regal.

Chattopadhyay, Purba. 2013. 'Consumption and Austerity in the Age of Globalization: A Critique of Capitalist Development in India', *Artha Beekshan: Journal of Bangiya Arthaniti Parishad*, 22(3): 45–57.

Connor, Gerry. 2001. 'Representation and Youth', http://henleycollegemediablog.blogspot.in/2011/05/section-b-representation-of-youth-by.html.

Deivanai, P. 2013. 'A Study on Determinants of Customer Satisfaction towards Fast Food Industries in Madurai District', *Intercontinental Journal of Marketing Research Review*, 1(9): 35–42.

Department of Agriculture and Cooperation (DAC). 2014. *Guidelines for Special Programme on Oil Palm Area Expansion*. New Delhi: Ministry of Agriculture, Government of India.

Department of Agriculture and Cooperation, www.agricoop.nic.in.

Directorate of Economics and Statistics, http://eands.dacnet.nic.in.

Drucker, Peter E. 1954. *The Practice of Management*. New York: Harper and Row.

European Journal of Clinical Nutrition (EJCN). 2012. Macmillan, www.nature.com/ejcn/archive/index.html.

Giddens, Anthony. 1991. *Modernity and Self-Identity: Self and Society in the Late Modern Age*. Stanford, CA: Stanford University Press.

Government of India (GoI). 2012. *Annual Report 2011–12*. New Delhi: Department of Animal Husbandry, Dairying and Fisheries, Ministry of Agriculture.

Hall, Stuart. 1997. *Representation: Cultural Representations and Signifying Practices*. London: Sage and The Open University.

Hampton, K.N., Rainie, L., Lu, W., Dwyer, M., Shin, I. and Purcell, K. 2014. 'Social Media and the Spiral of Silence', *Pew Research Center*, Washington, DC, 1, www.pewinternet.org/2014/08/26/social-media-and-the-spiral-of-silence;. http://tatagrowmorepulses.com/media_kit_pulses.pdf; www.iimahd.ernet.in/assets/snippets/workingpaperpdf/5337679172012-08-02.pdf; http://indiabudget.nic.in/es2012-13/estat1.pdf; www.tradingeconomics.com/india/imports.

Krishnaswamy, Kamala. 1999. *Obesity in Urban Middle Classes*. New Delhi: Nutrition Foundation of India.

M S Swaminathan Research Foundation (MSSRF). 2008. *Report on the State of Food Insecurity in Rural India*. Chennai: M.S. Swaminathan Research Foundation.

Malhotra, Amit. 2010. 'Fast Food Grows in India', *DESIblitz Web Magazine*, www.desiblitz.com/content/fast-food-grows-in-india.

Marcuse, Herbert. 1991. *One-dimensional Man: Studies in Ideology of Advanced Industrial Society* (2nd ed.). London: Routledge.

Moya, María Eugenia Fernández. 2012. 'Purchase and Consumption of Luxury Goods', DEPARTAMENTO DE ECONOMÍA DE LA EMPRESA, UNIVERSIDAD CARLOS III DE MADRID, Getafe, enero.(DOCTORAL THESIS), p. 11, http://e-archivo.uc3m.es/bitstream/handle/10016/14070/mariaeugenia_fernandez_tesis.pdf?sequence=1.

NACR. 2015. 'An Analysis of Changing Food Consumption Pattern in India 1956–2014', A research paper prepared under the project Agricultural Outlook and Situation Analysis Reports, New Delhi: National Council of Applied Economic Research.

Patnaik, Utsa. 2009. 'Origins of the Food Crisis in India and Developing Countries', *Monthly Review*, 61(3), July–August, http://monthlyreview.org/2009/07/01/origins-of-the-food-crisis-in-india-and-developing-countries.

Pingali, Prabhu and Khwaja, Yasmeen. 2004. 'Globalisation of Indian Diets and the Transformation of Food Supply Systems'. Food and Agriculture Organisation, www.fao.org.

Pramanick, S.K. and Ramanuj, Ganguly (eds.) 2010. *Globalization in India: New Frontiers and Emerging Challenges*. New Delhi: PHI Learning.

Sethia, Savneet. 2013. 'India's Changing Consumption Pattern', *GYANPRATHA-ACCMAN Journal of Management*, 5(2), http://accman.in/images/june13/4.pdf.

Sharma, Vijay Paul. 2012. 'Food Subsidy in India: Trends, Causes and Policy Reform Options', W.P. No. 2012–08–02, August, Ahmedabad: Indian Institute of Management, www.iimahd.ernet.in/assets/snippets/working paperpdf/5337679172012-08-02.pdf.

Shetty, P. 2002. 'Nutrition Transition in India', *Public Health Nutrition*, 5(1A): 175–182.

Subramanian, S. V., Perkins, J. M. and Khan, K. T. 2009. 'Do Burdens of Underweight and Overweight Coexist Among Lower Socioeconomic Groups in India?' *American Journal of Clinical Nutrition*, 90: 369–376.

Subramanian, S. and Smith, G. D. 2006. 'Patterns, Distribution and Determinants of Under- and Over Nutrition: A Population Based Study of Women in India', *American Journal of Clinical Nutrition*, 84: 633–640.

Swaminathan, M. S. 2009. 'The Media and the Farm Sector', *The Hindu*, November 11.

Swaminathan, M. S. and Sinha, S. K. 1986. 'Global Aspects of Food Production', in *Building National and Global Nutrition Security Systems*. Dublin: Tycooly.

16 Transnational higher education (TNHE) trends in India and China

Comparison of Euro-American and Chinese models

Siri Gamage

There is a need to problematise the continuing legacy of colonialism, modernity, and metropolitan educational discourses and practices as well as educational policymaking processes couched in terms such as internationalisation and globalisation in countries of the global periphery and analyse their true intents, trends and implications. One question to ask is whether internationalisation has the potential to address the challenges facing public higher education systems in the global south in areas such as quality maintenance, meeting unmet demand and so-called international standards? Policymakers, academics and other writers propose strategies while different countries have taken various steps to internationalise their higher education provision. Some measures adopted by governments have been to strengthen their publicly funded higher education systems whereas others have encouraged private investment in higher education. Both measures have their own problems and challenges.

Since the invention of modernity and modern education in the Western European and North American countries which were later transported to Australia, New Zealand and other colonised parts of the global south including India and Sri Lanka (formerly Ceylon), the English language and modernist education acquired a superior status in colonised countries. The knowledge imparted by institutions located in the global north was perceived by those in the global peripheries as a benchmark to be followed in knowledge production and dissemination. Qualifications received from same institutions were treated as superior to those received from the institutions located in the southern peripheries.

In the process of knowledge production and dissemination within higher education institutions in the global south, this distinction could be observed clearly by the way references are made to authors, books and journal articles produced in Western European countries and in North America.[1]

During the post–Cold War era, countries of the global south have been adopting a neo-liberal economic logic and associated discourse in the name of neo-liberal globalisation and internationalisation to acquire knowledge and training from countries of the global north – that dominate the production and dissemination of knowledge. In some ways, this is a continuation of modernist paradigm that became dominant during the colonial period and its aftermath in the global south with significant consequences for the indigenous knowledge production, e.g. subversion of indigenous knowledge production.

Internationalisation of higher education is seen today by countries of the global south as a necessary step to address issues and challenges facing their domestic higher education sector. Consequently, in countries such as India, publicly funded higher education institutions and private sector institutions compete to establish partnerships with institutions in the global north. Higher education institutions in the global north also wish to internationalise education partly as an income generating activity and partly as an avenue to enhance and expand their research cultures and profiles. In this process, a greater diversity of players have emerged globally, among them research-poor, newly formed institutions wanting to market their degree programs along with the research intensive universities. This chapter examines this diversity by taking two countries as examples: China and India. The extent to which the Western (or global) model is reproduced in the global periphery is also discussed while paying attention to any signs of truly Indian or Chinese models of higher education emerging in Asia.

Though some writers have indicated that there is a shift in the global core-periphery relation in economic and even educational terms, (for example Welch) with a movement to Asia, in particular China, and even argue that the traditional knowledge society that existed there has been subsumed by the neo-liberally informed global economy with implications for higher education, this chapter argues that it is by using Southern Theory perspective that one can truly start to build an alternative vision and strategy for higher education in the Asian region that will enable countries to move away from the dominant constructions by the rich, developed countries for their own benefit (see Connell 2007; Alatas 2010).

Transnational higher education (TNHE) in Asia and internationalisation

Many writers on higher education in the global south compare and contrast the higher education systems in their own countries with those of the developed global north and talk about 'an international standard'. To them, this means a standard established by higher education institutes and bodies such as the Organisation for Economic Co-operation and Development (OECD) located in the global north. The argument goes that if the institutions in the global south are to improve their quality, standards, international recognition etc. these institutions have to internationalise by adopting various measures such as establishment of partnerships with internationally recognised universities in the global north, obtaining higher education qualifications by the faculty from universities in the global north, adopting curricula and text books from the same region, and even reproducing the (scientific and professional) knowledge in their locations. Thus finding solutions to local problems in the higher education institutions in a country like India has been articulated as one requiring more – not less – internationalisation. Looking at local solutions to local problems from their own contexts, resources, and cultural or intellectual traditions is not somehow considered as the fashionable thing to do.

With globalisation of economies along neo-liberal free-market principles, liberalisation of financial markets, and the better facilitation of cross border movements since the 1980s, provision of education to students in the global south – both at school and university levels – by institutions located in the global north increased in numerous ways. This included (1) establishment of international schools on fee-paying basis, (2) establishment of university campuses and agencies on fee-paying basis, (3) movement of fee-paying post-graduate students to institutions located in the global north (and Australia, New Zealand), (4) involvement of experts located in the global north (plus Australia and New Zealand) in educational policymaking process with the backing of bilateral and multilateral funding agencies such as the World Bank, Asian Development Bank, and (5) the provision of educational resources, including policy and curriculum materials plus text books, generated in the global north to institutions located in the global south, (6) increased levels of cross-border movement of researchers from the global south to global north for knowledge work, and (7) increased levels of exchanges and partnerships between the two regions. These initiatives had a considerable impact on the development and implementation of educational policies and processes pertaining to the domestic state sponsored educational sector also.[2]

Paul (2009: 37) outlines several trends in countries of Asia in terms of internationalisation of higher education: (1) study abroad as the most visible mode, (2) foreign institutions setting up campuses or partnerships with local institutions, (3) Education hubs to attract foreign students in technical and professional subjects (Singapore attracted 16), (4) Distance learning expansion. These contribute to increased levels of transnational higher education (TNHE) globally.

Saying that we have witnessed a boom in the international trade in education, in particular higher education, Naidoo (2009: 310), observes that an increasing number of new or alternative providers have entered the market including media companies such as Pearson (United Kingdom), Thomson (Canada), multinational companies such as Apollo (United States) and Informatics (Singapore), corporate universities, and professional associations, are also engaged in TNHE activities (citing Knight 2005a).

TNHE is a worldwide phenomenon whose scale of activity has grown exponentially in recent years (Naidoo 2009: 326). International student flow increased from 149,590 in 1955 to 2.7 million in 2004. 'This trend depicts a shift in overseas study from an elitist experience to one involving mass movements' and 'no longer overseas study limited to those earning scholarships and fellowships' leading to the emergence of a global education industry as a key service industry (Naidoo 2009: 311).

Naidoo's conclusion from a secondary analysis of data is that

> Mode 3 TNHE occurs mostly in the Asia-Pacific region, the Middle East, Eastern Europe, and in South America. Australian, British, and US institutions most often undertake it. Wholly owned branch campuses and joint venture operations currently represent a very small share of the Mode 3 TNHE landscape.
>
> (2009: 320)[3]

Commercial presence of educational services – Mode 3 – refers to the commercial establishment of facilities abroad by education providers (e.g. 'local branch campuses' or partnerships with domestic education institutions). In 2004, Mode 3 accounted for 50% of the total world trade in services (Naidoo 2009: 313).

In terms of the providers of higher education, Naidoo presents further interesting findings:

> Australia is by far the most active exporter of programme mobility. With 1,569 education programmes and 37 institutions operating

in the programme mobility landscape, the overall 'intensity' of Australia's activity was 42.4 programmes per institution, compared with 12.7 programmes for U.K.-based institutions. In absolute terms, the United States is the third most active exporter of TNHE programmes followed by New Zealand and Canada. Ireland has some export activity but not on the scale of market leaders.

(Naidoo 2009: 321)

However, the intentions of such education exporting countries are not always academic. According to Altbach and Knight they have financial objectives as well as a dominating effect in the implementation:

> International higher education initiatives exist in almost every country. But the developed countries – especially the large English-speaking nations and, to a lesser extent, the larger EU countries – provide most services. By any measure – such as flows of international students, franchisers of academic programs to foreign providers, international accreditors or quality guarantors, or controlling partners in 'twinning' arrangements – these countries reap the main financial benefits and control most programs.
>
> (Altbachand Knight 2007: 294)

When we look at importers of TNHE in Asia, 'the hotspot of programme mobility is in Singapore, Hong Kong, and Malaysia in descending order. China and India are emerging markets with each, respectively, having 410 and 249 TNHE programmes' (Naidoo 2009: 321).

In the next section, I discuss international higher education mainly in two countries in Asia with a view to discerning the trends, shape, challenges, contemporary issues as well as the diverse nature of internationalisation. It becomes clear that TNHE is an important spoke in the wheel of globalisation as a tradable commodity.

India

When we talk about internationalisation of higher education today, generally we do tend to focus on the importation of Western higher education scholarship, models, paradigms and knowledge from the rich countries of the global north to countries of the global south in many forms. However, going back in history, it becomes clear that 'India heralded internationalization of higher education for the rest of the world. Internationalization was not an addendum, but the very creed that defined the ethos of higher education' (Yeravdekar and

Tiwari 2014b: 374). For example, in AD 5 the University of Nalanda, a residential university, 'attracted scholars and students from as far away as Tibet, China, Greece and Persia' (2014b: 374).

Exchange of cultural ideas across regions was common in the ancient and medieval periods of history. In the ancient world,

> internationalization was indicative of the process of exchange of ideas, and the movement of students, and itinerant scholars across territories. It was a common feature of the first academies in Pakistan, India, Egypt, China and Persia (Takschashila, Nalanda, Al-Azhar, Yuelu, Gandishapur) in the 7th and 9th centuries BC, attracting students from all over Asia and the Middle East.
>
> (Britezand Peters 2010: 37)

Examples cited include how Greek science passed to the Arabic world, how Christianity became a Hellenising force. In fact, 'the historical specificity in which the internationalization of ideas, the movement of scholars, and the exchange of artefacts, the development of connections and the direction and means of cultural mediation were established' (Britezand Peters 2010: 38) is an important focal point for investigation.

In the later historical periods,

> Developing nations like India have acted as sources, rather than sinks, of student and faculty circulation in international higher education. This is especially true for exchange with developed nations in the Northern hemisphere. Although there are substantial inflows from other developing countries, especially those in South and Central Asia and Africa, exchange with respect to the developed world is almost entirely outward.
>
> (Chakrabarti et al. 2010: 184)

Early in the 21st century, the Association of Indian Universities arranged a round table discussion on 'Internationalization of Indian Higher Education' at the University of Mysore. They discussed the mechanisms to promote internationalisation of Indian Higher Education at select Indian universities and adopted the 'Mysore Statement' (International Association of Universities Newsletter, July 2001 cited by Mitra 2010). This statement acknowledges:

- Accepting that internationalisation of higher education is a fact of life in the new 'knowledge era';

- Realising that internationalisation would lead to an improvement in the quality of education, promote Indian culture abroad, produce understanding and yield financial benefits;
- Recognising that partnership and networking are essential to enrich the teaching learning and to improve quality of research;
- Believing that it is necessary to act in earnest immediately;
- The government, academic institutions and the Association of Indian Universities take necessary steps to promote Indian higher education internationally.

The statement recommended various actions to the government and higher education institutions (see Mitra 2010: 107–108). Mitra discusses various advantages of internationalisation of higher education for Indian institutions (2010: 108–109).

Expansion of higher education in India

Higher education in India has expanded many folds in the last few decades. Since independence of the country in 1947, the higher education has grown 33-fold in number of institutions making availability of education to the masses. The number of universities has increased from 20 in 1947 to 378, and student population in higher education from 1 lakh in 1950 to over 112 lakhs in 2005.[4] The growth in capacity of higher education has improved enrolment ratio from less than 1% in 1950 to around 10% (Mitra 2010: 106).

The education providers include public non-profit, private non-profit and private for-profit institutions and have a mixture of public and private institutions. There is no boundary between public and private institutions as many public universities now look for private financing and charge a tuition or service charge. On the other hand, private institutions are eligible for public funds and engage in social non-profit actions (Mitra 2010: 106).

In 2009, India had 350 universities and 15,600 colleges, most of them public, graduating 2.5 million students each year. Every year, 350,000 students graduate with degrees in engineering – twice the number of engineering graduates in the United States, but still a tiny fraction of the total population of 18-to 24-year-olds (Chakrabarti et al. 2009: 186). According to the authors, 'India's public education system is lagging behind international standards. Apart from the ten most highly respected public universities in India, the education received from the remaining public Indian schools is far below international standards' (2009: 186).

Though India 'is the third largest after US and China with 10 million students continuing study in about 16,000 institutions' (Mitra 2010: 108) and 'It is one of the world's largest markets for foreign universities' for higher education access, the country has a significant unmet demand. Only 10% of the age group receives university education currently. It is half the rate in China. This is well below the rate in most developing countries (Mitra 2010: 109).

Mitra provides further comments about privatisation of higher education in order to meet the demand and low investment:

> Though higher Education in India has expanded many folds in the last few decades, with the expansion in state funded institutions, private operators are also been allowed to supplement education. The road ahead for India is related to creation of quality Higher Education Institutions to meet the challenge. The Government resources for higher education are not enough and investments in this sector from private and foreign sources are welcome.
>
> (Mitra 2010: 110)

In the case of India, several factors have contributed to the expansion of scale and modes of higher education. Among them are the opening up of the economy through new policies of liberalisation, easier capital flows and access to new technologies. 'Liberal policies have created opportunities for education service providers, both within the country and abroad, to invest in a big way in setting up new institutions or joint ventures to offer educational programmes that are in great demand' (Paul 2009: 36). The main players in this are from the private sector.[5]

According to Paul (2009: 36), what is new in terms of internationalisation of higher education 'is the much larger scale of such activities and inputs today, and the adoption of new modes of delivery of higher education' (2009: 36). Examples are foreign universities or colleges opening branch campuses or offering joint programs of study in partnership with local institutions. At the same time, 'With student and faculty circulation between Indian and Western institutions increasing, competition has developed within the Indian higher education market for attracting foreign institutions of higher education into collaborative partnerships and exchange programs' (Chakrabarti et al. 2010: 197). They have discussed the need for better student support services for enhancing such endeavours.

Several features stand out regarding the internationalisation of higher education in India:

1 India is following the same path as China and countries in SEA in establishing partnerships with higher education institutions in the rich countries of the global north. The private sector institutions have come into partnerships with foreign higher education institutions as well as student exchange programs. Chakrabarti et al. (2010) examine these in detail (pp. 186–190). In 2005, 'there were 131 foreign education programmes being offered in India in partnership with Indian institutions' (Paul 2009: 37). Moreover, 'Hundred percent foreign investment in higher education is now permitted by law in India' (2009: 37).

2 Brain drain:[6] India is a main source country for students in rich countries of the global north. 'Since the 2000–2001 academic year, the number of Indian students (studying overseas) has risen from approximately 55,000 to more than 90,000 in 2007–2008' (Chakrabarti et al. 2010: 187). According to Paul, in 2009, about 100,000 Indian students were studying abroad. Many do not return after study (Paul 2009: 36). It is stated that 'If more Indian students completed their education in India instead of enrolling abroad, they would be far more likely to ultimately seek employment in the growing Indian industrial sector' (Chakrabarti et al. 2010: 184).

3 In-bound students: In 2006, 2,627 came from the United States and those from south and central Asian countries consisted of 3,812 (30%) students. From SEA, there were 1,609. Totally, less than 13,000 students were studying in India (Chakrabarti et al. 2010: 187 citing UNESCO 2008 and other sources). According to them, 'student migration trends indicate that the massive outflow of university students from India shows no sign of abatement and cannot be compensated for by incremental increases of inflow from other nations' (2010: 188).

4 India plays a regional capacity building role in terms of higher education provision to neighbouring countries. According to Yeravdekar and Tiwari, India's 'predominant position as provider of quality higher education in pockets of the developing world, such as the South Asian region (SAR) has been documented and demonstrated in several studies' (2014b: 376). India 'has traditionally drawn students from countries which are developing economies and previously colonized – countries in the "periphery" in the

lexicon of neo-colonialism or "low and middle income countries" '(2014b: 375). This consists of about 95% of students who come to study in India (citing Power 2012: 243). They further point out that in countries from where students come to India for study, higher education systems are unsatisfactory, particularly in skill-oriented disciplines like science, technology, medicine, management, and professional-vocational (Yeravdekar and Tiwari 2014b: 375). However, 'the beneficiaries are often contractually bound to return to the home country and contribute to such projects as are compatible with the government's development agenda' (2014b: 376).

Emergence of private providers of higher education in India 'has propelled internationalization of higher education into an unprecedented momentum' (Yeravdekar and Tiwari 2014b: 378). Yeravdekar and Tiwari predict that 'India will continue to contribute to the human capital base, and in so doing, promote knowledge economy in several regions in the developing world' (2014b: 378).

However, in comparison to the developments in China and elsewhere in the region, 'India's forays into internationalization have been modest' (Paul 2009: 37). Some concerns exist about any rapid expansion of internationalisation in higher education as well as the domestic sector. For example, there is 'no effective and coherent strategic or regulatory framework to monitor and assess these activities' (Paul 2009: 37). It was also felt that foreign universities must not be allowed to encourage in gross commercialisation of higher education (Mitra 2010: 110).

One weakness in the Indian structure of higher education is the fact that 659 Indian universities, based on the 'London model', are burdened unmanageably by affiliated colleges – over 35,000 in number. The system continues 'undifferentiated' without institutional diversity. 'There are no mandates to stratify institutions by mission and concentration, and so funds are apportioned in butter-like spread' (Yeravdekar and Tiwari 2014a: 370). Multiple jurisdictions also have become an obstacle. The neglect of the private sector, which is growing faster than the public sector, is another issue facing the Indian higher education sector. In 2012, 64% institutions were private.

The government's inability to grapple core challenge in the universities is exemplified by the National Knowledge Commission established in 2005. Likewise the recent project to launch 14 'innovation universities' has also been subjected to a range of criticisms. On the contrary,

the success of Chinese policies rests, partially, on operationalizing differentiation, resulting in effective 'massification' of tertiary education in the face of resource constraints, while allowing select institutions to deliver excellence to a greater scale than would otherwise have been possible. And China has been at it for over two and a half decades.

(Yeravdekar and Tiwari 2014a: 371)

These authors believe that the Chinese higher education system has shown great results from radical policy actions. Most of it has to do with phenomenal spend, but the rest of it is about exemplary policy formulation and execution (2014a: 371). In the case of India, 'it suffers from gross underinvestment, but much worse is the affliction of policy paralysis' (Yeravdekar and Tiwari 2014a: 371. Endless disagreements and obstructions characterise the policy field. Their prescription for India is to implement goal-oriented projects like in China.

Further prescriptions

How far should India's strategy on internationalisation of higher education be for the mitigation of existing problems in the domestic sector? According to Paul, India's strategy should be directed toward this goal. However, the liberalisation policies 'have induced foreign providers to focus only on certain technical and professional fields of study that can earn them good market returns' (2009: 36). His prescription for India is

> To design a strategy that taps foreign universities and institutes of acceptable quality to work together with Indian universities. Institutes to improve both access and quality. Augmenting and strengthening the capacity to produce more faculty in selected fields through such partnerships will help public universities play a more effective role in higher education.
>
> (Paul 2009: 36)

He suggests measures to improve quality and access in the Indian higher education system. They include further increasing movement of students from India to other countries for higher education, opening more distance education from other countries to Indian students, allowing foreign university campuses in India, facilitating joint program offerings with foreign institutions, collaborations with reputed foreign universities and Indian universities, entertaining foreign students in top Indian universities, encouraging Indian institutions to set up campuses in other countries (Paul 2009: 39). Paul further suggests that the government of India should (1) identify the areas in which foreign inputs are most useful; (2) allocate adequate resources to pay for the service providers; and (3) put in place an effective regulatory framework to assure quality (Paul 2009: 41).

Yeravdekar and Tiwari (2014a) compare TNHE in India with that of China and provide useful observations. To them, China's hard fought battle 'proves that the centre-periphery paradigm in international education is not a foregone conclusion' (2014a: 369). In terms of budgetary allocations as well as policy engineering, the two countries set apart. China spends $250 billion and India 37.13 billion on higher education. In 2011, India produced 45,172 research publications whereas China produced 156,574. China has increased postgraduate enrolment while India records high undergraduate enrolment. China has increased its international competitiveness also. The number of US students in China in 2011 was 23,360 (8%) while in India it was 782 in 2012. This is a remarkable achievement given China's official medium of instruction is not English. India has no policies to attract international researchers of Indian origin either (2014a: 370).

While India is grappling with issues and challenges in its own domestic higher education sector such as the quality, unmet demand, and looking for ways to utilise the new found drive by the private sector within India and foreign partner institutions to capitalise on knowledge acquisition and capacity building in its higher education sectors – private and public – India plays a crucial role in providing higher education opportunities for students coming from the developing countries at a lower cost. This level of 'binary integration' is a special characteristic to be noted. Education is provided in English rather than Hindi. This is also a special feature compared to countries like China and Japan that insist in learning through their own languages. India's role in providing higher education to less developed countries in the region is part of its public diplomacy, and use of soft power to maintain its hegemonic position, though some writers emphasise the intention of spreading democratic ethos (Yeravdekar and Tiwari 2014b: 377). Many returning students become high achieving professionals in their own countries in administration, governance and policymaking. Any increase in inbound mobility of students should be credited to the emergence of private participants in Indian higher education (Yeravdekar and Tiwari 2014b: 380 citing Agarval, N.D.A.).

However, according to Yeravdekar and Tiwari, this is a pattern observable in the South Asian region, Gulf region in general. The establishment of the South Asian University as a South Asian Association for Regional Cooperation (SAARC) initiative is a unique experiment when branch campuses of foreign universities in rich Western countries are being established elsewhere to capitalise on the international student market. Socio-cultural similarities between India and source countries are also a contributory factor to the cross border mobility between India and other developing countries. A challenge India and even other countries of Asia and the global south face in this globalisation era is how to distinguish between those Western institutions that are motivated by profit and those that are genuinely interested in research, education, and training collaboration for mutual benefit. In this regard, a question has to be asked as to why do foreign universities and education companies would enter the Indian market? In this regard, Mitra's following comments are useful to clarify the issue:

> Everyone wants to extract profits – mostly by offering programs in fields that are in high demand. Foreign providers are not interested in investing in high-cost academic infrastructures and research. They wish to maximize the profit minimizing the investment. Some countries, including the United Kingdom and Australia, have a national policy to earn profits from higher education exports. The British Council and similar organizations help British educational institutions to increase their export potentials.
>
> (Mitra 2010: 109)

China

Internationalisation of higher education in China in the last few decades has seen significant transformations from taking advantage of the 'Western model' to promoting a 'Chinese model' in the current phase along with its increasing status as an economic power globally. Priorities in the higher education field in China have shifted in the last three decades.

With the open-door policy of 1978, China encouraged internationalisation of higher education. 'The idea was to bring back Western expertise into fields in which the country was lacking knowledge' (Jokila 2014: 130 citing Hayhoe 1984). Aspiration to modernise four areas was the rationale: industry, agriculture, defence, and science and technology. Three student generations were sent abroad for education. Based on Shen (2007), Jokila identifies three periods in this process: (1) post-cultural revolution and open door policy period (1978–89), (2) post-Tiananmen period (1989–2001) and (3) the period after the 2001 terrorist attacks in the United States. Because it was difficult for Chinese students to obtain visas to the United States, a diversification of destinations occurred. The trend changed from government-funded students going abroad to self-funded students. In 1978, 17,622 Chinese students went abroad. By 2002 the number increased to 125,179. In 2008, Chinese students were the largest in OECD countries with 17.1%. United States and Japan were the most popular destinations (Jokila 2014: 131, citing various sources).[7] During the late 1990s, 'China started to change its higher education from elite education to mass education'. Importantly, 'China runs the largest higher education system in the world with 2263 higher education institutions and 20,210,000 university students in 2008' (Hou et al. 2014: 310). 'However, places at a desirable university are still very competitive' (2014: 310). Therefore, 'potential students choose to study abroad through participation in the TNE programmes and institutions' (2014: 310). TNE is also viewed as a gateway to upward social mobility.

In the earlier phase, China adopted neo-liberal reforms in the education sphere in order to be competitive in the global knowledge economy. Achieving world-class status for its universities was one particular aim of such reforms.

> The popularity of international league tables has intensified the competition in the global higher education market. Countries across the world, including China, have participated in global ranking exercises, aiming to enhance the competitiveness and reputation of their higher education systems globally.
>
> (Wang 2013: 308)

One driver of internationalisation of higher education in China is to enhance quality to meet international standards. 'International activities can be considered a way for Chinese universities to improve their standing compared with other Chinese and international universities' (Jokila 2014: 129). The project 985 launched in 1998, 'funds 39 nationally eminent universities to become global actors and strive for world class status' (Jokila 2014: 129 based on Hayhoe and Liu 2010). These universities are based on the project 211 – a generous funding scheme in China.

Actually, the stated aim of TNE in China is to introduce high-quality education resources from other countries to enhance the international competitiveness of Chinese institutions (Hou et al. 2014: 308 citing Zhou 2006). For the Chinese government, 'higher education is not a commodity, but a service for public interest. This aim stands in contrast to the UK motivation for TNE' (2014: 308). However,

'The Chinese government is reluctant to accept the current role of the country being a sender in TNE' (2014: 308).

> Collaboration with developed countries in higher education has been greatly encouraged to obtain world-leading experience and to improve Chinese research and innovation capacities. Through cooperative TNE programs, Chinese universities are expected to integrate urgently needed curricula and textbooks of world-class levels.
>
> (Hou et al. 2014: 309)

There are 577 Chinese higher education institutions today hosting TNE. This comprises of 21% of the Chinese higher education institutions (Hou et al. 2014: 309). The Chinese government cooperates with foreign institutions to running schools.

> Chinese universities and foreign universities cooperate to set up programmes or institutions to recruit Chinese students. These students either stay in China to finish the whole course or go abroad in their later stage of study. The cooperation of institutions in Taiwan, Hong Kong and Macao with the institutions in Mainland China is also considered as part of Chinese TNE.
>
> (Hou et al. 2014: 308)

These programs appear in two formats: setting up institutions or programs. 'China currently operates 1979 TNE programs, which amount to a total of 450,000 students enrolled in TNE and 1.5 million graduates from TNE' (Hou et al. 2014: 308 citing MOE 2013).

Hou et al. (2014: 303) identified significant features of current Chinese TNHE on the basis of a documentary analysis amounting to 1652 documents on TNE. They drew certain themes and issues from this analysis for constructing the arguments in their paper and identified 511 TNE programs and institutions at undergraduate and postgraduate levels. They are mainly located in well-developed eastern coastal regions. However, by 2010 there are two exceptions: in Heilongjing, an economically less developed province, there were 152 undergraduate programs and four postgraduate programs, many of which were in cooperation with Russia (74). The province's location next to Russia and the widespread use of Russian as the second language make this a unique case. However, Shanghai has the second largest number of TNE programs.

It has five TNE institutions cooperating with universities in the USA, the UK, Germany, France and Belgium. Among its 52 undergraduate programs, the partner universities are from 13 countries or regions: the USA (15), the UK (7), Germany (7), France (5), Australia (4), Canada (3), Netherland (2), Italy (2), Japan (2), New Zealand (1), South Korea (1), and Hong Kong (1). The capital city Beijing has the largest number of postgraduate programmes. The USA (12), Australia (12) and Hong Kong (7) are the three most favored cooperative countries in the region.

(Hou et al. 2014: 311)

The second feature of TNE is 'that partner institutions are based in 21 economically developed countries or regions'. To elaborate further, 'The UK ranks the first with 114 programmes and institutions. The USA and Australia are both runners up with 84 each. The other top countries or regions are Russia (75), Canada (39), Hong Kong (30), Germany (24), France (18), South Korea (8), and Netherland (7)'. Other countries with fewer than five are Ireland, New Zealand and Japan (5 each), Belgium, Italy, Sweden, Singapore, Austria, Norway, South Africa, and Taiwan. These figures show that the TNE arrangements by China are overwhelmingly with the institutions located in the global north – even though countries like Hong Kong 'is ambitious to become the regional education hub through the internationalization of its higher education campuses' (Hou et al. 2014: 312).

It is obvious that 'Attracting international students has been recognized as a way to internationalize university campuses worldwide' (Jokila 2014: 131). The number of foreign students in Chinese campuses has increased in recent decades. In 2008, the number of foreign students was about 180 times more than at the beginning of the open-door policy' (Jokila 2014: 132 citing Jiang and Ma 2011). There were 36,386 in 2006 and by 2008 it increased to 51,038. Between 1950 and 1964, the majority came from Vietnam, the Soviet Union, and Eastern Europe. Later from 1973–78, majority came from developing countries (66%). The rest came from developed countries. By 2011, majority came from China's neighbouring countries. In 2010, only 12.6% came from Europe, 11% from America and 3.1% from Africa. 'The top sending countries were South Korea (21.3% = 62,442), the United States (8.0% = 23,292), and Japan (6.1% = 17,961)' (Jokila 2014: 132). A majority came for non-degree courses although an increase in degree course following numbers is on the rise. In addition to students, China is also attempting to attract talent on a global scale under the 'One Thousand Talent Scheme'.

These numbers show two-way traffic, even multiple way traffic, in terms of student mobility indicating a desire on the part of global learning community to access multiple sites of learning and education. The motives of various student cohorts and groups can be quite complex. Those from the developed world obviously want to enhance their language and cultural knowledge while being exposed to a potential super power. Future employment prospects in a globalised economy can also play a part. On the part of Chinese students also a similar motive can be at play along with migration objectives in some cases.

According to Hou et al. for the government, 'the essence of the cooperation should be for the Chinese institutions to introduce and absorb high-quality educational resources through which their own education system can be improved'. In this sense, 'it should not be simply about sending Chinese citizens abroad'. We must avoid 'TNE simply becoming a recruitment tool for overseas institutions' (Hou et al. 2014: 314). To achieve this goal, the government now conducts audits. It is 'only partner institutions who pay attention to the quality can be awarded the license from the Chinese government' (2014: 314).

Using education for soft diplomacy

According to Wang, today 'education is used as an important tool to expand China's influence, as it provides suitable channels to introduce the Chinese values and culture to the world' (2013: 306). The article by Wang examines 'How does China use education to expand its cultural influence internationally?' Through initiatives like Confucius Institutes established outside China with central government funding, China is attempting to educate those interested in Chinese language and culture. Notably, '2300 universities in about 100 countries offer Chinese language courses. In many countries, including South Korea, Japan, France and the United States, Chinese will become the fastest growing language in schools' (Wang 2013: 310 citing Ding and Saunders 2006).

It is worth further noting that 'By the end of 2006, 96 countries hosted a total of 322 Confucius Institutes and 369 Confucian classrooms' (Jokila 2014: 134 citing Confucian Institute Online 2012). 'One ambitious goal of Confucius Institutions is to train 100 million new Chinese speakers in the first 5 years. The global promotion of Chinese appears to live up to the expectation to raise the popularity of Chinese' (Wang 2013: 309). These Institutes represent a wider imagination of internationalisation of higher education as it shows China 'is not only a receiver of foreign knowledge but also a sender of its own knowledge' (Jokila 2014: 135 citing Yang 2010). Moreover, 'these institutions can be seen as a step away from traditional activities of the internationalization of higher education including people moving to institutions and projects moving' (Jokila 2014: 135). Though 'previous studies support the idea that the imagination of internationalization has widened over time in many respects', Jokila observes that 'the relative share of the institutions capable of enrolling foreign students has not increased' (Jokila 2014: 135).

A critical question in the process of internationalisation is about the subjects being taught under various programs. They can shed some light on the nature of knowledge acquisition and construction or reproduction as applicable to China as a country and the global economy where the Chinese play a crucial role in contemporary world. According to Hou et al., 'the most prominent cooperative subjects are Economics, Business Administration, Electrical Engineering and Computing Science, and Foreign Language Studies' (Hou et al. 2014: 312). In these programs, quality assurance has become an issue. Duplication of programs offered by multiple institutions is another issue.

What the recent policy changes by Chinese education authorities indicate is a different interpretation of internationalisation, that is instead of importing Western education model, exporting a Chinese education model (for details see Wang 2013). This not only reflects growing complexities in the internationalisation of higher education but also the multipolar nature of the world system.

Observations

China seems to be moving to the centre in terms of the internationalisation of higher education. The question is whether its education provision mechanisms are 'exploitative' of the students financial and epistemological resources as much as those emanating from the rich countries of the global north including America? Another question is whether Chinese higher education provided to others is domineering similar to the ones from the rich Western countries to the extent of subverting their own cultural and academic values and practices? In this regard, the relationship between the global and the local needs to be critically examined. Different participants may hold different understandings and perceptions of what the Chinese internationalisation of higher education means – even though the government policy may dictate a certain set of objectives. Jokila's article does not offer much help about these questions or indeed the qualitative content on global cultural flows via education and internationalisation. Therefore, these questions need further investigation and discussion. Analysing Chinese aid to Africa, Wang says that the uniqueness in the Chinese education policy in international contexts is its emphasis on equality of partners and mutual respect, among others. 'China presents itself as a brother or friend who also experiences poverty as a developing country, rather than as a donor from an advantaged background' (Wang 2013: 313). These comments highlight a different disposition characterised by the Chinese approach.

According to Jokila, often local cultural values in China can come into conflict with the global model of higher education promoted by rich Western European and American countries. On the other hand, there is evidence of a complex array of linkages that Chinese universities have established with higher education institutions in Europe, America, and Australia indicating a degree of compatibility and collaboration or even integration for mutual benefit.[8] However, Jokila points out that 'despite the emphasis on international activities, an emphasis on retaining cultural characteristics is in place' (2014: 129). This is reflected in the fact that the term internationalisation is used in Chinese policy documents to refer to international cooperation. 'The differences in the usages of the concept of internationalization illustrate the different imaginations of the agents and the disjuncture in the flows of ideas' (Jokila 2014: 129).[9]

One other aspect of internationalisation of education and cultural flows that is not explained here is the perceptions held by those in the higher education sphere in the Western world about China. In this respect, Suspitsyna's study based on an analysis of representations of China in the *Chronicle of Higher Education* – being the mostly read source of higher education in the US – is important. The study focused on how the US education media construct the image of China? The conclusion is that 'China is constructed as a binary to the US' (Suspitsyna 2014: 28). Yet 'The old geopolitical configuration of TNE and the view of some developed and, especially English-speaking countries acting as suppliers of education and others receiving or purchasing their product is now more complex' (Hou et al. 2014: 315). Hou et al. predict that 'It is likely that these distinctions in TNE will become less clear-cut, with perhaps many countries acting as both suppliers and receivers' (2014: 315).

While there is some debate about the aims and role of the Chinese model and Confucian Institutes, what is important for our discussion is whether the knowledge about Chinese culture, language and values promoted through the Confucius Institutions represent an alternative type of educational initiative compared to Western education provided by rich countries of the West and United States to Chinese (and other Asian) students? Such a question can be raised about any other education provided by Chinese educational providers on the mainland and in other countries through Chinese aided campuses to students in the region (e.g. Malaysia). What philosophical and ideological differences underlie these two types of education, in particular higher education, needs further assessment.

Thus, if we adopt critical perspectives on globalisation and internationalisation of education in the Asian region, it can open up new study points for investigation and clarification. According to Suspitsyna 'The opening up of globalization as governmentality to critical scrutiny will also decenter the Eurocentric perspective and offer new observation angles for viewing Chinese forms of governmentality' (2014: 34). To elaborate further, 'Chinese government's selective adoption of market-driven policies in the name of national economic development (Ong 2006), the rapid commercialisation of higher education and the ubiquitous involvement of Chinese university administrators in entrepreneurial activities (Xie & Wang 2008), and the rising ideology of Occidentalism in response to Western dominance (Lary 2006) are all part of that governmentality' (Suspitsyna 2014: 34). For Suspitsyna, this allows for new ways of embodying Chineseness and commodification of Chinese culture along with the subversion of the Western gaze.

In essence, these responses by the Chinese reflects imitation of the Western model in some phases of its higher education internationalisation policy process and a counter narrative based on what they perceive as the Chinese model. It is in this counter narrative that one has to critically examine the extent to which commodification of knowledge and marketisation exists as it can imply whether the so-called Chinese model of higher education internationalisation is truly different from the metropolitan, Western model? Similarly, 'the dismantling of the construction of China and Asia as the West's Other' (Suspitsyna 2014: 34) can have profound implications for the Western and Chinese models.

South East Asia (SEA)

Since the region has a high degree of integration with China, we can look at the situation in SEA countries for comparison. While all SEA states 'assert the importance of knowledge and knowledge industries to their future development, significantly different profiles exist across the region' (Welch 2013: 201). Each nation treads a different path. No any single state in SEA shows a similar scale to that of China. Welch examines the profiles of five SEA states (i.e. Indonesia, Malaysia,

Philippines, Thailand and Vietnam). In his analysis, Welch notes the dense relations between China and SEA countries. One index of this growing regionalism 'is the growth of intra-regional student mobility between China and ASEAN' (2013: 201). Between 1999 and 2007, Chinese students studying in ASEAN countries increased 712% – an increase from 1,387 to 11,262. On the reverse side, the ASEAN students in Chinese HEI's rose from 4,975 to 23,700, an increase of 376%. Welch says, 'this increase in mobility, paralleled by an increase in research collaboration among China ASEAN academic staff, and added to by the significant Chinese diaspora throughout Southeast Asia, is re-shaping the contours of regionalism in Asian higher education' (Welch 2013: 202). This has implications for the knowledge society in the region.

Next he discusses significant differences in the higher education profiles in five countries (2013: 202–204). Differences exist among them in terms of the density of researchers, and measures of research and development expenditure. Malaysia performs better compared to Philippines. 'The gap between Southeast Asia and the developed world, in terms of either total R&D spending, or the proportion of GDP expended on R&D, is particularly striking' (Welch 2013: 203). In terms of papers and citations, Philippines is the worst performer whereas Vietnam the best out of the five. In the case of world-class universities, out of the 500 in the world, only Singapore has one whereas China (except Hong Kong and Taiwan) has 22. Different countries in the region are taking steps, however, to address the situation, for example new model' multidisciplinary research universities in Vietnam, more autonomy for universities in Malaysia.

On a note of caution, Welch says the brain drain and corruption limit the development of regional knowledge societies. In his analysis, he problematises the notion of region due to its internal complexities and differences, especially when China is used as a benchmark.

Though Welch distinguishes between knowledge economy and knowledge society, the problem with his analysis is that unlike Connell, Alatas and so forth, he does not expand on the latter concept in a way that those in Southeast Asia are able to comprehend an alternative in terms of the concept or strategy to the knowledge economy discourse. The distinction made between knowledge economy and knowledge society by Welch in the article is minimal. He does not go beyond the recognition that the people in countries of East Asia and Southeast Asia have venerated teachers and knowledge for centuries or even millennia while doing their best to provide a good education for children (2013: 198). One gets the sense that knowledge society to him means the adoption of Western model of higher education along with key indices used by developed countries to measure the success.

Welch's analysis itself uses criteria established by the world powers – and those faithfully following the same – to measure world-class university status and research and development indices. If we are to make use of the concept for visualising an alternative internationalisation process of higher education, further conceptualisation of 'knowledge society' compared to 'knowledge economy' is necessary.

Discussion and conclusion

The story of TNHE and the internationalisation in the case of China and India is more complex than simply following a global (Western) model. However, such following seems to be the case more in India than in China. Being a former British colony and English being a language of preference by the middle to upper classes, India has had a near natural inclination to look West in its higher educational partnerships for knowledge exchange, research and academic collaboration. However, this is balanced by its regional role as a provider of higher education to those less advantaged students from the developing countries primarily in the global south. In contrast to this, China has been conscious of its own cultural and philosophical traditions of scholarship and the need to balance its higher educational internationalisation policies to counter the push by institutions and governments in the global north with home-grown variety of education and scholarship. Confucius institutes exemplify this. In addition to this, China is also attracting substantial numbers of students from the global south and elsewhere to its university campuses.

Both countries still send out large numbers of fee-paying students who want to capitalise on the opportunities available in rich countries of the global north, Australia and New Zealand. Nonetheless, the dominance exercised by higher education institutions in the global north over those located in China and in India may encounter responses by way of policies, regulation, auditing and quality control in time to come.

One inevitable consequence of international education under globalisation in the current phase is the brain drain of educated youths from Asian countries to developed countries of the global north, Australia and New Zealand.[10] To some extent, this topic has been side-lined in recent discourses of international education. This may be because of the other advantages of globalisation that countries in the global peripheries receive due to free trade etc. Nonetheless, it is a crucial factor in reducing the human resource pool available for development and education in the sub-continent. The lack of expertise resulting from this process is being compensated by international experts as part of externally funded programs to a certain extent. The knowledge production process is affected due to the absence of a vibrant section of educated youths and skilled professionals who seek greener pastures outside.

Through international education it is claimed that new opportunities are opened for young people to obtain an education provided by the rich countries in the English-speaking world and subsequently migration and work opportunities. Some join multinational corporations operating globally and in the region after completion of studies that are recognised in this international sphere of work. Some academics who could have played a crucial role in rethinking knowledge in various fields in their home countries in fact join these corporations, universities, research institutions located in the rich countries, or multilateral organisations such as the World Bank and provide services as economists, education, health and other specialists to governments and non-governmental organisation (NGO) sectors in Asia, Africa and Latin America. Sometimes such specialists are sent to their own home countries as specialist consultants with messages from above. They are an army of experts appropriated and re-constructed by the rich countries and multilateral agencies that operate with the blessings of rich countries in the global north in order to maintain the dominance in knowledge fields.

This raises important questions about international education. Does it aim to reconstitute intelligentsia from the periphery in the image of metropolitan intelligentsia, professional and managerial class? Does it contribute to the surplus labour extraction process in such a way that it serves the interests of the metropolis rather than the periphery? Does it aim to transport packaged knowledge products produced in rich countries in the name of modern knowledge to the periphery with new labels and higher value?

In this context, it is useful to remember that current process of internationalisation under globalisation in the global south as in countries of Asia is founded primarily on the principles and practices of neo-liberalism and knowledge economy. Educational institutions in the rich countries such as in Euro-America have entered into various partnerships with local private and public sector educational institutions in Asia and governments to promote internationalisation but the suppliers of education from the rich countries and the recipients in the peripheral countries seem to have different motives.

Metropolitan institutions have 'an income earning objective' to supplement their national incomes. Maintaining the dominance they exercise in the world knowledge industry and economy is another drive. English speaking rich countries promote language and linguistic power also in promoting Western knowledge, literacy, and communication skills. The partner institutions in the peripheries have aims such as the acquisition of new knowledge and technology, professional skills and training for their young people and middle level professionals who otherwise face difficulties in connecting with the global economy and the employment market to realise upward social mobility. Enrichment of their research institutions and capabilities is another aim.

However, these two-way collaborative activities in terms of internationalisation is creating an academic dependency for countries of the global south, in particular Asia. This dependence is counterproductive and even negates the virtues of Southern knowledge systems and traditions, which have been undermined for centuries by colonisation, modernisation and the neo colonial projects including modernist education.

Though there are some signs of expanded education provision by countries like China in the Asian region, following in the footsteps exhibited by Northern metropolitan institutions of the rich countries of Europe and America to reach a level of global dominance, it will take another decade or more for any tangible expansion in this direction. In the Chinese case, questions have been raised about the use of soft power in global diplomacy – which may or may not have a bearing on the future directions of educational internationalisation.

Therefore, Peters warning is particularly important for our era.

> In the age of knowledge capitalism the next great struggle after the 'culture wars' of the 1990s will be the 'education wars', a struggle not only over the meaning and value of knowledge both internationally and locally, but also over the public means of knowledge production.
>
> (Peters 2003: 376)

Promotion of the Chinese model seems to have merits in this regard if it is founded on the local knowledge and education, pedagogies, principles and methods. It is because the world of education requires diversity – not uniformity. Higher education narrowly defined to suit the global economy and its needs in an instrumental way is not the answer. Searching for this diversity in local cultural, philosophical, religious and historical traditions is the task of contemporary social scientists in the global south and Asia.

Therefore the challenge facing educational institutions in the global periphery like India is to conceptualise a different kind of education rooted in their own histories, traditions, philosophies, cultures and forms of living. A serious critical reflection about the modernist and neo-liberal foundations of international education under globalisation have to be undertaken to evaluate the dominating impact of educational products coming from the rich countries of the global north and their destructive effects on societies in spheres other than employment. For such a task, useful ideas can be drawn from recent publications on Southern Theory.

Notes

1 In countries such as Sri Lanka, such an attitude and practice had a significant impact on the way indigenous knowledge production and dissemination occurred resulting in its marginalisation and even exclusion from the mainstream intellectual activities (see Gamage 2016).
2 See S. Dhar 2015. Subvention and Governance Reforms in Secondary Education in Bangladesh: Actors, Acquiescence and Resistance in the Policy Processes, PhD thesis, University of New England, Armidale, Australia.
3 See Naidoo (1990: 323–324) for student numbers in Australia, New Zealand, Canada, the United States and so forth.
4 1 lakh of rupees is equivalent to Rs. 100,000.
5 This trend is based on two other factors: (1) unmet demand for higher education in India and (2) failure of the state to increase investment in higher education. Paul believes that 'as a result of these factors, further internationalization of higher education is already in progress in India' (Paul 2009: 36).
6 For more on brain drain see (Welch 2013: 206–207; Chakrabarti et al. 2009: 184).
7 From the government point of view, human talent development was a primary aim of promoting such study abroad. Today, the value of studying abroad is not as high as before as large numbers of students who have done so have returned to China (Jokila 2014).
8 In East Asia and Singapore, 'the Confucian model is considered to have specific characteristics. One notable trait is the nation state's strong role in higher education policy' (Jokila 2014: 128 citing Marginson 2011).
9 In terms of educational aid to Africa, Wang says the Chinese strategy is different from the traditional Western paradigm of educational aid as 'China's education aid focuses on training human capital for economic development through vocational and higher education' (2013: 311). Another important characteristic is the refusal of China to establish a donor-recipient relationship. Rather the relationship is focused on mutual benefit – though there are signs that this is changing recently.
10 Another area of human movement is the global refugee movement.

References

Alatas, S. F. 2010. 'The Definition and Types of Alternative Discourses', in M. Burawoy, Mau-kuei Changand M. Fei-yu (eds.), *Facing an Unequal World: Challenges for a Global Sociology*. The Institute of Sociology, Academia Sinica & Council of National Association of the International Sociological Association (Conference Proceedings).

Altbach, P. and Knight, J. 2007. 'The Internationalization of Higher Education: Motivations and Realities', *Journal of Studies in International Education*, 11(3/4): 290–305.

Britez, R. and Peters, M. A. 2010. 'Internationalization and the Cosmopolitan University', *Geopolitics, History, and International Relations*, 2(1): 34–61.

Chakrabarti, R., Bartning, A. and Sengupta, S. 2010. 'Developing Globally Compatible Institutional Infrastructures for Indian Higher Education', *Journal of Studies in International Education*, 14(2): 183–199.

Connell, R. 2007. *Southern Theory: the global dynamics of knowledge in social science*. Crows Nest, NSW, Australia: Allen & Unwin.

Ding, S., & Saunders, R.A. 2006. Talking up China: An Analysis of China's rising cultural power and global promotion of the Chinese language, *East Asia*, 23, 3–33.

Gamage, S. 2006. 'Buddhism and Southern Theory: Buddhist Knowledge Production and Education in Colonial and Post-Colonial Sri Lanka', *Journal of Post Colonial Education*, Special issue, 5 (1), Colombo. www.um.edu. mt/newspoint/news/features/2016/06/postcolonialdirectionsineducationvol. 5no. 1.

Hayhoe, R. 1984. Chinese-Western scholarly exchange: implications for the future of Chinese education. In R. Hayhoe (ed.), *Contemporary Chinese Education*. New York, NY: M.E. Sharpe, pp. 205–229.

Hayhoe, R., & Liu, J. 2010. China's Universities, Cross-border education, and dialogue among Civilizations. In D. W. Chapman, W.K. Cummings, & G.A. Postiglione (eds.), *Crossing Borders in East Asian Higher Education*. Hong Kong: Springer, pp. 77–100.

Hou, J., Montgomery, C. and McDowel, L. 2014. 'Exploring Diverse Motivations of Transnational Higher Education in China: Complexities and Contradictions', *Journal of Education for Teaching: International Research and Pedagogy*, 40 (3): 300–318.

International Association of Universities Newsletter, India. 2001. 7 (3), July, India.

Jiang, K., & Ma, X. 2011. Overseas Education in China: Changing Landscape and policies. *International Higher Education*, 63, 6–8. Doi: 10.1177/1028315307303542.

Jokila, S. 2014. 'The Internationalization of Higher Education with Chinese Characteristics: Appadurai's Ideas Explored', *Asia Pacific Journal of Education*, 35 (1): 125–139.

Knight, J. 2005a. 'Borderless, Offshore, TNHE and Cross-Border Education: Definition and Data Dilemmas', www.obhe.ac.uk.

Larry, D. 2006. Edward Said: Orientalism and Occidentalism. *Journal of the Canadian Historical Association*, 17(2): 3015. Doi: 10.7202/016587ar

MOE (Ministry of Education of the People's Republic of China). 2013. Current Situation of Chinese-foreign Transnational education since the implementation of the National Medium and Long term Program for Education Reform and Development (in Chinese). http://www.moe.gov.cn/publicfiles/business/htmlfiles/moe/s7180/201302/147776.html

Mitra, S.K. 2010. 'Internationalization of Education in India: Emerging Trends and Strategies', *Asian Social Science*, 6 (6): 105–110, June.

Naidoo, V. 2009. 'Transnational Higher Education: A Stock Take of Current Activity', *Journal of Studies in International Education*, 13 (3): 310–330.

Ong, A. 2006. *Neoliberalism as exception: mutations in citizenship and sovereignty*. Durham, NC: Duke University Press.

Paul, S. 2009. 'Internationalisation of Higher Education: Strategic Implications, Perspective', *Economic and Political Weekly*, XLIV (9): 36–41.

Peters, M.A. 2003. 'Education Policy in the Age of Knowledge Capitalism', *Policy Futures in Education*, 1(2).

Power, K.B. 2012. *Expanding Domains in Indian Higher Education*. New Delhi, India: Association of Indian universities Publications.

Shen, W. 2007. International Student Immigration: The case of Chinese 'seaturtles'. In D. Epstein, R. Boden, R. Deem, F. Rizvi, & S. Wright (eds.), *Geographies of Knowledge, Geometries of Power: Framing the Future of Higher Education*. New York, NY: Routledge, pp. 211–231.

Suspitsyna, T. 2014. 'Cultural Hierarchies in the Discursive Representations of China in the Chronicle of Higher Education', *Critical Studies in Education*, 56(1): 21–37.

UNESCO Institute for Statistics. 2008. *Global Education Digest*. Montreal, Canada: UNESCO.

Wang, L. 2013. 'Going Global: The Changing Strategy of Internationalisation in China', *Journal of Higher Education Policy and Management*, 35(3): 305–315.

Welch, A. 2013. 'Different Paths, One Goal: Southeast Asia as Knowledge Society', *Asia pacific Journal of Education*, 33(2): 197–211.

Xie, S., & Wang, F. 2008. Chinese Education in the era of Capitalist Globalization. *Boundary 2*, 35(2): 107–124. doi:10.1215/01903659-2008-006

Yang, 2010. Soft Power and higher education: An examination of China's Confucius Institutes. *Globalisation, Societies and Education*, 8, 235–245. Doi:10.1080/14767721003779746.

Yeravdekar, V.R. and Tiwari, G. 2014a. 'China's Lead in Higher Education: Much to Learn for India', *Procedia: Social and Behavioural Sciences*, 157: 369–372.

Yeravdekar, V.R. and Tiwari, G. 2014b. 'Internationalization of Higher Education in India: Contribution to Regional Capacity Building in Neighbouring Countries', *Procedia – Social and Behavioural Sciences*, 157: 373–380.

Zhou, J. 2006. Higher Education in China. Singapore: Thompson Learning.

17 Globalisation, IT and governance

Implications for social justice and inclusivity

Siddhartha Mukerji

The Indian informational technology (IT) sector has witnessed tremendous growth in last two decades in the global market. Indian IT and software companies like Infosys, Satyam, TCS (Tata Consultancy Services), Wipro, and a whole range of SMEs (small and medium enterprises), BPOs (business process outsourcing) and KPOs (knowledge process outsourcing) which dominate the international market in software and other technical support services today have contributed towards making India an economic superpower. A NASSCOM (National Association of Software and Service Companies) report states that the growth of the service outsourcing industry has touched the mark of $2.9 billion. It further observes that the IT-BPO sector is estimated to generate revenues of $88.1 billion by the end of the FY2011 with IT and software service sector accounting for nearly $76.1 billion. While its contribution towards national gross domestic product (GDP) has increased from 1.2% in 1998 to 6.4% in 2011, its share in total Indian exports witnessed a steep rise from less than 4% in 1998 to 26% in 2011. Additionally, direct employment in the sector is estimated to be nearly 2.5 million in the current financial year[1] The rapid growth of the IT sector depicts the prosperity and economic might of India at the global level.

The other belief is that using the benefits of IT for development and social inclusion still remains a distant goal. Disparities among regions and communities still remain core characteristics of Indian society. These disparities can be gauged through what can be termed as a digital divide between urban and rural areas, elites and the masses, and the states of India. Digital divide signifies that while the privileged regions or communities may have proper accessibility to modern technologies, a large mass of people and the backward regions may be totally excluded from it. Henceforth, it is a form of exclusion that exists at all levels of marginalisation. Ironically, IT has the potential to create wonders in the lives of people who are at the periphery and struggle every day for earning their livelihoods. The technological innovations could provide better access to health, education, banks, legal aid and so on to the marginalised communities and regions.

Exclusion, marginalisation and isolation may also assume new dimensions within the industry. This may be visible in the challenges faced by the software employees and professional at their workplace. Since the software industry does not come within the purview of the Factors Act, the management has free hand to control the employees and their working conditions. While the IT sector has the distinction of employing a large pool of women engineers and professionals, the increasing pressures of work conditions places additional burdens as a result of certain gender-specific requirements.

This chapter attempts to understand inclusion in and through IT. The first part of the chapter locates the background in which IT and software emerged as an economically and socially significant industry in the 1980s and the way it received the assistantship of the state for its development. This is followed by a comprehensive understanding of e-governance initiatives taken by central and certain state governments in promoting connectivity and inclusion of the backward regions and communities in the mainstream. This marks a paradigm shift in defining the developmental goals and meeting them with the innovations in IT and software. The next section attempts to identify different dimensions of exclusion and isolations within the IT-BPO industry particularly interrogating the gender and labour right questions.

The background

The IT industry received its initial start-up during the mid-1980s when the focus of electronics policy began shifting in the direction of export-led growth from import-substitution strategy of industrialisation. A radical restructuring of the industrial policies during this period is observable on two complimentary premises, namely encouraging private investment in several industrial spheres particularly those that were technology-intensive and providing special policy benefits for those industrial sectors that exhibited a certain degree of comparative advantage in the international market.

The political context of the mid-1980s that laid favourable conditions for the emergence of the software sector in the export front can be gauged at three levels, namely the technocratic vision of Rajiv Gandhi, a quick shift in the orientation of the DoE (Department of Electronics) from protectionism to liberalisation and the support of liberal, business-friendly visions of the prime minister's economic advisors. Although the triple alliance of political leadership, bureaucracy and private industry worked towards the goal of establishing an export-oriented IT and software industry, the vision of the political leadership went much beyond the confines of export-led growth strategy. Rajiv Gandhi's technocratic ideas sought to link the new technological-industrial drive with the developmental goals of the state. In other words, he was strongly committed towards a meaningful application of technology in delivery of a whole range of public services and bring technology close to the lives of the people particularly the ones at the grassroots level. In one of his inaugural speech at the National Convention on Small Industry, New Delhi on 17 September 1986, Gandhi stated that 'we want the sophisticated computer to study the monsoon so that we can tell the farmer when to plant and what the rainfall is likely to be accurately'.[2]

However, since the late1980s the software policies remained exclusively focussed on the promotion of export-oriented firms. The advancement of the Computer Software Export, Development and Training Policy announced on 18 December 1986 was the first step in the direction. It sought to remove all licensing restrictions on export-oriented software firms placing the imports of hardware, electronics components required for the export of software in the OGL (open general license) category. Under the new dispensation, the hardware imports could be procured through the EXIM (Export-Import Bank) route. Those applying through the latter route were entitled for a 50% rebate.

Similarly, since 1991 the government introduced the STP (software technology park) scheme with the objective of providing special policy benefits for the export-oriented companies. This primarily included tax exemptions and infrastructural support like provisions of continuous supply of electricity and high-speed data links. Other maintenance and technical support services offered within STPs were network design, system integration, installations, and operations and maintenance of application networks (STPI website home page). There has been a consistent rise in the number of export companies registered with STP. The Annual Report of STPI shows that number of exporting units in STPI has increased from 4279 in 2001–02 to 5814 in 2009–10 (STPI Annual Report 2009–10).[3] The overemphasis on export-promotion led to dereliction of the domestic market until very recently. As

Mascarenhas comments, 'While Indian software developers have put India on the IT world map, they have unwittingly become the target of the critics who question the undue emphasis given by the government to the export of software' (Mascarenhas 2010: 171).[4] The software and IT sector exhibits the distinctive character of having maximum forward and backward linkages with industry and other sectors of the economy. Consequently, it provides immense business opportunities in the domestic market. Its application in several social and economic sectors like health, education, banking, rural development and management and agriculture is particularly crucial from the standpoint of its implications for the overall development of the economy. This could be achieved by facilitating the process of delivery of public services or improving the quality of public services with the help of IT and software technologies.

Additionally, IT-driven development also entails computerisation and wide-scale application of IT in the government administration so as to reduce the onus of complicated filing that becomes a basis of frequent delays and disposal of cases. It has been observed that the application of IT in efficient public administration and good governance can enhance quality of life of citizens making administration responsive, citizen-friendly and citizen-caring, ensure accountability secure freedom of expression, reduce cost and improve quality, increase productivity of employees, minimise corruption, and remove arbitrariness in exercise of authority.[5] In broader terms, it lays a strong foundation for ensuring transparency and accountability in public administration.

E-governance and inclusion

E-governance has become a watchword in the plans and programs of the governments and public administration in contemporary world. It is a product of public-private partnership whereby the government in collaboration with the private sector seeks to introduce a whole range of services and facilities particularly in rural areas for facilitating accessibility to public services. It serves as an important means of social inclusions as it helps in connecting people and regions at the periphery to the mainstream. On the contrary, its confinement to certain regions and sections of the society may create a digital divide at all levels. The digital divide can lead to exclusion in two ways:

1   Differences in access to technology.
2   Differences in knowledge of accessing technology.

The second form of exclusion becomes more serious in the Indian context as providing access to technology will still be meaningless if the recipients of the facility do not have proper training in using such technologies. The elite-mass division thus gets manifested in differential access to technology and its required knowledge and training. While both central and few state governments in collaboration with private sector have undertaken preliminary steps to improve accessibility and connectivity in rural areas and started several developmental projects to extend the benefits of ICT (information and communication technology) to rural and poor communities, the objective of disseminating the required knowledge and training for using such technologies remains unattended.

The other area where ICT has the potential to play a vital role is its substantial use in administrative functions. E-governance necessitates the use of ICT in reducing paperwork and expediting the administrative processes involved in execution of government's plans and programs. It is found to be extremely useful in maintaining existing and old records of land, finance, accounts, property, and so on.

The concept of e-governance in India was first introduced by the former chief minister of Andhra Pradesh Chandrababu Naidu in 1996 with objective of eliminating the digital divide between urban and rural areas and the elites and the common masses. Therefore, Andhra Pradesh holds the distinction of being the first state to propose a comprehensive IT policy for e-governance. In this regard, the government of Andhra Pradesh has initiated several programs like eSeva, eProcurement, eSuvidha (complete application for municipalities), financial accounting system for Gram panchayats, Computer Aided Registration of Documents and Citizen Friendly Services of Transport. In order to develop statewide networking of data, voice and video services the Andhra Pradesh government launched the APSWAN (AP-State Wide Area Network) that seeks to connect state headquarters with 23 district headquarters and 1,088 mandal headquarters. It also attempts to develop broadband connection rural areas. For the management of administrative files and promote paperwork administration the government has introduced the KM-ATOM system.

The government of Andhra Pradesh has worked in collaboration with the private sector in several projects on IT-driven inclusion. In 2002, it undertook the project 'World e-Inclusion' with Hewlett Packard at Kuppam in Chittor district (Official website of IT Department Government of Andhra Pradesh).[6] The objective of this project was to develop ICT technology and products for rural development and make extensive provisions for internet facilities in the rural areas. It also initiated training programs for the youth, women and the panchayats.

The Karnataka government has been equally active in making e-governance meaningful with the introduction of several programs. One of the most prominent software system developed by the STPI-Bangalore for its use in the Karnataka Finance Department called Khajan. The government has also established several kiosks meant for providing easy payment of the water, electricity and phone bills. A kiosk is a computer terminal designed of specialised hardware and software to access information and for its application in delivery of public services. Karnataka government's Bhoomi project was started in 2004 that sought to computerise 20 million land records of 6.7 million land owners in 176 taluks of Karnataka were computerised. Under this project, kiosks were established for the farmers in getting a quick access to their land records. They were freed from the burden of going all the way to the taluk headquarters for procuring the land records. Similar kiosks have been established in rural areas by the Andhra Pradesh government through three of its major e-governance projects namely Rural eSeva, Rural Service Delivery Points and Rajiv Internet Village Centres.

ICT has also been in used to disseminate information on the modern methods of agricultural practices by government and non-government agencies. One such innovation is the establishment of Kisan call centres to keep the farmers updated of the latest advancements in the field of agriculture. The objective of the scheme is to make agriculture knowledge available free of cost to the farmers. Highlighting the goals of Kisan Call Centre scheme, it is observed that,

> the Indian agriculture is on the threshold of a second revolution . . . the next leap will come from the information and the knowledge intensity transfer to the agriculture sector . . . the real challenge before the policy maker is to overcome the information asymmetry between farmer and farmer, village and village, region and region and country as a whole with other countries. The developments in the field of information and communication technology in India will make it possible.[7]
>
> (Official website of Department of Agriculture
> and Cooperation, Ministry of Agriculture,
> Government of India)

The Kisan call centres is one of the recent projects of government's agriculture extension program the success of which will depend on its ability to connect the remote and most inaccessible regions and farming communities in the country.

Another such project called 'National Agriculture Technology Project' was undertaken by the National Institution of Agriculture Extension Management, Hyderabad. To begin with, the project was applied to 10 villages in Rangareddy district where multimedia CDs on several aspects of agriculture, rural development, health and education were distributed to different groups of people.[8] Since then people have been making maximum use of internet connectivity provided by the project.

In order to pursue its plan of action on e-governance the central government introduced the NeGP (National e-Governance Plan) on 18 May 2006. Its underlying aim is to

> make all government services accessible to the common man in his locality through common service delivery outlets and ensure efficiency, transparency and reliability of such services at affordable costs to realize the basic needs of the common man.
>
> (Department of Information Technology,
> Ministry of Information and Communication
> Technology, Government of India)

The implementation of NeGP will take place at three levels, namely the common service centres for providing services at a convenient location and reasonable cost; statewide networks for electronically shared information between various government institutions, and 27 mission mode projects for speedy implementation of high priority areas of public services.

The successful implementation of NeGP will depend on the extent to which it is able to promote inclusive development the watchword of the 12th Five Year Plan. Mascarenhas points out that the benefits of ICT are only reaching the economically and educationally well-off who are able to access these services (Mascarenhas 2010: 152). Empowerment and transparency of the marginalised and vulnerable sections of the society through ICT will make e-governance realise the goal of substantive development. Therefore, organisation of training programs on IT and its uses for the rural masses, panchayats and the local administration will help facilitate the process of knowledge and information dissemination. Second, it is observed that there have been regional differences in terms of e-governance initiatives taken by the state governments. E-governance has received serious attention in states which have witnessed rapid growth of the IT sector like Andhra Pradesh and Karnataka. The success of e-governance will be determined by the extent of its coverage and inclusions in both class and regional terms.

One of the significant innovative schemes of PPP in ICT for development and inclusion at the national level is the introduction of UID (unique identity) and the establishment of Unique Identification Authority of India under the chairmanship of Nandan Nilekani. The UID which will be issued for every resident in the country will assist the government and the service providers in identifying the recipients of several welfare schemes like MGNREGS (Mahatma Gandhi National Rural Employment Guarantee Scheme and PDS (Public Distribution System). Underscoring the significance of UID for inclusive development, Nandan Nilekani observes that,

> The Unique Identification project is a part of an approach to growth that Indian governments have embraced since the early decade – growth with an emphasis on inclusion . . . the urgent need to make our social programmes more effective and ensure inclusive growth has been an impetus behind the UID project.[9]
>
> (Nilekani 2011: 194–195)

Providing for proper identification the UID the government will be in a better position to ensure that the funds and benefits meant for the poor and vulnerable sections reach them successfully. The UID is also said to provide easy accessibility to banks and insurance services by the economically marginalised sections of the society. The identity details of the UID include demographic and biometric information. This will assist in identifying the user's age, socio-economic status which will further help in recognising particular needs of the individual. For instance, a child belonging to BPL (below poverty line) category will be entitled for getting health vouchers that will further help the parents in getting free immunisation from any hospital. Similarly, UID-linked education vouchers will allow children to get enrolled in schools of their choice (ibid.: 1999).

Therefore, there has been a paradigm shift in the perceptions of the government and business about the contributions of IT towards development in recent times. The scope of knowledge-based industries in social and economic sectors countrywide has given a new developmental orientation to the IT industry. The government policies and programs during the initial stages of development focused exclusively on promotion of exports. Its utility for developmental purposes was unrealised by the government and the industry. It is observed that the recent policy shifts towards e-governance and encouragement for PPP has been driven by the goal of achieving inclusive growth. The new measures taken in this direction have also been conditioned by the realisation that IT can no more be cited as an elite-based sector. Its mass utility provides tremendous scope for its expansion in the domestic market and socio-economic development.

Forms of exclusion and violation of rights in the IT-BPO industry

The advent of global capitalism under the neo-liberal regime has resulted in new forms of discrimination, exclusions and marginalisation in the society and economy. The advocates of globalisation appreciate rising employment opportunities in the market with the entry of multinational companies and the expansion of domestic entrepreneurship in innovative areas of production and investment like IT, BPO and telecommunications. Such an advocacy obscures the possibilities of identifying exploitative tendencies of the new players in the market. The situation gets further complicated by superimposition of traditional hierarchies that promotes differentiation and discrimination on the basis of caste, gender and colour in India.

IT industry which is a direct progeny of global capitalism also faces the brunt of new kinds of exploitation and marginalisation today. The exploitative tendencies in the IT-BPO sector could be analysed at two levels:

1 Lack of labour regulations in the IT sector makes the position of software and BPO employees vulnerable.
2 Gendered forms of segregation and marginalisation.

The IT industry does not come under the purview of labour regulation laws in India neither has it faced the brunt of unionism. Lack of unionism and the resultant existence of labour discipline in the sector stem from the fact that the IT-BPO sector does not represent a desirable political constituency. This is in contrast with sectors such as textiles, steel, pharmaceuticals where trade unions politics has been a common practice. Recent studies have shown that new forms of exploitation and violation of basic human rights have emerged within the IT industry. A glaring reflection of this could be seen in the work conditions of the young people at the call centres.

Ernesto Noronha and Premilla D'Cruz (2006)[10] in their field survey attempted to explore the subjective meanings and interpretations of work experiences of the employees in the IT-BPO sector at Mumbai and Bangalore. In their study, they observed myriad forms of humiliation and discriminatory practices being faced by the professionals at their workplace. It is seen that listening to racial comments from the customers based in United States, Australia, the UK and Canada in the phone calls is an everyday practise. This is often done to avenge the job losses in their respective countries arising out of outsourcing. In this regard Noronha and D'Cruz observe that,

> When customers identified the agents as Indians, they had to face the ignominious situation of callers hanging up. Agents were help-less when customers reacted this way due to the loss of jobs in the west. However, racial overtone of callers were to be handled with a professional fineness.
>
> (Noronha and D'Çruz 2006: 2117)[11]

They found that working in night shifts for client companies based in US, UK, Canada or Australia resulted in several health disorders like loss of appetite, sleeplessness, fatigue, drowsiness, change in body weight and indigestion among the professionals at the call centres. Resultantly, it was inferred that a substantial portion of their salary was spent in medical treatments. Even the breaks for lunch/dinner were extremely limited and strictly time-bound. Those appearing late for office, after the breaks had to face the abuse and humiliation of the bosses.

These accounts of exploitative tendencies reflect the violation of some of the basic rights of the workers at call centres. The right to dignity and self-respect is compromised to a large extent. The luxury of the physical environment at the workplace like a well-equipped, air-conditioned office; a canteen or a cafeteria with an exhaustive list of food items; and so on cannot overcome the mental harassment and the health disorders that are associated with the work environment.

Similarly, Babu P. Ramesh (2008)[12] in his study of the work conditions at call centres in Noida observes a series of unethical practices that put the workers at the mercy of the team leaders and the management. He points out several instances of stringent and exploitative work environment at call centres. The most prominent among these are difficulties in getting leaves and holidays. It is observed that even leaves taken in averse to illness is often treated as unauthorised unless it receives the consent of the team leader 4–6 hours prior to the shift.[13] Second, as the call centres serve the clients in the United States, UK, Canada, Australia, Singapore, and so on they work as per the time schedule of these countries. As a result, they are not entitled for leaves during Indian national holidays.

The call centre workers function like cogs in the machine and the 'panoptic' work conditions represent the Taylorite 'Shop-Floor Management System'. In this regard, Carol Upadhya and A. R. Vasavi observe that 'the informatics workers are subjected to the gaze of computer, the gaze of supervisor, the manager, the fellow production worker, and finally the internal gaze of the self').[14] They face subordination at all levels that generates a sense of alienation among them. Redressal mechanisms are almost absent in the informatics industry particularly the BPOs and KPOs. While most of the HR departments are entrusted with the responsibility of redressal of grievances, they are completely controlled by the top management of the company.

The second most observable yet neglected issue of discrimination or subordination is that of the female employees. Sanjukta Mukherjee (2008)[15] observes gendered forms of subordination and alienation in the IT and software industry. First, the increasing intake of female employees in the industry is overshadowed by the observation that they constitute hardly 16%–20% of the total workforce. Second, it is noticed that even within this category women are mostly involved in low-skilled programming jobs like data entry and human resource positions. This leads to exclusion of women from high-value added jobs like turnkey management projects, software products and packages and projects involving large-scale R&D. A NASSCOM report has noted that women constitute approximately 31% of the total workforce in the IT-BPO sector which makes their position better than their counterparts in other industries. However, only 6% of them have been able to occupy top leadership position in the industry (Official Website of NASSCOM, New Delhi).[16] A study conducted by NASSCOM clearly shows the exclusion of women employees from managerial and directorial positions. The information is provided in Table 17.1.

The report clearly indicates the dominance of male members in higher positions within the industry. The substantial increase is mainly

Table 17.1 Position of women in the IT industry (in percentage)

Year	Top-level	Directorial level	Managerial level	Entry level
2006	6	5	12	77
2007	6	6	13	75
2008	7	7	14	72

Source: NASSCOM, New Delhi

found at the entry level. Nevertheless, the attrition rate is higher among women. Men and women employees also shift jobs for different reasons. While men drop-out due to economic factors like better job profile and better compensations, for women its personal reasons like family pressures, marriage, pregnancy and family relocations that matter more. Also most women leave the jobs in their late twenties and thirties, the most critical time of the career.

On a different note, C.J. Fuller and Haripriya Narasimhan (2008)[17] locate a mixed package of empowerment and constraints on women by citing the experiences of women professionals in Chennai's software industry. Quite contrary to the observation made by Sanjukta Mukherjee, they find a steady increase in the entry of women in the software industry. In majority of cases cited, the authors found a strong sense of empowerment and self-confidence among women in the software industry. Nevertheless, the gender-based burdens and responsibilities at home often tampered with the equal and just position of women at their workplace (Fuller and Narasimhan 2008: 190–210).[18] The double burden of household responsibilities and pressures at workplace often increased the vulnerabilities of professional women vis-à-vis their male counterparts. It is observed that, 'women have constraints which in practise means that gender inequality within the wider society can significantly affect women's ability to take advantage of equality at work' (ibid.: 200).

The existing surveys on the gendered practices in IT and software industry suggest that gender-based inequalities and differences manifest in varied forms at workplace. This is to say that even if the benefits and burdens may be equally distributed in the concerned organisation, the engendered roles at home translate into disadvantages for women folk in every sphere of life. For instance, while working in night shifts at call centres or software firms may generate a sense of equality and self-confidence among women, it may invite the wrath of the family members. In many cases, the young girls are forced to drop-out as working in call centres for night shifts and getting influenced by the Western lifestyle at the workplace is denounced by family members. Families feel reluctant to allow their daughters to work in call centres both for security reasons and the social prejudices against the nature of job. On the other side, the women employees hardly get any support from the managers of the organisation in dealing with the double-burden. The inability to meet project deadlines as a result of domestic pressures is taken as a mark of irresponsible behaviour on the part of the female employee.

In general, software professionals or call centres workers constitute a community that faces several forms of domination at their workplace. The pressures of the global market that may be severely disruptive of one's creativity, dignity and self-confidence at the workplace has brought the question of the protection of basic human rights of young men and women professionals at the centre stage. Additionally, the absence of redressal of grievances at workplace and the exclusion of the IT-BPO industry from the purview of labour regulation has institutionalised the discriminatory and exploitative practices. This has contributed towards increasing the vulnerabilities of the employees in this industry.

Conclusion

The Indian IT industry is at the forefront of being a leader in the international market. Its increasing success rates have affirmed the comparative advantage of technology and knowledge-intensive industries in the developing countries. It has been a torchbearer to other countries of Asia like Philippines, China and Taiwan which have witnessed tremendous growth in IT and software in recent years. The popularity of Indian software engineers and professionals in the international market has encouraged migration and even permanent settlement in the advanced countries of the West and East.

The growth trajectory of the IT industry since the mid-1980s limited its expansion and utility in the domestic market. It is ironical that an industry that contributed towards making India an economic superpower remained neglected in the developmental processes within the country. The export-oriented policies of the government were driven by the pressures of the global market. However, the recent penchant for IT-driven development and the associated policies and programs of the government has been conditioned by the goals of inclusive growth and political repercussions against outsourcing in the United States. The latter has limited the scope of service exports and has correspondingly encouraged penetration in the domestic market.

The recent programs and initiatives of e-governance in collaboration with the private industry needs to be complimented by framing new regulation and standards that check the emerging exploitative tendencies and discriminatory practices within the IT-BPO sector. Second, recognising the gender-specific needs of the women employees in the industry special arrangements and concessions may be made in the firm's policies and guidelines. Although there has been a substantial increase in the number of women employees in past few years, women have remained confined to low-skilled positions and have failed to occupy top positions of management in the industry. The success of the industry in future will depend on its ability to promote inclusivity and diversity by recognising the rights of employees at workplace and making special arrangements for the upliftment and progress of its women employees.

Notes

1 Strategic Review 2012, NASSCOM, New Delhi, official website of nasscom (www.nasscom.in)
2 'Rajiv Gandhi's Selected Speeches and Writings: 1986', 2 May 1989, 116
3 www.stpi.in/writereaddata/links/2534218955annuarl1.pdf, Annual Report 2009–10, STPI, Government of India
4 R.C, Macserenhas, Indian Silicon Plateau: Development of Information and Communication Technology in Bangalore, Orient Black Swan, New Delhi, 2010, p.171
5 Murali Patibandala, Deepak Kapur and Bent Peterson, "Import Substitution and Free Trade: A Case Study of India's Software Industry", Economic and Political Weekly, April 8, 2000, p.122-123
6 www.apit.ap.gov.in, Official website of Department of Information Technology, Government of Andhra Pradesh
7 www.agricoop.nic.in, Official Website of Department of Agriculture and Cooperation, Ministry of Agriculture, Government of India
8 Ramachandraiah, C. 2003. 'Information Technology and Social Development', Economic and Political Weekly, 38(12/13): 1193, May 22–April 4, P.1193
9 Nilekani, Nandan. 2011. 'The Potential of the Unique Identity Number in India', in R.K. Shyamsundar and M.A. Pai's (eds.), Homi Bhabha and the Computer Revolution. New Delhi: Oxford University Press, pp.194-95
10 Noronha, Ernesto and D'Cruz, Premilla. 2006. 'Organizing Call Centre Agents: Emerging Issues', Economic and Political Weekly, 21 (14), May 27–June2
11 Noronha, Ernesto and D'Cruz, Premilla. 2006. 'Organizing Call Centre Agents: Emerging Issues', Economic and Political Weekly, 21 (14), May 27–June2

400   *Siddhartha Mukerji*

12 Ramesh, Babu P. 2008. In an Outpost of the Global Economy: Work and Workers in India's Information Technology Industry. New Delhi: Routledge
13 Ibid., p. 243
14 Upadhya, Carol and Vasavi, A.R. 2008. In an Outpost of the Global Economy: Work and Workers in India's Information Technology Industry. New Delhi: Routledge, p. 30
15 Sanjukta Mukherjee, "Producing the Knowledge Professional: Gendred Geographies of Alienation in India's New Hi-Tech Workplace", in Upadhya, Carol and Vasavi, A.R. 2008, ed., In an Outpost of the Global Economy: Work and Workers in India's Information Technology Industry. New Delhi: Routledge
16 Report on Diversity and Inclusion', official website of NASSCOM, New Delhi, www.nasscom.in
17 Fuller, C.J. and Narasimhan, Haripriya. 2008. 'Empowerment and Constraint: Women, Work and Family in Chennai's Software Industry', in Carol Upadhya and A.R. Vasavi (eds.), In an Outpost of the Global Economy: Work and Workers in India's Information Technology Industry. New Delhi: Routledge
18 Ibid., pp.190-210

References

'Rajiv Gandhi's Selected Speeches and Writings: 1986', 2 May 1989, 116, www.agricoop.nic.in, Official Website of Department of Agriculture and Cooperation, Ministry of Agriculture, Government of India
www.apit.ap.gov.in, Official website of Department of Information Technology, Government of Andhra Pradesh.
www.stpi.in/writereaddata/links/2534218955annuarl1.pdf, Annual Report 2009–10, STPI, Government of India.
Fuller, C.J. and Narasimhan, Haripriya. 2008. 'Empowerment and Constraint: Women, Work and Family in Chennai's Software Industry', in Carol Upadhya and A.R. Vasavi (eds.), *In an Outpost of the Global Economy: Work and Workers in India's Information Technology Industry*. New Delhi: Routledge.
National E-Governance Plan, Department of Information Technology, Ministry of Information and Communication Technology, Government of India, Mascarenhas, 152.
Nilekani, Nandan. 2011. 'The Potential of the Unique Identity Number in India', in R.K. Shyamsundar and M.A. Pai's (eds.), *Homi Bhabha and the Computer Revolution*. New Delhi: Oxford University Press.
Noronha, Ernesto and D'Cruz, Premilla. 2006. 'Organizing Call Centre Agents: Emerging Issues', *Economic and Political Weekly*, 21 (14), May 27–June 2.
Ramachandraiah, C. 2003. 'Information Technology and Social Development', *Economic and Political Weekly*, 38(12/13): 1193, May 22–April 4.
Ramesh, Babu P. 2008. *In an Outpost of the Global Economy: Work and Workers in India's Information Technology Industry*. New Delhi: Routledge.

Strategic Review 2012, NASSCOM, New Delhi, official website of nasscom (www.nasscom.in)

Upadhya, Carol and Vasavi, A.R. 2008. *In an Outpost of the Global Economy: Work and Workers in India's Information Technology Industry.* New Delhi: Routledge, 30.

'Report on Diversity and Inclusion', official website of NASSCOM, New Delhi, www.nasscom.in.

18 Risk and vulnerability in the neo-liberal order

Assessing social security in India

Manisha Tripathy Pandey

The discourse of risk society (Giddens 1991; Beck 1992; Douglas 1992) describes the stresses and strains characteristic of contemporary social life. Risks are result of the process of modernisation which get heightened in the neo-liberal age where market is a deciding factor. This chapter differentiates between risk and social vulnerability. Risk is a methodical way of dealing with threats and insecurities induced by modernisation. It means anticipation and management of calamity and disaster, be it ecological, financial or social. Vulnerability is the outcome of neo-liberal order and refers to the incapacity and failure of the state and society to withstand the consequences of an aggressive market. Whereas risks can be managed, vulnerability persists as threats and problems to the state and society at large. The susceptibility to the neo-liberal order and the difficulty of the poor and the weak in coping with the exposure to contingencies and stress of the market forces leads to a risk-prone and vulnerable society. The shrinking of the state in the contemporary phase of globalisation leads to withdrawal of the welfare state in areas of employment, work, education and health. Social security is a public measure which provides protection against low and declining standards arising out of the contingencies in life. With joint family giving way to nuclearisation of households in India, people's social security needs are threatened. Social security to the workers in the organised sector is provided through various central acts. But the workers in the unorganised sectors have very little or no security coverage and this worsens with the withdrawal of the state. There is an increase in unorganised labour force in India with increasing migration, urbanisation, demographic and economic factors. The chapter reviews and analyses the National Pension Scheme 2004 for the organised sector and the Unorganized Workers' Social Security Act 2008 for the unorganised sector to understand India's social security system. The vulnerability due to market forces makes the society insecure, uncertain and catastrophic. The catastrophe could be rise in insurgencies, riots, conflict and anxiety. Thus, socially vulnerable society is the result of inevitable structural form of the neo-liberal order. The neo-liberal market develops crisis-related safety nets but these are not permanent, redistributive and sustainable.

Mapping risk

Risk has become a crucial point for sociological imagination. It is associated with the emergence of modernity and industrialisation. It is the probability or threat of quantifiable damage, injury, liability, loss, or any other negative occurrence that is caused by external or internal vulnerabilities, and that may be avoided through pre-emptive action. It is synonymous with all the fear and uncertainties related to rapid social transformation and creates a culture of panic.

Risk is now a fundamental defining characteristic of both personal and public life. The meanings and use of risk are associated with the emergence of modernity and industrialisation, which itself incorporates capitalism, the institutions of surveillance and nuclear weaponry. All these changes are seen as contributing to a particular way of understanding the self and the world that differs dramatically from earlier eras. For the individual, it is argued, these changes are associated with an intensifying sense of uncertainty, complexity, ambivalence and disorder, a growing distrust of social institutions and traditional authorities and an increasing awareness of the threats inherent in everyday life. Beck and Giddens have discussed the increasing influence of unintended consequences which the technological growth machinery bestows upon us.

Ulrich Beck in *Risk Society* (1992) argues that risk is defining characteristic of our age. In advanced modernity the central issue is not wealth but risk and how it can be prevented, minimised or channelled. Risks do not derive from undersupply of technology or wealth but from overproduction. He defines risk as a systematic way of dealing with hazards and insecurities induced and introduced by modernisation itself. Risks, as opposed to old dangers or hazards (famines, plagues, natural disasters), are consequences of modernisation and globalisation. He discusses the long-term transition from a pre-industrial, through an industrial to a risk society. The contemporary world is now characterised by its uncertainties and the risks these uncertainties bring with them, risks which operate at a global environmental level, as well as a more immediate personal level. Risk seems to strengthen class society. The wealthy can purchase safety and freedom from risk. For Beck, the emergent 'age of catastrophes' forces us to move from the calculable to the incalculable future, or more precisely from governing through risk to governing by reliance on 'uncertainty'. Statistical risk techniques, he asserts, can no longer predict the global 'modernisation risks' that are the most significant threats to our existence. Global warming, global terrorism, holes in the ozone layer, nuclear disasters and so on are all examples of human-generated catastrophes not recognised until their effects become manifest. To deal with these, it is argued that governmental prediction must abandon the precise probability techniques of risk, and enter the realms of 'uncertainty' – meaning that only estimation and imagination can prepare us for the future.

Anthony Giddens (1991) describes modernity as a risk culture. It 'reduces the overall riskiness of certain areas and modes of life, yet at the same time introduces new risk parameters largely or completely unknown to previous eras'. Giddens (1990) identifies four key aspects of risk in his earlier work on modernity:

1　The increasing role of *surveillance* in society as expressed through the control of information and people. This apparently extends the threat of a totalitarian power base.
2　The emergence of an era of 'total wars' which superseded the age of the more limited wars that preceded it. Thus, the *threat of nuclear war* leaves the shadow hanging over the modern world, above and beyond the increased fatalities associated with war during the 20th century in general.
3　The threat encapsulated in the uncertainty and *unpredictably of economic change.*
4　The subsequent threat of *ecological disaster* and decay caused by the erraticism of capitalism and its propensity to create inequality. Capitalist accumulation is therefore perceived to be a major cause of environmental degradation.

Mary Douglas (1992), giving a cultural conception of risk, argues that risk and danger are culturally conditioned ideas shaped by pressures of everyday life. Risk has apparently become central to our social lives precisely because of the move towards a global society. We are liberated from the constraints of local community but at one and the same time are bereft of traditional forms of protection and support. Nobody can apparently agree as to what is and what isn't risky therefore suggests that risk fulfils the forensic needs of a new global culture, the shift to a world community having constructed a new set of political priorities. As such, she describes risk as a generalised 'weapon of defence' which fills the needs of justice and welfare.

Making sense of vulnerability

Vulnerability derives from the Latin word *vulnerare* (to be wounded) and describes the potential to be harmed physically and/or psychologically. It is often understood as the counterpart of resilience, and is increasingly studied in linked social-ecological systems. It refers to the inability to withstand the effects of a hostile environment. It is a concept that links the relationship that people have with their environment to social forces and institutions and the cultural values that sustain and contest them. It is the inability of people, organisations, and societies to withstand adverse impacts from multiple stressors including abuse, social exclusion and natural hazards, to which they are exposed. These impacts are due in part to characteristics inherent in social interactions, institutions, and systems of cultural values.

In the 1970s the concept of vulnerability was introduced within the discourse on natural hazards and disaster by O'Keefe, Westgate and Wisner (O'Keefe et al. 1976). They insisted that socio-economic conditions are the causes for natural disasters. The work illustrated by means of empirical data that the occurrence of disasters increased over the last 50 years, paralleled by an increasing loss of life. The work also showed that the greatest losses of life concentrate in underdeveloped countries, where the authors concluded that vulnerability is increasing.

Vulnerability refers to the susceptibility or potential for harm to social, infrastructural, economic, and ecological systems. It is the result of a set of conditions and processes that influence the way that these systems are harmed by natural and technological hazards or extreme events. Vulnerability is closely associated with resilience which involves the capacity of these systems to bounce back from disasters or their capacity to both respond to and cope with extreme hazard events. Expressed in a different way, vulnerability is the result of our exposure to hazards and our capacity to cope and recover in a sustainable manner (Pine 2009).

Social vulnerability is partially the product of social inequalities – those social factors that influence or shape the susceptibility of various groups to harm and that also govern their ability to respond (Cutter et al. 2003).

In this chapter, social dimension of vulnerability is taken. Social vulnerability is high in India as it has less capacity to cope with poverty, lack of infrastructure for health, education and skill building. Social vulnerability suggests a differential capacity of groups and individuals to deal with the adverse effects of hazards, based on their positions within the physical and social world. Social vulnerability often refers to the capacity of human societies and their social systems to cope with and recover from environmental changes and disasters. It also refers to the extent to which human societies, each with differing levels of resources and abilities available in their social systems, will be impacted by the environmental hazards and disasters.

Risk, from the point of view of rational-legal authority, is an empowering thing. When a man or a group takes lakhs of rupees as a loan from a bank and makes investment, it is called entrepreneurial and risk. When a poor man depends on micro-finance, it is vulnerability. For example, a vegetable seller takes a loan in the morning to buy vegetables and sells it during the day, it is vulnerability. Thus social vulnerability is associated more with the poor and the downtrodden whereas risk affects people of all echelons of society. Risk displays an 'equalising effect'. Everyone is threatened by risk of global repercussions.

What is neo-liberalism?

Globalisation has expanded, intensified and accelerated social relations across time and space. The 'end of history' served as a catalyst to firmly establish the neo-liberal order of deregulating national economies, liberalising international trade and creating a single global market. Neo-liberalism is the reigning economic paradigm that rose to prominence in the 1980s propagating free or self-regulating market and 'rolling back' of the state. Neo-liberalism is a revival of liberalism. Liberalism has undergone a process of initial growth, intermediary decline, and finally a recent rejuvenation. Alternatively, neo-liberalism might be perceived of as a distinct ideology, descending from, but not identical to liberalism, proper. It builds on the convictions of classical liberalism that market forces will bring prosperity, liberty, democracy and peace to the whole of humankind.

David Harvey (2005) stands out as being one of the few who tries, in his *A Brief History of Neoliberalism*, to give the concept a wide-ranging definition:

> Neoliberalism is in the first instance a theory of political economic practices that proposes that human well-being can best be advanced by liberating individual entrepreneurial freedoms and skills within an institutional framework characterized by strong

private property rights, free markets and free trade. The role of the state is to create and preserve an institutional framework appropriate to such practices. The state has to guarantee, for example, the quality and integrity of money. It must also set up those military, defence, police and legal structures and functions required to secure private property rights and to guarantee, by force if need be, the proper functioning of markets. Furthermore, if markets do not exist (in areas such as land, water, education, health care, social security, or environmental pollution) then they must be created, by state action if necessary. But beyond these tasks the state should not venture. State interventions in markets (once created) must be kept to a bare minimum because, according to the theory, the state cannot possibly possess enough information to second-guess market signals (prices) and because powerful interest groups will inevitably distort and bias state interventions (particularly in democracies) for their own benefit.

(Harvey 2005: 2)

Harvey proposes with his definition to view neo-liberalism, not as the rejuvenation of liberalism in general, but as a distinctive economic theory which in recent times has replaced a more mild-mannered embedded liberalism, that is Keynesian approaches to macroeconomic governance inspired by modern liberalism. It is apparent that Harvey sees neo-liberalism not as a continuation of liberalism proper, but as something which lives independently of mainstream liberal values and policies. With his definition, which incorporates everything from Thatcherism to socialism with Chinese characteristics, Harvey emphasises that neo-liberalism is 'a theory of political economic practices rather than a complete political ideology.

Besides being an ideology, neo-liberalism is a mode of governance (Steger and Roy, 2010). A neo-liberal governmentality is rooted in entrepreneurial values such as competitiveness, self-interest and decentralisation. Neo-liberalism also connotes a concrete set of public policies expressed in the D-L-P formula: deregulation of the economy; liberalisation of trade and industry; and privatisation of state-owned enterprises. Related policy measures include massive tax cuts; reduction of social services and welfare programs; replacing welfare with 'workfare'; tax havens for domestic and foreign corporations willing to invest in designated economic zones; new commercial urban spaces shaped by market imperatives; anti-unionisation drives in the name of enhancing productivity and 'labour flexibility'; and regional and global integration of national economies.

Understanding social security

Social security is a comprehensive approach designed to prevent deprivation, assure the individual of a basic minimum income for himself and his dependents and to protect the individual from any uncertainties. Social security is guaranteed by the Constitution of India to every individual and household. The right of workers to social security has been recognised as inalienable and, therefore, must accrue to every worker under any system of labour law or labour policy. Provision of social protection is enshrined in Articles 38 (securing a social order for the promotion of welfare of the people), 39 (certain principles of policy), 41 (right to work, education and public assistance in certain cases), 42 (just and human conditions of work and maternity relief) and 43 (living wage, etc.) of the Constitution of India as a part of the Directive Principles of State Policy. Important social security, poverty alleviation and social welfare measures are being implemented by various ministries/departments of state governments and by civil society organisations.

Why do we need social security?

Social security protects not just the subscriber but also his/her entire family by giving packages in financial security and health care. Social security schemes are designed to guarantee at least long-term sustenance to families when the earning member retires, dies or suffers a disability. It acts as a facilitator – it helps people to plan their own future through insurance and assistance.

India has always had a joint family system that took care of the security needs of all the members provided it had access/ownership of material assets like land. There was a shared sense of responsibility towards one another. With increasing migration, urbanisation, demographic and economic factors, there has been a decrease in large family units and with joint family giving way to nuclearisation of households in India, people's social security needs are threatened. This is where the formal system of social security gains importance.

The state bears the primary responsibility for developing appropriate system for providing protection and assistance to its workforce. There is no existing universal social security system in India. Only about 35 million out of a workforce of 400 million have access to formal social security coverage in the form of old-age income protection. This includes private sector workers, civil servants, military personnel and employees of State Public Sector Undertakings. Out of these

35 million, 26 million workers are members of the Employees' Provident Fund Organisation. Social security to the workers in the government organised sector is provided through various Central Acts. But the workers in the unorganised sectors have very little or no security coverage and this worsen with the withdrawal of the state.

As India addresses the challenges of the 21st century and manages its rise globally, constructing and implementing a modern social security system represents one of its major imperatives. A modern social security system can enable India to cushion the burden on workers of restructuring public and private organisations; to increase the legitimacy of further reforms; and to encourage individuals and firms to engage in entrepreneurship and make creative career choices. All three are essential for India to emerge as a resilient knowledge-driven economy and society.

The organised sector includes primarily those establishments which are covered by the Factories Act 1948, the Shops and Commercial Establishments Acts of state governments, the Industrial Employment Standing Orders Act 1946 and so forth. This sector already has a structure through which social security benefits are extended to workers covered under these legislations.

The unorganised sector on the other hand is characterised by the lack of law coverage, seasonal and temporary nature of occupations, high labour mobility, dispersed functioning of operations, casualisation of labour, lack of organisational support, low bargaining power and so forth. All these make it vulnerable to socio-economic hardships. In rural areas it comprises of landless agricultural labourers, small and marginal farmers, share croppers, persons engaged in animal husbandry, fishing, horticulture, beekeeping, toddy tapping, forest workers, rural artisans etc. In urban areas, it comprises mainly of manual labourers in construction, carpentry trade, transport, communication etc. and also includes street vendors, hawkers, head load workers, cobblers, tin smiths, garment makers, etc.

India's unorganised workers who work long hours (when they get any employment at all), are forced to migrate to find work, toil in dangerous and often inhuman conditions, and have no fixed employer or any assurance of minimum earning constitute 92% of the country's workforce. They start working as children and continue till they are too old or till illness or disability overtakes them. They are the 'unfree' – bound by grinding poverty, exploitation, discrimination and constant flux. These 'unfree' people include 95% of all female workers and 89% of all male workers in India and together they contribute more than 60% of the country's gross domestic product.

Social security laws in the organised sector

The principal social security laws enacted in India are the following:

1 *The Employees' State Insurance Act 1948*, which covers factories and establishments with 10 or more employees and provides for comprehensive medical care to the employees and their families as well as cash benefits during sickness and maternity, and monthly payments in case of death or disablement.

2 *The Employees' Provident Funds and Miscellaneous Provisions Act 1952*, which applies to specific scheduled factories and establishments employing 20 or more employees and ensures terminal benefits to provident fund, superannuation pension, and family pension in case of death during service.

3 *The Workmen's Compensation Act 1923*, which requires payment of compensation to the workman or his family in cases of employment related injuries resulting in death or disability.

4 *The Maternity Benefit Act, 1961*, which provides for 12 weeks' wages during maternity as well as paid leave in certain other related contingencies.

5 *The Payment of Gratuity Act, 1972*, which provides 15 days' wages for each year of service to employees who have worked for five years or more in establishments having a minimum of 10 workers.

Separate Provident fund legislation exists for workers employed in coal mines, seamen and tea plantations in Assam.

Defined benefits pension and GPF (prior to 1 January 2004)

It is important for a country to have a well-defined pension arrangement enhancing strong social structure. Pension and retirement benefits provide sense of security to an individual and also acts as a source of investment. The central government employees who were in service as on 31 December 2003 have a defined benefit pension scheme. The New Pension Scheme is a contribution based pension scheme in which any individual can contribute towards their retirement fund. Those appointed prior to January 2004 get their post retirement amounts through a pension plan, which defines the benefit type. There is a monthly payment, which is equal to 50% of last drawn salary. Minimum payment to retired employees as pension through this old scheme is Rs. 3,500. Those above the age of 80 get an additional pension in the range 20%–100% of basic pensions. Besides, there is also dearness relief, based on All India Price Index for Consumers. Again, there is a medical allowance fixed, which deals with expenditure related to health care.

The main features of the old scheme are as follows:

- Pension
- Commutation of pension
- Service gratuity
- Retirement gratuity
- Death gratuity
- Leave encashment
- Family pension
- Group Insurance.

Types of pension

1   Superannuation – calculated as 50% of average emoluments of last 10 months' salary drawn subject to the minimum of Rs. 3,500 and maximum of Rs. 45,000.
2   Family pension – At the rate of 30% of basic pay subject to the minimum of Rs. 3,500 and maximum of Rs. 27,000.
3   Voluntary retirement – Maximum of five years weightage in the Qualifying Service.

Commutation of pension

- Can commute a lump sum payment not exceeding 40%.
- Reduced pension in proportion to the % of commutation and age factor.
- Commuted portion of pension shall be restored after the completion of 15 years.
- Lump sum amount received on commutation of pension is not liable for Income tax.
- Dearness relief calculated to the original pension not on the reduced pension.

Gratuity

- Retirement gratuity: admissible (along with pension) on retirement after completion of 5 years of qualifying service. Calculated at one-fourth of a month's Basic Pay + DA for each completed six monthly period of qualifying service. Maximum retirement gratuity payable is 16 times of emolument limited to Rs. 10 lakhs.

- Death gratuity: payable to the nominee in the event of employee's death.
- Service gratuity: entitled for service gratuity (and not pension) if total qualifying service is less than 10 years.

The National Pension System 2004 (defined contributory pension scheme): choice or coercion?

The New Pension Scheme (NPS) is an effort of the government to reduce its pension liability and also helping general public to decide where to invest their money. It is a two-tier contribution based investment structure in which an individual has full authority to decide where to invest his money. The NPS is a defined contribution based pension system launched by the Government of India with effect from 1 January 2004. Like most other developing countries, India did not have a universal social security system to protect the elderly against economic deprivation. As a first step towards instituting pension reforms, Government of India moved from a defined benefit pension to a defined contribution based pension system. Unlike existing pension fund of Government of India that offered assured benefits, NPS has defined contribution and individuals can decide where to invest their money.

The scheme is structured into two tiers:

Tier-I account: This NPS account does not allow premature withdrawal and is available to all citizens from 1 May 2009. Contribution to Tier-I:

- 10% of Basic Pay + Dearness Allowance contribution by the government servant every month.
- Equal matching contribution by the government.
- Kept in non-withdrawable pension Tier-I account.

When a government servant exits at or after 60 years of age:

- 60% of pension wealth can be withdrawn lump sum.
- 40% of pension wealth to invested in annuity – mandatory – to provide pension for lifetime for self and dependent.

When a government servant leaves the scheme before 60 years of age:

- 80% of pension wealth mandatory for investment.

- Benefit of Invalid pension, Disability pension, Family pension, Extraordinary Family pension are extended.
- Retirement Gratuity for discharge from duty to Disease/Injury or invalidation also extended.

Tier-II account: This voluntary NPS account permits withdrawal for exceptional reasons only, prior to the retirement age. Tier-II contribution will be kept in a separate withdrawable account.

Since 1 April 2008, the pension contributions of Central Government employees covered by the National Pension System (NPS) are being invested by professional Pension Fund Managers in line with investment guidelines of Government applicable to non-Government Provident Funds. A majority of State Governments have also shifted to the defined contribution based National Pension System from varying dates. Pension Fund Regulatory and Development Authority (PFRDA) will regulate the pension market. The six pension fund managers are ICICI Prudential Pension Funds Management Company Limited, IDFC Pension Fund Management Company Limited, Kotak Mahindra Pension Fund Limited, Reliance Capital Pension Fund Limited, SBI Pension Funds Private Limited and UTI Retirement Solutions Limited.

Old and the new pension schemes: an analysis

The basic difference between the old and the new scheme is that while the earlier system was defined, the new one is totally based on contribution and investment returns along with accumulations until retirement age, annuity type and its levels. In order to protect the interests of NPS subscribers, government has implanted various measures including a flexible pattern of investment, placement of a regulator, and creation of low cost modern NPS architecture.

There is a lot of dissension from various quarters regarding the safety, and benefits associated with this new pension scheme. Earlier pension systems in the country used to be provided only by employers (private and public). But new pension scheme introduced by the government is a flexible mode of retirement scheme in which any individual in the country can start investing towards retirement fund. This is easily the best investment scheme in the country to maintain standard of life after retirement.

Benefits of new pension scheme

- *More people are going to benefit than before*: those employed within the private sector and the self-employed people are brought in this scheme. Up to now, only 11% of Indian population came under this post retirement scheme.

- *Availability of flexible schemes*: It is up to the employees to decide which scheme they want to go for ensuring the growth of money. One needs to give a monthly contribution that includes 10% salary and dearness allowance.

- *Withdrawal account*: Another additional benefit of the NPS (Tier II) is that those who want can set up their very own withdrawal account, which is free of government interventions completely. However, in such cases, there are no equal contributions.

- *Voluntary withdrawal*: Those who complete their total service tenure of 60 years can consider their withdrawal from this new pension scheme any time they want. However, this is possible only after the purchase of 40% worth of an annuity from their pension wealth during withdrawal.

- *Cost-effective*: The cost of investing in new pension scheme is almost negligible whereas the cost of investing in alternate funds like mutual funds is very high.

- *Freedom to entry*: New pension scheme allows anyone from the age of 18 till 55 years to enter and invest into this pension scheme.

- *Investment opportunities*: The new pension scheme has a unique feature that provides every opportunity to an individual to invest in variety of funds and yielding maximum returns from their investments. Returns from investments in turn help an individual to reach and attain their investment objectives and future goals.

- *Tax implications*: There is no tax implication for an individual if he chooses to invest in new pension scheme. An individual is provided tax benefit over and above Rs. 1 lakh under section 80C of income tax laws.

- *Security to the nominee*: In case of death of the contributor, the nominee to the beneficiary receives the accumulated amount in lump sum. So, it provides sense of security to the nominee as well.

The scheme was compulsorily thrust upon the central government employees who are two-way losers. One, the huge costs savings for the government in pension payout by the switch over to the *defined contribution* pension system from the *defined benefit* pension system is a direct charge on the overall remuneration package employees are entitled to. Two, they do not have a window to air their grievances in this respect because the loss is not immediately felt and the full impact of the change will be felt only after 30 years or so when those who joined the service in January 2004 start retiring. It is also true that the anticipated savings in pension expenditure will also start accruing to government only by then. A time tested social security arrangement available to a section of employees has thus disappeared without any alternative system in place. When one refers to social security arrangement, one has in mind all the pension benefits, including family pension. While in the private sector and profit making public sector undertakings employees have an opportunity to bargain and settle remuneration based on their skill and market realities, government employees and those employed in quasi-government and statutory bodies are a helpless lot whose bargaining power is stifled in the name of public interest.

While introducing the NPS, the government had argued that DBS is unsustainable because the pension expenditure is increasing at a very high rate. What the government did not mention is that the government's pension expenses as a percentage of GDP is quite negligible in India (less than 0.1%). In South Korea or in Hong Kong it is about 2%. In Italy, France and Germany where the coverage under DBS pension is wide, the pension expenses as percentage of GDP is much higher in these countries. In Italy it is 14%; in France and Germany the ratio is 12%. In Japan 9% of the GDP is spent on DBS pension. One wonders how it becomes unsustainable in India where the expense on DBS pension is so low. The argument that DBS would render all governments 'bankrupt' thus appears to be untenable. Why should the small pensioners who usually do not have savings to tide over the crisis be driven to uncertain situation? Global capital does not have any moral obligation to honour the right of the citizen to live with dignity even in the retired life.

The Unorganised Workers' Social Security Act 2008

This is an Indian Act enacted by the Government of India to provide for the social security and welfare of the unorganised workers (meaning home-based workers, self-employed workers or daily wage workers). The Act provides for constitution of National Social Security Board at the Central level which shall recommend formulation of social security schemes, namely, life and disability cover, health and maternity benefits, old age protection and any other benefit as may be determined by the Government for unorganised workers. As a follow up to the implementation of the Act, the National Social Security Board was set up on 18 August 2009. Section 3(4) provides formulation of schemes relating to provident fund, employment injury benefits, housing, educational schemes for children, skill upgradation, funeral assistance and old age homes by the state governments. According to the Ministry of Labour, the term 'unorganised labour' has been defined as those workers who have not been able to organise themselves in pursuit of their common interests due to certain constraints, such as casual nature of employment, ignorance and illiteracy, small and scattered size of establishments and so forth. They constitute nearly 93% of the workforce. Majority of workers in the unorganised sector are employed in agriculture sector, some in construction and remaining in manufacturing activities, trade and transport, communication and services. A large number of them are home based and are engaged in occupations such as *beedi* rolling, *agarbatti* making, *papad* making, tailoring and embroidery work. The combination of life insurance, health insurance and old age pension is a requirement for a single scheme by the Government of India.

Overview of the various schemes

The Act does not define the exact schemes that will comprise the social protection floor for all workers. The central and the state governments will from time to time agree on the schemes that are relevant to the workers however the act lists the following schemes all of which are pre-existing schemes and offered by various government departments:

Indira Gandhi National Old Age Pension Scheme: Old people above 65 years of age belonging to BPL category are eligible for a monthly pension under this scheme. The persons living below poverty line and above the age of 60 years are eligible for old age pension of Rs. 200 per month. For persons above the age of 80 years, the amount of pension has been raised to Rs. 500 per month.

National Family Benefit Scheme: This provides for Rs. 10,000 to the family of an unorganised worker belonging to BPL category in case of death due to natural or accidental causes.

Janani Suraksha Yojna: All BPL women above 19 years, delivering at home, both in the Low Performing States (LPS) as well in the High Performing States (HPS) are entitled to cash assistance of Rs. 500 per delivery up to two live births.

Janshree Bima Yojna: This is implemented by LIC, 50% of the annual premium of Rs. 200 is paid by the Government of India and other 50% is paid either by the beneficiary, nodal agency or the state government. The beneficiaries are given Rs. 30000 on natural death, Rs. 75,000 on accidental death, Rs. 75,000 on total permanent disability and Rs. 37,500 on partial permanent disability. Rs. 300 per quarter per child is also paid as scholarship for two children in IX to XII.

Aam Aadmi Bima Yojna: This is confined to the members of the landless unorganised workers in rural households, in the age group of 18–59 years, provides insurance against death and disability to landless rural households and is also implemented by LIC.

Rashtriya Swasthya Bima Yojna (RSBY): This provides insurance cover of Rs. 30,000 to the unorganised sector workers in BPL category and their family members (a unit of five). Transportation costs (actual with maximum limit of Rs. 100/visit) within an overall limit of Rs. 10,000 are also covered. Smart cards are provided for cashless treatment for select diseases which require hospitalisation. However there is no provision to cover outpatient treatment which constitutes a major part of the medical expenses.

Handloom Weavers' Comprehensive Welfare Scheme: All handloom weavers benefit under this scheme which covers the handloom weaver, his wife and two children. The health insurance component is implemented through ICICI Lombard General Insurance Company Ltd.

Handicraft Artisans' Comprehensive Welfare Scheme: This scheme covers all handicraft artisans with their three family members. The health insurance component is implemented by ICICI Lombard General Insurance Ltd. The Government of India pays Rs. 650 and the artisans have to contribute Rs. 150 per annum.

Pension for Master Crafts Persons: This is limited to the recipients of National awards merit certificates and state awards in handicrafts and whose annual income is less than Rs. 15,000 with no financial assistance from any other source. Pension of Rs 1,000 per month is paid by central government.

National Scheme for welfare of Fishermen and training and extension: The central and the state governments share the funding in the ratio of 50:50. Rs. 40,000 is provided for the construction of houses, Rs. 30,000 for tube wells for drinking water, and Rs. 175,000 for the construction of common work places or community halls. Fishermen are paid Rs. 300 per month for three months for marine and for four months for inland fishers during the fishing ban period.

Critique

As the first attempt to legislate security for 93% of the workforce, the Unorganised Workers' Social Security Act 2008 is welcome. But the Act itself has been criticised for not defining a minimum social security floor that is enforceable by law and for not providing institutional powers to ensure effective implementation. Though the Unorganised Workers Social Security Act was passed in 2008, there has been dismal progress on the ground. The National Social Security Board for Unorganised Workers, constituted in August 2009, is limited to an advisory role, and does not have sufficient powers to implement, monitor or enforce social security. With the exception of a few states such as West Bengal, Chattisgarh and Karnataka, a majority of the states have not even set up their state level welfare boards.

However, it does not make it mandatory for the government to introduce new welfare schemes. It unfairly divides unorganised workers into those below the poverty line and those above, and is silent on a national minimum wage, improving working conditions and the problems of women workers like unequal pay and sexual harassment at the workplace. Also, these existing schemes are for the BPL category only (Goswami 2009). The shortcomings of the act are many. In reviewing the effectiveness of the Act, Goswami (2009) focuses on the following issues:

> The Act seems to be *a compilation of existing BPL schemes*. Also, these existing schemes are for the BPL category and by dividing the unorganised workers into BPL and nonBPL categories grave injustice is being committed against the latter. A minimum level of social security for all workers should be ensured.

Not an inclusive definition of unorganised worker: Section 2 of the Act gives the definition of an unorganised worker including those relating to self-employed and wage worker. Many key worker segments are not included: contract/casual workers, cooperative sector, ad-hoc employment opportunities like event management, entertainment/cultural activities and placement jobs and workers such as Anganwadi workers who are not covered in either in the organised or unorganised sector. Moreover, thousands of organised workers are not covered by this Act such as contract labour and casual labour. The Act also excludes workers dependent on livelihood systems such as forest workers and fish workers, who cannot be brought within the ambit of home-based workers, self-employed workers and wage workers. Most importantly, rural agricultural workers are excluded who comprise 65% of the unorganised workers.

Special problems of women workers, migrant workers and disadvantaged groups such as sex workers, eunuch, abandoned old/sick people have not been ignored by the Act. While specific segments of the workers (e.g. street vendors, domestic workers, coastal fisherman) often do not have any proof of their identity as workers and exercise their entitlement to various social protection measures, other workers face last mile challenges in leveraging the schemes and benefits targeting them.

Wage issues: The minimum wage is fixed by state governments, according to regions within a state, and according to occupation and skill of the labour. The minimum wages are neither revised on time by the state governments nor enforced with any modicum of seriousness. The act is silent on the crucial issue of national minimum wage. There are no penal sections to curb malpractices like nonpayment of wages, paying less than minimum wages, delays in payment, unequal remuneration, etc.

Benefits: The Act should have a clear definition of social security as measures by the government in collaboration with employer, worker or otherwise, designed to meet the contingencies in life of a worker including old age pension, unemployment benefits, maternity, livelihood loss compensation, accident and medical care and child care support.

Grievance redressal: The Act does not clearly address the issue of grievance redressal (with penalties) and dispute settlements. The grievance redressal should be based on the tripartite model of employers, worker representatives and the government.

Important terms not defined: The term 'social security' is not defined in the law and also the terms 'social security' and 'welfare' are used interchangeably. The emphasis seems to be on schemes of welfare rather than social security as a whole.

Moreover, the term 'family is used in a very restricted manner (a spouse and two children). What happens to the dependant parents, dependent widowed sister or dependent widowed daughter-in-law? In India family ties are so extended and strong, that nuclear family definition does not really help.

Charity, not rights: The language of the Act is not one of giving rights to the unorganised sector workers at par with workers in the organised sector, but rather confine their status as beneficiaries of government schemes. The Right to Working Conditions is also missing as an essential right of the worker.

The Right for dignified life is denied if social security systems are not in place. After reviewing the two Acts, in the context of the organised sector as well as the unorganised sector, it can be said that there is an adverse effect on social security in India in the neo-liberal age. With the revision of pension schemes for the government employees in India, the idea of pensions being rights of workers has been thrown into the neo-liberal dustbin. The return under NPS is market driven. There is no guaranteed/defined amount of return. One can never be sure that the returns from equities would always be better than the guaranteed returns. The returns generated through investments are accumulated and is not distributed as dividend or bonus. Thus the implications are quite deep.

For the millions of workers in the unorganised sector, the fundamental issue of employees' right to a life of dignity is not there. There is a declining interest on savings which increases insecurity among senior citizens. There is an increase in contractual labour now as this is also favoured by the multinational corporations. There is increasing unemployment especially rural non-agricultural and urban informal employment. The hire and fire system followed by many private firms and also MNCs, cause disruption of family and social life. The professionals are thrown out of jobs when the market is not doing well. Moreover, entitlements of maternity leave and provision of crèches are denied in most of the private sector jobs. This social vulnerability is the result of market-driven economy.

Why did it take nearly 60 years for the government of India to enact a law for the unorganised sector which constitute 92% of the workforce? The unorganised sector seemed to be socially dangerous as there was a lot of discontent and class unrest among them. The social costs of this were manifest in various conflict-like situations between the employers and employees (for example Maruti case in Gurgaon) and also increase in the rate of crime among the people belonging to the unorganised sector.

Rise and intensification of a socially vulnerable society

The logic of the market is economic, that of profit and efficiency, while the logic of state is political, that of legitimacy and welfare. The two logics are unconnected but always affect each other. The very nature of the neo-liberal market is truncated as there is concentration of economic power in fewer hands. There are widening socio-economic inequalities and disparities as only urban educated population is benefitting. Because of privatisation, the reservation policy for the marginalised sections of the population has been affected. Amassing of wealth (by few MNCs and private players) by deprivation and denial (of the masses) as in the case of the SEZs (Pandey 2011), leads to weakening of the social safety-nets and social vulnerability of the poor and marginalised.

With apparent ecological and social limits to neo-liberal globalisation and development, the current matrix of social security is unsustainable, inequitable, and inaccessible to the majority of humans in India.

The idea of risk is related with the development of instrumental rational control, which the process of modernisation promotes in all spheres of life – from individual risk of accidents and illness to export risks and risks of war. Social vulnerability is a political economy concept. It is the conceptual nexus that links the relationship that people have with environment to social forces and institutions and the cultural values that sustain or contest them.

In the neo-liberal age, vulnerability of people is pushed to the limits. The bread-winner of a family is supposed to be giving social security to all his dependents. His social boundaries would crack if he is unable to do so. But does he have the capacity to do so? The demand on a person to perform does not match with his capacity to exist and pay. Capacity is building human skills for information and knowledge society. Capacities mean creating abilities not only for food, clothing and shelter but also means to education and health in market-reliant economic growth. A person's capacities get depleted with rising cost of living in the age of the market. This is social vulnerability. The triumph of the market at the expense of the state increases vulnerability of the poor as there is increasing concentration of economic and therefore political power in the hands the multinational corporations. Besides increase in economic disparities, the market process has varied social consequences such as the intensification of marginalisation of the lower classes, deepening underdevelopment, ethnic conflict and instability. The insecurities of the neo-liberal order through withdrawal of state in important areas of welfare, unemployment of unskilled and semi-skilled workers, hire and fire system of the market, breakdown of traditional forms of social support and individualisation of experience plunging into chaos, have led to extreme form of social vulnerability which is difficult to address.

This social discontent is derived from paradoxical, hegemonic and uneven nature of liberalisation and globalisation. There is an inverse relationship between economic and social development. There is worsening social security, widening social justice and social tension and conflict. This leads to a socially vulnerable society which is more problematic than risks of ecological or financial kinds.

References

Beck, Ulrich. 1992. *Risk Society: Towards a New Modernity*. London: Sage.
Cutter, S. L. et al. 2003. 'Social Vulnerability to Environmental Hazards', *Social Science Quarterly*, 84 (2): 242–261, June.
Douglas, Mary. 1992. *Risk and Blame: Essays in Cultural Theory*. London: Routledge.
Giddens, Anthony. 1990. *The Consequences of Modernity*, Cambridge: Polity Press.
Giddens, Anthony. 1991. *Modernity and Self-Identity: Self and Society in the Late Modern Age*. Cambridge: Polity Press.
Goswami, Paromita. 2009. 'A Critique of the Unorganized Sector Act 2008', *Economic and Political Weekly*, 44 (11), March 14.
Harvey, David. 2005. *A Brief History of Neoliberalism*. New York: Oxford University Press, http://labour.gov.in/upload/uploadfiles/files/ActsandRules/SocitySecurity/TheUnorganisedWorkersSocialSecurityAct2008.pdf, accessed on 17/2/2014. http://pensionersportal.gov.in/, accessed on 17/2/2014.
O'Keefe, P., Westgate, K. and Wisner, B. 1976. 'Taking the Naturalness out of Natural Disasters', *Nature*, 260: 566–567.
Pandey, Manisha T. 2011. 'Ventilating Predicament of Development: New Economic Enclaves and Structural Violence in India', in Ravi Kumar (ed.), *The Heart of the Matter: Development, Identity and Violence* (77–104). New Delhi: Aakar Books.
Pine, John C. 2009. *Natural Hazards Analysis: Reducing the Impact of Disasters*. Taylor & Francis.
Steger, M. B. and Roy, R. K. 2010. *Neoliberalism: A Very Short Introduction*. New York: Oxford University Press.

Index

For Product Safety Concerns and Information please contact our EU
representative GPSR@taylorandfrancis.com
Taylor & Francis Verlag GmbH, Kaufingerstraße 24, 80331 München, Germany

www.ingramcontent.com/pod-product-compliance
Ingram Content Group UK Ltd.
Pitfield, Milton Keynes, MK11 3LW, UK
UKHW020936180425
457613UK00019B/421